On Psychological Prose

On Psychological Prose

Lydia Ginzburg

Translated and edited by Judson Rosengrant
Foreword by Edward J. Brown

PRINCETON UNIVERSITY PRESS

PRINCETON, NEW JERSEY

Copyright © 1991 by Princeton University Press
Published by Princeton University Press, 41 William Street,
Princeton, New Jersey 08540
In the United Kingdom: Princeton University Press, Oxford

All Rights Reserved

Library of Congress Cataloging-in-Publication Data

Ginzburg, Lidiia, 1902–1990
[O psikhologicheskoĭ proze. English]
On psychological prose / Lydia Ginzburg ; translated and
edited by Judson Rosengrant ; foreword by Edward J. Brown.
p.   cm.
Translation of: O psikhologicheskoĭ proze.
Includes bibliographical references and index.
ISBN 0-691-06849-6 — ISBN 0-691-01513-9 (pbk.)
1. Psychology in literature. 2. Prose literature—History and
criticism. 3. Psychological fiction—History and criticism.
I. Rosengrant, Judson, 1941–   . II. Title.
PN56.P93G513   1991
809'.93353—DC20   90-21136   CIP

This book has been composed in Adobe Sabon

Princeton University Press books are printed on acid-free paper
and meet the guidelines for permanence and durability of the
Committee on Production Guidelines for Book Longevity of the
Council on Library Resources

Printed in the United States of America by Princeton University Press,
Princeton, New Jersey

1 3 5 7 9 10 8 6 4 2
1 3 5 7 9 10 8 6 4 2
(Pbk.)

In memory of Lydia Ginzburg

_____

CONTENTS

FOREWORD

LYDIA GINZBURG is one of the most distinguished and original minds to
have worked on the nature of verbal art, its processes, and its position
within a particular culture. Such a statement will come as no surprise in
the contemporary Russian intellectual world, where her contribution to
modern literary theory is regarded, justly in my opinion, as quite comparable to that of Bakhtin and as a healthy complement and correction
of poststructuralist tendencies in the West. The appearance of Judson
Rosengrant's English translation now guarantees that Ginzburg's unique
contribution will have its proper measure of recognition among us also.

On Psychological Prose is an investigation of the methods used, both
in historical genres and in fiction, to portray the human consciousness. It
illuminates the presence of an aesthetic component in all such writing,
and thus is a prime contribution to the contemporary discussion of the
"poetics" of historical and even scientific writing. Ginzburg was a student
of the formalist theoretician Iurii Tynianov, whose important contribution was the idea that the boundary between literature and nonliterature,
and therefore the distinction between so-called literary and other kinds of
language, is not a fixed and stable one. Kinds of writing that for one
generation had only historical interest, another may elevate to the level of
verbal art. The ancient Russian chronicles were prime examples, as were
letters and memoirs at a later period.

Ginzburg deals in the main with the evidence of Russian literary and
historical writing, evidence located precisely in the nondefined area on the
borderline between historical and poetic creation. Thus the letters of Belinskii, in their conscious effort to give direct verbal evidence of the
human drama in which the writer felt himself to be a participant, and
immersed as they are in the language and the concerns of contemporary
literature, provide a psychological portrait of his generation that, as
Ginzburg puts it, leads directly to the analytic method of Tolstoi. The
products of Russian literature, in Ginzburg's hands, seem particularly
suited to address the important questions about the relationship between
literature and history. And she deals brilliantly also with similar texts
from other literatures, particularly the *Mémoires* of Saint-Simon and the
psychological method of Marcel Proust.

This book deals systematically with the idea of the aesthetic in its widest application to historical and other kinds of writing. Ginzburg demon-

strates in a magnificent passage that the story of Napoleon as preserved
in the popular imagination has all the ingredients of a consciously plotted
tragedy, with a proper beginning, middle, and end: "Everything in the
Napoleonic legend, from the bridge at Arcole, to the banner in the hands
of the young Bonaparte, to the island of St. Helena, is apprehended as a
finished aesthetic structure. The broad strokes of history are accompanied by precise details: the three-cornered hat, the close-fitting gray frock
coat, the arms folded across his chest. The events are so tightly bound up
with their details that it is as if those details were a deliberate invention."
But of course it was not that way at all. "The island of St. Helena was not
something that had been foreseen." In novels, on the other hand, the same
aesthetic effect may be produced by deliberate contrivance: the end is
indeed "foreseen" from the beginning. The novel *Anna Karenina* begins
with its ending, the tragic snuffing out of a life at a railway station, then
works its way back to it again with the suicide of Anna under a railway
carriage. But the problem of aesthetic organization, as Ginzburg's book
beautifully demonstrates, extends also to the structuring of historical accounts, even to the fashioning by an individual of his or her own life; to
the effort of a real Anna Karenina, for instance, to escape from contin-
gency into meaning. "Anna could have chosen another way to end her
life," as Milan Kundera put it in *The Unbearable Lightness of Being.*
"But the motif of death and the railway station, unforgettably bound to
the birth of love, enticed her in her hour of despair with its dark beauty."

The final third of this critical work is devoted to the "psychological
prose" of Lev Tolstoi, particularly in the two great novels *War and Peace*
and *Anna Karenina.* Ginzburg's discussion of those two novels constitutes a rediscovery of Tolstoi as a predecessor of the modern novel. She
points out that Tolstoi was the first to abandon literary "stereotypes" in
the presentation of character and to show instead the instability of "character traits" and the presence of contradictory urges in one and the same
character. We recognize his characters as who they are only after generalizing from a welter of contradictory thoughts and actions, much as we do
in "real life." And the thoughts and remarks of each character are embedded in a meaningless chaos of everyday trivialities and gross, inappropriate details that ought to be beneath the notice of a serious artist: the hair
on Dolokhov's arms observed by Nikolai Rostov during his agony of
losing the family fortune to him at cards; the faint moustache on a little
princess's upper lip. Tolstoi's emphasis on minor matters usually considered inappropriate to artistic structure produces an uncanny sense of reality in the account of a character's mental experience. Ginzburg argues
very plausibly that Tolstoi "foretold the future." An important ingredient
of the modern novel, she argues, is present in Tolstoi's "stream of consciousness," and the fractured details of many modern narratives are

foreshadowed in his obsessive emphasis on synecdoches, parts of a scene that stand for the whole in the memory of a character, the artist, and the reader. Tolstoi, it might be said, took the first steps in the modern tendency to "foreground" the data of consciousness as detached from, and even calling into question, the real world itself. Thus Tolstoian "realism" contained in itself the seeds of its own destruction.

The appearance of this important book in Professor Rosengrant's exemplary translation should give new life and possibly a new direction to modern critical theorizing.

EDWARD J. BROWN
STANFORD UNIVERSITY

TRANSLATOR'S PREFACE

HOWEVER ELABORATE its arguments and however historically and generically diverse the material from which it takes them, *On Psychological Prose*[1] is still quite able to speak for itself. It will therefore not be my purpose here to examine its critical assumptions or principal themes, or even to provide an overview of its author's life and scholarly career, as interesting as those topics might be.[2] Instead, I shall consider the book merely as a problem in translation, as a text whose Russian version required a certain kind of analysis and a certain kind of solution if it was to be rendered in English in a way that would be genuinely useful to its new readers. In other words, I shall try to explain what I have done in this edition and why I have done it that way.

On Psychological Prose presents the translator with two main kinds of difficulty—stylistic and editorial. The stylistic difficulties may conveniently, if somewhat arbitrarily, be divided into the "intrinsic" and the "extrinsic"—into those features that pertain to Ginzburg's own style and those that reflect the styles of the many authors she cites in the course of her discussion. The editorial difficulties, on the other hand, derive from the cross-cultural and multilingual character of Ginzburg's scholarship and from the consequent need to adapt her text and apparatus for English-speaking readers.

The intrinsic stylistic features of *On Psychological Prose* consist of those elements—key words and phrases, persistent collocations, characteristic tropes and rhetorical devices—that are "text bound," that acquire their full meaning from the involutions of the text itself, or rather that take that meaning from their continual elaboration within it, so that one's idea of their import emerges from and is conditioned by the numerous contexts in which they have occurred. These elements constitute something like the "idiolect" of *On Psychological Prose*, and in particular they include Ginzburg's peculiar vocabulary and terminology—her distinctive application of the idioms of criticism and linguistics, of semiotics and structuralism, of psychology and the other social sciences. They also include (though less directly) her sometimes abrupt syntax—her occasional impatience, as I would describe it, with explicit transition and linkage—as well as the other, more general qualities of her style: its combination of pithiness, rigor, and abstraction, its intellectual authority, and its refreshing independence from academic fashion and cant.

Although these intrinsic stylistic features naturally implicate a considerable portion of the book's usages, they are in fact quite resistant to analysis, at least of the discursive variety, since that analysis would properly have to avail itself of massive quotation and minute examination of progressive shifts of contextual meaning. Indeed, anyone rash enough to undertake such an analysis might quickly find himself drawn into something that in sheer scope and detail was tantamount to the replicatory process of translation itself, but that unlike translation was in fundamental conflict with its own ostensible purpose of useful reduction, simplification, and clarification. He would, in other words, find himself caught up in something rather like the absurd predicament of Borges's Pierre Menard, who "did not want to compose another *Quixote*—which is easy—but the *Quixote* itself."

Yet however resistant these intrinsic stylistic features may be to purely discursive investigation, they remain the real stuff of translation, the level at which the text's denotational and structural arrangements are most extensively and subtly revealed, and the level thus requiring the most tactful representation in the new version. With regard to the particular involutions and elaborations of *On Psychological Prose*, I hope it will therefore be enough to say that although the different strategies of my translation certainly strive to be scrupulously accurate in conveying the line and detail of Ginzburg's argument and style, they are not literalist—they do not subscribe to the crude notion of translinguistic synonymy, of a kind of automatic transference of unscathed meaning from one vessel to another. Instead, those strategies are based more on the principle of semantic than of lexical equivalence. Accordingly, I have on occasion allowed myself to depart from a verbatim rendering of the Russian, especially when it seemed to me that the original formulations were unnecessarily taciturn or obscure or had a very different resonance in Russian than they could have in English.

The extrinsic stylistic features of *On Psychological Prose*, in contrast, are easier to discuss. Semantically, they are less determined by immediate context, and like the subjects and methodologies they invoke, they are for the most part quite capable of being identified, ordered, and transposed. In the great variety of their historical and cultural reference, they are an excellent index of the reach of Ginzburg's scholarship. Among the areas in which these features are most apparent are citation and allusion.

Part of Ginzburg's argument concerns French literary monuments, and she therefore quotes from a number of masters, including Montaigne, Saint-Simon, Rousseau, Constant, Stendhal, Sainte-Beuve, Taine, Flaubert, and Proust. In relation to Saint-Simon, Rousseau, and Proust, that quotation is quite extensive, since in Ginzburg's view these authors represent important aspects of or stages in the development of psychological modeling in literature—of psychological prose. All of the quotation, however, involved the problem of working back from the largely unidentified translations used in the Russian text to their French originals, and then either translating directly from the French (using *Pléiade* editions wherever possible), or employing a respected and readily available English version (such as Donald Frame's Montaigne, J. M. Cohen's Rousseau, or the Moncrieff-Kilmartin Proust). Sometimes there was a discrepancy between the Russian translation supplied by Ginzburg and the original French or standard English version. This was usually the result of two unavoidable factors: that French, English, and Russian have different semantic structures—they model the world differently—so that precisely congruent translations among them are rarely possible; and that any translation, even the most avowedly literal, inevitably entails an interpretation of and selection from those structures by a particular translator. If individual (and cultural) perception of both the means and the ends of the translation of any text may differ, it follows that the versions arrived at must also differ, and if those versions are produced by translators working in different languages, then of course they can be expected to differ even more. In any event, whenever there was a discrepancy, the English was adjusted in order to ensure its conformity with the French. Very rarely, however, did that mean altering Ginzburg's own text in any significant way, and never did it mean violating the sense or spirit of her exposition and argument.

In addition to French monuments, Ginzburg also quotes extensively from German sources: Goethe, Eckermann, Hegel, Schopenhauer, and Marx, among others. She also cites a book called *Self-Knowledge* by the British moralist and popular psychologist John Mason (in a Russian translation by the eighteenth-century Freemason Ivan Petrovich Turgenev), and of course she quotes a number of Russian figures: Zhukovskii (his correspondence and diary, which show the influence of Mason), Bakunin, Stankevich, Belinskii, Herzen, the better known nineteenth-century Ivan Sergeevich Turgenev, Dostoevskii, Tolstoi, and Gor'kii, to name only the most important. Ginzburg's Russian citations, moreover, represent a variety of genres, ranging from the familiar letter and the diary to the memoir, and thence to the novel and tale; as one might expect, she supports her observations with quotation from secondary sources as well, including monographs, critical studies, literary histories, and psychology and philosophy texts in Russian, French, German, and English. This additional primary and secondary material, at least with regard to the German sources, presented much the same difficulty as did the French. The Russian citations, however, because they include so many different generic, period, and individual styles, required particular care, lest the distinctive features of those styles be lost and the lineaments of Ginzburg's argument lose clarity.

This last problem assumed special importance in the rendering of "The 'Human Document' and the Construction of Personality," with its rami-

fied discussion of the epistolary prose of Bakunin, Stankevich, and Belinskii in the 1830s and 1840s. One of Ginzburg's main tasks in this section of the book is to trace the application of an adopted terminology or
phraseology, with its attendant set of conceptions and attitudes, to psychological and ideological questions, and then to examine its modification, or "modernization," under the pressure of new empirical insights.
The most striking example of this phenomenon is Belinskii's adaptation
of a secondhand philosophical-psychological terminology derived principally from Bakuninian Hegelianism (and consisting of direct borrowings
from the German, Russian calques for German expressions, and Russian
words whose semantic fields were influenced by German usages), in order
to secure new perceptions about the nature of human psychological processes and their connection to overarching ethical questions. Ginzburg
brilliantly analyzes the significance of these terms and their associated
meanings for Belinskii's moral and intellectual development and, by extension, for the development of subsequent Russian realism, indicating
the dynamic and reciprocal relationship between sign and signified, between the adopted terminology and the emerging complex of ideas and
feelings that it came to designate. Ginzburg's discussion of this issue is of
course quite intricate, touching as it does on the shifting semantics of
obsolescent romanticism and nascent realism, but I shall cite one brief
passage here by way of illustrating both the nature of her essentially
philological method and the kinds of obstacles it presents to the translator. The passage follows a substantial quotation from Hegel's *Philosophie des Geistes*, in which he enjoins against confusing his conception of
psychology (which concerns the mind's perception of itself) with vulgar
psychology, that is, with the psychology of everyday life:

> It was precisely what Hegel was warning against here that his Russian fol-
> lowers, with their passionate interest in ethical issues and in self-analysis,
> were concerned with (and productively so). Terms like "stage" [*moment*],
> "definition" [*opredelenie*], "spontaneity" [*neposredstvennost'*], "unenlight-
> ened" [*neprosvetlennyi*], "subjectivity" [*sub"ektivnost'*], "accident" [*slu-
> chainost'*], "illusion" [*prizrachnost'*], "true life" [*istinnaia zhizn'*], "free-
> dom" [*svoboda*], "necessity" [*neobkhodimost'*], "concreteness" [*konkret-
> nost'*], and the like were at once applied to the solution of psychological
> problems. Also frequently met with is the very important expression "soul-
> beauty" [*prekrasnodushie*, meaning "self-indulgent idealism"], employed
> by Belinskii to stigmatize the remnants of Schillerian idealism.
>
> "Soul-beauty" was an ironic derivation from the German *schöne Seele*,
> although in circle usage a doublet for the term appeared, the odd little word
> "self-grinning" [*samoosklablenie*]. Belinskii used the latter term frequently
> in his letters of the late 1830s. It would be no easy matter to establish its
> precise meaning, had not Bakunin deciphered it in his foreword to [the Rus-

sian translation of] Hegel's *Gymnasialreden*. "Self-grinning," it turns out, was a synonym for "soul-beauty."

The appropriate quotation from Bakunin then follows. The translator has several options in dealing with material of this kind. He may simply render the Hegelian-Bakuninian-Belinskiian terminology contained in this passage with direct English equivalents; he may opt for the rebarbative but more precisely informative expedient of interpolating the original Russian, including, if necessary, an English paraphrase; or he may, as a kind of Nabokovian last resort, erect a competing edifice of explanatory footnotes. Yet whatever his solution (or combination of solutions), he should at least try to find English variants that not only convey something of the special meaning the Russian expressions had when they were first used, but also give a sense of their composite or appropriated character, so that the reader, regardless of the degree of his own philological knowledge, may comfortably follow the modulations of Ginzburg's cross-linguistic and cross-cultural exposition.

To be sure, it is not very often possible to find English equivalents that can actually do this—that can convey the complex morphological and semantic structure of the Russian terms—with the result that a choice must usually be made between structure and referential meaning. A good example of this particular problem is the above-quoted calque *prekrasnodushie (Schönseeligkeit)*. I have rendered this with the neologism "soul-beauty" (thereby inverting the structure of the Russian and German terms, which literally yield something like "beautifulsouledness" or perhaps even "lovelimindedness") and glossed it in the interpolation as "self-indulgent idealism," although "starry-eyed idealism," the translation favored by the second edition of *The Oxford Russian-English Dictionary*, would do just as well. By themselves, the paraphrastic or dictionary translations probably do manage to convey the bare denotational meaning of the Russian-German phrase, but function and tone have been lost since the allusive structure of the Russian and the fine irony contained within it have been jettisoned. Conversely, while the neologism may suggest something of the morphology of the Russian (and German) term, its denotational meaning remains obscure—which raises yet another question. In addition to the problem of accurately rendering the complex semantic structure and tone (insofar as this is possible) of individual lexical items, there is the equally important problem of the reader's general apprehension of the text. The ability to follow Ginzburg's analysis sometimes depends on a sense of the rich meaning of terms like *prekrasnodushie*, and if that meaning is not capable of being conveyed by means of translation alone, or is capable of being conveyed only partially, then it must, in order to protect the larger themes of which it is after all only a concrete example, be provided somewhere else, either in an explanatory interpolation or footnote or in an appended analysis like the one engaged in here. In short, although the translator may strive for ideal, multidimensional accuracy in his translation, he must also be prepared to realize that even the most conscientious and resourceful effort may prove inadequate in overcoming the limits imposed by his own language and cultural tradition, with their perhaps comparable yet still very different historical conditions.

This matter of rendering a characteristic authorial or period diction in *On Psychological Prose* is not, however, restricted to expressions of European provenance alone; native Russian words and phrases also play their part. In the case of Belinskii and his circle, for example, many of these latter terms were taken from the writings of Nikolai Gogol'. Unlike the abstract, Germanic rhetoric of philosophy and psychology invoking the recondite world of speculative thought, this Gogolian language served to conjure up in striking and often humorous fashion a specifically Russian everyday social life; it brought a discourse that might have been in danger of losing itself in the romantic empyrean back down to a firmer and more realistic earth. This aspect of early nineteenth-century circle usage is no less important for Ginzburg's analysis:

> Gogolian turns of phrase, usually in a somewhat altered form, are pervasive in Belinskii's letters: "You want to be a general so you can wear the ceremonial ribbon over your shoulder" [*Khochetsia byt' generalom, povesiat tebe kavaleriiu cherez plecho*], "My dear Triapichkin" [*Dusha moia* Triapichkin], "You want to take up something lofty but the fashionable crowd does not understand" [*Khochetsia zaniat'sia chem-nibud' vysokim, a svetskaia chern' ne ponimaet*], and so on. One also encounters surprising collocations of Gogol' and Hegel that produce terms of a new type. In July 1838 Belinskii wrote to Bakunin, "Botkin told me the scene that begins *Wilhelm Meister*, and my soul trembled with delight. But one needs to know just what is there—more essence and actions [*sushchnost' i postupki*], that is—yet I know nothing." Belinskii was concerned in this letter with the transition from an illusory, ideal love to an earthly, real one, and that certainly involved "actions." The word itself, however, originated as an ironic quotation. In the first act of *The Inspector General* (third scene), Bobchinskii says of Khlestakov, "He walks around the room, and there is such reasoning and character in his face, . . . such important actions. . . ." This formula combining Bobchinskii's little word with Hegel's "essence" occurs several times in Belinskii's letters. It is a joke, of course, but one expressing a very important insight for Belinskii about the unity of idea and action, of idea and phenomenon.

In dealing with passages of this kind, one must be circumspect both with the quoted material and with the authorial commentary, so as, once again, not to weaken the dynamic correspondence between these expressions and the complexes they invoke. As a practical matter, this means identifying the sources whenever possible and adjusting the translation to them—in the present instance to the appropriate works by Belinskii and Gogol'. Very rarely, however, may it mean more than that, since the phrases that give such passages their special stylistic flavor in Russian can obviously never have the same kind of implication in English, and it would be fatuous to pretend that they can. Here, as in the rendering of the Germanized Russian above, one is faced with an inescapable fact of all translation, whether of the artful arrangements of verse or of the supposedly more pedestrian and tractable elaborations of scholarly prose: it is at once a kind of struggle and a kind of dance, a continuous movement back and forth between opportunity and constraint. It follows from this fact that the essence of good translation begins with an awareness of the need to balance naturalness and fluency in English with fidelity to the original language. Taken absolutely, these principles are of course irreconcilable. Understood contingently, making the constant adjustments of diction, tone, syntax, and rhetoric required by the original at each of its innumerable points, they may sometimes reach a kind of two-part harmony, wherein the translator, the always secondary interpreter of the score, has at least a chance of convincing and accurate performance.

The editorial difficulties presented by *On Psychological Prose*, since they did not directly involve linguistic issues, were less contentious than those presented by the book's various styles. Essentially, these difficulties entailed five kinds of solution: the identification of fugitive quotations and original texts and (in order to avoid potential confusion and maintain consistency) the restoration of their titles to the original German and French forms; the inclusion of bracketed interpolations to assist the reader in identifying biographical and bibliographical references unlikely to be familiar; adaptation of the book's scholarly apparatus to conform to Anglo-American conventions and to reflect the substitution of original non-Russian sources, and the translation either directly from those sources or the employment of standard English translations, as mentioned above; the addition of thematically explicit headings and the corresponding enlargement of the table of contents in order to make the book more accessible to the selective reader; and finally the preparation of a full index to further increase that accessibility. It should go without saying that whenever material was added or adapted, it was done so with the author's consent. All changes, whatever their nature, have been identified in the notes with the symbol "(Tr.)." The one exception to this rule (aside from the bracketed interpolations in the text and the added headings and expanded table of contents) is the inclusion in the English of original volume and chapter citations—for example, "vol. 2, pt. 1, chap.

6" for the appropriate section of *War and Peace*, or "pt. 8, chap. 9" for *Anna Karenina*, and so on—in order to assist the reader who may wish to consult the quoted passages in their original Russian or in one of the available English translations. Similarly, volume and page numbers—for example, "20:481" for Gor'kii's *Klim Samgin*, or "413; 385–386" for the French and English versions, respectively, of Rousseau's *Confessions*—have been inserted wherever a quotation has been translated or taken from a generally available Russian, French, German, or English academic (or otherwise standard) edition, and either Ginzburg herself failed to provide the necessary bibliographical information, or that information was necessitated by an editorial substitution on my part. I should also add that all translations in the text are my own, unless otherwise indicated.

The last issue to be addressed here concerns the method used to transliterate Russian titles, words, and names in the text and in the apparatus. Given the scholarly nature of *On Psychological Prose*, I have, with a few exceptions (such as established names like Herzen, Ketscher, Kitty, Betsy, Pierre, Maria, and Lydia), opted for the Library of Congress system without diacritical marks, so as to provide a reliable guide for any readers who may wish to consult the original material. This system may of course prove irritating to some users of the book, since from a certain English-speaking point of view it arguably provides distracting and even superfluous phonetic information, but I remain convinced that, in regard to the citations at least, the clear advantages of utility outweigh the presumed disadvantages of inelegance.

I would like to express my thanks for material assistance in the preparation of this volume to the Provost of Reed College, the Indiana University Russian and East European Institute, and the Andrew W. Mellon foundation. I would also like to thank those students of criticism, translation, and Russian and European literature who in one way or another have contributed to the project during its long and sometimes difficult gestation. Olga Matich and Sarah Pratt, colleagues during my stay as a Mellon Fellow at the University of Southern California, kindly consented to read chapters of the translation and to share their comments; Irina Paperno and Boris Gasparov of the University of California at Berkeley lent their expert knowledge of Russian literature and of Lydia Ginzburg at a crucial early stage; Alice Stone Nakhimovsky of Colgate University, during discussions of a version of "The 'Human Document' and the Construction of Personality" (included under a somewhat different title in her and Alexander Nakhimovsky's Cornell anthology, *The Semiotics of Russian Cultural History*), gave me the benefit of her translator's perspective; William Ray, a former colleague at Reed, answered questions about the intricacies of Rousseau's French; Caryl Emerson of Princeton University and Jane Gary Harris of the University of Pittsburgh, thanks to their thoughtful reading of the entire manuscript, prompted me to refine certain points of interpretation and presentation; Lydia Ginzburg, at whose request I first undertook the translation, herself helped in the solution of certain editorial problems (most notably through the identification of much of the original Saint-Simon material) and lent the project her considerable moral support; and Edward J. Brown of Stanford University and William Mills Todd III of Harvard University, first graduate advisers at Stanford and later friends, gave the entire enterprise their benevolent assistance from its inception to its conclusion. I owe an exceptional debt of gratitude to my wife and abiding colleague, Sandra Rosengrant of Portland State University, who read a very large manuscript more times than she would perhaps care to remember, but who always did so with unfailing grace and invaluable insight. Needless to say, whatever errors of conception and execution remain are entirely my own.

BLOOMINGTON, INDIANA

On Psychological Prose

_____

INTRODUCTION

THE PROBLEM from which this book takes its departure is the relationship between the conception of personality characteristic of a given era and social milieu and the artistic representation of that conception. It is in this sense that one should understand the book's title, not confusing the broad view of psychological prose with that psychologism whose particular methods were worked out by nineteenth-century literature. The cognition of spiritual life is traced in this book on the basis of material taken not only from canonical artistic literature but also from memoiristic or documentary writing, which in our time has aroused the intense interest of readers and writers all over the world.[1] That cognition is examined on several levels—letters (which reflect the life process in an unmediated way), memoirs, and finally the experience of the psychological novel, the most highly organized form in this group.

In keeping with its procedure, the book consists of three parts arranged according to the degree to which the material investigated in them is structured, is aesthetically organized. That is why the phenomena discussed here are not necessarily examined in chronological order, although each is unfailingly related to its actual historical context.

This book is conceived as a theoretical work, although the theory of literature too is concerned with historical material. The historical method in literary scholarship involves the study not merely of the literary process, but also of the very structure of the work in relation to the dynamics, the changing function of its elements.

Literature may undoubtedly be studied productively on a number of different levels, but its semantic level is already a historical one. It is impossible to read through a literary work as a system of signs without understanding what those signs meant to the artist who created them, without discovering, that is, the meanings engendered by a historically formed and socially determined cultural complex.

Even when he is examining an aesthetic structure intrinsically, the researcher involuntarily and inevitably takes its historical character into account. And it is not only the researcher who does this. The least sophisticated reader, whenever he takes an old book in his hands, knows in advance that he is entering a world where even the most familiar words will not mean quite what they do today. This is the unsophisticated reader's historical intuition. As for the literary scholar engaged in the solution of one theoretical problem or another, the historical nature of the material may become a tacit assumption or an implied premise, or it

may serve as an explicit context for the development of theoretical propo-
sitions. It is the second of these orientations that is the more congenial to
me, and it is the one that determines the approach to the issues studied in
this book.

Aesthetic activity goes on unceasingly in the human mind; art is merely
its ultimate, highest stage, just as science is the ultimate stage of logico-
cognitive activity, which also goes on unceasingly. There is an unbroken
chain connecting artistic prose to the history, the memoir, the biography,
and ultimately the "human document" of everyday life. The nature of this
correlation is complex and has varied from one epoch to another. Depending on the historical preconditions, literature has either withdrawn
into special, pointedly aesthetic forms, or it has moved closer to nonliter-
ary discourse. The intermediate, documentary genres, without losing
their specificity, without turning into either novel or tale, have accordingly sometimes acquired the status of verbal art.

The normative aesthetics of classicism originated in the strict demarca-
tion of art from the other areas of human spiritual activity. By every one
of its tenets, it strove to create a particular sphere of the beautiful, a carefully elaborated system of the distinctive means of artistic expression.
That normative system included everything—from genres, which were
conceived as definite, fixed aspects in the representation of reality, down
to the individual word, whose place in the poetic lexicon was assigned by
taste. The requirement that verbal material have a preordained aesthetic
quality gained impetus from the fact that the language of literature was in
essence the same as that of verse. Prose remained outside the boundaries
of the classical hierarchy of genres, in a sense therefore outside the boundaries of verbal art itself.

Romanticism legitimized prose. But understanding art either as divine
revelation or as the self-expression of an elect personality, the romantics,
in keeping with those conceptions, for the most part also used means of
verbal expression that had acquired heightened aesthetic effect (even
though they had been liberated from a stable norm).

Nineteenth-century realism emerged during the rise of historiography,
and it developed side by side with the development of the exact sciences.
Realism, because it depicted concrete reality in terms of its causal conditionality [obuslovlennost'], both social and historical, had no need either
of a distinctive sphere of the beautiful or of a specifically artistic verbal
medium. The very existence of such a medium had lost its philosophical
meaning, and the previously inviolable boundary between belles lettres
and the other forms of writing was thereby erased.

Hegel, who took a dim view of what he called the "debasement" of art,
indicated as early as the 1820s the potentiality (and from his perspective,

the danger) of the elimination of that boundary. Classifying the forms of art in his *Ästhetik*, Hegel stressed the fundamental difference between poetry and the other arts. Unlike architecture, painting, and music, poetry does not employ sensuous material. Its material is the word, understood not in its phonetic but in its semantic capacity. "Poetry runs the risk of losing itself in a transition from the region of the senses into that of the spirit. . . . In poetry both content and material are provided by our inner ideas. Yet ideas, outside of art, are already the commonest form of consciousness and therefore we must in the first place undertake the task of distinguishing *poetic* from *prosaic* ideas."[2] Returning to this theme again and again, Hegel demanded that poetry retain a special language (of poetic figurativeness) and warned it against the danger of beginning to speak in the language of scientific thought and "prosaic" reason. What Hegel regarded as the destruction of literature, as its dissolution in an alien prosaic element, would in two or three decades become the guiding principle of the new aesthetics being advanced by maturing realistic thought. In particular, it was Russian realistic aesthetics that elaborated the principle of the convergence of science and art.

In his article "A Survey of Russian Literature in 1847," Belinskii proposed the following formulation (apropos of the works of Herzen): "They wish to see in art a kind of intellectual China, sharply delineated by precise boundaries from everything that is not art in the strict sense of the word. But in fact those borderlines are more hypothetical than real; at least you cannot point to them with your finger as you can to the boundaries of a state on a map." In the same work Belinskii declared that "memoirs, if they are written with skill, constitute something like the final frontier of the realm of the novel, themselves sealing it off."[3]

Art is closed off neither from logical cognition nor from actual life—on that point the theoreticians and practitioners of French realistic prose in the second half of the nineteenth century also insisted, although they did so from a different vantage than did the Russians. They welcomed the introduction of a scientific element into the very fabric of the artistic work, and they recognized the aesthetic significance of the genres lying outside the boundaries of traditional aesthetics. The principles of a new conception of man, and the connection of those principles to contemporary political, historical, psychological, and ethical views, are from time to time especially apparent in such intermediate genres of the middle and second half of the nineteenth century as the biography and the autobiography.

Nineteenth-century literature clarified and realized the aesthetic potentialities of the documentary genres, although those potentialities had earlier existed in unregulated form. In previous eras historiography had fulfilled its own peculiar functions, to a certain extent thereby taking the place of artistic prose. Such, for example, had been its role in antiquity and during the Renaissance. In seventeenth-century France, memoirs and the other documentary genres acquired a similar significance. Seventeenth-century France was in fact the true birthplace of the memoirs of the new age. For people of the seventeenth century, memoirs were history, although as a practical matter the genre performed literary tasks as well. The aesthetics of classicism regarded verse language as the only true language of art (making a partial exception for comedy) and almost completely ignored the novel. Yet outside the boundaries of aesthetic hierarchy and regulation lay not only the novel; there also flourished an intermediate prose that had even greater importance for the seventeenth century: memoirs, letters, *maximes*, and *caractères*. In contrast to the abstract and ideal world of high poetry, the world of these genres was a concrete and sober one of penetrating observation and persistent analysis of the "mainsprings" of behavior. Embodied in it was an epochal conception of the human being that was contiguous on the one hand with the discoveries of classical tragedy and comedy, and on the other with everyday knowledge of the self and the surrounding world. Interest in documentary literature thenceforth grew ever more keen. And the point here is not only the cognitive significance of the authenticity of the events described in the documentary work; it is also that literature located outside traditional canons is sometimes able to furnish unusual, even startling insights into spiritual life, thereby anticipating the future discoveries of artists. Rousseau's *La Nouvelle Héloïse*, an immensely successful novel in the mid-eighteenth century, had by the nineteenth already become dated. His *Confessions*, however, will never cease to be a vital, astonishing precursor of nineteenth- and twentieth-century analytical prose.

Fiction draws its material from reality, incorporating that material into an artistic structure. The factual reliability of what is depicted, in particular its origin in the personal experience of the writer, is aesthetically irrelevant (although it is of course essential for the work's creative history). Documentary literature, however, thrives on the open correlation of and struggle between these two principles.

The destinies of people as they are recounted by historians and memoirists may be tragic or absurd, beautiful or ugly. And yet the distinction between the world as it actually was and that of poetic invention is never erased. The special quality of documentary literature lies in that *orientation toward authenticity* of which the reader never ceases to be aware, but which is far from always being the same thing as factual exactitude.

The controversial and apocryphal in memoirs may be explained not merely by the imperfect operation of memory or by intentional suppressions and distortions. Inherent in the very essence of the genre is a kind of ferment of "unreliability." Only pure information (names, dates, and so forth) can completely coincide in the accounts of different memoirists; beyond that point selection, judgment, and point of view come into play.[4] No conversation, unless it has been transcribed at once, can years later be reproduced in all its verbal detail. No event of the external world can be known to the memoirist in all the abundance of its participants' thoughts, experiences, and motives; he may only speculate about them. Thus, the writer's own point of view reshapes the material, and imagination ineluctably strives to fill in the gaps—to retouch, to render more dynamic, to bring to a conclusion. It is understandable that great artists and thinkers have in their autobiographies and memoirs particularly yielded to these temptations.

Factual deviations, however, by no means cancel out either the orientation toward authenticity as the work's structural principle, or the peculiar cognitive and emotional possibilities deriving therefrom. It is that principle that makes documentary literature *documentary*, whereas it is aesthetic organization that makes it *literature* as a phenomenon of art.[5] It is not invention that is necessary for aesthetic significance, but organization—the selection and creative combination of elements reflected in and transfigured by the word. In the aesthetically apprehended documentary context, the real-life fact undergoes profound transformation in the very act of its expression. And this does not mean stylistic ornamentation or superficial figurativeness. The words may remain unadorned—may be "bare," as Pushkin said—but they must possess the special quality of artistic images.

The artistic image is always symbolic; it always stands for something else. It is a particular sign of generalizations, the representation of broad strata of human experience, both social and psychological. The artist creates signs that embody thought, and the latter may not be separated from the former without being destroyed. The memoirist follows a different path, the converse as it were. He cannot create the things and events that are most convenient to him. Events are given to him, and he must reveal in them the latent energy of historical, philosophical, and psychological generalizations, thereby transforming them into the signs of those generalizations. He paves the way from the fact to its significance. And aesthetic life is thereby awakened in the fact; it becomes the form, the image, the representation of an idea. The novelist and the memoirist begin at opposite poles, so to speak, and meet somewhere along the way in a unity of meaning and event.

If one were to schematize these relations, one might say that in fiction the image emerges in the movement from an idea to the individual instance giving it expression, whereas in documentary literature it emerges in the movement from the individual and concrete instance to a generalizing idea. The two ways of writing are at once different modes of generalization and cognition and different ways of constructing artistic symbolism.

Fiction, as it departs from experience, creates a "second reality"; documentary literature provides the reader with a dual cognition and a twofold emotion. This is because his experience of the authenticity of the real-life event remains unmediated by any art at all. A few lines of newsprint affect us differently than does the greatest novel.

The artistic symbol in documentary literature has a distinctive structure. It contains, so to speak, the reader's independent knowledge of the thing being portrayed. The peculiar dynamic of documentary literature lies in the commensurability yet incomplete congruence of two different levels: that of the real-life experience and that of its aesthetic interpretation.

Real-life symbolism finds a place both in the thinking of historians and in the conceptions of historical events and figures present in the consciousness of a society. Everything in the Napoleonic legend, from the bridge at Arcole, to the banner in the hands of the young Bonaparte, to the island of St. Helena, is apprehended as a finished aesthetic structure. The broad strokes of history are accompanied by precise details: the three-cornered hat, the close-fitting gray frock coat, the arms folded across the chest. The events are so tightly bound up with their details that it is as if those details were a deliberate invention. But of course they are not. The island of St. Helena was not something that had been foreseen.

Herzen, a connoisseur as well as master of artistic investigations of the nonfictitious, once compared the indeterminacy yet nonarbitrariness of real-life facts to the objective reality of a biological specimen, and then contrasted the latter with an "anatomical specimen made of wax," which, in his words, is what the heroes of novels are like. "The wax mold may be more expressive, more normal, more *typical*; everything the anatomist knew may be rendered in it, but not *what he did not know* . . . , for in the wax specimen life itself, with all its accidents and mysteries, has dried up, has come to a halt and grown rigid."[6] The accidents of which Herzen is speaking here are indeed accidental in comparison to the carefully weighed characteristics created by the artist as he strives to express his conception in the most perfect way. But they cease to be accidental when a track has been laid from them to the meaning of an event, and when a context has awakened symbolic significance in them. We are surrounded by symbolism of this kind. Aesthetically significant images crop up in life itself, and this pertains above all to the main thing—a person's image or personality [*kharakter*].

Personality in memoirs and in autobiography may be a fact of the same artistic significance as in the novel, inasmuch as it too is a kind of creative construct, and the aesthetic activity giving rise to it goes even further into that everyday knowledge of ourselves and of those around us and encountered by us that is and always has been an indispensable condition of human social interaction.

Images of human beings are constructed in life itself, and an everyday psychology accumulates in the traces of letters, diaries, confessions, and other "human documents" where the aesthetic principle is present to a greater or lesser degree of conscious realization. Aesthetic intention may reach the point in letters and diaries where they become literature clearly meant for a readership, sometimes posthumous and sometimes even contemporary. Memoirs, autobiographies, and confessions are almost always literature presupposing readers in the future or the present; they are a kind of plotted structuring of an image of reality and an image of a human being, whereas letters or diaries fix the indeterminate process of life with its as yet unknown denouement. A forward-looking dynamic is replaced by a retrospective one. The memoiristic genres thus approach the novel without becoming identical to it.

Aesthetic structuring increases as one moves from letters and diaries to biographies and memoirs, and thence to the novel and tale. An immense distance separates the letter replete with psychological revelations from the psychological novel. But there is a unifying principle. The letter and the novel, according to this view, represent different levels in the structuring of images of personality [*lichnost'*], and at any level in that structuring the aesthetic element is inevitably present. Not only is literary personality a structure, but so is personality as we are concerned with it in sociology and history and even in everyday life, a structure that derives from our observations of both internal processes (introspection) and external ones.[7]

Contemporary psychology favors a dynamic conception of personality. Certain trends in twentieth-century Western psychology connected with pragmatism and neorealism have dissolved personality in a ceaseless flux of psychic states. Behavioral psychology has rejected not only the categories of personality and character, but even that of consciousness (an individual's behavior is regulated by the mechanism of "stimulus-response"). Soviet psychologists occupy very different positions, but they too have proceeded far beyond the earlier static view of personality. While revealing the personality's underlying, relatively stable elements, they also insist on a dynamic, functional analysis of its construction. S. L. Rubinshtein, for example, writes that "the personality of a human being is a system of generalized . . . impulses consolidated in an individual. . . . In order for a motive (impulse) to become the attribute of a personality, to become 'stereotyped' in it, it must be generalized in relation to the situation in which it originally occurred, as well as extended to all those other situations that in their essential features are homologous to the first with respect to the personality in question."[8]

Such a conception of personality neither deprives it of its objective preconditions nor condemns it to an elusive fluidity, yet neither does it regard it as a mere datum that acquires figurative dynamism only in literature. Personality is an ideal conception, a structure created by the individual himself in consequence of his self-conception, and continuously created in everyday life by everyone on the basis of observations of other people or of information about them. It is clear that everyone's personality will be subject to a series of interpretations, some sharply divergent, others differing merely in certain details and nuances. Rubinshtein puts particular stress on the unreliability of the results of introspection. "An individual's own version of himself is far from always being the most trustworthy."[9]

But if even everyday personality is a kind of construct, then it follows that in daily life there takes place a continuous selection, omission, and correlation of the elements of personality, that there takes place work, in other words, that is potentially aesthetic, and that reaches its most highly organized form in art. Art is always organization, a struggle with chaos and nonbeing and the transience of life. How naive, therefore, are certain contemporary efforts to turn verbal art—an art that works directly by means of the most universal and powerful tool of organization, the word—into a mouthpiece for formlessness. The word will not perform tasks that are alien to its nature.

"Stream of consciousness," for example, is a completely conventionalized form for depicting a mental process. Using both words and a syntax that, however disjointed, is characteristic of language as a means of generalization, the writer conveys that inner speech that has not yet attained, or that has only partially attained, organized embodiment in the word.

Where, then, at what threshold, does the aesthetic character of psychological constructs emerge? There is no precise boundary here, but there are a number of transitional phenomena, and of course one and the same real life phenomenon may be seen as either aesthetic or extra-aesthetic, depending on the point of view or orientation of the observer. The aesthetic begins, obviously, whenever there is a characteristic experience of the absolute identity and therefore equivalence of the sign and the signified—an experience of significant form and of formalized idea. The beautiful in art, says Hegel, is "an individual formalization of reality" possessing the specific ability "to embody and reveal the ideal."[10]

To a certain extent, personality, the image of a person formed in reality, may itself become just such an "individual formalization" and at the same time extension of that reality. Without this aesthetic potentiality, the well-known fact of the mutual interpenetration in life and in literature of images of personality would be impossible and incomprehensible.

Even Goethe spoke of that interpenetration. In *Dichtung und Wahrheit* he recounted how the creation of *Werther* had been a kind of catharsis for him, a way of resolving a difficult spiritual crisis, and how the book had impressed young minds and produced a rash of suicides. "But, while I felt relieved and enlightened by having turned reality into poetry, my friends were led astray by my work; for they thought that poetry ought to be turned into reality, that such a moral was to be imitated, and that, at any rate, one ought to shoot oneself."[11]

Human social life is shot through with the process of self-organization (whether conscious or automatized). Out of chaos and flux social man identifies and combines those elements that are most valuable and suitable for the situations in which he finds himself—social, professional, domestic, emotional, and so on. He passes, so to speak, through a series of images that are oriented toward shared norms and ideals, images that not only have a social function but that also possess aesthetic coloration. The aesthetic criterion accompanies a person from his very first lessons in social decorum ("It is unattractive to eat with your hands," a child is told, thereby revealing to him the world of acceptable forms of behavior) to the highest ideal of personality developed by an age. The aesthetic stands out most vividly in those periods or circumstances where behavior has a ritual or ceremonial character or a particularly organized form. This is especially true whenever its symbolism is conspicuously material or involves pageantry. The tunic of the military man, the chasuble of the priest, and the gown of the jurist are all symbols of professional conduct, which is not the same thing as the private behavior of the individual soldier, clergyman, or judge.

Psychology has long since raised in this connection the question of the different ways in which someone may structure his individual personality, and of how a particular personality may not necessarily correspond to a single empirical *individuum*. As early as the end of the nineteenth century, William James was maintaining that in practice everyone "has as many different social selves as there are distinct *groups* of persons about whose opinion he cares."[12] Jung, in his well-known book *Psychologische Typen* and in other works as well, also insisted on the possibility of there being more than one personality in the mind of a single (normal) person. Jung proposed the conception of the "mask" (or "persona," from the mask worn onstage by the actors of antiquity). The individual knows of his mask that it is "oriented on the one hand by the expectations and demands of society, and on the other by [his own] social aims and aspirations."[13]

Whether one agrees with these theories or not, the interesting thing about them, at least in the aspect that concerns us, is that they involve the "creatability" of psychic structures by means of the selection, correlation, and symbolic interpretation of psychic elements—by means, that is, of a method analogous to that used by art. Contemporary semiotic literature has proposed the idea of the model and of modeling for phenomena of this kind.

In the course of discussions of structuralism in literary studies, some have noted the danger of substantial changes in content and function occurring whenever the concepts of one terminological language are translated into another. At the same time, however, a new term is indeed called for whenever it really is necessary, whenever it consolidates a new act of cognition. When applied to those structures of human personality that are created in literature and in life itself, is not the idea of the "model" an instance of an unnecessary duplication of terms? Could not one be satisfied with the word "pattern," for example? In the present case one could not. A pattern is more the object of a direct imitation—a replication—whereas the relationship between actual people and the conceptual structures of personality is a complex one. It implies a reproduction that is neither complete nor direct but rather functional, and at the same time it implies cognition of its object. The term "ideal" has, by the same token, not so much a cognitive as a valuational content, and it embraces by no means all of the modes and possibilities of structuring individual personality.

In *The Encyclopedia of Philosophy*, Iurii Gastev defines the model as "a conventional image (representation, schema, description, etc.)" that "serves to express the relationship between human knowledge of objects and the objects themselves."[14] Models may be subdivided into the material and the ideal (imaginary, speculative, conceptual), and the ideal into those that function as figures or images and those that function as signs.

The psychological structures that a person constructs and apprehends in life and in literature may be regarded as kinds of imaginary figurative models. The world of such images of personality exists not according to the principle "pattern equals copy," where the intention is to apprehend the object directly and completely; rather, they reproduce their object schematically, sometimes in only a few of its functions. At the same time, they stimulate definite forms of behavior. Models exist "as a specific image of reality in which are combined elements of the logical and the sensory, the abstract and the concrete, the general and the particular, the visible and the invisible."[15] If one applies these definitions to the modeling of the individual as it occurs in actual life, then the aesthetic potentialities of that modeling become obvious. The idea of the model thus has a specificity that is important to the subject being touched upon here. At the same time, however, one should neither forget the conventionality and approximateness that this term has in the humanities, nor expect of it the precision that it has in the exact sciences and in technology.

Along with the cognition of human beings by means of the philosophy, historiography, and art of an age, an everyday modeling also takes place

Romanticism was accustomed to wanting the impossible, to striving for the unattainable. In this sense too "life-art" was entirely romantic, inasmuch as it was a problem known to have no solution. Life as a whole cannot be aesthetically organized. Art presupposes the linking of signs in time or space, and not merely the organization but also the unity of its material (words, sounds, colors). Its laws cannot be removed to the qualitatively different world of reality with impunity. Even in the theater, where material unity is lacking, there is still the spatial unity of the stage and the temporal unity of the performance. In life there are utterances, conversations, written attestations, gestures, and actions that are inwardly and outwardly combined in a conventional unity. But what remains unassimilated in the aesthetic structure carries too much weight. What should have been the triumph of art in fact destroys its specificity. Conventional images grafted onto life run the risk of being crudely materialized, like the ghosts of spiritualists that rap, speak, and cough.

These destructive and sometimes even comical potentials are especially evident in the "life-art" of twentieth-century symbolism.[29] The romantic confounding of life and art was made possible by the fact that in life itself an ideal sphere had been secured that was closed off to base reality. The "new poetry" of the twentieth century came after realism, an experience that had not failed to leave its mark on all concerned. The "life-art" of the symbolists was thus unable to shake off completely the dust of everyday reality, and for that reason it degenerated into grotesquerie and "mystical clowning." Where, for example, is the line separating buffoonery and idealism in the cult of Liubov' Dmitrievna Blok, whose votaries Andrei Belyi and Sergei Solov'ev proclaimed themselves in the first decade of the 1900s? Even Blok took a dim view of that confusion of the transcendental and the mundane that could not even believe in itself.

There is an interesting correlation between "life-art" and documentary literature. While translating life into its own language, documentary literature at the same time accepts the obligation, so to speak, of preserving the integrity of the facts it takes from life. Thus, if "life-art" structures life according to the laws of art, then the reverse is true of documentary literature: it strives to reveal those relations in life that have not yet been mediated by the plot inventions of artists.

Different periods and cultural stages have perceived the relationship between art and reality in different ways and have had at their disposal different principles for the socioethical and aesthetic modeling of personality. Rationalist ethics operated on the basis of the "norm." The norm was a prescribed type of behavior, abstractly rational, albeit derived from the characteristics of the "natural man" (as was the case with the eighteenth-century philosophes). Characteristics opposed to the norm were relegated to the satirical genres. Within the limits of caste-oriented thought, the norm was externally and uniformly applied to people of a particular social category. Beyond that, however, the possibility was accepted that such people might have various other personal characteristics, and those characteristics were fully tolerated, provided they did not interfere with adherence to the norm.

Romantic ethics, on the other hand, was concerned with the whole personality (despite the polarity of its "mundane" and "divine" principles and the struggle between them). The romantic *ideal* was fundamentally different from the classical and Enlightenment behavioral *norm*, above all in that it was not addressed to a particular social group, nor in any way intended for mass reproduction. Indeed, the very essence of the romantic personality lay in its separateness from the "crowd." The hero and the man of the "crowd" could not share one and the same psychological structure or the same principles of behavior, although the "crowd" could follow the hero, and the hero could show compassion for the "crowd" and sacrifice himself for its sake. The romantic ideal was not a behavioral norm, but a spiritual limit posited only for an elect. Precisely because romanticism was concerned with an elect, it could even allow itself to include vices in its ideal. But of course they were vices of a very special kind. Born of the romantic hero's tragic fate, they possessed a sort of ethical and aesthetic value. Such was the case with romantic demonism, although even the most demonic of romantic heroes was always bound as well to unconditional social and moral values, albeit sometimes in complex and contradictory ways. Decadence later tried to liberate demonism from those values and to justify the depravity of its heroes on exclusively aesthetic grounds.

By the middle of the nineteenth century, a new approach to the study of human beings had emerged, one that proved decisive for the realistic and psychological method in literature. That method did not prescribe a norm for the processes of life; rather, it studied their results. That is why the social type created by nineteenth-century realism was so different from the types of classical comedy or satire. There the author proceeded from a norm established by reason, even depicting the negative type as an antinorm. The social type of nineteenth-century literature, however, was not applied to life from the outside but rather derived from within—by means, obviously, of complex artistic transformations. This did not mean, of course, that the socially and biologically conditioned type of realism was devoid of ethical significance. Literature is too much a matter of values for that. Not infrequently the social type was an indictment, or, on the contrary, a model against which contemporaries might measure themselves. To a greater or lesser degree, this happens whenever any social group becomes aware of the need for the advent of a "new man." What was Bazarov? Not a norm, not an ideal, and certainly not a set of positive characteristics. Among the junior staff of *The Contemporary*, he was even denounced as a lampoon of the younger generation. But Bazarov fought off all attacks and became—with his positive and his negative traits—a standard for the "new men." Moreover, his negative traits (rudeness, cruelty, repudiation of the aesthetic, and so forth) received positive valuation as the signs of a new social position.

The relationship between literary roles and their sources in social life varies from one historical period to another. It has occurred both as an *ideal* relation, presupposing a high degree of aesthetic generalization of the material drawn from life, and as a *real* one, in which literature has sought spontaneous, unstylized contact with reality. There have been great works of verbal art in both these keys.

Symbolic ideality is an integral part of archaic forms of literature and of folklore. The historical development of literature has been marked by a decrease in aesthetic formalization (although, to be sure, the contrary impulse has also found its place). With nineteenth-century realism, the material taken from social life finally broke through stylistic barriers.

The identification of the hero was now no longer oriented toward models that had undergone stylistic modification, but rather toward a typology that had been derived from life itself. Without this underpinning in the reader's apperception of "social roles" (doctor, teacher, student, landowner, government official), the greatest achievement of post-Tolstoian realism, the system of Chekhov with its enormous range and its unprecedentedly minute and sensitive differentiation of current phenomena, could never have come into being. Chekhov referred the reader to everyday social conceptions and at the same time, like any great writer, he actively shaped those conceptions, returning them to public consciousness as aesthetic facts.

Realism obscured the boundary between the organized narrative and the "human document," thereby giving expression to yet another tendency of the perpetual interaction of art and reality. Two models of personality had converged: in relative terms, the *natural* or documentary, and the *artificial* or that freely created by the artist. They had converged, but they had not become identical. Reality and the experience of life were and are the source of both. But in the first instance, that experience keeps invention on a tether and carries on a struggle, as it were, with its structural principle. In the second instance, experience merely provides material for the untrammeled exercise of invention and design.

The novelist may keep to the sequence and interconnection of his prototype events, or he may move a good distance from them. In either case, he knows that he can and that he must create according to his own understanding of things. Tolstoi was fond of preserving the interconnections of life right down to the tiniest details, but even he said in this regard, "Andrei Bolkonskii is no one, just like any other novelist's character."[30] The novel (the third part of this book is devoted to the psychological novel) created an ideal structure, at the same time allowing poetic invention the utmost liberty to organize the elements it required in the most perfect, purposeful, and expressive of unities.

If the strength of the documentary genres lies in their indeterminacy, in the fact that they are not something "made up," then the strength of fiction lies conversely in its unlimited possibilities of organization, in the potential perfection of its freely emerging plan. As Pushkin said, "The very idea of the *Inferno* is the fruit of great genius" ("Retort to Kiukhel'beker's Articles in *Mnemosyne*").

Supreme aesthetic organization is a powerful force, one capable of driving a culture. Tolstoi, Dostoevskii, and other great novelists have shown what a "second reality" imagined by genius can be for the spiritual life of mankind. Tolstoi was a veteran of the Sevastopol' campaign, yet he did not write memoirs about it. He—the creator of worlds—transformed his military experience into the artistic revelations of the *Sevastopol' Stories* and of *War and Peace*. But the new in art does not invalidate the old, and highly organized forms do not supersede those that are less organized or that are organized on different principles. The latter too have their own irreplaceable possibilities.

I have touched in a preliminary way in this introduction on a number of questions that will subsequently be immersed in the study of concrete historical material. The two theoretical poles between which that study moves are the structuring and cognition of historical personality and the analysis of individual spiritual life. These phenomena are interrelated, to be sure, and both are investigated on a number of different levels, from letters to the psychological novel. The subject of investigation on each of those levels is the phenomena that are most characteristic of it. In the familiar correspondence of Russians of the 1830s, the structuring of historical personality took place in a highly charged atmosphere of moral inquiry and psychological self-analysis. Saint-Simon's *Mémoires*, Rousseau's *Confessions*, and Herzen's *My Past and Thoughts* are indispensable for investigation of the characteristic problems and methodologies of memoiristic evidence about the human being. The writings of Lev Tolstoi—a main topic of the third part of this book—are the high point of nineteenth-century analytical novel.

Was this moral and at the same time psychological self-examination a fundamentally new phenomenon in Russian culture?

Sentimentalism, with its uniform ideal of the natural and sensitive man, had also fostered a heightened interest in inner life. As is well known, the special identity of Russian sentimentalism lay in the fact that it was advanced not by the bourgeoisie, as had been the case with Western sentimentalism, but by the social stratum that later came to be called the "educated nobility."

The members of this group were military officers and government officials, sometimes very prominent ones ([the poet] Ivan Dmitriev, for example, was an actual privy councillor and minister of justice), and could not, of course, have conducted themselves according to the rules governing sensitive hearts.[3] But no one expected them to. Their mode of life was determined by other norms based on caste. Yet the history of Russian cultural thought at the end of the eighteenth and the beginning of the nineteenth centuries was acquainted with other kinds of phenomena as well. There was, for example, the intimate circle of the Turgenev brothers, which included [the writers] Voeikov, Merzliakov, Andrei Kaisarov, and the young Zhukovskii. In his *Zhukovskii: The Poetry of Feeling and "Sincere Imagination,"* Aleksandr Veselovskii notes the characteristic features of the spiritual life of that circle: close attention to the inner man, self-absorption, the ideal of self-perfection, the moral significance of journals and confessions (which Zhukovskii would continue to insist on), and friendship conceived as a means of self-knowledge and mutual cultivation.[4] All this anticipated, as it were, the forms of circle social life in the 1830s.

The freedom-loving, civic mood that captivated part of the membership of the Turgenev circle did not immediately replace the spiritual habits inculcated in their youth both by the Freemason Prokopovich-Antonskii, who headed the university Nobility Pension where the Turgenev brothers and Zhukovskii had studied, and by Ivan Petrovich Turgenev, whose moral authority was beyond question not merely for his sons, but also for their comrades.

I. P. Turgenev, one of the most important representatives of Moscow Freemasonry, in 1783 translated and published [the British moralist] John Mason's popular book *Self-Knowledge.* The young Zhukovskii read it carefully, and it served him as a practical guide for self-improvement. Mason's book is a typical blend of Masonic mysticism, political loyalism, and pragmatic moral-psychological excursions into the sphere of self-knowledge, including a description of appropriate exercises and of various techniques for the observation of one's own spiritual life. The purpose of these exercises is religious purification of the soul and the achievement of mystical union with God, although the suggested means are often marked by a kind of psychological concreteness. Thus Mason mentions the necessity of knowing one's own temperament or "constitution," and of acting "decently and in keeping with" one's own character. The book is rife with appeals for a cultivated and skeptical self-scrutiny, which is compared to the examination of things "through a magnifying glass": "For in order to a true *self knowledge*, the human mind, with its various powers and operations, must be narrowly inspected; all of its secret bendings and doublings displayed. Otherwise our self acquaintance will be but very partial and defective; and the heart after all will deceive us."[5] Accordingly, chapter 12 of the book's first part is entitled, "Everyone that knows, is in a particular manner sensible how far he is governed by a Thirst for applause." Chapter 11 of the first part is called "Concerning the secret springs of our Actions" and contains the following: "Another considerable branch of self acquaintance is, to know the true motives and secret springs of our actions. . . . It is not only possible, but very common, for men to be ignorant of the chief inducements of their behavior; and to imagine they act from one motive, whilst they are apparently governed by another."

There are other statements of the kind in the book: "We may meet with frauds and faithless dealings from men; but after all, our own hearts are the greatest cheats; and there are none we are in greater danger from than ourselves" (pt. 3, chap. 1). And: "Would you know yourself, you must very carefully attend to the frame and emotions of your mind under some extraordinary incidents. Some sudden accidents which befall you when the mind is most off its guard, will better discover its secret turn and prevailing disposition than much greater events you are prepared to meet" (pt. 3, chap. 7).

If we turn from these reflections to the journals of the young Zhukovskii, the latter's provenance becomes clear. "What am I like? What is good in me? What is bad? What is occasioned by circumstance? What by nature? What can be acquired and how? What must be corrected and how? What can be neither acquired nor corrected? . . . What kind of happiness is possible for someone of my character? These are problems on whose solution some (much) time will have to be spent. They will be solved bit by bit in the course of my journal" (entry for June 13, 1805).[6]

The entry for July 30, 1804, begins, "Today was spent most unpleasantly. I was dissatisfied with myself, upset, disheartened." There follows an analysis of "today" in the form of a conversation between two speakers that fixes the psychological consequences of the most fleeting impressions. This is also a tendency of Protestant religious-moralistic and Masonic literature. The author of *Self-Knowledge* frequently reminds us that in the evening "we should review and examine the several actions of the day, the various tempers and dispositions, we have been in, and the occasions that excited them" (pt. 3, chap. 1). The journals of the young

Zhukovskii are a monument to the early attempts of Russian thought to analyze the inner human being. The moral program of that self-analysis was oriented toward a kind of self-sufficient ideal of the sensitive and virtuous man. A person's merits or defects were measured against that preestablished ideal; they were not individualized. In his early journals and letters, Zhukovskii dwells in particular on such of his own defects as sloth, idleness, and lethargy—defects that had also been envisaged by Masonic literature, with its own requirement of individual activity and vigor. John Mason's chapter called "Self-Knowledge promotes our Usefulness in the World" is devoted to the question of the maximal utilization of one's gifts. Discussed in it are those who "live away whole days, weeks, and sometimes months together, to as little purpose, . . . as if they had been asleep all the while" (pt. 3, chap. 7). On August 26, 1805, Zhukovskii wrote in his journal:

> In my present frame of mind I don't even feel the need to think: such moments are very close to nothingness, or are even worse than nothingness, since you feel something unpleasant. . . . How did I spend my youth? I lived in complete idleness. . . . No one showed any particular concern for me, and . . . whatever concern was shown seemed like charity to me. I was not abandoned or cast out, I had a place of my own, but . . . I did not feel anyone's love; consequently, I could not be grateful out of genuine feeling, but only from a sense of obligation. . . . That made me cold. . . . Whoever is isolated from others has no subject for reflection. . . . His character is made timid, indecisive, listless, indolent, for character too is formed through activity.[7]

Zhukovskii is concerned here with the circumstances in which his character was formed; they are biographically concrete, but not individualized. Social disadvantage (in particular, an illegitimate birth), an unhappy childhood, and a lonely youth were all traditional motifs of sentimentalism, but they were also part of Zhukovskii's actual experience. From that experience, he selected and formulated precisely those elements that fit already existing general formulas, just as the poetry of sentimentalism had done.

The theme of activity, of the struggle against idleness and sloth, is present too in Zhukovskii's early correspondence. "How excellent it would be if we could all live together—and by living I don't mean *breathing*, *sleeping*, and *eating*, but *acting* and taking pleasure in one's activity; it follows that that activity must lead to something lofty, or else how could one take pleasure in it?" (letter to Aleksandr Turgenev of September 11–16, 1805).[8] The same thing occurs in a letter written five years later (November 7, 1810): "All my past life is shrouded in a kind of fog of *spiritual inactivity* in which it is impossible to discern anything. . . . So, my dear friend, *activity* and *its object, utility*—these are what inspire me now."[9] It is clear from the letters as a whole that Zhukovskii conceived of such activity as inner work on the self and as the business of the writer.

Zhukovskii reflected a great deal in his early letters on the nature of true friendship. It is very hard for an isolated person to be active and virtuous. Friendship in a special, moralistic interpretation is the central act of spiritual life. It is at once the condition and the consequence of action and virtue. "We must labor and act together, so that we may later be made worthy of friendship and therefore become friends. Friendship is a virtue; it is everything, only not in one person, but in two (or even in three or four, but the more the better). If it should be said of me: he is a true friend, that would be the same as saying: he is a virtuous, noble person who is animated by a *single* flame in concert with another being who is his equal, who sustains him, and who is sustained by him. That is how I understand friendship" (letter of September 11–16, 1805).[10]

The forms of familiar intercourse, so various in different epochs and milieus, are important indications of prevailing conceptions of the human being and of his psychological structure and purpose in life.

The beginning of the nineteenth century saw the emergence of yet another line in the development of the Russian educated nobility, one leading to Decembrism (in the broad sense) and the generation of Pushkin. That generation included people either connected with the noblemen's rebellion or located on its periphery, people who (before the Decembrist catastrophe) had been engaged in practical tasks, and who preferred the legacy of the French and Russian Enlightenment to the traditions of Anglo-German sentimentalism. People of this stamp were characterized both by civic zeal and Voltairean skepticism, and by a hidden inner life. That life was revealed neither in conversation with one's friends, nor in letters and journals (as demonstrated by the diaries of Pushkin, the notebooks of [the poet] Viazemskii, and so on). It was opened only by the key of poetry, where it became, in aesthetically transmuted form, the possession of all who could read. Such people could have applied to themselves the words of Montaigne: "Many things that I would not want to tell anyone, I tell the public; and for my most secret knowledge and thoughts I send my most faithful friends to the bookseller's shop."[11] Neither the psychic trouble of Batiushkov, which led to mental illness, nor the severe hypochondria of Viazemskii, nor the tempestuous emotional life of Pushkin left much trace in their voluminous correspondence. People of Pushkin's day used vulgar language in their letters as a matter of course, but they concealed the secrets of their hearts with stubborn modesty. They would have turned away with astonishment and disdain from the incredible admissions of the familiar correspondence of the 1830s and 1840s.

The cult of friendship remained intact from the circle of the young Zhukovksii and the Turgenev brothers, to the Pushkin circle, and thence to the Stankevich circle, although its forms changed dramatically. For

Zhukovskii, friendship had been a means for self-improvement and the achievement of moral perfection. For Pushkin, friends were the comrades of one's childhood games and youthful feasts, one's soulmates and boon companions. "Chaadaev, you remember how it was?" ["To Chaadaev," 1826].

In the 1830s friendship was strenuous, demanding, and utterly candid. It cultivated the skills of psychological analysis, which took the form of a kind of mutual reflection in response to the expanded personality's need for continuous self-realization and self-revelation.

Post-Decembrist romanticism was marked by an intense interest in the inner life of the personality—the *elect personality*, obviously. Later on it will be necessary to say more about the paradox of romantic individualism, in consequence of which its elect personalities were not individual at all, but reproduced a shared model: that of the Byronic demon, say, or the Schellingian poet.

Authentically individual analysis and individual treatment of universally significant moral values emerged at the end of the 1830s and the beginning of the 1840s in a time of transition, of severe crisis in Russian romantic thought. It emerged in the circles of that era, the outposts of the passionate intellectual life of young Russia.

Romanticism as such was not self-analytical. It was more interested in the image of personality than in the mechanisms that set it in motion. To be sure, minds raised on the Enlightenment and rationalist philosophy had not delved very deeply into examination of the "inner man" either. Zhukovskii broke that inner man down into predetermined virtues and defects. For later positivism, already widespread in the Russia of the 1840s, life was not primarily an ethical fact. That is why the Stankevich circle, with its romanticism in retreat before Hegelianism (in a peculiarly Russian version), is of such interest. It was here in fact that the question of personality as a historical phenomenon and as an individual psychological unity was first posed in earnest, as were the corollary questions of destiny, behavior, and the personality's moral responsibility in regard to its own qualities. Reality was viewed as the embodiment of spirit, of Reason, and everything that took place within that reality, everything that happened to the individual, could therefore have philosophical and ethical significance.

Three extraordinary figures stand at the head of circle intellectual life: Stankevich, Bakunin, and Belinskii.

The striking thing about Mikhail Bakunin's biography is that he seems to have lived several lives. The Bakunin of the 1830s was a romantic, a Fichtean, a Hegelian, a member of the Stankevich circle, a friend and adversary of Belinskii, and the inspirer of the "Premukhino Idyll." The 1840s for Bakunin were years of study, of wandering, and of association with the international revolutionary movement—he was one of the organizers of the Dresden uprising of 1849. The 1850s saw him in Russian and Austrian jails, in exile in Siberia, and finally, in 1861, at the age of forty-seven, escaping from Siberia abroad, where he became an active collaborator in Herzen's publishing ventures, and subsequently the leader of world anarchism.

The young Bakunin was one of the last and most brilliant expressions of Russian romanticism. The numerous letters that have survived from the 1830s document both the manner in which he constructed his personality and the ways in which its image was refracted in the minds of his family and friends, especially the members of the Stankevich circle. There were many different perceptions of Bakunin, but all concerned agreed that his personality had an especially structured quality, with sharply pronounced features tending toward clear-cut historical and moral attributes. It was indeed for this reason that literature did not pass him by. Bakunin became the prototype (in one case certainly, in the other probably) of the heroes of novels by Turgenev and Dostoevskii. The Bakunin archives show very clearly how this young man, whose lot until then had been merely that of a private being, at a certain point began to ally himself with the historical life of his time.

Premukhino, the name of the Bakunin family estate in the Tver' district, has a permanent place in the history of Russian culture. The "Premukhino Idyll" or "Premukhino Harmony" was a whole complex with its own ideology and style. That style, moreover, had a dual manifestation. In the 1810s and 1820s it was something quite consciously, even systematically, created by Aleksandr Mikhailovich Bakunin, Mikhail Bakunin's father and the head of the immense patriarchal family. Later on, in the 1830s, the spiritual life of Premukhino was dominated by the young people under the inspiration of the oldest brother, Mikhail, and Premukhino then became one of the focal points of Russian romanticism, especially of the romantic cult of femininity. Bakunin's four sisters served as the objects of that cult, which was maintained by Mikhail's brothers and friends, including Belinskii, Stankevich, Botkin, and Kliushnikov.

In 1828 the fourteen-year-old Mikhail Bakunin was appointed to the Artillery School in Petersburg and left Premukhino for five years. In the letters of the young military-academy pupil there is as yet no evidence of either individual or historical personality. Instead, one finds a politically conformist youth who obviously lacks those intellectual interests that were already familiar to Herzen and Ogarev at an even earlier age, a youth with rather naive literary tastes and ideas who spoke of the historical novels of [the second-rate] Bulgarin with esteem, and then remarked of the just published *Boris Godunov* that "Pushkin's passionate admirers see only beauty in it. But there are defects as well."[12] Nonetheless, even in

Bakunin's early letters (1832–1833), his spiritual experiences were oriented toward a definite literary model, one formulated in accordance with the rules of sentimentalism.

> Your letter, dear Varen'ka, disappointed me [Bakunin wrote to his sister Varvara]. It proved to me that my thoughts and my hopes are an empty chimera, that tender friendship, that precious gift from on high, does not exist for me, poor wretch, since I could not find it in a sister, one whom I adored. . . . For it is she who has destroyed my infatuation with her. But what is to be done? That is the way of the world, and I am only now beginning to understand the full truth of something Auntie once said: "How many more times will you be disappointed, dear Michel, how many more times will your hopes and dreams be dashed, how much longer will it be before you begin to accept the world as it is!" (1:98–99)

It is no accident that a Karamzinian flavor, one obviously quite dated by the early 1830s, predominates in the young Bakunin's letters. It was in fact that cultural legacy that he received from his parents. Aleksandr Mikhailovich Bakunin was a freethinker (there is even a suggestion that in the most circumspect way he took part in the drafting of the charter for the [Masonic] Union of Welfare) who had mellowed with time and exchanged his nonconformism for moderately conservative views. He was an enlightened late eighteenth-century Russian nobleman, and it followed that for him the literature of sentimentalism was the most advanced.

Aleksandr Mikhailovich also inculcated that style of life and literature in the numerous members of his family. The Premukhino way of life was conceived as the embodiment of a kind of sentimentalist and Enlightenment, and at the same time feudal, utopia. Its program was set forth by the dilettante poet Aleksandr Mikhailovich in the 1820s in a lengthy poem (preserved in the family archive) called "Osuga," the name of the small river on which Premukhino was situated.

> I see the peaceful village filled
> With labor-loving peasant folk;
> I haven't any notion why
> Our intellectuals call them slaves!
> With labors well within their reach
> They render our established share.
>
> · · · · · · · · · · ·
>
> The house is large, without parquet,
> No lavish carpets spread around,
> Nor other cherished bric-a-brac,
> *Not even tables laid for cards.*
>
> · · · · · · · · · ·

When at the turn of eventide,
The family comes to gather round
Like swarming bees within the hive,
I'm more contented than the Tsar.
I'm surrounded by familial love,
The Tsar by courtly masquerade;
To me fly honey-laden bees,
While drones consume the Tsar's largesse.[13]

The poem expresses very definite sociopolitical and moral assumptions and ideals, stylistically shaped under the immediate influence of Derzhavin's "Life at Zvanka" [1807] and the sentimentalist epistles of the elder Karamzinians.

The mode of life and epistolary style of the Bakunin sisters were, in essence, permanently formed by sentimentalism, despite all the later accretions of romantic features. Mikhail Bakunin too was for a long time unable to cast off the view of life of the "man of sensibility."

In a long letter to his father written in December 1837, Bakunin reviewed his past, returning to the values and standards prescribed by the Premukhino utopia. His childhood had been a time of sacred love and friendship linking all the members of the family, a time when the children's inquisitive minds had been nurtured under the enlightened and humane guidance of their father. Then came the years of study at the Artillery School, a period of spiritual defilement and devastation yielding to a new moral fervor. The Bakunin of 1837 already saw the world quite differently, of course, but in his letter he was singling out certain elements of his complex spiritual life. He appears there as the man of sensibility, clad in the appropriate style, one familiar to his father and easily understood by him. A happy childhood, youthful lapses, impulses to purification—all this is very general and could be characteristic of any disciple of the sentimentalists; it makes no claim to being in any way exceptional. Nevertheless, awareness of his own exceptional nature did in fact develop in Bakunin with extraordinary force—to the degree that he worked out his historical personality while coming to grips with romanticism and romantic philosophy.

The intellectual life of the 1830s was varied and chaotic. Romanticism at that time embraced a wide variety of different spheres—from the academic, where it flourished in the soil of careful study of contemporary philosophy, to the philistine, where it was transformed into a foolish craving for effect. The elasticity of the boundaries separating the different "romanticisms" made possible the eclecticism of the period. The young had already absorbed the romantic legacy in its entirety, simultaneously adopting Pushkin and [the Byronic] Bestuzhev-Marlinskii, Zhukovskii

world and yield to desecrating it. . . . You see how reasonable I am: others flee the blows of fate, but I seek them out in order to secure my independence forever. (1:187)

Bakunin's attitude, as we see here, was a fully conscious one. The elements he incorporated into his personal image were few in number, but they were reiterated in letter after letter. Above all they included the celebration of single-minded will and the stern renunciation of earthly blessings and pleasures and of one's external "I" for the sake of enriching that "I" by means of the higher life of the spirit (again the romantic dialectic of the universal and the personal): "I think *my personal I* has been destroyed forever; it no longer seeks anything for itself, and its life will henceforth be lived in the absolute, where my *personal I* has found more than it has lost" (1:398).

All this had little in common with the extremely careless and disordered empirical existence of the young Bakunin. But that did not disconcert him in the least. In constructing his image, Bakunin proceeded not from psychological particulars, but from his theories, intentions, and ideals. He proceeded from everything that moved him deeply, that claimed his passionate attention, and that he therefore saw as the highest reality. His self-affirmation was carried out entirely on an ideal plane, and for that reason it knew no limits: "Great storms and thunderclaps, trembling earth, I do not fear you, I despise you, for I am a man! . . . I am a man, and I shall be a god!" (1:262). And in another letter, written later: "Jesus Christ began as a man-animal and finished as a man-god, such as we all must be" (1:384–385). In his own way, the twenty-three-year-old Bakunin here anticipated a problem that would later interest Dostoevskii: Kirillov's basic idea in *The Devils* that whoever overcomes the fear of death becomes a god.

In creating his "man-god," Bakunin performed a kind of artistic act. His titanic conception of himself had its own style nourished on the precepts of 1830s Russian romanticism. The latter was an amalgam of many romanticisms that omitted, however, those elements that were unnecessary to its system: the irony of the early German romantics, for example, or the folkloristic interests of the late. But above all it was an amalgam of sensibility and emotionalism, the sources of which were diverse. There was the still unexhausted legacy of sentimentalism, there was Jean-Paul interpreted in a one-sided way without his irony, there was Schiller, and there was the febrile writing of the French, especially the novels of George Sand, which were becoming increasingly influential. The affective style of the young Bakunin's letters was much more direct and uniform than that employed by Herzen in his own letters of the 1830s. There were two reasons for this (in addition to the psychological ones). In the first place,

Herzen, unlike Bakunin, was already turning himself into a major writer and was involuntarily breaking stylistic molds; in the second, Herzen was writing to his betrothed and to his friends in his native language, whereas Bakunin's letters to his sisters were for the most part written in French, a fact that deprived their style of its creative source.

The young Bakunin elaborated the titanic image of the prophet and "man-god" principally in his letters to his sisters and to their friends Aleksandra and Natal'ia Beer, but he also did so in his letters to his younger brothers. As has often been observed in the biographical literature devoted to him, Bakunin's messianism in the 1830s was above all of a domestic variety.

Herzen was no stranger to domestic romantic messianism either. It was a phenomenon characteristic of the era and it followed logically from the philosophy of "life-art." Thus, while living in exile in Viatka, Herzen was surrounded by young friends whom he introduced to a lofty spiritual life. Natal'ia Zakharina had her proselytes as well. She was the object of devotion for several young girls whom she educated in a religiously romantic spirit.

There were, of course, not a few heterogeneous admixtures in this everyday messianism: inborn imperiousness, youthful conceit, and even the habits of the manor. As if guessing at the possibility of such a reproach, Herzen wrote to his betrothed in 1836 about her lady's maid and companion, the serf Sasha Vyrlina, "Tell your Sasha, so she won't lose hope. I give her my word as a nobleman that, as soon as it is possible, I shall purchase her freedom, and she can serve you the rest of her life—for serving you is no humiliation; if you were a noblewoman, I would not advise it, but you are an angel, and if the whole human race were to kneel down before you, it would not abase itself, but only do what it had once done before another Virgin" (21:106).

For the young Herzen, however, domestic romantic propaganda merely accompanied more important goals. He had already experienced the practical work of the social struggle, even suffering imprisonment and exile. For him the idea of a calling or mission now meant historically meaningful behavior. The Bakunin of the 1830s was another matter, an activist on behalf of a cause he himself still did not know, someone entirely preoccupied with his own inner life and with questions of moral perfection. For Bakunin, the domestic world was no less the dominion of absolute spirit than the universe itself.

The future leader of the Dresden armed insurrection and stalwart of world anarchism expended enormous energy to insure that the lives of the members of his domestic circle developed along the lines of the program he had set out for them. There were numerous pretexts for exercising that energy, since the relationships in the circle were distinguished by a fundamental disorder. Bakunin's sister Liubov' was engaged to Stankevich. He had ceased to love her and with difficulty tried to hide that fact from his betrothed as long as she remained alive. Belinskii was unhappily in love with Aleksandra Bakunina, who subsequently had an unsuccessful romance with Botkin. Bakunin himself regarded his sister Tat'iana with a tenderness that patently exceeded the bounds of brotherly feeling and left him vulnerable to pangs of jealousy. Especially great upheavals and family convulsions accompanied the struggle to "liberate Varen'ka," Bakunin's attempt to obtain the divorce of his sister Varvara Aleksandrovna from her husband, D'iakov, since their marriage had failed to satisfy the philosophical demand for ideal spiritual harmony between husband and wife.[19]

Extraordinary disarray and confusion reigned in 1836 in the Beer household as well. Aleksandra Beer was planning to enter a convent. Natal'ia Beer, who not long before had been hopelessly in love with Stankevich, suddenly revealed that she was in love with Bakunin, although until then she had been thought to nurture an adoration of him on purely philosophical grounds. All of this was accompanied by tiffs and reconciliations between the Beer sisters and their young lady friends at Premukhino. Bakunin and his friends occupied themselves with making philosophical sense of these peripeties, although the latter would have provoked only ridicule from the people of Pushkin's time. One must keep in mind, however, the great interest taken by the Russian romantics of the 1830s in the inner life of those around them, and their search for ways to evaluate and explain it; one must keep in mind, that is, all that would later sustain Russian literary psychologism. Even nervous noblewomen had their value here, as did much else that in its initial domestic guise might have seemed merely ludicrous or tedious. "It was complete chaos," Natal'ia Beer wrote the Bakunin sisters in regard to a meeting she had had with Mikhail, "a profusion of sensations and ideas that utterly astonished me. . . . There were moments (oh, for me those moments were truly hellish) when I wanted to purchase . . . with the most terrible of misfortunes the power to revive him or to be destroyed myself, and by my death to bestow new life on a new woman, a woman who would give him happiness, who would take care of him and be his guardian angel. At those moments I wanted to have the power of God."[20]

It was precisely this ecstatic milieu that accepted without modification the image of the prophet and "man-god" that Bakunin created. He would never have dared to present that image in pure form to his friends in the Stankevich circle; they would have given it a harsh rebuff.

Great ideological movements frequently have not only their vulgarizers but also their parasitical following, which transforms their ideas into a fad or game. We are confronted here with a phenomenon that might be called "feminine romantic parasitism." Rationalistic culture produced a number of notable women, from La Fayette and Sévigné to Madame de Staël. But in order to obtain recognition in the seventeenth and eighteenth centuries, a woman had to have her own gifts and accomplishments. In this sense she was faced with requirements that were, in a manner of speaking, broadly human. German romanticism also brought to the fore a number of talented women: Caroline Schlegel, Rahel Varnhagen, Bettina von Arnim (although, except for Bettina, they wrote almost nothing but letters). The romantics put the question differently, however. Romantic culture assumed and required the presence of woman in the guise of beautiful lady, as bearer of the principle of the eternally feminine, and so forth. This stimulated the women of romantic circles to play a definite role that was independent of their personal qualities and gifts. Hence their occasional ideological mimicry or their distorted and shallow reflection of the complex spiritual life of the true ideologues. Natal'ia Aleksandrovna Herzen was unquestionably both a talented writer and a talented person. One cannot say the same of the Bakunin sisters, with their exaltation inculcated in them by Michel. As for the Beer sisters, that exaltation had already passed over into hysteria.

In 1848 Turgenev published the story "Tat'iana Borisovna and Her Nephew," in which there appears a female character who, though minor, is nonetheless important for an understanding of the narrative. She is an "old maid of about thirty-eight and a half, the kindest sort of creature, but warped, strained, and given to transports of rapture." She "fell in love with a young student who was passing through, and at once began a vigorous and ardent correspondence with him. As is customary, she gave him her blessing in her missives for a sacred and beautiful life, sacrificed her 'whole being,' asked merely the name of sister, abandoned herself to descriptions of nature, alluded to Goethe, Schiller, Bettina, and German philosophy, and of course drove the poor youth to black despair."

These lines are known to be a pitiless depiction of Tat'iana Aleksandrovna Bakunina, and they refer to her unsuccessful romance with Turgenev, which began in 1841. The style of Tat'iana Bakunina's love letters (and of those of all the women in her circle) is portrayed with great precision.[21] It may be that Turgenev dealt especially harshly with that style because he himself had been compelled to pay it tribute. In entering the Premukhino world, he behaved in accordance with its romantic precepts. The following are some lines from a farewell letter he wrote to Tat'iana Bakunina (on March 20, 1842):

> You alone will understand me: it is for you alone that I would be a poet, for you, with whom my soul is in some ineffable and miraculous way conjoined, so that I hardly need to see you at all, or feel the need to talk to you . . . ; and

in spite of that, never, in hours of creativity and deep and solitary bliss, do you leave me; it is to you, to you, my excellent sister, that I read whatever issues from my pen. . . . Oh, if only once I could walk with you some spring morning down that long, long avenue of lindens, if only I could hold your hand in mine and feel our two souls merging.[22]

A passage in German follows in which figure the words "blessing," "sister," and "best and only friend." Thus, not only the rapturous "old maid," but also the "young student who was passing through"—Turgenev himself, that is—was answerable for the parodied style. The romantic milieu required accommodation even from those natures that were poorly suited to it.

It should be said that the world of Premukhino remained true to its precepts in even the most tragic of circumstances. Varvara Aleksandrovna Bakunina met Stankevich abroad in 1840, and they came to an immediate understanding and declared their love for each other. Five weeks later Stankevich died. For Varvara Aleksandrovna this was a catastrophe in which all her hopes for happiness and a new life had perished. Yet the very next day, while seated by Stankevich's body (he had died during their joint trip from Rome to Milan), she wrote down her thoughts and feelings in accordance with all the rules of the Premukhino style. The page with these notes in German (the language of romanticism) has been preserved in the Bakunin family archive:

Oh no, no, my beloved, I have not forgotten your words; we met and we recognized each other! We are joined together for eternity; our separation is brief, and that new kingdom that has already been revealed to you—it will be mine too, for there love is infinite, there the power of the Spirit is infinite! . . . That faith was yours! It is mine too. Brother, do you recognize me, does the voice of a sister reach you in eternity? I shall recognize you in your new strength and beauty. . . . And you also will recognize her, you will divine her—that sister you left far behind!

A frankly philosophical discourse then follows in which the voice of Michel is clearly audible:

In and of itself the material world is nothing, and only through its internal union with the spirit has my being, my *I* received its reality. Only through that for me incomprehensible conjunction of the infinite and the finite has my *I* become an *I*, a living, independent being. When I say "I," I become conscious of myself, I become known to myself. Through a reverse convergence with the Universal, I of necessity lose this consciousness of myself—my individuality disappears; I am no longer I, and only the Universal remains. Spirit for itself. Thus, I am nothing! What then is death? There is little comfort in this.[23]

These words were written by a woman seated next to the remains of her beloved, who had just passed away. If romantic philosophy in that circle was a fashion imbibed secondhand, it was nevertheless one that was lived with great seriousness. That is why Bakunin relied so heavily on the audience of young ladies and adolescent brothers he himself had trained. Among his friends, however, Bakunin's preaching took forms that were much more cautious and less consistent with his inner sense of himself. The style of his letters to his friends is accordingly also of a quite different nature. The letters are more colloquial, simpler, and philosophical ideas are expounded in them in a dry and specialized language.[24] Bakunin was obviously intimidated by Stankevich with his sober judgments and his unquestioned authority in the circle, and in his letters to Stankevich there is neither the edifying nor the oracular tone. On the contrary, there are even complaints about his own spiritual inadequacy: "To end my life [if he does not manage to go to Berlin to study] as an artillery lieutenant or as an actual state councillor makes no difference to me: I am neither the first, nor shall I be the last who has been stopped short of his ideal aspiration, which anyway is quite often nothing more than the agitated movement of young blood. I have remained the same decent and absurd fellow you once knew. . . . And so you see, my dear Stankevich, neither my external, nor my inner life deserves much attention" (2:297).[25] From prophet to lieutenant of artillery—such was the range of Bakunin's self-definition. No less variegated were the ways in which he was perceived by those around him. The proselytes bowed down before the prophet, but their father, irritated by his son's philosophical experiments, declared that Michel was puffed up with egoism and "blind self-regard," and that he cared only for flatterers and longed "to hold sway in the family."[26]

Granovskii was frightened of Bakunin's "abstract energy" ("For him there no subjects, only objects"), and in 1840 confided to Ia. Neverov, "I have never before encountered such a monstrous creature. Until you get to know him better, it is enjoyable and even useful to talk to him, but on closer acquaintance, it gets oppressive—*unheimlich* somehow. I am afraid he will run into Stankevich again somewhere. He will torment him the same way he did Botkin."[27] But the Botkin who (in 1838) had been tormented by Bakunin wrote to him, "All the hostility I felt for you is gone, and reborn are those sacred moments when you were for me the evangel of the secrets of a higher life."[28] The contrast between these two judgments warrants the linking of Bakunin with Dostoevskii's Stavrogin, who either destroyed those people he came into contact with or acquainted them with the "secrets of a higher life."

Bakunin's personality breaks up into a series of divergent images created by himself, by the members of his family, by his friends, and later on by the memoirists and writers for whom he served as a prototype. Furthermore, his friends perceived him differently at different periods in their association with him. It follows that there was no ready-made, reliable Bakunin personality that had only to be taken from reality and depicted, although this certainly does not mean that it lacked objective qualities. Bakunin's psychological makeup manifested itself in a variety of ways, and interpretations and evaluations of it were therefore just as various, yet underneath them all, if one looks closely enough, there is a rather stable behavioral mechanism. Whether praising Bakunin or excoriating him, his contemporaries continually returned to the contradiction between the speculative power of his mind and the insufficiency of his concrete grasp of life, between the indefatigable energy of his spirit and a sort of deficiency in human feeling. Belinskii called Bakunin a prophet and a god of thunder "whose organism lacks passion." One had only to weaken or remove one of the components of that contradiction for the mechanism of Bakunin's behavior to collapse.

It is precisely for this reason that Turgenev met with failure when he used Bakunin as the prototype for his Rudin. Turgenev retained Bakunin's abstractness and hortatory fervor in his Rudin, but he deprived the character of force. The vast logical speculations of the young Bakunin were turned into the impotent introspection of the superfluous man. Whatever resemblance there might have been was therefore immediately dissolved. Herzen said in this regard, "Turgenev, taken with God's practice in the Bible, created Rudin in his own image and likeness; Rudin is a second Turgenev who has been thoroughly exposed to the young Bakunin's philosophical jargon" (11:359). Chernyshevskii, after calling Rudin a "caricature," added, "as if a lion were a fit subject for caricature."[29] In revising his novel, Turgenev gradually moved away from the task of rendering Bakunin's portrait (the original, obviously more portraitlike versions have been lost), yet he never repudiated the parallel. With Bakunin in mind, he declared in a letter written in 1862, "I presented a rather true portrait of him in Rudin; now he is the Rudin *not* killed on a barricade."[30] Turgenev gave a number of Bakunin's individual features to Rudin, but he disrupted the functioning of the basic principle underlying his character—the initial contradiction between his inner coldness, his deficient humanity, and that "leonine quality" that Belinskii spoke of even in times of bitter conflict with him.

The Bakunin problem assumes a different form in Dostoevskii's *Devils*. Leonid Grossman, in arguing that Bakunin was the prototype for Stavrogin, has enumerated twenty points of resemblance. Viacheslav Polonskii and other opponents of Grossman (V. Borovoi, N. Otverzhennyi) have endeavored to refute those points and to demonstrate that Stavrogin has a much greater affinity with Speshnev, [one of the leaders] of the Petrashevskii Circle.[31] It is true that he does, but that does not entirely dispose of the matter. The noisy, tirelessly active Bakunin has no reflection whatever in the behavior of Stavrogin. On the other hand, there is in Dostoevskii's character a structural contradiction between power of intellect and the inadequacy of an abstract, ungrounded nature. And there is also Dostoevskii's utilization of what Bakhtin has called "prototypes of ideas."[32] Bakunin's views on the tactics of revolution, especially during the time of his association with [the terrorist] Nechaev, must have served as the "prototype" for those of Stavrogin's ideas that inspired Petr Verkhovenskii.

The most remarkable image of the young Bakunin in all his energy and intensity, however, belongs neither to the artists nor to the memoirists. That image was created by Belinskii in his letters to Bakunin and to their common friends. He created it and destroyed it, and then created it anew. Reflected in the microcosm of that amity and that enmity, of that love and that hate, were shifts of epochal significance—the breakdown of romantic consciousness and the formation of a new consciousness in its stead. Russian culture was moving inexorably toward a conception of man that was concretely historical, social, and psychological. On that path, the path from the young to the mature Herzen and from Bakunin to Belinskii, there was one other important intermediate link—Stankevich.

All who have written about Stankevich have noted the paradoxical inconsistency between the meagerness of his philosophical and literary legacy and the power of his influence on his contemporaries. Herzen mentions it in *My Past and Thoughts* (9:17), and Annenkov goes into it in particular detail in his biography of Stankevich, where he calls him "one of those . . . remarkable figures who have left nothing behind." According to Annenkov, "the reason for Stankevich's complete and irresistible influence was to be found in his lofty nature, in his ability to forget himself entirely, and, without the slightest sign of boasting or self-regard, to carry everyone away with him into the realm of the ideal."[33]

Stankevich truly was surrounded by a very special aura of love and enthusiastic veneration. "It is impossible to convey in words," Turgenev says in his recollections of Stankevich, "what kind of respect, almost reverence, he inspired."[34] Belinskii's letters abound with reverential judgments of the same sort: Stankevich was summoned to "a great cause"; "I have met only one person in my life to whom I have unconditionally deferred, to whom I now defer, and to whom I shall always defer." After Stankevich's death, Belinskii called him "a divine personality," and declared that he was indebted to him for everything human in himself. "Think only of what each of us was," he wrote to Botkin, "before we met Stankevich or people imbued with his spirit" (11:193, 265, 547, 554). Granovskii responded to Stankevich's death with a similar admission:

"He was our benefactor, our teacher, a brother to us all; each of us owes him something. I more than anyone."[35]

Herzen, Turgenev, and Annenkov sought the reasons for Stankevich's significance and influence in the fact that he was the conscience of the people in his circle, the purest embodiment of their moral aspirations. But there was more to it than that. The meaning of the distinctive Stankevich cult becomes clear only in relation to the profound intellectual crisis that occurred at the end of the 1830s and the beginning of the 1840s. Bakuninian romanticism had by then run its course. The idea of concrete reality entered Belinskii's purview in 1838, perhaps even in the fall of 1837, when he first became acquainted with the aesthetics of Hegel. The year 1838 was a turning point for Lermontov too; it saw the beginning of his work on *A Hero of Our Time*. And Herzen, Ogarev, and Botkin had all abandoned romanticism by the beginning of the 1840s (the fact that the people of the 1830s retained certain features of romantic consciousness until the end of their lives is another matter).

The powerful new intellectual movement, already termed "realism" by Herzen, was above all distinguished by its universality. It involved a new method, which was applied to the most varied spheres of human activity, and it therefore also involved the formation of the new realistic man.

The need for a new order of consciousness, for a new epochal hero, was intensely felt. For the moment, however, that new epochal image lacked definition. Indeed, the very term "realism" remained vague and elastic for a time, since it had not yet broken free of its purely philosophical meaning, of the speculative formula opposing the ideal and the real. A model for the new personality still had not taken shape, and during the transitional period the requirements for it were therefore largely negative ones. The first thing was to eliminate the characteristics of the obsolete romantic idealism—stiltedness, illusion, and cant. Stankevich satisfied these increasingly pressing demands through his own personality. He was an early and in a certain sense a negative embodiment of the sought-after realistic man, and in this lies the solution to the question of his unerring power and authority over other minds.

Stankevich was a "man without cant." Annenkov spoke of this quality, and so did Konstantin Aksakov in his *Recollections of Student Days*.[36] Belinskii's perception of Stankevich was the same. And Turgenev in his memoir of Stankevich wrote, "There wasn't a trace of cant in him; not even Tolstoi would have found any."[37] Turgenev's memoir was written in 1856, and he had in mind of course the relentless moral inquiry and psychological candor that were already characteristic of Tolstoi's early works. The remarkable thing, however, is that Tolstoi himself sensed a peculiar inner affinity with Stankevich. In 1858, after reading Stankevich's correspondence, which had just been published by his brother, Tolstoi wrote, "Never has any book made such an impression on me. Never have I liked anyone so much as this man, whom I never saw. What purity, what gentleness, what love permeated his whole being."[38]

Tolstoi was just ten years old when in a letter to Stankevich (1838) Belinskii attempted to define the "Tolstoian" basis of Stankevich's personality. "Friend, a great change has taken place in me. At last I understand what you call (and have long called) *simplicity* and *normality*. You were no less vulgar and idealistic than we were, but you always retained a vigorous sense of your vulgar idealism and your idealistic vulgarity, as well as of the need to find a way out into *simple,* normal reality" (11:307).[39]

With his common sense, the clarity of his abstract thought, and his appetite for practical action, however modest, with his affability, his ready sense of humor, and his fondness for jokes and "farces" remembered by all who knew him, Stankevich was indeed perceived by his contemporaries as someone who had found a way out into "normal reality."

Stankevich evolved from idealism to more sober views along with all the other remarkable people of his generation. His development, however, had its own individual character. It seemed to lack a material expression. It was embodied not in written works but in his personality itself. And that personality was devoid of any signs of the romantic mold on the basis of which—in its several varieties—so many of his contemporaries had constructed their own personalities. Stankevich had a nonromantic personality. Unlike many others, however, he did not try to force it into the romantic patterns provided by the age. He left his personality in a state of rather amorphous freedom and elegant simplicity. And it was that quality in particular that captivated those who were tired of obsolete yet persistent stereotypes.

Stankevich belonged to an intermediate, transitional stage, and one that was, moreover, not all that clear-cut. He took up the spiritual legacy of romanticism, above all the problems of the ideal and of an all-embracing love. The foundations of his thinking had been laid by romanticism and by German idealist philosophy.[40] Even the philosophy of the real, which completely absorbed him at the end of his life, revealed reality to him in terms of Hegelian logical categories, but without those powerful breakthroughs into the social and the concrete that were characteristic of Belinskii's Hegelianism from the very beginning.

The very application of ideological formulas to life, their biographical substantiation, reveals Stankevich as someone linked to romanticism in a number of ways. Even the experiences that the romantic was supposed to have, such as a simultaneously earthly and ideal love, happened to him. Yet that whole romantic set of problems and even that romantic practice left his personality untouched, without forging the emerging features of the new man into a romantic mask. At the time of that man's maturation, it was just such negative accomplishments that were the most important—the absence of a mask, of cant, of a pose, and of a typological mold. Stankevich was not only a man not given to cant; he was also someone without a role, someone who therefore demonstrated to his contemporaries that a historically effective spiritual life was possible even without a role, even without a set, easily recognized form.

In direct contrast to Bakunin, Stankevich did not construct his personality consciously; his friends and contemporaries did that for him. They gave it a one-dimensional form: the ideal of the lofty mind and pure heart. This image of Stankevich served them as a weapon in the struggle against illusion, stiltedness, and cant. But Stankevich himself, astonishingly free as he was of self-love and intellectual coquetry, was inclined toward critical self-analysis and stern self-judgment. Hence the striking disjunction between Stankevich seen from the outside and the same person viewed from within. His contemporaries required the idealized image of him for their own spiritual maturation. That image was constructed by means of a rigorous selection, a sifting of complex and contradictory spiritual experience. But the person whose experience it was could not (unless he was a Foma Opiskin [from Dostoevskii's *A Friend of the Family*]) recognize his inner self in such one-dimensional, idealized categories.

Inner self-realization was more likely to be possible in the forms of romantic demonism, which even in its generalized form assumed, or even presupposed, contradiction. Furthermore, the romantic personality could in the process of its self-realization push aside as inessential or empirically irrelevant anything that did not fit its preconceived lofty formula. This was in fact how Bakunin proceeded. Stankevich, however, was the sort who could brush nothing aside—he wanted to account for the full measure of his experience. He knew that a person passes through a great number of impulses, desires, and momentary reactions before he reaches the point of action or of behavior that is apparent to those around him. If he is someone of an analytical bent, he judges, condemns, or justifies those impulses, but by no means does he ever discount them as irrelevant to any ideal definition of himself.

A person cannot regard himself from within as a crystalline, pure, and ideally harmonious personality, and not merely from modesty or an aversion to the crudeness of that kind of self-admiration. He cannot see himself as such because saintliness, purity, and harmony are not psychological definitions at all, but completely judgmental formulations of a behavior that has been generalized and abstracted from the empirical complexity of inner life. For self-realization of that judgmental kind, it is necessary to withdraw a good distance from oneself and construct one's image from an external point of view as an object whose significance is as much aesthetic as it is ethical. For Stankevich that was not necessary.

Stankevich conceived the transition to a philosophy of reality in terms of abstract Hegelian categories. The actual substance of his personality, its set of day-to-day concerns, was to a great extent still linked to romanticism. It is for this reason that the ideal image of Stankevich held by his contemporaries lacked firm outlines. Its only feature was the negation of cant, stiltedness, illusion, and falsehood. The positive content of the new personality had not yet been defined. A recognizable model of the new man from which individual personalities could be derived, which could give people form and open up new possibilities for typology and classification, still had not been created. That is why Stankevich was poorly suited to be a prototype.

It is common knowledge that Turgenev was a celebrated master of historical typification. In each of his novels he endeavored to fix an image (usually the main hero) that would define the features of a generation. Yet Turgenev's portrayal of two of his famous contemporaries (Bakunin and Stankevich) proved inadequate. And that was no accident. Turgenev's early tale "Andrei Kolosov," although partly about his own unsuccessful romance with Tat'iana Bakunina, is even more a reflection of the image of Stankevich and of the latter's unsuccessful romance with Liubov' Bakunina. Turgenev had no ready-made form for Stankevich's personality. He combined it with autobiographical recollections and memories of Belinskii. The Belinskiian elements destroyed the personality's structure. Turgenev turned Kolosov into a plebeian intellectual, whereas Stankevich was a typical late product of the Russian educated nobility. It was precisely this social background that Herzen stressed so insistently in his rendering of Stankevich in *My Past and Thoughts*. Belinskii has left us evidence in his letters of the nervous hyperintensity produced by the bitter uncertainty of the plebeian intellectual's life. In "Andrei Kolosov," Turgenev attempted to conjoin that difficult, penurious mode of existence, whose desperation was unhappily familiar to Belinskii, Dostoevskii, and Nekrasov, with the inner freedom, harmony, and clarity of mind that were characteristic of Stankevich.

The forced juxtapositions were unavailing. The hero of the tale was apprehended variously, even as a petty egoist and vulgarian.[41] The fundamental conflict in his personality was inevitably turned into something else. After becoming convinced of the inadequacy of his feelings for her, Stankevich had resolved to break with his betrothed, Liubov' Bakunina, since according to the doctrine professed by him and his friends, a marriage without love would have been a profanation of love, a desecration of the spirit. Looking at Kolosov in a similar situation, we find something rather like the theory of free love that would later assume an essential place in the worldview of the plebeian intellectuals, even though that idea is still only dimly sketched in the 1844 Turgenev tale.[42] Druzhinin wrote of "Andrei Kolosov" that "the trouble with the story is that its *conception is at variance with its construction*, that the type born in the mind of the gifted storyteller has in the story lost all of its meaning."[43]

The young Turgenev's failure is of theoretical interest. It attests to the difficulty of creating an integrated literary personality when the structure of the corresponding historical personality type that is its mold has not yet taken shape, or has not yet been clearly grasped. It was of course Turgenev who subsequently found the key term "nihilist," and who in Bazarov created a model for whole generations. The category of the "superfluous man" was no less clear to him. But the personality of Stankevich eluded Turgenev, and not only in "Andrei Kolosov," but also in the much later *Rudin*, where the character of Pokorskii is modeled on Stankevich, and unsuccessfully so by Turgenev's own admission.

The figure of Pokorskii is ideologically more clear-cut, but his personality is based on the same principle as Kolosov's; he is Stankevich with an admixture of Belinskii, a composite of harmony and the mode of life of the indigent plebeian intellectual.

Turgenev was unable to find a model for the image of Stankevich and his complex transitional nature. Bakunin, however, he relegated to an already familiar category, one that he himself had formulated, that of "superfluous men." Both Herzen and Chernyshevskii objected to this stereotyping of Bakunin. Bakunin was not, of course, a "superfluous man." He was a tirelessly active organizer who was fanatically devoted to his own, not infrequently abstract, goals. Such he had been, and such he remained in every period of his life, from the struggle to "liberate Varen'ka" to leadership of the world anarchist movement. Even so, Rudin is endowed (as many have admitted) with a number of Bakunin's more recognizable traits. As if afraid they might pass unnoticed, Turgenev brought them all together in Lezhnev's famous characterization of Rudin: "He is a remarkably intelligent person, although essentially an empty one. . . . He is a tyrant at heart, lazy, and not particularly knowledgeable. . . . He likes living off other people, he plays a role, and so on . . . , all of which is in the order of things. But what is bad is that he is as cold as ice. . . . As cold as ice, and he knows it, although he pretends to be passionate" (chap. 6). References to all these qualities may be found in the letters of Belinskii, Botkin, and others written during periods of struggle and polemic with Bakunin. In becoming Rudin's qualities, however, they were deprived of the basic principle that set them in motion. Turgenev shaped them into a different structure, that of the "superfluous man."

A number of Stankevich's more recognizable traits are concentrated in Andrei Kolosov as well—from the universal love surrounding him to his affability and even humorousness combined with a lofty spiritual life. Andrei Kolosov is characterized by "a clear, simple view of life" and "the absence of any indulgence in cant." These were of course the very features that constituted the basis of Stankevich's image in his circle. Neither Kolosov nor Pokorskii really resembles Stankevich, however. Combining Stankevich and Belinskii in a single image brought together phenomena possessing very different social natures and belonging to quite different (if chronologically proximate) stages in the movement of Russian culture toward realism.

Belinskii went much further than Stankevich had. And that is the reason why it was in fact Stankevich who was regarded by the idealists of the 1830s as their teacher and exemplar. Stankevich was for them a guarantor of clarity and harmony. Belinskii's extreme solutions, his terrible consistency, his whole spasmodic, torturous development, frightened and repelled other minds.

Stankevich judged himself to be unemotional and freely admitted it. It is a motif that recurs with remarkable persistence in his letters.

> Empty or emptied—I don't know what to call my mind. Emptied? What was in it then? . . . Dear friend, there was something in it once, and there still is, but it is so meager and poor. And I had hoped for such a rich, full life. That was my mistake, my error. . . . Love is a religion, the only one possible, and a religion must fill up every moment, every instant of one's life, or else the person who knows himself even a bit cannot love; but in order to be capable of such a love, one has to be more developed, one has to be a spirit, whereas I was only a mind, and moreover one that suffered from self-indulgent idealism.[44]

This May 1837 letter to Bakunin (the original is in German) explains a great deal not only about Stankevich's own ethical position, but also about the whole temper of his circle. Above all, it explains how Stankevich, although revered by his comrades, was able to judge himself unsparingly and without any trace of pretense or posturing. He advocated an unattainable ethical idea, a love that would fill "every instant of his life." Actual moral practice could not help but fall short. That is why there emerged in the minds of Stankevich and Belinskii the moral categories of "apathy," "torpor," "coldness," and "lovelessness," which were regarded as defects, as sins against the spirit. Aridity and apathy were inimical to the requirement of love; indolence, to the requirement of an intense life of the spirit; and lack of will, to the requirement of self-perfection. This was already a departure from the romantic conflict engendered by that embarrassment of spiritual riches that separated the hero from the crowd and that left him vulnerable to romantic disenchantment. Now, on the contrary, the source of evil was spiritual lack. In a letter to Granovskii, Stankevich said that "human nature ... needs to have demands made upon it. It needs to rise to them" (449). This meant that the highest demands made on the soul did not come to it in ready-made form.

The most concrete expression of love was love for a woman (as Stankevich maintained in his letters). On this level, the philosophical conflict, although still philosophical, acquired additional psychological features. Stankevich had taken his infatuation with Liubov' Bakunina for an ideal love that opened up the possibility of an ideal marriage. He soon realized his error. According to the ethical code accepted in his circle, a marriage without love was the greatest possible sin against the spirit. The cruelty of a break seemed the lesser evil. But since Liubov' Bakunina was seriously ill, it was necessary to postpone that break—it was necessary to dissemble (a role for which Stankevich was particularly ill-suited).

According to the code of honor observed by the nobility, Mikhail Bakunin ought to have called Stankevich out for deceiving his sister. Instead, he submitted the episode to philosophical scrutiny, and Stankevich for his part analyzed himself in a letter to the brother of his jilted fiancée:

> I have never loved. For me love has always been a whim of the imagination, idle fun, a game of self-love, a crutch for faintheartedness, the only interest that could occupy a mind devoid of base desires yet still lacking any real, substantial content (speaking in the language of philosophy). The field of action for the truly strong is reality. The weak mind lives in *Jenseits*, in striving, in indefinite striving; it needs *something* (since there is nothing definite in it to shape its nature and its wants). As soon as that indefiniteness has been made *etwas*, has been made definite, the mind once again reaches beyond the bounds of reality. That is my story, and it is obviously the reason for all the trouble. What Belinskii regards as genius is merely vileness. (650)

Stankevich here rejects the ideal personal image proposed for him by his friends, and from within he constructs another, in which aridity, apathy, and coldness predominate.

> I have kind friends [he wrote to Varvara Aleksandrovna D'iakova in 1837] who are prepared to say that my wants are too great to be satisfied and too strong to leave me in peace. Not so! My head was confused, my mind was empty and weakened. . . . I had no definite desires, and so there was nothing to satisfy; I wanted a regeneration that would give me the desires themselves. . . . Could such a weak, broken mind love? Isolated from the world— *die schöne Seele*—it created pale images for itself and then sought their sem-

blances among people. . . . Encounters, mistakes, contradictions, crises were necessary. I understood my predicament, my former insignificance, without changing it in the least; I cursed that *Schönseeligkeit*, but was not reconciled with the world. From this comes that arid struggle that has taken up so much of my time and energy, and even now I am still unable to free myself of that servile doubt, those tormenting thoughts that turn so agonizingly and torpidly in my mind. (723)

For Stankevich, "aridity" and "torpor" were at once ideological sins and agonizing physical states. In another letter written to Varvara D'iakova three years later, Stankevich declared that she would find in him "a homunculus hovering between heaven and earth, who is aware of his glass abode but who lacks the strength to break it" (738). Stankevich has in mind here the homunculus or artificial man hatched in the retort in the second part of Goethe's *Faust*. Even so, the image of an ineffectual creature "hovering between heaven and earth" is also very close to Baratynskii's "The Stillborn" [*Nedonosok*], a poem first published in *The Moscow Observer* in 1835 (and later included in the collection *Twilight*), and one that Stankevich would certainly have been familiar with.

> I come from the race of spirits,
> But not of the Empyrean tribe,
> For scarcely do I reach the clouds,
> Than I weaken and fall back down.
> So small and poor, how shall I live?
> Beyond the surging clouds, I know,
> Lies paradise; I drift suspended,
> A winged sigh between earth and sky.

Who was right, then—Stankevich's contemporaries, who saw in him an irreproachable chevalier of the spirit, or he himself with his baring of his faults? Stankevich was undoubtedly what his friends believed him to be, a man of great rectitude and elegant simplicity. But he was not given to playing up his own virtues. He was concerned with something else. He continually measured himself against the idea of an all-pervasive love and of all consuming desires, and he found himself wanting. He discovered aridity, coldness, and a lack of spiritual energy and will in himself, and he viewed those qualities as ethical defects. Overcoming them became the starting point for the personal psychological and moral program that engaged him until the end of his life.

Stankevich's spiritual life and the forms in which it found realization were clearly gravitating toward later Russian psychologism with its interest in moral issues. Belinskii proceeded even further in that direction. He regarded himself as profoundly obligated to Stankevich and invoked him repeatedly in relation to the concerns of his own "inner life." But in Belinskii the contradictions had become so intolerable that they demanded a way out and solutions, and those solutions were always extreme. Belinskii's letters of the 1830s and 1840s are for this reason a unique record of the maturation of the new historical consciousness.[45]

Part Two

BELINSKII AND THE EMERGENCE
OF REALISM

PSYCHOLOGICAL INSIGHTS not yet possible at a certain stage in the established, canonical genres, or only beginning to come to light in them, are often possible in the more peripheral forms of literature—in letters, diaries, memoirs, and autobiographies. Numerous cultural monuments attest to this fact, including the letters of Belinskii.

Belinskii invented a new kind of critical essay, but for a number of reasons he was unable to include in it the full range of his complex spiritual life. He was bound by the nature and functions of the genre, above all by the impossibility of talking about himself (which of course is just what the young Herzen did so extensively in his autobiographical sketches of the period). He was bound too by the censorship, by the expectations of the journal in which he published, and by the need to address, especially at the end of the 1830s, a wide circle of readers. "I write neither for you nor for myself but for the public," Belinskii informed his Moscow friends soon after moving to Petersburg (11:438).

From the very beginning, his work for *National Annals* [*Otechestvennye zapiski*] was marked by this expressly didactic purpose. At the same time, however, Belinskii experienced during those and the preceding years a series of psychological conflicts that were remarkable for their intensity and their degree of conscious realization. And it was in his letters that Belinskii gave expression to this vast work of the soul.

In his role as literary critic and historian, Belinskii was the true founder of Russian realism. His own theory of realism (even if he still did not actually apply that term to art) corresponded to the stage reached by Russian literature during his lifetime—that of the Gogol' school. Belinskii both reflected and gave shape to that movement. Soon after the appearance of Tolstoi's *Childhood, Boyhood,* and *Sevastopol' Stories* and Turgenev's *Rudin,* Russian literature moved decisively into the new, psychological phase of its development, but that occurred only after Belinskii's death. Belinskii thus remained the theoretician of a literature concerned with the socially typical and characteristic. Psychological analysis for him had not yet become a special theme in its own right, even in the articles on Herzen's *Who Is to Blame?* and Goncharov's *A Common Story.* This is obvious if one merely compares those pieces to Chernyshevskii's famous

1856 article on Tolstoi's early works. Belinskii's early letters, however, are extraordinary documents of unique psychological introspection—the material, as it were, that directly prepared the way for the Russian psychological novel.

From the time of Aleksandr Pypin's *Belinskii: His Life and Correspondence*[1] to our own day, Belinskii's letters have been a primary source both for the reconstruction of his biography and for the study of his ideas in their complex period development. There is of course an extensive literature devoted to these subjects. What interests me, however, is that each phase in the evolution of Belinskii's philosophical and sociopolitical views had a psychological dimension as well. Each was a stage in the gradual maturation of the new "real" man, and it is here that their objective historical meaning is to be found. What for Belinskii was subjective psychological analysis, or concern with the nature of his own personality, was in a sense derived from the probings of his always troubled conscience. It is this that permits the inclusion of his letters in the artistic and ethical sphere of the Russian problem novel.

The salient feature of Belinskii's evolution was his ever-increasing appetite for reality. Each phase, even within a single period of development, was subsequently rejected as insufficiently concrete and real, and always in comparison with whatever new concreteness had been achieved, which in its own turn was also dismissed as inadequate. The problem of Fichtean "ideality" was resolved in the crisis of 1838. The abstractly conceived Hegelian reality adopted in its stead was then supplanted by the reconciliation with the world as it actually was, although by 1840 Belinskii had pronounced that world "vile" and had repudiated his earlier reconciliation with it. But even before this last, essentially political rejection, Belinskii had already admitted while still in his Hegelian phase the *unreality* of the newly discovered reality. He had felt the need even then to penetrate still deeper into the real. In a confessional letter to Stankevich written in 1839, he observed, "we have understood 'reality' very poorly, although we thought we understood it well. . . . In the beginning, we discussed it very nicely, even elegantly, and we did a bit of writing, but in reality we implemented it terribly *unrealistically*" (11:388). The change in Belinskii's political views came soon afterward, as did his admission that the Hegelian Universal had been an illusion too, this time in comparison with the concreteness of personality now regarded in relation to its actual social existence.

This process of acceptance and rejection proceeded on two fronts simultaneously. The first was Belinskii's articles and journalistic activity. The other was the relationships he maintained among his circle—their friendships and antagonisms, confessions and conflicts—with his letters serving as the material substratum, so to speak, of that intellectual life.

Although not intended for publication, that epistolary activity had as its primary function the formation of a new man, of a new epochal personality type. Belinskii's source for this enterprise was his friends and himself—his own personality, which thereby acquired universal and objective meaning. It was precisely this universality and objectivity that demanded a fully realized self-image, a clearly defined personality structure.

That image was constructed in the dialectical interaction of two elements: self-affirmation and self-condemnation. Both elements were necessary for the solution to the problem. Self-affirmation was the recognition of the value, merit, and significance of one's own personality as the repository of the philosophical and moral issues of one's time. The idea of self-condemnation, on the other hand, came from the fact that a great deal was asked of such a personality, that there was much that it had to answer for, so that it was always aware that it had fallen short of the demands of its own conscience.

Belinskii's extant familiar correspondence begins in 1837—during his Fichtean period, that is. Stankevich and his friends began with romantic premises, and moreover late romantic ones, which put great emphasis on romantic dualism and on all the polarities that it implied: heaven and earth, dream and base reality, spirit and flesh, feeling and reason, and so on. This habit of thinking in terms of antitheses persisted from the end of the 1830s until the 1840s, the period that was most crucial for Belinskii. Later on, I shall look at the evolution of the different stages of this period, with their different ways of conceiving the human being.

In 1836 and 1837 romanticism was given a Fichtean interpretation in the Stankevich circle. The focus of attention was Fichte's doctrine of love as the wellspring and prime mover of life. As always in that circle, these philosophical principles were at once applied to the issues of self-improvement and human purpose that preoccupied the membership. They were translated, so to speak, into psychological categories that were then applied to the members' own spiritual life and to the spiritual life of their friends. The ideas of happiness, the life of the spirit, ideal love, and so forth, took on psychological meaning, and thanks to the dualism of romantic thought, they soon acquired contrary or negative qualities as well. Thus, ideal love for a woman had as its antithesis sensuality, happiness was opposed to the lower, rule-bound existence of duty and rational morality, the "true life in the spirit" was contrasted with the illusory external world, and so on. These polar dualities converged, on the one hand, in the ideal of the Schillerian heroic personality and, on the other, in the image of the vulgarian, or, to use Belinskii's expression, the "soulless man." Self-affirmation and self-condemnation had very clear places in this schema. A person affirmed himself as endowed with the capacity for love and a longing for the ideal, and condemned anything in himself that interfered with that longing or that stood in the way of that ideal. In measuring himself against his ideal, he continually discovered "unworthiness," another of Belinskii's formulas.

The young Belinskii's initial sense of himself was formed on the basis of this romantic dialectic. "Only the infinite exists; everything finite is an illusion," he declared in a letter to Nikolai Satin in October 1837. But it was precisely at this point that Belinskii was beginning to disavow romantic stereotypes.

According to romantic norms, finite man was supposed to strive perpetually for the infinite, although he could never attain it. Pitfalls lay in wait for him; he was overcome by vices and passions. The aesthetic view of this wickedness—its idealization—gave rise to romanticism of the demonic variety.

With Belinskii it was different. Everything was transformed by his organically relentless search for the individual and the concrete. He applied the romantic polar schema to his own personality, which he subjected, even at that early stage, to intense and very careful scrutiny. For the time being, however, he was unable to move beyond dualism, to avoid thinking in terms of paired positive and negative elements. The result was a unique combination of ideal schema and unexpectedly real content.

A great deal has been written about Belinskii's dispute with Bakunin on the subject of "kopecks" and their role in human life (the letters of August 16 and November 1, 1837).[2] Behind those symbolic kopecks lay the important issue of the status of *external life*.

"Ideal and actual life had in fact always been separate in my thoughts: the Premukhino harmony and acquaintance with the ideas of Fichte convinced me for the first time that it was the ideal life that was real, positive, and concrete, and the so-called real life that was negative, illusory, insignificant, and empty," Belinskii declared in his romantic phase (11:175). But, unlike the pure romantic Bakunin, he immediately restored the rights of that "so-called real life"—of the external one, that is.

External life was the baser form, yet as it turned out, it was the one that required the most assiduous attention. When governed by human will and organized by reason, it became the occasion for a higher existence; otherwise it was merely the source of evil and degradation. "Could I, while still shackled to the external life with iron chains, have raised myself to the level of the absolute? I saw myself as devoid of honor, as base and indolent and incapable of anything, as a pitiful, abortive sort of person, and it was only in my external existence that I found the reason for it all. . . . No sooner was an awareness of strength born in me, no sooner was I warmed by faith in myself, than the apartment, the grocery store, frock coats and trousers, debts, and all the loathsome things in life would immediately kill off my strength and faith, and I was capable only of trumps or checkers" (11:177, 178). Belinskii's psychologism already encompasses here not only selected facts of spiritual life but potentially any facts, including those that gentry intellectuals, educated in the culture of romanticism, were used to leaving beyond the threshold of consciousness. One finds in Belinskii's letters the same shifts that one finds in literature as it came to terms with the realistic method. The quotidian ("the grocery store, frock coats and trousers, debts") has been freed here from the comical associations that it necessarily had for the romantic consciousness. It has become the drama of life exposed to the gaze of the thinker and artist, who sees in it the source of the most intimate and far-removed spiritual states.

The Belinskii of 1837, however, still had not by any means achieved a fully realistic conception of life. To skip over the subsequent stages of his development would only be to simplify and impoverish it. For the Belinskii of this period, the nature of the world was still dual, still to be explained in terms of the romantic hierarchy of the sublime and the mundane. This philosophical schema inhibited the growth of a concrete, individualized psychological content. The realm of everyday reality, the realm in which rational morality and duty held sway, was still lower in comparison with the ideal of a life of blissful love. But external life and the inner life were interconnected, and a blissful life in the absolute was impossible without first satisfying the demands of duty and common sense. "Yes, brother Michel, no matter what you say, it is still *thoroughness and the most scrupulous attention to kopecks* as a means and not as an end in life that is, when united with striving for life in the absolute, the true perfection of man. Life in the absolute means the unbounded freedom of the spirit, but is he free whose every moment depends on the influence of external circumstances?" (11:180).

Here the ideal ("the true perfection of man") is given a new formulation. It is no longer merely the Schillerian exalted personality but a personality that lives "in the spirit," yet is still capable of governing the external elements of its life. This formulation brought with it a number of new ethical polarities: order and disorder (or carelessness), will and the lack of it, and capacity for work and laziness.

Lack of will, laziness, and carelessness were sins against the spirit. They hindered its "unbounded freedom" and therefore its ability to achieve happiness, and they reduced it to a state of degradation. These new polarities required observation of the concrete, individual human being. Consequently, they radically transformed the earlier romantic premises of his personality.

Belinskii called his excessive fervor, his extreme impulses and reactions, and the inordinate demands he made on himself, his "furiousness," and he remained acutely aware of it all his life. In 1837 this maximalism took a form derived in part from Schiller's *Die Räuber*: "I despise and hate virtue without love. I would rather hurl myself headlong into an abyss of vice and debauchery, I would rather obtain my daily bread on the highway with a blade in my hand than trample my feelings and my reason in the dirt and become a good Quaker, a vulgar *raisonneur*, a puritan, a sectarian, good by calculation, honest out of self-interest . . . ; it is better to be a fallen angel—a devil, that is—than an innocent, sinless, but cold and slimy toad" (11:167, 168). The person presented here was endowed by nature with a furious craving for love and a furious striving for the truth—the features of his self-affirmation. But that self-affirmation took public forms that were opposed in every way to accepted norms of behavior—hence Belinskii's eccentricity, his fierceness, and his outland-ishness.[3] "Or have you still not guessed that [I am] not quite like every-body else, but belong to the race of *cranks*?" (11:119), Belinskii wrote as early as 1835 to his relatives, the Ivanovs.

To a certain extent, of course, this image of himself was based on the romantic eccentrics immortalized by Hoffmann (the very idea of crossing Hoffmann with Schiller was typical of the motley romanticism of the 1830s). Their grotesqueness, their outlandish behavior expressed the eternal incompatibility of the exalted spirit and the vulgar forms of every-day life. Yet, as always with Belinskii, there was a real-life dimension as well. Outlandishness was characteristic not merely of the exalted spirit out of tune with the actual world, but also of the disorganized spirit un-accustomed to work. Thus the theme of eccentricity, refashioned in psy-chologically concrete terms, simultaneously contained within itself both self-affirmation and self-condemnation.

Opposed to the craving for love and the striving for truth were lack of will and idleness, which gave rise to "disorder." Disorder was itself re-garded as something that fostered a person's innate defects. This by now completely unromantic conception was worked out in detail in the above-mentioned 1837 letters to Bakunin. "What then, I ask you, what then is the reason for the futility of all my outbursts, my intellectual passion, and the many excellent gifts that nature has not denied me?" (11:169–170). The answer is "a disordered life." Even sensuality is seen here not as a source but rather as a consequence of disorder. Poverty, debts, and the impossibility of discharging one's material and moral obligations reduce a person to despair. "And what was the reason for all this? Carelessness, a disordered life, and groundless hopes for the future. And so I threw myself into debauchery and sought oblivion in it, as a drunkard seeks it in wine; and the reason for my sensuality was that same disordered life again, that same carelessness, that same contempt not only for kopecks, but also for banknotes and gold. . . . What should I do? Here is what: *destroy the cause of evil, and all the evil in me comes from carelessness, a disordered life, and those despised kopecks*" (11:172).

The mechanism of self-affirmation and self-condemnation worked by means of paired positive and negative qualities, which had strictly defined places. Together they formed the image of someone who was tormented by his "unworthiness," but only in relation to the high ideal that had been revealed to him.

The issue of worthiness versus "unworthiness" could not, of course, be settled without reference to external life. Later on, Belinskii would perceive the conditionality of external life in increasingly social terms. His psychologism would become more and more deterministic and analytical. But it would be a gross oversimplification to regard the later development of Belinskii's ideas of psychic life as a direct outgrowth of the notion of social conditioning. Those ideas in fact had a much more complicated genesis. Belinskii was not only the founder of later Russian realism; he was also the most typical exponent of the intellectual life of the 1830s and 1840s. This meant that not only his philosophical and political ideas but also his psychological analysis and self-analysis necessarily had to pass through the peculiarly Russian version of Hegelianism.

For Russian intellectuals of the time, every aspect of life was capable of philosophical interpretation, and therefore any fact could in principle be explained theoretically, could be turned into a problem. Annenkov speaks in his biography of Stankevich of the latter's tendency to analyze "his own private spiritual life" (Stankevich's expression), and in the same passage he characterizes the atmosphere prevailing in the Bakunin household: "The other members of that family surrendered themselves with tireless energy and astonishing zeal to the mystical and quasi-philosophical explanation of life's phenomena. . . . Their thirst to discover the spiritual principle underlying all existence and to immerse themselves in it was truly unquenchable."[4] Annenkov observes that Mikhail Bakunin abandoned himself with particular energy to the philosophical "explanation of life's phenomena," and adds that for Bakunin, "all life was revealed . . . through the prism of abstraction, and he spoke of it with conspicuous animation only when it had been translated into an idea."[5]

Herzen describes precisely this tendency of mind in chapter 25 of *My Past and Thoughts*: "Everything *in fact* spontaneous, every simple feeling, was raised to an abstract category and then brought back without a drop of living blood, as a pale algebraic shadow. . . . The very tear welling in the eyelid was rigorously assigned its proper place: either *Gemüt* or 'the tragic in the heart'" (9:20). Herzen's judgment is harsh and ironical, as is understandable in someone who himself had to struggle to overcome the habit of raising life's phenomena "to the level of an abstract category." Yet it should be remembered that this habit of detailed and at the same time generalized examination of psychic life laid the groundwork for the psychological novel, since the characteristic feature of the Russian sociopsychological novel is, after all, that in it ideology permeates the material of ordinary social life, and that the facts of private life are raised to the level of philosophical generalization.

Romanticism produced its own stereotypes, its own fixed patterns. They found their way into Russian romanticism as well, although the philosophical interests of young Russia in the 1830s radically altered them. At the beginning of the decade, social utopian ideas decked out in Saint-Simonian terminology became part of the demonic image, producing a peculiar new variety of it, the demon with a hint of optimism and faith in social progress. By the end of the 1830s Hegelian terminology had begun to be used as an instrument for the analysis of spiritual life. This development sharply transformed the outline of the romantic personality.

Several of Bakunin's philosophical articles and drafts belong to this period (including his foreword to the translation of Hegel's *Gymnasial-reden*, in which the idea of "reconciliation with reality" was first enunciated). These pieces are saturated with the terminology that Herzen treated so ironically in *My Past and Thoughts*, and that was used in the circle to characterize individuals and to elucidate their relationships.

Especially interesting in this regard is a draft called "My Notes" (1837), a variation on the theme of Hegel's *Phänomenologie des Geistes*, which Bakunin was studying at the time. Also reflected in the draft is Bakunin's familiarity with the book of Hegel's disciple Karl Rosenkranz, *Psychologie, oder die Wissenschaft vom subjektiven Geist*, which had just been published.[6] The terms that Bakunin was presenting to his Russian readers there were largely calques for the terminology employed by Hegel in his doctrine of subjective spirit.

> The *finite man* [wrote Bakunin] is he who is not completely imbued with *self-conscious spirit*, in whom there are still *spontaneous* elements *unenlightened* by spirit.... A person's *unenlightened* aspects hold him back; they interfere with his union with God and make him a slave to accident. The accidental is a lie, an *illusion*; in the *true and real* life nothing is accidental; everything there comes from sacred necessity, from the *grace* of God. The accidental is powerless against *true reality*; and it is only illusions, only a person's illusory interests and desires, that are subject to the accidental.... The accidental is the dark, unenlightened side ... of life. *Consciousness* is *liberation from spontaneity*, the illumination of human nature by spirit.... It is only the illusory that perishes from the accidental, and the illusory must perish. *Illusion* destroyed by illusion—that is the liberation of man. (2:71)

The terms I have italicized here served in circle usage as means for the analysis of intimate spiritual experiences, although to be sure they had been intended for entirely different purposes by Hegel himself. Indeed, in the introduction to the *Philosophie des Geistes*, he condemned the psychology of everyday life and stressed that his doctrine of the spirit's perception of itself was by no means to be taken in a concrete psychological sense:

> *Self-knowledge*, in the usual trivial sense of an investigation of the foibles and faults peculiar to the individual, is of interest and importance only to the individual, not to philosophy. Even with regard to the individual, however, its value diminishes to the extent that it fails to concern itself with knowledge of the general intellectual and moral nature of man, and, disregarding the duties which constitute the true content of the will, degenerates into the individual's being self-complacently absorbed in his own precious peculiarities. The same is true of the so-called *knowledge of human nature*, which is also concerned with the peculiarities of particular minds.[7]

It was precisely what Hegel was warning against here that his Russian followers, with their passionate interest in ethical issues and in self-analysis, were concerned with (and productively so). Terms like "stage," "definition," "spontaneity," "unenlightened," "subjectivity," "accident," "illusion," "true life," "freedom," "necessity," "concreteness," and the like were at once applied to the solution of psychological problems. Also frequently met with is the very important expression "soul-beauty" [*prekrasnodushie*, meaning "self-indulgent idealism"], employed by Belinskii to stigmatize the remnants of Schillerian idealism.[8]

"Soul-beauty" was an ironic derivation from the German *schöne Seele*, although in circle usage a doublet for the term appeared, the odd little word "self-grinning" [*samoosklablenie*]. Belinskii used the latter term frequently in his letters of the late 1830s. It would be no easy matter to establish its precise meaning, had not Bakunin deciphered it in his foreword to Hegel's *Gymnasialreden*. "Self-grinning," it turns out, was a synonym for "soul-beauty." "The result of Jakobi's system was what Hegel called 'soul-beauty' (*Schönseeligkeit*), and what might also be called 'self-grinning.' This is what the beautiful but poor and feeble soul does whenever it gives itself up to the contemplation of its own excellent but sterile qualities and mouths empty phrases, not because it wants to mouth them, but because the living word is the expression of a living reality, and the expression of emptiness is perforce also empty and dead" (2:171). And so the beautiful soul, grinning, admires itself.

All of Bakunin's biographers and all of the editors of his letters, from Annenkov to Aleksandr Kornilov and Iurii Steklov, have been unanimous in observing that the Bakunin of the 1830s regarded both his own life and the lives of those close to him as a direct manifestation of absolute spirit. As such, those lives had universal interest and were subject to collective philosophical discussion. And Bakunin, certainly not one to stand on ceremony, transformed not only his own personal qualities and the private affairs of his comrades into subjects for public philosophical discourse, but also the most intimate experiences of his own sisters. The Hegelian categories were brought to bear on these and other phenomena without any modification whatever. Bakunin was not in the least intimidated by the possible comic effects of such a direct application of Hegel to the young noblewomen. "Place your hand over your heart," he wrote to Natal'ia Beer, "and ask sincerely whether you are entering the absolute in that frame of mind. No, you certainly are not. . . . You say, 'Since I don't have what I want, I shall begin to live in the absolute.' But that is a sacrilege in the true sense of the word. The absolute, dear friends, is a living whole; it includes everything, and anything not included in it has no life of its own" (2:68–69).

And here are some lines from an 1838 letter to his sisters: "Remember that two *I*s reside in you, one unconsciously true, infinite—your substance—and the other your conscious, finite *I*—your subjective definition. All life consists of making subjective what is substantial in you, of elevating your subjectivity to the level of your substance and making it infinite. You are splendid girls, and infinity is in you, so do not fear for yourselves, but believe, love, reason, and boldly go forward" (2:142).

Thus, by means of Hegelian terminology, Bakunin analyzed the behavior of his proselytes and at the same time attempted to control them. In demanding that his sister Varvara divorce her husband, he invoked the "true life" and the "absolute": "You wish to live with him in absolute love? That is interesting too. Then tell me, if you have found that your husband lives in the absolute, then in what way is he connected to it? By potatoes and the fatuous things he says? No, Varen'ka, he stands outside the absolute; he and the absolute are two extremes that will never come into contact" (1:396–397).

The new ideas quickly gained currency in Bakunin's family circle. His proselytes took up the appropriate phraseology and applied it to themselves. Preserved in the Bakunin family archive is an unmailed letter from Aleksandra Aleksandrovna to Belinskii, who for several years had been hopelessly in love with her: "You saw me in a morbid state this summer; I was completely possessed by a dark, *unenlightened* feeling. . . . A white church loomed over me, and next to it was my sister's grave . . . ; her death seemed to tear something from my heart, and yet I was united with her more than ever, united not in a life of illusions, dreams, and fantasies, but in a sacred, *real* one. You are right, I still have not arrived at a *true realization* of my *inner life*; I am frequently carried away by *illusion*, but faith and love are not in vain."[9]

If even the young women of the Bakunin circle were attempting to formulate their own spiritual states in terms of Hegelian philosophical categories (overheard in bits and pieces), then how much more willing to do so were those of Bakunin's comrades who felt his influence most

strongly? Thus, for example, the twenty-year-old Mikhail Katkov wrote
Bakunin in 1839: "There can be nothing higher or sweeter than the feeling you have when you begin to be aware of yourself as a lawful citizen
of the kingdom of spirit, when you begin to have a profound respect for
your own *I*, not the earlier spontaneous, natural one that was defeated,
but the enlightened, spiritual, concrete one of a life shared with others.
. . . Our main error was that we worried overmuch about our relationships: they have to emerge freely from the personality and be considered
real to the degree that the person himself is real."[10]

The most characteristic examples of the psychological application of
philosophical terminology, however, are provided by Botkin's letters of
the late 1830s.

> I understood and acknowledged in you, Misha, that which makes up the
> sacred essence of your life, beyond all your excesses and idiotic subjectivi-
> ties. That hidden essence of your being is what I love, and with it, with that
> essence, which forms your true *I*, I shall always feel at one. . . . I am not
> talking about the fact that my rebirth is fused with you, that it was *first*
> through you that I came to know those ideas that caused the blindfold to
> drop from my eyes, and I entered the free realm of being, where my soul,
> weary from the dark convolutions of reason and from every sort of doubt, at
> last breathed freely and easily. . . . I am not referring to those moments when
> we accepted each other completely, when there was no end, no limit to my
> immersion in you, and the deeper I was immersed, the more magnificent and
> luxuriant the organization of your soul was revealed to me. . . . Here is the
> essence of my relations with you. In them there is neither lie, nor duplicity,
> nor anything illusory. Yet how very far have our subjectivities, our mutual
> excesses, our petty vanities, and self-grinning cast us apart. . . . Yes, Misha,
> we have been cast apart, and only the *rational experience* of life can reunite
> us concretely. But I say again: it is your insufferable pride, your shallow
> sense of the people close to you, and your puerile recklessness that have
> played the principal role in this. So far you have not been fond of *reconcilia-
> tion*, but have only been a master of breaking off.[11]

Botkin is a convincing example of how epochal intellectual movements
attract and transform people of even the most unsuitable psychological
characteristics. Botkin's subsequent evolution revealed his authentic, organic features—a characteristic blend of positivism, artistic sensibility,
and the most refined sybaritism.[12] He remained true to his passion for
music and gastronomy even on his deathbed. He died (in 1869) paralyzed
and nearly blind, but he arranged magnificent concerts and dinners at his
bedside and declared, "Celestial birds are singing in my soul."[13]

In what way, then, was Botkin a romantic of the 1830s? He wholeheartedly and sincerely carried out all that was required of him by the
model of romantic conduct accepted in his circle. His letters of those years

reflect passionate quarrels and reconciliations with his friends, a predisposition to "demonism" and the beyond, and ideal love and introspection. A quick intelligence and flexible mind for him took the place of that authentic spiritual experience that Bakunin, Stankevich, and Belinskii, each in his own way, possessed to the highest degree. It was from these characteristics that Botkin's eclecticism derived—not only intellectual, but psychological as well. He easily combined the incompatible. As Boris Egorov has written, "It is curious that even in the most 'romantic' period of his life, he still kept industry and commerce in mind."[14] Kornilov, citing Botkin's letters to Aleksandra Bakunina full of complaints about his spiritual torment, notes that that torment "in no way prevented his taking an active part" in concerts, amateur theatricals, suppers with friends, and the other amusements of his circle.[15]

This does not at all mean, of course, that one should dismiss the young Botkin's romantic experiences and philosophical conflicts. Fashion too is an important phenomenon, a symptom of cultural processes. But the case of Botkin is not just one of fashion; it also clearly demonstrates how a historical personality type originating in fashion may be superimposed on empirical personalities, both suitable and unsuitable. Young minds are compellingly drawn to the possibility of such an incarnation, since for them it promises escape from a private and as it were accidental existence into a historical one. To give expression through one's own personality to the motivating ideas of one's time is an irresistible temptation. Life later tests the reality of those symbolic incarnations. Some pay in full measure, while others, after playing for a while at that seductive game, mellow with the years. So it was with Botkin.

Belinskii unquestionably felt the influence of Bakunin's vigorous mind too. But here strength came up against strength. Belinskii also passed through a period at the end of the 1830s and the beginning of the 1840s when he applied Hegelian categories to the analysis of his own and others' spiritual life. But for him that process led to other conclusions and it revealed other possibilities.

The psychological turn taken by Bakuninian Hegelianism in the 1830s ultimately proved to be just another version of romantic consciousness. Using new means, Bakunin recreated the image of the man of great destiny and providential purpose. True, the basic features of that personality were now "reality" and "concreteness," but that Hegelian concreteness was in fact unity in diversity, and that reality, the essence of things as apprehended by the spirit. These features could thus become attributes of the romantic man, who, as before, remained opposed to base empirical reality. It was precisely this that permitted, without the need for any supplementary modification, the introduction of the philosophical ideas of Bakunin's Hegelian psychologism into the usage of his family and friends.

In the first phase of his own interest in Hegel (the spring and summer of 1838), Belinskii still drew a theoretical distinction between abstractly conceived reality and concreteness, but he was already overwhelmingly attracted to another kind of reality and another kind of concreteness. He continued to apply philosophical ideas to the analysis of spiritual life, but unlike Bakunin he reworked those ideas; he saw details and he correlated the ideas with particular objects.

Belinskii at this point was still under the sway of dualism, was still thinking in terms of antitheses, but the emphasis had shifted: the positive had become the negative. The old Schillerian idealism was now pronounced an empty dream, an illusion. Dream and reality had exchanged places, thereby in accordance with the laws of romantic polarity engendering a new set of corollary oppositions arrayed in a new terminology.

The Hegelian idea of "substance" was removed to the psychological plane, where in circle usage it came to denote a person's true essence. Opposed to that essence were the "phenomena" of spiritual life—the individual's external, private "definitions," and the "stages" of his development, which not infrequently distorted his true substance (or essence).

The first period of Belinskii's development had been characterized by the cult of feeling, which stood opposed to crass rationalism. Now, however, the objective stood higher than the subjective, and the polar opposite of "rationalism" became "reason." Feeling had not lost its standing, but in order for it to be regarded positively it had to be illuminated by reason, lest it give rise to the negative phenomenon of "unenlightened spontaneity." Instead of Fichtean love, the highest ethical state was now "harmony" or organic spiritual life, with the contraries of harmony, "disintegration" and "introspection," becoming the principal obstacles on the path to the ideal. The drama of moral awakenings and degradations was ceaselessly played out within this philosophical-psychological framework. This drama found expression in the numerous letters that Belinskii wrote at the end of the 1830s, and I shall look at one of them, an especially remarkable example.

This is a letter written in June 1838 to Bakunin, and it is an important link in the highly complex history of the relationship between the two friends and adversaries. In the letter Belinskii summarizes the history of their relationship, at the same time reviewing and reevaluating such basic ideas for the intellectual and moral life of the circle as love, friendship, personality, and so forth. The letter is rife with circle phraseology.

> Michel, we have both been unfair to each other. We attacked in each other not those particular definitions, not those defects and vulgarities which are cast away and shaken off like dust, but our substances. . . . Our mutual illusions produced howling, morbid dissonances in the beautiful harmony that we had formed through our attraction to one another. . . . Except for love,

all is illusion and falsehood, and love suffers when its object is unworthy. . . . Yes, Michel, I sense that I have deeply offended you. . . . But I have no regrets about the past; it was a stage in the development of my spirit. . . . I was offended by your overweening pride, although I now see it as proof of your high calling, as evidence of the depth of your substance. You were never content with your definition; you always hated it both in yourself and in others. Entering a new stage, you expected us to enter it too, and you hated us, seeing that we were in our own stages and not in yours. That was subjectivity and narrowness on your part; yet how much there was that was beautiful, sacred, and great in that subjectivity and narrowness. In my eyes, you are now none other than a manifestation of elements in chaotic ferment. Your *I* tries to give shape to itself, but since it is fated to do so in monumental forms, that process is naturally painful for you: destruction takes place in it for the sake of creation, and decay, for a new fertility. (11:240–242)

The psychological application of philosophical ideas is exceptionally clear here. At the same time, the Hegelian categories in Belinskii's use of them are not abstract; they bear on the actual relationships of actual people. Later on in the letter they are employed in an analysis of the personality of Bakunin, someone in whom the philosophical alternated with ordinary social reality, resulting in their mutual transformation:

Your peculiarities, childishness, silliness, and vulgarity are all clear to me now. You were unfair to me in many ways, not personally, as I once thought, but as the result of a temporary condition of your spirit. Now I understand you fully, and so my love for you is deep: love is understanding, that sacred and *organic* understanding where there is one unspoken feeling, or if it is spoken, then not as an abstraction, but as something that is also a feeling. Yes, I love you now as you are, love you with all your faults, your narrowness, love you with your long hands, which you wave about so gracefully in moments of transport, and with one of which (I do not remember whether it is the right or the left) you so picturesquely, so vividly—holding the two longest fingers together—demonstrate and prove to me that there is no capacity for speculation in me, "and that is all there is to it"; I love you with your curly head, that fountain of wisdom, and the smoking chibouk in your mouth. Michel, love me too as I am. Wish me infinite improvement, help me to reach my lofty goal, but do not punish me with proud contempt for my deviations from it; respect my individuality, my subjectivity, and be tolerant of my lack of enlightenment. . . . Michel, one can only love the substance—I understand that; but, you see, that substance is itself an illusion: it is recognizable only through the definition. And in a person it is only the definition as the expression of his substance that one can love. (11:245)

This last declaration was an absolutely fundamental one for Belinskii. Individual "definition" was now seen as a concrete psychological manifestation of human essence. And it is therefore no accident that the philosophical terms suddenly yield here to the picturesque image of Bakunin with his pipe and his large hands (it would be impossible to find anything of the sort in Bakunin's letters of the period).

But it is not just the picturesqueness that is important here; more to the point is the fact that with the aid of philosophical terminology Belinskii was able to fix the processes taking place within an individual consciousness and to trace a sort of dialectic of the soul.

> I have always felt the need to speak out, and a rage against that need. The result of that struggle had to be despair, an impoverishment of life, its manifestation in convulsive gleams, in momentary raptures, and in days and weeks of deadly apathy. And so it was with me at Premukhino. It was there that I first came face-to-face with thought, and was horrified at my own emptiness. That was a terrible time in my life, but I now realize its necessity. . . . I suffered because I was noble; I sacrificed all of my feelings, beliefs, and hopes, my self-esteem and my personality, for the sake of my finite definitions. (11:243)

In addition to a distinctive use of Hegelian terminology in the correspondence of Belinskii and his friends, one also finds phraseology of an entirely different provenance—words derived from a variety of linguistic strata but serving in circle usage as terminological counters for certain basic ideological and psychological ideas. This phraseology includes such frequently encountered expressions in the correspondence of the young Belinskii as "apathy," "articulation," [vygovarivanie], and "scrutiny." The idea of "apathy," so important to the system prevailing in the Stankevich circle, was tied to the whole notion of idleness and lack of will as indicative of the "condition of degradation." Similarly, "articulation" and "scrutiny" were connected with self-absorption and self-analysis, with unrestrained candor, and with those forms of friendship that Belinskii accepted at the time, but later denounced so vehemently.

Ordinary words, albeit bookish in origin, thus became terms or formulas for the initiated. The same kind of denotation was sometimes also given to quoted words and phrases, often of completely unphilosophical origin. In the second half of the 1830s Stankevich and his friends were attracted to Gogol'. In the fall of 1835 Belinskii's brilliant article "On the Russian Tale and the Tales of Mr. Gogol'" was published in The Telescope. Gogolian images and expressions soon afterward became an integral part of the intellectual currency of the circle and of the correspondence of its members. Belinskii turned those Gogolian expressions into a kind of specialized terminology, which was then incorporated into his system of philosophical antinomies. Toward the end of his Fichtean period, for example, the ideas of "Khlestakov" and of "Khlestakovism" stood in opposition to those of duty and moral responsibility. Later on they became the antitheses of simplicity and concrete action. "Khlesta-kovism" was in fact one of the most important concepts in the early Belinskiian ethical system.

Gogolian turns of phrase, usually in a somewhat altered form, are pervasive in Belinskii's letters: "You want to be a general so you can wear the ceremonial ribbon over your shoulder" (11:348), "My dear Triapichkin" (11:428), "You want to take up something lofty but the fashionable crowd does not understand" (11:528), and so on. One also encounters surprising collocations of Gogol' and Hegel that produce terms of a new type. In July 1838, Belinskii wrote to Bakunin, "Botkin told me the scene that begins *Wilhelm Meister*, and my soul trembled with delight. But one needs to know just what is there—more essence and actions, that is—yet I know nothing." Belinskii was concerned in this letter with the transition from an illusory, ideal love to an earthly, real one, and that certainly involved "actions." The word itself, however, originated as an ironic quotation. In the first act of *The Inspector General* (third scene), Bob-chinskii says of Khlestakov, "He walks around the room, and there is such reasoning and character in his face, . . . such important actions."[16] This formula combining Bobchinskii's little word with Hegel's "essence" occurs several times in Belinskii's letters. It is a joke, of course, but one expressing a very important insight for Belinskii about the unity of idea and action, of idea and phenomenon.

The expression "it dances" or "it does not dance" (in the sense that it is or is not "working out") comes from the tale "An Enchanted Place" ("No, it does not dance, and that is all there is to it!") and it turns up quite often in the letters. In 1839, at the height of his struggle for concrete reality, Belinskii wrote to Stankevich, "Time is the test of all inclinations, feelings, and ties—*reality has begun to dance*" (11:366). This is once again the linking of a philosophical idea with a Gogolian turn of phrase that renders that phrase a term for the initiated.

Such bold linguistic experiments are fully in keeping with the whole stylistic tenor of Belinskii's letters, a motley and uneven one (in contrast to that of Bakunin's letters). Accompanying the analytical mode are friendly banter, jokes, and rough vulgarisms, and sometimes the language of romantic idealism breaks through the philosophical or colloquial tone. Thus, in an 1838 letter, Belinskii says of Bakunin's sister Aleksandra, "No, falling passionately in love with any other woman in the world is out of the question. Any other woman, however exalted, is merely a woman, while in her are heaven and earth and hell, for she is a pure shining cherub of the living God; she is heaven, remote, profound, limitless heaven without a single wisp of cloud—a single azure expanse illumined by the sun!" (11:241). This kind of language, however, was a remnant of earlier idealistic tendencies that were becoming less and less possible for Belinskii.

The romantic personality with which the young Russian philosophers of the 1830s had begun had its own schema, which, though modified by philosophical ideas, remained essentially intact. The personality corresponding to the new philosophical phase, however, had to be created anew. This new image emerged in Belinskii's letters of 1838: the universal and historically significant image of a man who had not yet freed himself of his romantic past, but who was already just as passionately and sometimes just as futilely attracted to reality as, not long before, he had been attracted to dreams. In the structure of this new personality, harmony was opposed to disintegration and introspection, and feeling enlightened by reason, to "unenlightened spontaneity."

But Belinskii did not stop there. His thirst for the real carried him still further and, for a while, brought him to the notorious "reconciliation with reality," to acceptance, that is, of the political conduct of the autocratic state. The new image of personality had inevitably to reflect the new image of reality.

Belinskii endeavored to accept "what exists," but the sense of reality that prompted him to do so also guarded him against idyllic notions about the nature of the world. In September 1838 he wrote to Bakunin, "Reality is a monster armed with iron claws and a huge mouth with iron jaws. Sooner or later it will devour all those who live out of harmony with it and resist it. The only way to free oneself from reality and to see it not as a monster, but as the source of happiness, is to *face it*" (11:288). Defined here, in essence, is the personal, psychological dimension of philosophical and political reconciliation. The highest virtue of the human being was to be found not in Schillerian heroics (which, after all, had already been dismissed as "soul-beauty" and empty dream), but in enduring all the burdens imposed by that terrible reality and transforming them into the source of happiness. Such resignation was possible thanks to the unconditional dominance of the "rational universal" over the accidental and the private, and of the practical demands of the state and of society over the desires and subjective feelings of the individual. The once-proclaimed primacy of the objective over the subjective was thus now redefined as the primacy of the universal (in the Hegelian sense) over the particular and the individually human. All of the personality's other oppositions of positive and negative qualities underwent a corresponding redistribution.

To the dismay of his philosophical friends, Belinskii now understood reality not only as a unity of essence and phenomenon consciously accepted by the spirit, and not merely as the political conduct of the state, but also as empirical everyday life, as the laws and demands of communal life and relations, which were obligatory for all alike, whether endowed with talents and gifts or lacking them. This now antiromantic principle served as the starting point for the creation of a new model of the human being and his behavior. Before, harmony had been regarded as the highest ethical state; now its place was taken by "simplicity."

Belinskii acknowledged in a letter written to Bakunin in 1838 that it was from him that he had first heard the word "reality": "But I have another word that I say over and over again, and it is my *own* word and a great one. It is *simplicity*. My Lord, how profound is its mysterious and *simple* meaning!" (11:293). In Belinskii's letters of these years, the word "simplicity" was repeated often in a variety of contexts, and it became a key to the whole issue of constructing personality. Associated with it were "normality" and "spontaneity." Simplicity and normality had their own antitheses: stiltedness, cant, "Khlestakovism," introspection, and distortion. These correlations had a dual significance for Belinskii's maturation. During the period of his "reconciliation with reality," they reflected the distrust of protest that he spoke of in his articles on [Griboedov's] *Woe from Wit* and on "Menzel as a Critic of Goethe" and in other essays. At the same time, however, they served to register a new phase in the continuous and productive evolution of his idea of reality.

Simplicity and normality became the basis for the reconsideration of those spiritual states and relations, above all love and friendship, that had been so decisive for the romantic mind. The ecstatic form of friendship that had held sway in the circle and that had originated in "scrutiny" and "articulation" (which in their own turn had been a response to the personality's acute need for self-realization) was now condemned, and celestial love for an idealized woman, an idea that had once presupposed unattainability and hopelessness, was now redefined as a negative phenomenon and dismissed as an illusory fantasy of the sort that someone may "burden himself with." Actual, consummated love now became the positive pole of the antithesis, giving rise to a new theory of love in which mutuality and equality were regarded as the necessary preconditions of true love and all else was dismissed as deluded dreaminess. As was always the case with Belinskii, this reorganization of his thought was nourished by material drawn from actual life, and that gave it a concrete psychological turn. In his letters of 1839–1840, he revised the account of his love for Bakunin's sister Aleksandra, now viewing it as an example of "soul-beauty" and of stilted and deluded dreaminess. Also subject to reconsideration were the images of the Bakunin sisters themselves, which not long before had been created in the likeness of Eternal Femininity. The sisters remained lofty and "sacred," but they were now seen as having been distorted by Michel, who had introduced disharmony and introspection into their "divine spontaneity" (during the period of his "reconciliation"

Belinskii accepted the Hegelian conception of women as incapable of abstract thought). But Belinskii judged his own relations with Mikhail Bakunin even more harshly: "I am sick of this beautiful-souled spinning around in empty circles of sham relations, sham friendship, sham love, and sham hate" (11:368).

This revaluation of ethical values did not imply, however, that they had now been safely mastered. Belinskii's new conception of himself was structured not in ideal terms but as a generalization based on existing psychological reality—as something that emerged from the struggle between his individual strengths and weaknesses. Belinskii's main strength now lay in the fact that he had curbed his romantic arrogance and had submitted himself to universal laws that extended from the state to everyday life. Accordingly, simplicity and normality became his new ideal. Belinskii did not, however, see himself as an ideal hero. Rather, he was someone who had grasped the value of reality, of concreteness and simplicity, yet who was still subject to stiltedness, introspection, "Khlestakovism," and timidness in a love that now demanded consummation. Taken together, these negative aspects were the antithesis of reality. But the very idea of reality was once again entering a new phase.

It is considered, and rightly so, that Belinskii's move to Petersburg and the impressions of the Russian imperial capital he received there greatly influenced the new departure in his worldview. But as early as September–October 1839, even before he moved to Petersburg, Belinskii had written an enormous confessional letter to Stankevich in which he summarized the Hegelian enthusiasms of the circle, his own relations with Bakunin, and a great deal else besides. This letter reveals how much Belinskii was even then prepared to reformulate the questions of what was real and what was not.

The cult of the universal and the preaching of "reconciliation with reality" reached their apogee in Belinskii's articles on the anniversary of the battle of Borodino. The second of these, a response to Fedor Glinka's "Essays on the Battle of Borodino," appeared in the December 1839 issue of *National Annals*, but by February 1840 Belinskii was already saying, "Oh perish that abominable universal, that Moloch that devours life, that self-grinning rattlesnake of egoism!" (11:467). The same February Granovskii wrote to Stankevich that Belinskii's "fanatical respect for reality is on the wane. He writes that he would give God knows what 'to get back the article on . . .'" (on the Battle of Borodino, that is).[17] The Moloch of "Russian reality" was already irrevocably condemned, and the private personality it trampled underfoot was restored its rights, its moral value, even though the painful transitional state of Belinskii's thought was to continue until he found new forms of the universal for that personality, until he solved for himself the problem of its social existence. The political significance of the transitional phase is obvious: Belinskii was freeing himself from the, for him, organically repellent idea of violence against the individual. But this phase was also extremely important for the realization of his own personality. In regard to Belinskii's development, the Hegelian crisis was distinguished by a particular psychological intensity. Moreover, the defining contradictions of that crisis led directly to issues that would concern the Russian psychological novel in the second half of the century.

Up to this point, the philosophical-psychological antinomies that had emerged in circle usage had been disposed in a rather clear-cut arrangement. Originally, the positive pole had been occupied by ideality, with base empirical reality on the negative side; later on, reality became a positive principle, with vulgar idealism serving as its negative pole. In keeping with the laws of romantic thought, the initial premises gave rise to corresponding sets of contrasting qualities.

Now, however, the formerly clear-cut opposition of values was gone. Reality was terrible; reality with its iron claws had turned into "vile reality." "The only good thing in life is dreams; if you do not know that yet, you will soon find out" (1840 letter to Botkin; 11:563).

Was this a return to the earlier romantic antithesis of dream and base reality? No, it was something else. Then, the dream had been the highest metaphysical reality; now it was merely an illusion. The opposition remained, but now it was no longer obvious which was the positive and which was the negative element. The earlier opposition had become a frankly unresolvable contradiction that, in its turn, gave rise to other contradictions—on the one hand, the Moloch of terrible reality and of an inhumanly abstract "universal," and on the other hand, human personality. Yet Belinskii understood the illusoriness of any idea of personality not subsumed in a system of shared values and relations, even if he was still unable to define those new relations clearly. "There lives but one universal, and we are Chinese shadows, waves in the ocean; there is only one ocean, but there have been, there are, and there will be many waves, and who cares about one or another of them?" (11:444).

The universal was inhuman, the value of individual personality, illusory. The valuative emphasis had now shifted, and the whole structure of antitheses had therefore been rendered unstable. Correlations emerged that were completely unexpected but that followed logically from the initial premises. Thus, "apathy" now occupied the positive pole. Apathy had been the contrary of love, an indication of the "condition of degradation." Now it had a different function. "It seems that I have forever lost the capacity for childish enthusiasm, thank God. I have decided that the deadliest, most brutish apathy is better, higher, and more noble than dreams and sham emotions" (11:534). Just as simplicity had in its time, apathy now took the place of harmony and stood in opposition to stilted-ness, cant, and "Khlestakovism." Needless to say, Belinskii regarded apathy as merely a "stage" in his development, as a symptom of sober-mindedness.

In the very first of Belinskii's extant letters from Petersburg, one writ-ten to Botkin, we read: "I do not have time for anybody now. I am not in love with anyone or involved with anybody, because the time came when I clearly saw that I either had to become what I must be or renounce all claim to any kind of life or happiness. For me there is only one way out—you know what it is; it is not in *Jenseits* or in mysticism or in anything that provides a way out for half-endowed natures and half-disillusioned souls. . . . Only one thing is left—either to make something real of myself or, as long as breath remains in my body, to sing this little ditty: 'I have wasted my life, and now it is gone Forever'" (11:416).

Such ideas as spirit, the absolute, and true substance could no longer serve, in this period of crisis and reconsideration of earlier positions, as the origin and justification of human values. Only one indisputable value remained—sober truth. "I would rather my heart were torn to pieces by the truth than made blissful by a lie," Belinskii wrote in February 1840 (11:438). And it is characteristic that in the above letter to Botkin, apathy was once more linked to sobermindedness as a symptom. Several lines after the passage just quoted we read, "You did a lot for me—I saw that; but I just did not care about it, as if it did not have anything to do with me. It was all the same to me—go or stay, live or die, bury you or see you alive." The idea of "sober truth" was an idea of its time, born of the movement of Russian thought toward realism. Somewhat later, at the beginning of the 1840s, it became a decisive idea in Herzen's worldview, as is exemplified by his letters, diaries, and articles, especially those on "Dilettantism in Science," in which he wrote that a man must "give every-thing to science and in recompense receive the heavy cross of sober knowledge" (3:66).

The stern wish for sober knowledge was becoming the basis of self-affirmation for Belinskii, as it later would for Herzen. A man should no longer attempt to reconcile himself with terrible reality, nor should he seek refuge from it in illusion; rather, he should master it by means of a fearless search for the truth—such was the new generalized image of him-self constructed by Belinskii at the end of the 1830s and the beginning of the 1840s. "I want to look every terror right in the face and reject nothing but confront everything" (11:553).

As always, however, Belinskii's conception of himself was as much a product of self-condemnation as it was of self-affirmation. Though a fear-less seeker of the truth, he was still stricken by the paralysis, vices, and weaknesses of character and will that were characteristic of the "introspective generation." Belinskii's self-conception had now become a fact of historical significance: it was the self-conception of a generation.

Belinskii discussed the introspective generation in his 1840–1841 articles on Lermontov, but in his letters of that period he gave the theme a much harsher and more outspoken treatment. "Fate has made a milksop of me: I belong to an unlucky generation weighed down by the curse of its time, an evil time! All transitional generations are a sorry lot: they have to answer not for themselves but for society. . . . The new generation gladdens me: it is full of life and devoid of the rotten habit of introspection" (11:521).

Belinskii now postulated a kind of ideal person endowed with qualities that stood in direct opposition to the weaknesses of the introspective generation (an ideal approached among the "young people" by Nikolai Bakunin, Michel's brother and someone with whom Belinskii was much taken at the time). Introspection was replaced in the ideal person by healthy spontaneity (which as "unenlightened spontaneity" had once been a defect), fragmentariness by wholeness and vitality, and the paralysis of the "wet hen" by the ability to master life's concrete blessings. During his "reconciliation with reality," Belinskii had already replaced ideal and disembodied love with actual love. Now he went even further, restoring to pleasure its rights and rehabilitating sensuality as a manifestation of spontaneity and vitality.[18]

The positive pole was now simultaneously occupied by boldness in the acquisition of knowledge and apathy, by apathy and sensitivity, and by lovelessness and the vitality of a spontaneous apprehension of life. The greater complexity of these correlations and the movement beyond romantic polarization and the bilateral contrasts that this complexity entailed were accompanied by an increase in psychologism (sustained by intense scrutiny of the "private personality"), a psychologism that was increasingly realistic, inasmuch as an understanding of the full extent to which spiritual life is socially conditioned grew stronger as the metaphysical antitheses grew weaker. A resolution of the crisis was now near at hand precisely because the contradictions were growing ever more intolerable.

The dream was beautiful, but it was an illusion, a concession to human weakness. Reality was terrible, but one could not break free of it. Emptiness and despair awaited the person who was incapable of reaching "beyond himself." "If it were not for the magazine, I would have lost my mind. If vile reality had not sucked my blood drop by drop, I would have gone mad" (11:563). Social activity was still presented in the 1840 letter as a means of self-affirmation and of the struggle with emptiness, but the basic structure of the romantic and Hegelian polarities had been destroyed once and for all. Both systems beset the man of the reflective generation with illusions. A solution would come after Belinskii had discovered the objective value and necessity of "social action," when that action had become an ethical act of the highest order.

Dating from June and September 1841 are Belinskii's famous letters to Botkin on Maratian love for mankind in general and on "sociality" [*sotsial'nost'*] ("sociality, sociality, or death!"). The idea of socialism, which for Belinskii had become "the idea of ideas, the reality of realities, the question of questions, the alpha and omega of belief and knowledge" (12:66), did not contradict the idea of personality rescued from absorption in the Moloch of the universal, since personality was now conceived in a new, social way—not as something lofty or isolated, but as both an individual and a collective phenomenon.

Sociality required public action. "I have now fully grasped what I am, have understood my own nature; either idea can be rendered fully by the word *Tat*, which is my element" (letter of 1840, 12:13; see also 12:38 for a discussion of "vital and rational *Tat*"). It was no accident that Belinskii used the German word for "deed" or "action." The new position followed logically from earlier spiritual experience—from the idea of action in *Faust* ("Im Anfang war die Tat") and from the Hegelian conception of activity. Soon afterward, Herzen would take up in the above-mentioned series of articles on "Dilettantism in Science" his own advocacy of "creative action" [*odeistvotvorenie*], or the transition from theory to practice.

The statement "I have now fully grasped what I am" was another typically Belinskiian view of the self from off to the side, the definition of that self in terms of psychological and historical categories. This time, however, he construed his own "nature" as complex and divided, apprehending that division as a consequence of the tragic disharmony between his inner spiritual experience and his social activity. "I am disappointed in everything, I do not believe in anything, and I do not love anybody or anything, even though the prosaic interests of life concern me less and less, and I am more and more a citizen of the universe. A terrible craving for love devours more and more of my inner life, and my sense of desolation grows more intense and insistent. This is mine, and it is the only thing that is. But I am occupied most by what is not mine. Human personality is the point on which I am afraid I shall go mad. I am beginning to love mankind in the Maratian way" (11:52). The individual image that emerges here comes from the conjunction of unrealized love for a woman and realized love for mankind. Love for mankind was an indisputable spiritual experience that convinced the person of the objective status of social values and goals. At the time of the crisis, terrible reality had been opposed to illusion, which saved even those who knew it to be illusion from fatal emptiness. But now the antithesis of terrible reality was the just and rational reality of utopian socialism, and the fearless contemplator of sober truth had been turned into the man of purposeful action (which in Belinskii's case took concrete form in his journalistic activity).

Belinskii's spiritual development, however, was never easy or direct. The "inner man," the private personality, had retained from the period of the crisis of faith in Hegelian ideas a host of unresolved questions. Such themes as apathy, baren suffering, and the incapacity for love continued to be heard in his letters of these years. The realm of useful social aspiration was consciously and persistently separated from that of private existence, which remained solitary, difficult, and permeated by a futile, "tantalizing" craving for happiness and love. "Both interest me, but inside I carry death and emptiness. Hopes, passions, and life still exist for me in general terms, but for myself there is nothing. It is all tedious, cold, and empty: there is no hope whatever for personal happiness. Ah, bitterness, bitterness! Life stands exposed" (April 1842; 12:106). Even earlier, in an 1841 letter to Nikolai Bakunin, Belinskii had clearly formulated his understanding of the separateness of the two realms of his spiritual life:

> You see, I am just the same as I was, still the same beautiful soul, reckless and loving. My heart has not cooled; no, it is not dying from coldness, but from a surfeit of fire that has nothing to nourish it. . . . The inner world is fascinating, but without external realization, it is a world of emptiness, mirages, and dreams. I do not, after all, belong with the purely inner natures; I am no more an inner person than I am an external one. Rather, I stand on the borderline between those two great worlds. My inner world cannot compensate me for an insufficiency of external activity, and for that reason it is merely a source of torment, coldness, and apathy—a dark and stifling prison. (12:76)

The split between the inner and outer worlds became during this critical period the basis for Belinskii's conscious realization and structuring of his own personality as a historically generalized version of the personality of the introspective generation. As did Herzen and the rest of his contemporaries who were attracted to the ideas of utopian socialism, Belinskii believed in the possibility of an ideal harmony between the social and the personal, although both he and they were convinced that that harmony was destined only for future generations. The split between the "two great worlds" in Belinskii's consciousness at the beginning of the 1840s should not, of course, be seen as a matter of personal "weakness." Rather, it was a fact of epochal significance, one indicative of a new stage in the development of Russian intellectual life, of that moment when introspective man broke free of romanticism and acquired a *real* orientation.[19] Sober knowledge and social activity—the dominant features of the real man—anticipated both the final stage of Belinskii's ideological development and the road that ultimately would be taken by the Russian revolutionary democrats. Yet what Belinskii termed his "inner world" was no less an anticipation of the future. The contradictions, the dissatisfaction, the avid self-scrutiny in response to terrible moral demands that, however personal and intimate, inevitably acquired universal meaning—all these opened the way to the psychologism of Russian prose in the second half of the century and to its crowning accomplishment, the unprecedented self-analysis of Tolstoi. At the same time, however, the psychological novel did not supersede the kind of self-knowledge achieved by the generation of the 1830s. That self-knowledge remained unique both by virtue of its intensity and its frank translation of philosophical issues into the language of spiritual experience. And it was indeed Belinskii who came closest, in the methods he used to define his own inner world, to the Tolstoian line in the development of Russian culture.

The model of the man of real orientation necessitated another shift in valuational accent. In spite of the earlier denigration of the introspective generation, introspection (now understood as protesting reason) was moved to the positive pole, and spontaneity to the negative (the converse of their placement at the height of the Hegelian phase). "Reason and awareness," Belinskii wrote in September 1841, "are the true foundations of human value and happiness. For me, to see someone enjoying the shameful happiness of spontaneity is the same as the devil being faced with suppliant innocence: I destroy spontaneity wherever I can, without reflection or remorse, and it does not bother me if the person then perishes in a domain of introspection that is foreign to him. Let him" (12:72).

Along with introspection, "subjectivity" was also rehabilitated, although it was now understood as the material of personality, which was itself regarded as an individual entity contained in the social whole. But subjectivity involved Schillerism and its heroics, which had not long before been subject to abuse. Opposed to Schillerism as its (negative) antithesis was the refined egoism of Goethe, even though Goethe had in Belinskii's earlier Hegelian phase been the epitome of the true life of the spirit, with Schiller opposed to him as the incarnation of illusion and dream. The system of antitheses thus continued to play a role in Belinskii's thinking, although, generally speaking, it was no longer used to structure personality. For the man of real orientation, other, different means were required.

For Belinskii and Herzen at the beginning of the 1840s, realism was essentially a method to be used in the building of a new, rational world.[20] Moreover, it was a universal method applicable to any sphere of human activity—knowledge and art, morality and the social struggle, love, family, and everyday existence. It introduced logical determinism, the search for causes and connections, into the conception of the human being.

Cause-and-effect relations therefore replaced metaphysically based antitheses as the structural principle of the new, real personality. To be sure, neither the idea that personality is conditioned, nor the analytical method for its investigation, was entirely new. Both had numerous sources and were the result of centuries of preparation. There was the great analytical tradition of Montaigne and La Rochefoucauld, which produced the analytical novel; there was the sensationalism of the philosophes and the ideas of Herder; and finally there was the issue of man's relationship to his environment as that issue had been redefined by young realism, both Western and Russian (the Gogol' school).

Of critical importance, too, was the fact that it was no longer possible in the nineteenth century to ignore the achievements and objectives of empirical psychology. Even Hegel's doctrine of subjective spirit assigned a place not merely to questions of sensory awareness and feeling, but also to much more private empirical factors. In the section called "Anthropologie" of his *Psychologie*, Rosenkranz followed Hegel in examining such matters as the peculiarities of race, sex, and age, the nervous and circulatory system and the doctrine of temperaments, physiology and phrenology, and so on.

These various sources were all available to Belinskii, just as they were to all the thinking people of his generation. What was striking were the conclusions that he drew and his concrete psychological application of ideas that were in the air.

Belinskii traced the psychological process in earnest in both its general significance and its individual specificity, but most importantly in its *details*, details that were still beyond the reach of the novel in the first third of the nineteenth century. In his letters, psychological determinism acquired ever-increasing importance, and in the beginning it did so almost spontaneously, thanks to the organic concreteness of his perception of life. Thus, as early as 1837, in the letter discussing the antithesis of internal (higher) and external (lower) life, he made a concession to external life in his theory of "kopecks" and their psychological significance. It was at that time too that he turned toward the study of temperaments, declaring that there was "only one" normal temperament, "the harmonious" one. Bakunin possessed such a temperament, according to Belinskii, and he did so because his father had led a temperate life and was a worthy man, "whereas my father drank and led a dissolute life, as a consequence of which I received a *nervous* temperament. . . . It is my belief that the spirit always triumphs over its material nature, that it is able to alter its temperament in spite of nature. But this means that the achievement of perfection is *harder* for me than it is for you. . . . In order to keep from distorting the truth whenever judging someone close to you, it is necessary to consider all the circumstances, organic and natural, of his upbringing and his external life" (11:196–197). Later on, especially during the period of crisis in 1840–1841, Belinskii sharpened his analysis of childhood trauma, of the biologically and socially conditioned nature of psychological complexes and conflicts.

In his letters Belinskii investigated in relentless and detailed fashion the basic conflict of his own *private* life, the conflict between unrealized love and his attempt to suppress his "terrible craving for love" by means of a sensuality poisoned by bitterness. At the end of the 1830s and the beginning of the 1840s, Belinskii was already interpreting that conflict as socially conditioned. He was interested in the feeling of social inadequacy and its consequences: timidity, a morbid awkwardness, and emotional inhibition or nervousness. For example, in an 1840 letter to Botkin remarkable for the power and precision of its details, he speaks of a childhood trauma as the source of his later morbid reactions:

> One thing bothers me terribly: my timidness and shyness are not diminishing, but increasing at a monstrous rate. I cannot show myself in public: my snout turns red, my voice trembles, my arms and legs shake, and I am afraid I shall fall down. . . . What is the meaning of this wild strangeness? I remember a story of my mother's. She was a lover of gossip and used to chase after it in order to have something to wag her tongue about. Once, when I was still a babe in arms, I was left with a nurse, a girl she had hired, who smothered me and hit me so I would not bother her with my screaming. Maybe that is the reason. . . . Later on my father could not stand me. He would swear at me, humiliate me, find fault with me, and beat me mercilessly and indecently—eternal memory to him! I was a stranger in my own family. Maybe that is the explanation for my absurd behavior. I am simply afraid of other people; society terrifies me. Yet if I see a fine female face, I die—my eyes fog over, my nerves go to pieces, as if I were looking at a python or a rattlesnake, and my breath grows faint and I am on fire. (11:512)[21]

By the beginning of the 1840s and his declaration of "sociality" as the "alpha and omega" of existence, realistic conditionality was becoming for Belinskii a conscious method to be used in the analysis of spiritual life. "The substance of social life is the source of interests, goals, and activity." This was a formulation of general character. But Belinskii portrayed in very concrete terms what happened to the man of real orientation whenever circumstances had denied that "substance" to him, as may be seen, for example, in a letter to the Bakunin sisters written in 1843:

> I am very far from blaspheming the sacred need of love for a woman out of the conceited vanity of imaginary wisdom, but if that need and its realization are not deeply rooted in the soil of reality and have become detached from the other aspects of life, then they may be vulgar. Examples of a cold and disappointed feeling that, having begun to expire of its own accord, is all of

a sudden extinguished without any reason are especially abundant in our society. Even lofty and profound natures are prone to it—I am referring to Pushkin. Where is the reason for that phenomenon to be found? In a society where everything human is completely divorced from reality, in a society that is savage, sordid, and insane, but that still has the right of force on its side and will have for a long time. I regard myself as one of the passionate souls. Give such a person a sphere of action suitable to his abilities, and he will be reborn and become a man and a human being, but that sphere—well, you already realize that it is nowhere to be found. . . . The heart of a person, especially one who is consumed by a burning hunger for rational action, but who goes unsatisfied, who has not even the hope of satisfying that agonizing hunger—the heart of such a person is always more or less subject to the arbitrariness of chance, for emptiness, whether voluntary or involuntary, can only yield more emptiness—and I, less than anyone, can vouch in the future for my on occasion rather strong, but more often than not distracted, nature. Yet there is one thing that I can vouch for with confidence, and that is that if God should once again empty the cup of his wrath upon me and, like an Egyptian serpent, once again poison me with that anguish without surcease, with that striving without a purpose, with that bitterness without cause, with that suffering that is contemptible and degrading even in my own eyes, then I would no longer be able to expose the pus of my spiritual wounds, and would find the strength to flee forever from those who might be offended or troubled by my shame. I was no stranger to pride before, but it was paralyzed by many things, in particular by romanticism and a pious regard for the so-called inner life—that fiend of German egoism and philistinism. (11:141–142)

Ideas about the laws governing social life have been projected here onto extremely private experiences, onto personal psychology, just as the philosophical categories of German idealism had earlier been projected onto them. In this letter Belinskii once again traces the image of someone who is profoundly committed to social action, yet who is severely restricted in his possibilities, someone whom personal happiness has passed by, and who has repressed in himself the unquenchable desire for it. The outlining of his own personal image was something that Belinskii would rarely return to, however. His realistic thought continued to develop, of course, but by 1844 self-analysis had disappeared from his letters completely; his spiritual energy was redirected to the social world. And after his marriage (at the end of 1843), he abandoned psychological revelations forever.

Belinskii was unique even among his famous contemporaries for the intensity and tirelessness of his moral life. For him, a new idea had inevitably to find expression in the concrete psychology of the new man, and he regarded his own psyche as the proper arena for that epic experiment.

During these years, he consciously created a series of models for the man of the new age, someone in whom the intellectual energy of the historical moment was concentrated.

And the point here really is the replacement one after another of different models of historical man—of the ideologue—since Belinskii's conception of his personal qualities remained relatively stable. During these tempestuous years of ideological searching and redirection, he continued to insist on much the same set of organic characteristics. He viewed himself as possessed of "a fantastic and ridiculous nature," as passionate and violent, and as being a person of extremes, and he did so because his "violent" outbursts alternated with sudden descents into spiritual torpor and paralysis. He was someone endowed with a great hunger for love, goodness, and truth, but impaired by a "vile upbringing," childhood traumas, and a lack of discipline, as a result of which he was overcome by indolence, lack of will, and disorder. His organic characteristics entered into complex interaction with whatever ideological phase he happened to be passing through. And, of course, for Belinskii ideology was itself always a passionate experience too, one that was capable of transforming a person's very essence.

The initial philosophical dichotomy changed, thereby engendering a whole sequence of secondary positive and negative redistributions. During Belinskii's romantic period (he himself called it Fichtean), the initial opposition was between "idealism" and "base reality." During his Hegelian period, that formulation was turned upside down, producing a new opposition between "reality" and "vulgar idealism." During his crisis of faith in Hegelian ideas, yet another opposition emerged, one between the "illusory dream" and "vile reality." And finally, with the resolution of the Hegelian crisis, illusion was itself replaced by objectively authentic "sociality."

Characteristic of each of these periods was a specific ideal of personality and a conception of the fundamental principle of its behavior. In the first period that ideal was the Schillerian heroic personality, with the vulgarian or "soulless man" standing as its contrary. In the next period the ideal was the "real man" (in the Hegelian sense), with the Schillerian personality serving as its antithesis in the guise of the despised "beautiful soul." "Soul-beauty" retained its negative position in the next period as well, when the "real man" was supplanted by the relentless seeker after knowledge, and then by the man of social action. During all these changes, however, the personality ideal was never fully identified with the actual image of its bearer. The historically generalized and psychologically concrete image constructed by Belinskii for each period of his development always remained the image of someone who was striving to attain an ideal, yet who was burdened by "defects" and negative "stages" that kept him from reaching it.

Attending each phase in the evolution of the personality ideal was a particular conception of that personality's fundamental ethical value or condition. Thus, at various points there emerged such secondary oppositions as love and apathy, harmony (fullness of life) and introspection, simplicity and stiltedness ("Khlestakovism"), truth and illusion, and so forth.

Depending on the initial philosophical premise and the changing personality ideal, these ethical values could become countervalues, and vice versa. Thus, during the Hegelian crisis, "apathy" became the positive contrary of "stiltedness" and "cant," and "introspection," the contrary of "thoughtlessness." The particular value assigned to the ideas of "subjectivity" and "objectivity" changed several times as well. Sensuality, once opposed to romantic love, was later rehabilitated as the polar opposite of "illusion" and lack of vitality.

In constructing this changing sequence of historical images, Belinskii used philosophical means and even a frankly philosophical terminology, just as his friends in the Stankevich circle were doing. For Belinskii, however, these theoretical categories adapted from contemporary thought had a very concrete psychological content. The changing historical images belonged to a single individual; they were closely correlated with each other, and their alternation was always governed by a search for ever-greater reality.

Among the oppositions that continued to inform Belinskii's thought at the end of the 1830s, a special place was held by the Belinskii-Bakunin antithesis, an opposition of two epochal personality types that was extremely broad in its range, and whose monument was their voluminous polemical correspondence of 1837–1840 (of which, unfortunately, only the Belinskii letters have survived). This correspondence had its own particular philosophical-psychological subject matter, which reflected the evolution of Russian thought from romantic idealism to Hegelianism and thence to realism. The human images constructed by Belinskii in the course of that evolution were constructed largely by means of the continual measurement of his own personality against that of Bakunin. Revealed in the process of that measurement were continual discord and an agonizingly close bond, which Belinskii characterized with the formula "love-hate."

In keeping with this formula, the image of Bakunin varied, but it was in fact that variability that constituted its essence. "I see your sad face before me, one that I have always loved. You are especially clear to me when you are sad, and your soul merges with mine. . . . If someone should capture in a portrait that mysterious expression, so familiar to me and so dear, then I would be glad to have it. It would be a true portrait, a portrait of your soul" (August 1838; 11:270–271).[22] This affection was the first part of the formula, but there was hatred as well: "Oh, what a vile, mean egoist he is, what a phrasemonger, a devil in philosopher's clothing!" (letter to Botkin, 1840; 11:497).

If Herzen and Chernyshevskii had accused Turgenev of trivializing Bakunin's personality, no one could reproach Belinskii for doing so. His Bakunin, whether loved or hated, was always monumental. He was either a spirit or a devil. The contradictory elements that had already become the main locus of Belinskii's characterization of Bakunin (intellectual force and great spiritual energy combined with silliness, irresponsibility, egoism, and an incapacity for love, whether "divine" or "mundane," and so forth) soon acquired hyperbolic scope. The dialectic of that personality was paradoxical: leonine spirit and fatuous juvenile. "He is a marvelous person, profound, original, a leonine nature—you cannot deny him that; but his pretensions, puerility, swaggering, dishonesty, and lack of scruples make friendship with him impossible" (11:350). "He is an abstract hero bound for his own and others' ruin, someone with a splendid mind, but utterly heartless, with the blood of a rotten salt cod in his veins" (11:522). Belinskii devised a dual, contradictory structure for Michel's character, simultaneously imposing on it yet another polarity, the opposition between Bakunin and himself, an opposition that rendered his own image more precise.

> You write to Botkin that I consider you a vulgarian and only make a carica-
> ture of your poor substance. No, I have always seen and still see in you a
> noble, leonine nature, a profound and mighty soul, an uncommon energy of
> spirit, outstanding gifts, infinite feeling, and a capacious mind. Yet at the
> same time I recognized and still recognize monstrous conceit, pettiness in
> regard to your friends, childishness, silliness, an insufficiency of sincerity
> and fellow-feeling, a high opinion of yourself in comparison with others, a
> desire to dominate, to hold sway, and an inclination to speak the truth to
> others but a reluctance to hear it about yourself. For me those contradictions
> form a single whole, a single person. You are a rich amalgam of the most
> excellent elements, but they are still in ferment and still need a great deal of
> work. . . . You have had a profound influence on my life, and I cannot deny
> a certain resemblance to you, which is based not only on the affinity of our
> two essences, but also on our individualities with all their differences. . . .
> We have something in common—a destructive element; and at the same time
> there is something opposed in us, something adverse. I cannot express my
> feelings for you other than as a *love that resembles hate, and a hate that
> resembles love.* . . . I know that concealed in the secret depths of your soul
> there is an inexhaustible source of love, but that love is for the time being
> directed toward the absolute, just as it is toward essences and not the phe-
> nomena themselves. Your blood is passionate and vital, but it flows (if one
> may use such a figure) not your veins but in your soul, whereas my soul is

in my blood, which is passionate and turbulent, and it moves in me whenever my blood seethes, and it is often hidden by my blood, both from my own and other people's eyes. I am either trembling all over with passionate, agonizing love, or I am simply nothing, the kind of rubbish you would throw away as soon as you would spit; and since love resides in me only momentarily, Michel, the rest of the time I know my own value very well. . . . It is because of this that I am jealous in friendship, and that every attempt to love is agony for me; it is because of this that my passionateness covers up and conceals my depth. . . . All these parallels between you and me are nothing other than an attempt to make sense of the strangeness of our relationship. (11:344–346)

This incisive analysis was hardly governed, of course, by the disinterested curiosity of the investigator. Rather, Belinskii was gazing intently at Bakunin as if into a strange mirror reflecting his own contrasting image. Belinskii's self-awareness passed through a series of such contrastive juxtapositions with Bakunin's personality: love and the incapacity for love, feeling and reason, a concrete apprehension of life and abstraction, timidity and despotism, self-revelation and self-importance, and so on. But these contrasts were not merely an abstract set of antitheses; they were bound up in concrete human personalities, in contrasting psychological structures, each with its own principle of inclusion, combination, and correlation of the elements that it had taken from reality.

The young Bakunin preached romantic dualism in its purest form; everything "base," everything inconvenient in empirical reality, was left outside the threshold of consciousness. In Belinskii's perception of the world, that romantic dualism was undermined at the very outset by his respect for "external life." The range of phenomenal life included by him was democratic, in the sense that any fact was for him potentially an ideological fact. The connection between this *social* quality and the aesthetic qualities of maturing realism is obvious, since anything in the realistic system could in principle become an artistic fact. At the same time, realism was a transition in the movement from romantic summary generalization to the cognition of life in all its multifaceted detail.

The very range of detail included in that cognition ultimately had ethical significance as well, since the phenomena embraced by consciousness were inevitably subject to judgment (positive or negative). Thus, there arose the problem of moral responsibility for one's everyday life, a problem that Belinskii and Bakunin debated, especially in their famous argument over "kopecks." In one of his 1837 letters, Belinskii spoke of the humiliations to which Bakunin had been reduced by his disorderly life and his dishonest attitude toward debts and business obligations. "Michel . . . , does not all this have a bad effect on your spirit, and does it not in any way disturb your inner life? If 'no,' then you are too lofty for me, and I am incapable of understanding you; if 'yes,' then your having seen evidence of eternal degradation in my letter about scrupulousness and kopecks means nothing. . . . You do not even want to hear about kopecks, but you want to have them—it makes no sense. You speak only of the inner life, but you pay a significant tribute to the external one; it is not logical" (11:170–171).

The antithesis between the infinite and the finite was transforming empirical reality into something like a domain of irresponsibility. The young Bakunin's view of life followed the characteristic pattern of romantic ethics. In an 1837 letter to the Beer sisters, for example, he wrote:

> We shall leave that poor sphere to the poor cramped souls who get by on their basic feelings and impressions; we shall live the life of the holy spirit; we shall consecrate our individualities to the sacred sphere of absolute love. Only there shall they be raised up to the truth, and believe me, those who live in poor independence from it are a lie that is not even worth mentioning; they are a momentary product of their organization and will be destroyed with it. Only that which has entered into the universal life of the spirit is real. And so, friends, for heaven's sake do not speak to me of the individual needs of my little soul, where it is better for it to live, with Tanichka or with Varen'ka, in what place or in what location. (2:51)

In another letter of the same year these views were given an even clearer formulation: "The only true life is that which issues from an awareness of the absolute; everything that is said and done outside that awareness is insignificant and utterly without reality" (2:69). The more insignificant the domain of everyday life, the less the processes taking place within it need swallow up one's spiritual energy, and the more one's personality might flourish in the realm of lofty spiritual values. These were the two facets of romantic ethics, the ethics of an elect, and they were inseparably linked.

Eternal dissatisfaction and striving for the unattainable were traditional features of the romantic hero. Yet that hero was contradictory too, in the sense that a kind of complacency was also characteristic of him. In essence, this is precisely what was meant in the Stankevich circle by the odd phrase "self-grinning." Romantic complacency was a logically inevitable consequence of election, for the romantic personality knew that it was the finest flower of humanity. This tendency of romantic consciousness found clear expression in the young Bakunin's messianism.

The romantic hero was a positive hero, but in a special way. However positive or even ideal he might appear, he still possessed defects (irreproachability was in fact rather more typical of the Enlightenment or sentimentalist hero). Indeed, the romantic hero could even be depraved—hence the whole demonic line in romanticism—although that depravity was grandiose, exceptional, and lofty. It was not so much the virtues and vices themselves that were important, but their spiritual scale, which was in no way limited by the requirements of commonly accepted morality.

If Bakunin found himself wanting, it was only because at one time or another he had been unworthy of the image he had constructed for himself. In January 1837 he wrote to his sister Varvara Aleksandrovna:

> The infinite cannot exist where it is confined, and one must admit that our friendship has taken too confining a form. It is not you who are to blame in this, but I alone. I brought too much egoism into it; I forgot that every external relation must be only an expression of inner life in the absolute, and I have made the absolute the basis of my personal life, of my own personal happiness. That was false; it went against my nature, and it *was degrading to me* [italics mine] and the source of that apathetic suffering that overcame me at Premukhino. . . . It is impossible for me to return to Premukhino. . . . I was so insignificant there, so unworthy of myself. . . . Now I am in possession of myself again, I feel once again, and once again I love deeply. Why is that? It is because I have become myself, and have understood again, better than ever before, that I do not have to seek for anything outside myself, that I must dissolve myself completely in the absolute. My dear friends, I have a fiery nature; my feelings are turbulent. This means that only life in the absolute can give me happiness and save my self-respect, for without the absolute I am capable of any crime. I am passionate, egotistical, and jealous, and in me, finally, are none of those feelings that accommodate other people to social life. I can be happy only in solitude. Oh, I am capable of great deeds—I sense that—but to do them I must forget myself, for otherwise my egoism will destroy my mission. (1:386–387)

The basic assumptions of the romantic consciousness are very clearly expressed in these lines—a great destiny (a mission) and lofty depravity as the mark of a "fiery nature," and egoism and a striving for the personal realization of universal values, without which the life of a great spirit would be impossible.

The hero whose lofty vices have been transformed into the spiritual energy of election may be found in the early Lermontov and, with their demonic motifs, even in the Herzen of the youthful autobiographical sketches and of the correspondence with his betrothed.

Belinskii was another matter. From the beginning he stood with the great self-revealers who did not turn away from the unseemly. A disposition to self-revelation is, to be sure, a matter of individual character, but in people of great creative and moral power it acquires historical value, becoming a means for the formation of a new, contemporary human being, one who has already begun to emerge but whose particular stamp still needs to be cognized and formulated.

The self-revealers had their own kind of self-affirmation too (without it no creative activity would have been possible), one nourished by an awareness of the universal significance of the moral and psychological problems they were endeavoring to solve.

The results for world culture of the self-absorption of a Rousseau or a Tolstoi are well known. Belinskii contributed to the history of that culture through activity of an entirely different kind. His letters, published years after his death, could not directly influence the maturation of Russian psychologism; nevertheless, they are an important reflection of those processes in the intellectual life of the Russian intelligentsia of the 1830s and 1840s that anticipated the method and prepared the material for the Russian novel of the second half of the century.

Self-revelation and "self-grinning" (to use the circle phrase) were a decisive antithesis in the Belinskii-Bakunin conflict, a conflict that had great constructive value for Belinskii since it was through constant reference to his friend and antagonist that he constructed his own image. Belinskii's compulsion to judge himself harshly was motivated by a high regard for the reciprocal accountability of life and of one's creative activity. That creative activity was nourished by empirical life, and every action that one took in life was answerable to one's ideas. This was a principle of interconnection that was fundamentally opposed to romantic "life-art," which was a kind of theatrical, playful act that used only selected aspects of life. Belinskii extended the responsibility of creative endeavor to the whole of life's content, and that content was itself entirely subject to the authority of conscience. Conscience was understood as the pressure of everything that a person was responsible for. The *real* man consciously immersed himself in the countless phenomena of everyday existence, in its *details*. For him, thought was capable of illuminating not merely life's loftiest peaks, but also any one of its nooks and crannies. The 1830s were a time of intense ethical experience for Belinskii, and that meant that philosophical ideas were capable of being translated into the language of any practical sphere whatever. The philosophy of the young Belinskii was in fact a kind of applied ethics.

The need to apply one's philosophy to one's own life was familiar to Stankevich too. In an 1839 letter to his friends the Frolovs he spoke of the need "to live with one's whole nature," adding, "otherwise, what would philosophy be?" And later in the same letter he raised the question of the ethics of everyday life and of antiromantic "details":

> One thing in your portrait of Bettina made me pause, Elizaveta Petrovna: "Elle sait le bien et le beau, dans leur essence et leur luxe, mais elle n'en sait pas les details positifs." That kind of general, abstract poetry started to lose its value for me a long time ago, just as the idea of the positive has never had any meaning for me outside its ideal one. . . . Everything that partakes of the

noble and the beautiful, everything that attracts you to itself, above all reminds you: reckon with life, with people, and come to terms at once with all
that is around you; otherwise, your pleasure in what is great will be illusory!
The great thing is to put the small things in order. Yet when you take a look
around, good Lord! It is all a muddle, nonsense, misunderstandings! How
can you come to terms with that? . . . There is a need to simplify it all. Well,
then, do it so that in everything you do, you remain as you really are, or
Jehovah will answer for the consequences! In addition to your awareness
that it would be wrong to heap misfortune like that on an old man with
whom your relations are not altogether of the closest sort, you involuntarily
wonder, where does it follow that everything that is an expression of me
must be good? And in every decision you make, you involuntarily suspect an
element of *self-love*, an element of sloth, or some sinful fondness for peace
and quiet, which you do not want to disturb without very good reason—my
goodness, so many *Rücksichten*. (679, 682–683)

Here are both a principled defense of details and Stankevich's characteristic self-condemnation. Yet for Stankevich, a transitional figure, all
this had not yet become a powerful motivating force, and he would not
have been able to say, as Belinskii did in a letter to him, "The processes
taking place in my spirit always find their realization in my life and are
reflected in circumstances that are for the most part disturbing and terrible" (11:365).

Among the oppositions that served as points of reference, so to speak,
in the polemic between Belinskii and Bakunin, one of the most important
was that between responsibility and "Khlestakovism." The latter formula
came to stand for a number of ideas that were current in circle life: "soul-
beauty," "stiltedness," and "cant," or the irresponsible use of words. At
the beginning of the forties, "Khlestakovism" was increasingly used, at
least by Belinskii, to identify the characteristics of the romantic: "Only
'romanticism' allows man to feel beautifully, to reason loftily, and to act
badly" (11:114). This is from an 1842 letter to Nikolai Bakunin, although it was of course Nikolai's brother Mikhail who was for Belinskii
the living embodiment of romanticism.

Belinskii nourished both a love for and a hatred of Bakunin: at one
pole he was a Khlestakov, and at the other, a [Lermontovian] Pechorin.
Belinskii's characterization of Bakunin in the June 1838 letter cited earlier
coincides in many respects with remarks contained in his 1840 article on
A Hero of Our Time:

Yet this man has nothing to fear: he has a secret awareness that he is precisely what he believes himself to be, and that he exists only in the present
moment. Yes, there is spiritual strength and willpower in him; something
great in him flashes like lightning in dark storm clouds, and he is beautiful

and full of poetry even in those moments when one's human feeling rises up against him. . . . He has a different purpose, a different path than you do. His passions are storms that cleanse the spirit. . . . Let him slander himself, taking the mere stages of his spirit for its complete development . . ; a triumphant time will come and contradiction will be resolved, the struggle will end, and the discordant sounds in his soul will merge into a single harmonious chord! (4:235–236)

This is in the same key as the portrait of Bakunin in the 1838 letter (although the image sketched in the article has a greater resemblance to Lermontov as Belinskii understood him at the time). Especially close to the Bakunin interpretation is the conception of Pechorin's weaknesses or deficiencies as developmental stages concealing a truly powerful essence.

Pechorin and Khlestakov corresponded, respectively, to the poles of love and hate, to the leonine spirit and to puerility and "swaggering." Several years later, however, Belinskii came to see Bakunin in terms of yet another, surprisingly different romantic avatar—Aleksandr Aduev [in *A Common Story*].[23]

In the 1840s Belinskii was already moving away from a typological conception of romanticism toward a historical one, and he held early romanticism in high regard (especially the writings of Zhukovskii). The romanticism that he and Herzen were combating in the 1840s was an obsolete contemporary version of it that was stubbornly refusing to make its exit from the stage and that was finding renewed life in the teachings of the Slavophiles, but that, more to the point, was still personally experienced and not yet completely played out. Belinskii's last word on romantic idealism was given voice in the second part of "A View of Russian Literature in 1847." The problem of romanticism is addressed in his celebrated comparison of the novels of Herzen and Goncharov, or more precisely, in his comparison of two of their characters: Bel'tov and Aleksandr Aduev. Bel'tov [in *Who Is to Blame?*] is a romantic intellectual, a type that had caught Herzen's eye in the idealist circles of the 1830s, and one that was also very well known to Belinskii. Aduev is the romantic type who has descended from the empyrean into the thick of provincial bourgeois-gentry life. Goncharov's conception was undoubtedly broader than this. He wanted to strike a blow against contemporary romanticism itself, but he was unable to define its ideological center. Apollon Grigor'ev observed very accurately in his article "Russian Literature in 1851" that "the striving for the ideal does not recognize its stepchild in Aleksandr Aduev and the irony falls flat."[24] Aduev is no longer an ideologue, but a kind of everyday, empirical romantic "who feels but does not philosophize," in Belinskii's classification of him. He continues: "Let us say a few words about the hardly new, but still interesting species to which this little romantic beast belongs," and there follows a detailed characterization of the everyday romantic, enumerating everything that romantics "call living the lofty life beyond the reach of the contemptible crowd, or soaring in the mountains while the contemptible crowd creeps along the valley."

This characterization was obviously directed against the "pseudo-majestical" person, the vulgar romantic, but it also had a covert polemical thrust. In Aleksandr Aduev, Belinskii was simultaneously stigmatizing both [the romantic rhetoric of the popular poet] Benediktov and something that was even more important to him—the culture of romantic idealism through which he himself had passed and from which he had finally broken free at the cost of considerable effort and pain: "They have long been fascinated by three sacred ideas: glory, friendship, and love." Belinskii then proceeds to a characterization of romantic friendship, with the image of the romantic bifurcating in his analysis: the provincial youth Aduev gives way to the "idealist of the thirties."

> They make friends according to a preconceived program in which the essence, rights, and obligations of friendship are precisely defined; the only thing they do not do is conclude contracts with their friends. They need friendship in order to astonish the world and to demonstrate to it how different the friendship of great natures is from that of ordinary people and the crowd. They are drawn to friendship . . . by the need to have someone around with whom they can talk endlessly about their own precious individualities. To put it in their own lofty style, a friend is a precious vessel for the pouring out of the most sacred and cherished feelings, thoughts, hopes, dreams, and so on, whereas in point of fact a friend in their eyes is a tub into which they dump the slops of their own self-love. (10:335–336)

All of this is said apropos of Aleksandr Aduev, but it obviously does not concern only him. The lines have other, hidden addressees; they are a refraction of memories of the kind of friendship that flourished in the circles of the 1830s, all of whose temptations and torments Belinskii had himself been forced to undergo. He very likely wrote this passage while recollecting the history of his friendship with Mikhail Bakunin. And in fact he had written in similar fashion to Bakunin in 1840:

> We are no longer friends, you say with regret, but only acquaintances. But were we ever friends? The basis of our relationship was a spiritual affinity—that is true—but was there not also mixed up in it an exchange of idleness, indolence, flattery—of mutual admiration, that is—and so on? At least . . . it is true that since the time we began to shake off your oppressive authority and dared, in our turn, to speak the truth to you and to teach you, we have gone our separate ways. You did not like that method of mutual instruction—you always wanted to be right and never in the wrong, and you viewed what you had earlier done with us as audaciousness. Who is at fault here,

Michel? I am truly glad, however, that that circle no longer exists, that circle in which there was much that was beautiful but little that was lasting, in which a few people tormented and made each other happy by turns. (11:486)

All of this is very like the depiction of romantic friendship in the 1848 article, especially the characterization of those for whom "a friend is a tub into which they dump the slops of their own self-love."

"Khlestakovism" was something like the quintessence of irresponsibility, and "Aduevism" a parody of romantic dualism. Lermontov had anticipated Aduev in Grushnitskii, who in his turn had been a parody of Pechorin. All of them were codes for Bakunin, whose contrasting image accompanied Belinskii throughout the period of his struggle to master reality. Those spiritual phenomena that Belinskii found at the end of the 1840s in Goncharov's novel had already been experienced by him in actuality at the beginning of the decade.

Belinskii's new realistic ethics embraced the totality of human experience. Unlike romantic ethics, it did not find support in the transcendental, and it was therefore forced to establish its standards on an entirely new basis. The problem of "obligation" is the greatest and most difficult issue faced by nonreligious ethics (I shall return to this question in the last chapter of the present book). Russian democratic ethics, among whose sources stands the mature Belinskii, sought to base obligation on a conception of the person as an unconditionally valuable entity, yet one that derived its full worth and content from society. Social theory found corroboration in emotion, in the spontaneous experience of kinship with and love for other people, and it accepted that emotion as an unconditional fact of moral life.

Belinskii's movement from Fichteanism and the "reconciliation with reality" to the ethics of utopian socialism (in its Russian revolutionary-democratic variant) was neither rapid nor smooth. There were doubts and detours, and the state of crisis lingered for a long time, with faith in the absolute already relegated to the past, but the foundations of the new morality not yet fully established. It still occasionally seemed to Belinskii at the beginning of the 1840s that he had voluntarily consented to live by the rules of illusion, that being the only way that action was possible and that he could preserve his human dignity and his feeling of love and sympathy.

In 1841 Belinskii wrote to Nikolai Bakunin, "I have no faith in my convictions, and I am incapable of betraying them: I am more ridiculous even than Don Quixote. He at least believed in his heart that he was a knight, that he was tilting with giants and not windmills, and that his fat and ugly Dulcinea was a beauty; but I know that I am no knight, but a madman—and all the same I play the knight. I know that I am tilting at windmills, and still I tilt; I know that my own Dulcinea (life) is ugly and repulsive, but I still love her—against all common sense and everything obvious" (12:76–77). The two Don Quixotes, one ideal, the other real, are of course a parable. One believes in the absolute and has no need of explanation (like Bakunin); the other no longer believes and is still unable to explain, but acts in keeping with the laws of social life, which are an enigma to him, but which dictate that a person may not live without goals and values, even if he is unable to find a rational basis for them.

The Belinskii of the final years of his life was a direct forerunner of the revolutionary democrats of the 1850s and 1860s. Yet his development as a whole was contradictory. His spiritual experience, with its clear-cut manifestations of the national self-consciousness, was multifaceted, and one may find in it numerous anticipations of phenomena that would be typical of later Russian culture, including the ideas and views that nourished the Russian novel in the second half of the century.

Chronologically, Belinskii's activity was of a piece with that of Turgenev and Goncharov. As the critic and theoretician of the natural school, he was the direct inspirer of their early experiments. But in his letters, those remarkable monuments devoted to his own personality and to the formation of a new human type, one finds evidence of a peculiarly "Tolstoian" element. That element may be seen in Belinskii's need to "articulate" and "scrutinize" (as the circle termed the thirst for analysis), but above all in the ceaseless operation of an ethically based impulse toward self-knowledge, and in the requirement that ideas be realized in life and that life be answerable to ideas.[25] The temporal difference here is of course not so very great as it might seem, inasmuch as the essential cast of Tolstoi's own mind was worked out in the 1840s.[26]

Tolstoi linked his own quest for the meaning of life (which for him was always inseparable from self-analysis) directly to the condition of skepticism and to the necessity, as he saw it, of finding a way out of that condition (I shall discuss this in more detail in the third part of this book). From Tolstoi's *Confession* we learn that it was the death of his brother Nikolai Nikolaevich that precipitated the crisis that brought him to the verge of suicide (the effect on Tolstoi of the deaths of his brothers Dmitrii and Nikolai was transmuted in *Anna Karenina* into the episode of the death of Nikolai Levin). Here is the way Belinskii responded to the death of Stankevich in 1840:

> Yes, it seemed to all of us impossible that death would dare to come prematurely to such a divine personality and turn it into nothingness. Into *nothingness*, Botkin! Nothing has remained of it but flesh and bones over which the worms are swarming now. He lives on, you will say, in the memory of his friends, in the hearts in which he fanned and kept alive the sparks of divine love. Yes, but will those friends live very long, will their hearts beat for long?

Alas, neither faith, nor knowledge, nor life, nor talent, nor genius is immortal! Only death is immortal, and its colossal, triumphant image proudly ascends a throne of human bones and laughs at hopes, love, and aspirations! . . . Can you see what a difference there is between the present century and the last? Then they still talked about the "hereafter," designating it as a kind of terra incognita in whose existence they themselves did not really believe; nowadays we do not believe in any "hereafter" either, like any nonsense rejected by reason, and that empty word is no longer used even in jest. Then they still wept and entreated; now, silent and proud, we stride with a resolute step into the insatiable maw of death. . . . The idea of life's vanity has for me destroyed even suffering itself. I do not know what it is all about or for; since we shall all die and rot anyway, what is the point of loving, believing, hoping, suffering, striving, or fearing? Men die, peoples die, our planet will die, and Shakespeare and Hegel will become as nothing. . . . It is a dreary world, but there is no other! (11:538–540)

The question of the meaning of life is posed here as one that depends on a solution to the problem of death, and the essence of that problem is that there is no "other world."

It is no accident that Belinskii's thought in 1840 was moving in a direction similar, in this instance at least, to that of Tolstoi in the 1870s. Both men were going through a period of rejection of the idea of the "hereafter"; both were at the moment giving voice to the essential dilemma faced by the nonreligious mind. Tolstoi escaped from that dilemma into his religious doctrines; Belinskii overcame it through faith in "sociality," through faith in the activity of social man. Belinskii's own solution would come later, however; for the time being, the logic of determinism was leading him ineluctably to the antinomy of the unconditional value of the individual human being, on the one hand, and of his inevitable destruction, on the other. In another letter written to Botkin the same year, Belinskii addressed this issue directly:

As far as personal immortality is concerned, whatever the reasons were that made you abandon that question and left you indifferent to it—just wait; a time will come when you will begin singing another tune. You will see that that question is the alpha and omega of truth, and that our salvation lies in its solution. I spit on any philosophy that contemptuously ignores that question merely because it does not have the means to solve it. Hegel disapproved of everything fantastical as by definition false. . . . You say you believe in your own immortality, but what is it then? If it is this thing or that, or anything you like—a glass of kvass, an apple, a horse—then I congratulate you on your faith, but I do not want it for myself. I too have a feeble little impulse to *believe* in this thing or that, but I do not have the strength to *believe*, and one wants knowledge that is certain. You say that when you heard about Stankevich's death, you were suddenly gripped by the question: but what has become of him? Is that so fatuous? Is acceptance really possible without an answer to that question? No, I shall not let go of that Moloch that philosophy has called the Universal; I shall keep asking it: where have you taken him and what has become of him? You say: for God's sake, let us rid ourselves of abstract reflection about the "hereafter" and the future life, since they deprive the present of its strength and vitality and are pointless anyway. Fine: but where is the proof that those reflections are merely abstract and not very much to the point? Next: I want to look every terror right in the face and reject nothing but confront everything. Finally: what will it give you, that "present" to which you (in keeping with an old habit) ascribe strength and vitality? What will it give you, the *smoke of fantasies*? Fight for it, Botkin, stand up for it with all your might, and do not ever admit to yourself how spitefully it mocks you! (11:552–553)

There are in Belinskii's writings on Stankevich's death virtual textual coincidences with Turgenev's "Enough" and Tolstoi's *Confession*.[27] And the Dostoevskii of the 1860s and 1870s, avidly and persistently studying the type of the atheist or theomachist, turned not only to contemporary "nihilists," but also to the people of his youth, to the men of the forties—Speshnev, Petrashevskii, and Belinskii.[28] In recalling Belinskii in *The Diary of a Writer* for 1873, it was in fact to that group—the Russian atheists—that Dostoevskii assigned him.

I found in him a passionate socialist, and he started right in on atheism with me. There was in it much that was meaningful to me, especially his remarkable flair and his exceptional ability to enter into an idea in the most profound way. The *Internationale* in one of its appeals a couple of years ago began at once with the sententious declaration that "Above all, we are an atheistic organization"; it began, that is, with the essential question. Belinskii began the same way. . . . As a socialist, he knew that first of all he had to depose Christianity; he knew that the revolution would have to begin with atheism. He had to depose the religion from which the moral foundations of the society he had rejected were derived.[29]

The intellectual life of the Russian intelligentsia of the 1830s and 1840s was the medium in which were first crystallized those ideas that later found expression in the spiritual experience and writings of Tolstoi and Dostoevskii.

The self-revelation and ethically and psychologically intense search for the meaning of life and death in Belinskii's self-analysis were indeed "Tolstoian" elements, but there were "Dostoevskiian" themes in his letters too, especially in those written at the end of the 1830s and the beginning of the 1840s. Above all, there is the theme of love-hate or friendship-enmity that runs through the correspondence with Bakunin (the "love-hate" formula defines Arkadii's attitude toward Versilov in *A Raw Youth*, for example).

It is possible to find in Belinskii's letters not only a love-hate, but also a happiness-suffering motif: "They spoke to each other with faces that shone with joy. I was not sure whether my tortured breast could endure that torment, although it was not from jealousy or envy. I knew very well that even if she had loved me, it would not have been any easier for me. I wished them both happiness. I loved them both, and all the same I suffered greatly and reveled in my suffering, like a drunk on a spree, because there was much in it that was human. And so I was drawn irresistibly to that house in order to enjoy my own suffering" (11:398).[30] And there are other anticipations of Dostoevskii's world in Belinskii's correspondence. Here is a letter written to Botkin on September 8, 1841, at a time when Belinskii was almost completely preoccupied with the idea of life in society: "*What do I care* that the universal lives, while the individual personality suffers? *What do I care* that earthly genius resides in the clouds, while the crowd wallows in the mud? What do I care that *I* understand an idea, that a world of ideas in art, religion, and history is open to me, when I am unable to share it with all those who ought to be my brothers in humanity and my fellows in Christ, but who are alien to me, and my enemies because of their ignorance? *What do I care* that there is happiness for an elect, when most do not even suspect that it is possible? *Away with happiness if it is to be mine alone out of thousands! I do not want it*, if it is not mine in common with my lesser brothers!" (12:69; italics mine). This is not very far from Ivan Karamazov's "returning his ticket" in the famous conversation with Alesha, even to the point of shared syntax and phraseology (I have italicized the parallels): "*What do I care* that no one is guilty, and that I know it—I need retribution, or else I shall destroy myself. . . . *I do not want harmony; out of love of humanity I do not want it. I would rather be left with the unavenged sufferings.* I would rather have my unavenged suffering and my frustrated indignation, *even if I am wrong.* Too high a price is asked for harmony, anyway; the entrance fee is too great. And so I hasten to give my ticket back. . . . It is not God I do not accept, Alesha; it is just that I most respectfully return Him my ticket" (pt. 2, bk. 5).

Dostoevskii began work on *The Brothers Karamazov* in earnest in 1878, but the maturation of the novel's plan, its crystallization, began earlier. Aleksandr Dolinin dates that beginning to 1877 and even in part to 1876.[31] In any case, in 1875 *The Herald of Europe* published Pypin's biography of Belinskii based on the latter's still unpublished correspondence. Cited in the biography's seventh chapter (which was published in the journal's February issue) is the above-quoted September 8, 1841, letter from Belinskii to Botkin, including the passage that is so similar to Ivan's "returning the ticket."[32] Dostoevskii was thinking about Belinskii in the 1870s, and he wrote about him in *The Diary of a Writer* for 1873 and 1877. One must suppose that he was also aware of Pypin's biography. Perhaps his creative memory retained Belinskii's phraseology and then used it in Ivan's monologue. The passages are not identical, of course. The main question for Belinskii is the fate of the majority, of his "lesser brothers"; for Dostoevskii, it is the moral impossibility of purchasing universal harmony at the price of the suffering of even one human being.

The issue here is not merely one of isolated parallels, however. The whole atmosphere of the correspondence with Bakunin—an atmosphere of love-hate, of revealing admissions and ideas bodied forth in life, and of passionate and changeable relationships—contained beginnings that were later investigated by Dostoevskii.

The movement toward Tolstoi and Dostoevskii, two summits of the Russian and world novel, may be traced back to the spiritual life of the Stankevich circle and especially to the letters of Belinskii. This is only natural. As a critic and historian of literature, Belinskii was the first to formulate the principles of Russian realism. Yet Belinskii was in fact a critic of such singular range and insight precisely because he was at the same time engaged in the unpublished, but immense and terribly difficult task of comprehending not only the social and moral problems, but also the psychological forms of the new, *real* human being.

Memoirs

THE LITERATURE of memoir, autobiography, confession, and *pensée* engages in direct discussion of the human being. It resembles poetry in that it involves the explicit and sustained presence of the author. An experimental boldness and latitude and an uninhibited and intimate relationship with the reader have long been characteristic of these intermediate genres, with their evasion of canons and rules. The dialectic of such genres lies in their piquant combination of free expression and constrained invention—constrained, that is, by what actually happened.

Memoir typology is extremely varied, ranging from the extreme self-revelation of Rousseau's *Confessions* to the chroniclelike political memoirs of Madame de Staël (*Dix années d'exil*), which begin with the sentence, "It was not to interest society in myself that I resolved to recount the circumstances of my ten-year exile. . . ."

Sometimes only the most tenuous line separates autobiography from the autobiographical tale or novel. The actual names of the characters may be changed, the resulting conventionality at once removing the work to another category, wherein the author obtains the right to invent. It was enough for this purpose for Stendhal to call the hero of his autobiography "Henri Brulard," or for Dostoevskii to introduce into *Notes from the House of the Dead* a narrator who had been condemned to hard labor for the murder of his wife. Because of the censorship, Dostoevskii could not allow a Petrashevskiian to tell the story. Yet whatever the external reasons for the replacement of the narrator in *Notes from the House of the Dead*, the result was that it became impossible to approach that work with the requirements and criteria of factual accuracy (which Dostoevskii often departed from for the sake of his general plan). Gor'kii used his own name in his trilogy, but he still called *Childhood*, *At Large*, and *My Universities* "tales," despite their autobiographical truthfulness, and they are indeed fully situated along the path of his artistic production.

In addition to those memoiristic writings contiguous with the novel or tale, there are others of a fundamentally different kind that, despite their inevitable ties with one literary movement or another, strikingly exhibit the particular identity of the genre, its special purposes and potentialities. I shall talk about three such works here: Saint-Simon's *Mémoires*, Rousseau's *Confessions*, and Herzen's *My Past and Thoughts*. These works reveal to the highest degree the identity of memoir writing, even though they are extremely diverse, and diverse not merely because they reflect different historical epochs but also because they possess different structures and undertake different cognitive tasks. Saint-Simon was the creator of a powerful stream of social and moral portraits or *caractères* fixing his contemporaries, Rousseau was concerned with the "inner human being," and Herzen addressed the human being in his dialectical-historical capacity. Each of these books was at once a historical and a "human" document, a creation of superb literary art, and a new stage in the cognition of reality and of the human being.

Part One

SAINT-SIMON'S *MÉMOIRES* AND
THE RATIONALIST SCHEMA

THERE IS an extensive literature devoted to the duc de Saint-Simon's *Mémoires*, and it has studied that astonishing book from a number of different vantages—as a historical resource, as a monument of its time, and as an artistic work. The present discussion, however, will look at the *Mémoires* only in regard to their solution of the problem of understanding and depicting individual character [*kharakter*].[1]

Sainte-Beuve called Saint-Simon the "spy of his age."[2] A unique work of world memoiristic literature, the *Mémoires* run in their various editions from twenty to forty or more volumes, covering the period from the 1690s to 1723 (the last twenty-five years of the reign of Louis XIV and the subsequent eight years of the regency). After Saint-Simon's death in 1755, the government of Louis XV, fearing what it might disclose, confiscated the whole enormous manuscript (along with other documents that had belonged to Saint-Simon). That manuscript then lay hidden in the archives of the Ministry of Foreign Affairs for almost seventy years, to be published in more or less complete form (rather than in individual excerpts) only in 1829–1830. The *Mémoires* were thus removed from the historiographical and literary culture of their time.[3]

It was once believed that Saint-Simon's memoirs were a journal in which he had made entries from day to day and to which he gave final form only in his old age. This idea derived from Saint-Simon's own statements that he had begun keeping systematic notes of a memoiristic nature as early as 1694, and it gained support from an extant letter written by him in 1699 to his spiritual guide Rancé, the abbé of the Trappist order. In this letter Saint-Simon asks Rancé to acquaint himself with some fragments of a memoir he has been working on. All traces of those first notes have been lost, however, or at least have not yet been found in the huge Saint-Simon archive.[4] Nevertheless, French historians have through careful investigation succeeded in establishing a rough picture of the *Mémoires'* genesis.

In 1729 Saint-Simon obtained a copy of the multivolume manuscript of the journal of Dangeau, a courtier who over the years had been scrupulously recording, although without commentary, the day-to-day life of the court of Louis XIV. Saint-Simon furnished that manuscript with his own observations and "addenda," sometimes brief and sometimes expanded into immense excursuses, which gradually evolved into the first version of the *Mémoires*.[5] This work on Dangeau's journal continued for almost ten years; then, in 1739, when he was sixty-four, Saint-Simon set to work on the final edition of the book, which he completed around 1750.

In the course of this labor Saint-Simon used a great quantity of materials that he had prepared himself—his "addenda" to Dangeau's journal (and perhaps his own notes, now lost); scholarly memoranda and treatises touching on various historical, genealogical, and political questions; diplomatic papers; historical investigations; letters; excerpts from the memoirs of contemporaries or from copies of ceremonial registries containing detailed information on court etiquette and rank; and a great deal else besides. Saint-Simon's own memory and imagination then transformed that mass of documentary evidence into an inimitable world of direct observation.

Saint-Simon often took issue with Dangeau and scoffed at his grandiloquence, but he relied extensively on his journal, taking from it a multitude of facts and adopting its general chronology.[6] Gone with the legend that the *Mémoires* came into being as a journal written hard upon events as they occurred is the notion that Saint-Simon was a literary dilettante. It was once believed that this great nobleman had not deigned to correct or revise what he had simply jotted down with a kind of aristocratic carelessness. As Chateaubriand put it, "He wrote offhand for posterity."[7] Saint-Simon himself provided the pretext for such opinions in his Conclusion to the *Mémoires*: "In order to improve on what one has written, one needs to know how to write well; it is obvious from this book that I can pride myself on no such thing" (7:399). The Saint-Simonian affectation of negligence taken up by the romantics has not withstood the test of scholarship. The most recent studies have shown that his complex, difficult style, far from being merely the result of aristocratic dilettantism, was a conscious instrument devised to deal with prodigious artistic tasks, and that Saint-Simon worked tirelessly on the text of the *Mémoires*. This new view is borne out merely by comparison of Saint-Simon's "addenda" to Dangeau's journal with his own finished versions of the same episodes. He compresses and expands the original narrative, he heightens or downplays it, he alters judgments (and sometimes even facts), he looks for and finds other words—in the same way that any artist does while working on a rough draft.

At first Saint-Simon's *Mémoires* were largely apprehended as a monument of their age and as a historical resource, and academic historiography accordingly judged and condemned their author in accordance with its own laws. A. Chéruel, the editor of the first scholarly edition of the

Mémoires, although paying tribute to Saint-Simon the artist, showed in detail how his turbulent passions, aristocratic prejudices, and political interests reshaped historical reality.[8] Gradually, however, a different viewpoint took hold. Saint-Simon was a great writer entitled to his own subjective vision of the world and even to the alteration of individual facts for the sake of a higher truth, both artistic and historical. This estimate of Saint-Simon originated in the 1850s in the writings of Sainte-Beuve, the leader of the romantic critical school (by then already a bit dated). For Sainte-Beuve, Saint-Simon was the creator of a vast and unique world, a writer given to hyperbole and metaphor who looked at life with a magnifying glass. Sainte-Beuve compared him to Rubens and Shakespeare and called him "a Tacitus at full gallop." "Any age," he wrote in 1856, "that has not had its own Saint-Simon, at once seems deserted, mute, and faded; there is something uninhabitable about it."[9]

Taine expressed himself in a similar spirit. He wrote that Saint-Simon's passion "deprives his style of all inhibition. Moderation, literary good taste, eloquence, nobility are all swept away and drowned. . . . The scullery, the stable, the pantry, the mason's shop, the servants' quarters, the house of ill-repute—he finds his expressions everywhere. He is crude and vulgar, and he molds his figures out of simple clay. Though still a great nobleman, he is popular; his magnificence brings it all together. Let the bourgeois purge their styles, in the cautious way of people subservient to the Academy; he is ready to drag his own in the gutter, like a man who is contemptuous of his dress and considers himself superior to any stain."[10]

Saint-Simon has subsequently been compared to the great writers of other ages as well, in particular to Balzac.[11] In his *Monsieur le duc de Saint-Simon et sa comédie humaine*, La Varende has suggested the following interrelated assemblage: Rabelais, Saint-Simon, Balzac, and Proust. Another investigator has declared that "this feudal duke is the spiritual contemporary of Zola," and has mentioned Tolstoi in the same connection.[12] And Herbert De Ley, the author of the monograph *Marcel Proust et le duc de Saint-Simon*, has noted that "the Saint-Simon described in the criticism of our day is in part a Proustian Saint-Simon. Just as in critical works on Proust a sentence on Saint-Simon is de rigueur, so in works about Saint-Simon a sentence on Proust has been obligatory ever since the appearance of *A la recherche du temps perdu*."[13]

Saint-Simon is Shakespeare, Rabelais, Balzac, Zola, Tolstoi, Proust. . . . Juxtaposing artistic methods in this way can be productive and interesting, but it requires caution, lest the differences between the seventeenth and eighteenth and the nineteenth or twentieth centuries, or between the novel and the memoir, be lost, thereby obscuring the work's cognitive specificity and its place in the history of the understanding and depiction of individual human beings.

Saint-Simon was unquestionably a great artist, but his book is not a novel. The special nature of his accomplishment lies in the fact that although he wrote about what actually happened, fitting his material to schemata—religious, political, and aesthetic—that had been provided by his age, that actuality, grasped as it was with an extraordinary power of vision, exploded those schemata at the same time that it derived its structure from them.

Saint-Simon wrote his *Mémoires* in the 1740s, that is, after Montesquieu and as a contemporary of Voltaire, but still as someone belonging to the end of the reign of Louis XIV. Yet Saint-Simon was archaic for the era of Louis as well. He gave vivid expression to a preclassical, baroque principle, one organically tied to his ideology. In the midst of the servile aristocracy that made up the court of Louis XIV, Saint-Simon held on to the utopian ideal of an aristocratic monarchy, at the apex of whose pyramid stood the king surrounded by his advisers, the dukes and peers. Saint-Simon was fiercely hostile to the leveling policies of Louis and to the bourgeois reforms of Colbert and Louvois, indeed, to anything that led to the ascendancy of bureaucrats, bourgeois upstarts, and Louis' bastards, whom the king preferred to his own legitimate offspring, since their greatness was entirely a matter of his own will. Yet Saint-Simon's ideology did not, on the other hand, derive from the feudalistic Fronde, which shook France at the end of the 1640s and the beginning of the 1650s. Saint-Simon was fanatically jealous of his own ducal status, despite the fact that he was himself the scion of an impoverished noble family, the son of a favorite of Louis XIII, on whom the latter had conferred the titles of duke and peer of France. In social origin, Saint-Simon belonged to the new aristocracy. He was himself a peer by dispensation, and he therefore ought not to have opposed the king's creation of new dukes. But he wanted kings to recognize in the people they created a kind of absolute, metaphysical status that was independent of its source. He wanted, in other words, the impossible.

Saint-Simon was confused in his politics, but the very contradictoriness of his basic assumptions proved to be a considerable asset in his capacity as "spy of his age." He was relentlessly opposed to everything—the despotism of the king, the arbitrariness of his ministers and bureaucrats, the pretensions of the bourgeois *Parlement*, the success of the new aristocracy, and the servility of the old, which was incapable of protecting its position of privilege.

Saint-Simon's true allegiance was to the reign of Louis XIII, his father's benefactor, as well as to the sympathies and antipathies of his father, who had retired from the court after Louis XIII's death. That stern background gave Saint-Simon the moral purity, religious and ethical rigorism, and archaic literary tastes and habits that he kept until the end of his life.

Archaism has its own dialectic, of course; it too may be a source of freedom from prevailing rules and canons. In great artists, it engenders new discoveries and anticipations of the future. And so it was with Saint-Simon.

Taine emphasizes that the archaic clutter and apparent confusion of Saint-Simon's style is not only an emotional, but also an intellectual fact; Saint-Simon wanted to say too much at once and to explain it all with too much precision:

> No one can grasp so many things so quickly all at once; that is the reason for the passionate compression of his style, its explanatory ideas attached as appendages to the main clause, which is choked by the lack of space and carried away with everything else as if by a whirlwind. . . . He begins, another idea bursts in, both streams cross, and he does not separate them but allows them to flow into the same channel. This is the reason for the disjointed sentences, the interlacings, the ideas tacked on crosswise and left protruding, for the prickly style that bristles all over with unexpected additions, becoming a sort of unkempt thicket where dry, abstract ideas and luxuriantly flourishing metaphors intertwine, pile up, and suffocate each other and the reader.[14]

A few people in the eighteenth century did manage to acquaint themselves with Saint-Simon's government-restricted manuscript. Their reactions were characteristic of the age: the memoirs were extraordinarily interesting but poorly written, the style was awful, and the portraits were failures. These verdicts of purism and classical good taste belong to two highly placed lady readers (Sainte-Beuve cites their reviews in his 1855 and 1856 articles on Saint-Simon). The romantics, on the other hand, were delighted with Saint-Simon's style and its characteristically preclassical element, its Renaissance and baroque figurative and linguistic features not yet under the sway of convention and rule. That style was of course championed by the same Sainte-Beuve who gave back to Frenchmen Ronsard and the other poets of the *Pléiade*, figures who since the classical era had been regarded as the epitome of fustian, obscurity, and bad taste.

Pointing out Saint-Simon's preclassical tendencies does not, however, exhaust the question of his literary antecedents. Saint-Simon endeavored to ignore the writers of the eighteenth century, but despite his obvious indifference to belles lettres, he alludes with respect in the *Mémoires* to almost all of the great figures of seventeenth-century French literature. And he does not merely allude to them. In their singular way, the *Mémoires* absorbed the achievements of classical tragedy, comedy, satire, and burlesque—of Corneille, Molière, Boileau, La Fontaine, and even Scarron, whom Saint-Simon held in high regard. The influence of these figures was oblique and indirect, but Saint-Simon's interest in the work of the historians, memoirists, and moralists was not only unconcealed but extraordinarily keen. He believed, after all, that he was writing *history*, and the method of the *Mémoires* was accordingly worked out on the basis of a variety of historical models (which is not to say, of course, that he merely copied them), ranging from the ancient historians (Livy, Plutarch, and Tacitus) to Saint-Simon's own seventeenth-century contemporaries, many of whom are mentioned in his book (Bassompierre, Retz, and Rohan).

Several basic kinds of memoir literature may be distinguished in seventeenth- and eighteenth-century France. There were chronicle memoirs concerned with political events (the history of the Fronde in the memoirs of Retz and La Rochefoucauld),[15] with military campaigns (the memoirs of the Maréchal de Villars and of other generals), with diplomatic demarches (the memoirs of Torcy), and so on. And there were intimate court chronicles consisting of courtly and fashionable anecdotes, such as the above-mentioned memoirs of Dangeau and the memoirs of Madame de Maintenon's niece, Madame de Caylus, or of Madame de Staal (de Launay), regarding the court of the duchesse du Maine.

All of these memoirs paid tribute, in one degree or another, to the incidental characterization of contemporaries—paid tribute, that is, to the fashionable seventeenth-century genre of the *portrait*. For Saint-Simon, however, the problems of portrait characterization had become fundamental, inasmuch as he had consciously set himself tasks that were not merely chronological but moral and psychological as well. He wanted to understand the individual human being—not man in general as in Pascal, and not the social-moral type as in La Bruyère, but the actual, living human being. He states explicitly in the preface to the *Mémoires* that events must seem chaotic so long as the people who took part in them remain undescribed and their actions unexplained. That is why such genres as the *portrait*, the *caractère*, the *pensée*, the *maxime*, and the epistle were as important to Saint-Simon as the memoir, if indeed not more so.

The moral reflections of Pascal and Nicole, the "mainsprings" of La Rochefoucauld, the social "masks" of La Bruyère, and the observations of Madame de Sévigné all left their traces in Saint-Simon's book. The *Mémoires* are a vast and unique synthesis of sources and traditions that combines the methods of the "intermediate" genres with those modes for the apprehension of life worked out by classical tragedy, comedy, burlesque, and satire. One finds in the scholarship devoted to Saint-Simon convincing collations of individual passages from the *Mémoires*, now with Molière's *Tartuffe* and *Le Malade imaginaire*, now with the sermons of Bossuet.

Classicism strictly forbade the mixing of genres. But memoirs were not a canonical form; they lay outside the rules of *L'Art poétique*. Saint-Simon accordingly allowed himself to combine the tragic and the comic, the elevated and the trivial. That this was a completely conscious decision is attested by his statement in the *Mémoires* that "the most awful spectacles are often accompanied by the most ridiculous contrasts" (1:909). Saint-Simon's narrative is heterogeneous. Latent in it is a variety of genres or at least of different kinds of prose. The abridged editions of the *Mémoires* are quite understandably concerned with the highlights—the great scenes and the characterizations of important historical figures—but they give no sense whatever of the structure of the work. The basis of that structure is a kind of informational chronicle (Dangeau's journal was its canvas) in which the great is confounded with the petty, and the public with the domestic—a succession of deaths, births, marriages, battles, diplomatic proceedings, theological controversies, and court receptions and dinners.

I shall cite the subhead of one chapter. The chapter divisions were the work of the *Mémoires*' publishers, but the subheads reproduce Saint-Simon's own notations written in the margins of his manuscript:

Death of the duchesse de Chaulnes—Death of Chamarande-père—*Problème* banned by order of *Parlement*—The sojourn of Mme de Nemours, the prince de Conti, and other pretenders at Neuchatel—The Treaty of Carlowitz—The Prince Elector of Bavaria is named inheritor of the monarchy of Spain; his death—Proclamation of the Ninth Electorate—Death of the famous Chevalier Temple—A treasure sought in vain by the king from the archbishop of Reims—Death of the chevalier de Coislin—Death of La Feuillée—M. de Monaco is ambassador to Rome; his unsuccessful demands—"Monseigneur" used by secretaries of state and to secretaries of state—The installation of the abbé de Cîteaux at the Estate Provincial of Burgundy—Mme de Saint-Géron is recalled—The marriage of the compte d' Auvergne and Mlle de Wassenaer—The embassy from Morocco—Torcy is a Minister; a strange oath—Reneville, lieutenant of the king's guard, disappears; Permillac kills himself. (1:603)

The flow of the basic chronicle is broken up by distinctive narrative forms, each with its own typology. The most common of these are the *portraits* (usually postponed to coincide with information about the death of the person in question). There are also structurally complete anecdotes and scenes, either very brief or elaborated with theatrical circumstantiality and vividness. And there are meditations, rhetorical digressions, and even occasional *maximes* interspersed in the text. Just as Saint-Simon had received the forms of his religious and political views from his own rationalist time, so he obtained from it the modes of his artistic thought. He did not, however, merely construct ideal images, whether tragic or comical or derived from the conventions of the *caractère* and *portrait*. He also wanted to recount what he himself had witnessed, and that witnessed reality burst through the literary forms provided by his time.

But to what extent was that reality actually witnessed firsthand? How is one to divide Saint-Simon's fame between memory and imagination?

Historians at first censured Saint-Simon for partiality, subjectivity, and a multitude of inaccuracies and departures from the truth. Then it was proclaimed that his *Mémoires* were not history but literary art. This latter point of view has been carried to its own extreme. Yves Coirault in *L'Optique de Saint-Simon* and in another book on the "addenda" to Dangeau's journal treats Saint-Simon as a brilliant visionary whose imagination produced and invented memories—not fiction, but in fact memories in which the real is no longer distinguishable from the imaginary.[16]

Notions of this kind are useful for characterizing Saint-Simon's artistic vision, but I would suggest that it is impossible to settle the question of the relationship between the real and the imaginary in his book without taking into account Saint-Simon's own conception of history, since without that conception one cannot explain the clear contradiction between his practice as a writer (with his casual attitude toward facts) and the undoubtedly sincere assurances of his own accuracy and truthfulness that are contained in the *Mémoires'* preface and conclusion (even though Saint-Simon admitted that complete impartiality is impossible).[17]

Saint-Simon sets out his view of historiography in his preface to the *Mémoires*, and it is the characteristic view of a time when historicism as it is conceived today still did not exist (modern historical thought actually begins with the writings of the French and German philosophes) and when there was as yet no clear distinction between memoirs and history. Saint-Simon draws a distinction between what he calls "general" and "private" history. General history involves the life of several nations or the events of several centuries. Private history "takes place before the author's own eyes," and its purpose is "to place [the] reader in the midst of the participants in all that is recounted, so that he will believe that he is not so much reading a history or memoirs, as that he himself is involved in the secret of all that is represented to him, and a spectator of all that is told" (1:4–5).

Kings, noblemen, the court, court cabals and intrigues, the replacement of lovers, ministers, and favorites, battles and diplomatic machinations were all appropriate subjects for memoirs. Indeed, in the seventeenth century, such subjects were regarded as the very substance of history. But Saint-Simon placed particular demands on history conceived in that way. He was opposed to the lifeless factuality typified for him by Dangeau's journal: "It is essential that a factual narrative reveal the origin of those facts, their causes, consequences, and relationships with each other. . . . It [is] necessary to reveal the selfishness, the vices, the virtues, the passions, the enmity, the friendship, and all the other mainsprings [*ressorts*], and not merely the principal ones, of the incidents, cabals, plots, and public and private actions that are part of the events being described, as well as all the divisions, ramifications, and consequences that have become the sources and causes of other cabals, and that have engendered other events" (1:4). History thus had to become an investigation of passions, interests, and "mainsprings" (the same ones that La Rochefoucauld had studied). The historian or memoirist (the distinction is immaterial) had to break through the strata presented to external observation by the events themselves into the realm of undisclosed and ulterior motives. And that inevitably led to conjecture and assumption, to hypothetical reconstruction of the world hidden from the observer. But that hidden world in its turn demanded visible embodiment from the memoirist; it required external signs and symbolically meaningful details. The work of the imagination was thus subject to competing claims, both external and internal.

Much attention has been given in the Saint-Simon scholarship to the singular, almost theatrical vividness of his great scenes with their numerous, minutely drawn characters: the court after the death of the Grand Dauphin, the duc d'Orléans' seizure of power at the 1715 session of *Parlement*, the convening of *Parlement* in 1718, to name but a few. I shall dwell for a moment on one of these.

Monseigneur, the fifty-year-old son of Louis XIV, has suddenly died, and the duc de Bourgogne, the king's grandson and Saint-Simon's patron, has become heir apparent. All the court relationships have been rearranged in an instant. Saint-Simon describes the night following the death of the Grand Dauphin:

> The expressions on the faces of those present were truly eloquent; one needed only eyes and not the slightest knowledge of the court to read the desires of some, while the countenances of those who had nothing to lose remained perfectly blank. . . . Those first moments revealed the first impulses in a true light, and for once free of the constraint of good manners. . . . Faces were sad or haggard, gestures more frequent than intended, and for the rest there was almost absolute stillness. . . . Those who were glad tried in vain to increase their appearance of gravity by looking sad or stern; yet all they could achieve was a thin veil, through which keen eyes might discover their real feelings. . . . Mgr le duc de Bourgogne wept in all sincerity, quietly shedding tears of compassion, piety, and prolonged strain. M. le duc de Berry was equally sincere, but he might have been weeping tears of blood, so bitterly he cried. Indeed, it was not merely sobs that came from him, but shrieks and howls, even bellowings. Sometimes he was quiet, but only because he was choking, and then his cries would break out again, so

loud, so monstrously loud, that they resembled the uncontrollable trumpet-ings of deep despair. Many others joined in these heartrending outbursts, goaded thereto by emotion or a sense of the proprieties. . . . Mme la duch-esse de Berry was beside herself. . . . The bitterness of despair was imprinted on her face. You could see as plainly as if it were written there a perfect frenzy of uncontrollable woe, not from grief or affection, but from pure selfishness: there were intervals when she was dry-eyed, but sullen-looking and angry. Then came torrents of tears and gestures, involuntary yet re-strained, betraying the deep anguish that resulted from her previous medita-tions. . . . Mme la duchesse de Bourgogne . . . comforted her husband, find-ing that easier than to show any sign of needing consolation herself. . . . A frequent use of the handkerchief reflected the sobs of her princely brother-in-law, and a few tears occasioned by the scene around her, and carefully hus-banded, were encouraged by artful rubbing to smudge her cheeks and make her eyes red and swollen; but all the time her furtive glances wandered over the bystanders and scanned the face of each one in turn. . . . To one who knows the inner life of a court, these first moments after some tremendous event are immensely gratifying. Each face reminds one of the cares and in-trigues, the laborious efforts to advance a private fortune or form and strengthen a cabal, the cunning devices designed and executed for such pur-poses, the attachments at varying degrees of intimacy, the estrangements, dislikes, and hatreds, the unkind turns played and the favors granted, the tricks, petty shifts, and baseness of some individuals, the dashing of the hopes of some in midcareer, the stupefaction of others at the summit who had thought their ambitions fulfilled. By the same blow a new importance was given to their adversaries in the opposing cabals; the force of the recoil at that same moment brought the affairs of some (notably myself) to a suc-cessful conclusion and consequently to extreme and unlooked-for joy, while fury was displayed on the faces of the rest, in spite of all their concern to hide it. . . . Such an amalgamation of ambitious people and momentous events is a delight to those who understand, and ephemeral though it may be, it pro-vides one of the greatest pleasures to be had at courts. (3:815–823)[18]

Saint-Simon's conception is clear: he has examined the inner main-springs of these people and is therefore easily able to read the external signs of their behavior, even taking malicious pleasure in it. Everything about that behavior is expressive—from the quick glance at a neighbor to the cries of the duc de Berry, which resemble "the uncontrollable trumpetings of deep despair." Yet the more expressive the description, the more conventional it is. Memory is incapable of accurately reproduc-ing, after thirty years or more, demeanors, gestures, and intonations. And people do not behave that expressively in real life anyway.

Saint-Simon's era regarded such questions differently, however. For them, external behavioral symbolism had to correspond to definite internal states. "One needed only eyes . . . ," Saint-Simon begins his description. Indeed, the movement here does not so much proceed from observation of behavior to the mainsprings that that behavior conceals, as it moves in the opposite direction—from investigation of those mainsprings to conjecture about their "expression." The description is thus more an example of rationalistic deduction than of empirical observation reproduced thirty years after the fact. Nevertheless, there is always an empirical element concealed in Saint-Simon's imagery, and it is that element that gives his writing its particular identity. Memories, even the most altered, remain unique and distinctive facts of his experience of life.

The key to Saint-Simon's departures from the truth is therefore to be found not only in his powerful imagination and fierce temperament, but also in the very nature of the problem he was endeavoring to solve, the problem of the historian as he conceived it. Saint-Simon takes a phenomenon and opens it up; he uncovers the motivations hidden beneath the surface. Yet he also wants the reader to see for himself the mechanisms that he has revealed, and he offers him the magnifying glass of his hyperbole and metaphor. The very nature of this process required the conjoining of memory and fiction at every step. It is for this reason that Saint-Simon could invent and yet sincerely believe in his own veracity.

Much has been written about Saint-Simon's remarkably keen eye for detail, some of it actually going so far as to draw comparisons with nineteenth-century literature. But the greatest writers, even those who anticipate the future, are still products of their time. This is at once their limitation and their strength. Saint-Simon's concrete use of detail is obviously still a long way from nineteenth-century realism, which sought to create a consistent material context for the existence of its characters.

The aesthetic assumptions of Saint-Simon's era are reflected in the fact that, for him, the concrete is still closely linked to comedy and burlesque (the lower genres of the prevailing system of literary classification). It is from this comedic and satiric tradition that his sharp rendering of detail derives. That detail is intended to be characteristic, but in an exaggerated way, even when taken in isolation. It is an expression of the basic nature of a character or event and a focal point of the author's judgment of his subject matter. To be sure, one may find other, more purely descriptive details in Saint-Simon, but they are less typical, less characteristic of his method of making things concrete. Whenever he writes about something touching or sublime, his depictions at once lose their splendid materiality.

The Saint-Simonian concrete detail has another significance as well, one originating at the intersection of his aesthetic and political views. It is common knowledge that Saint-Simon's era was one in which ceremonial and ritual thought had reached an extraordinarily high level of development, culminating in the activities of the very circle to which Saint-Simon himself belonged, the court of Louis XIV. Louis transformed the cult of etiquette and ceremonial formalism into a political fact: it served as a means for the consolidation of absolute power.[19] Yet even in that milieu, Saint-Simon's unrelenting and bitter struggle to secure even the most trivial of ceremonial privileges became the subject of jokes and mockery. It should not be forgotten, however, that all of Saint-Simon's sophistical concern with sitting and standing ladies (sitting and standing in the presence of the king, that is), with rights to armchairs and to stools and to chairs with backs and to chairs without them, and with the right to precede foreign princes or to stand in an illuminated room holding a superfluous candle while the king was being undressed at bedtime, and so on— it should not be forgotten that for Saint-Simon all these concerns masked ideas of aristocratic prerogative and political dignity that were in fact already illusory by his time.

Ritual thought in that circle had produced what in contemporary language might be termed extreme "semiotism," that is, a heightened feeling for form or a heightened perception of the symbolic or significative meaning of words, gestures, objects, and all the other things associated with particular people and circumstances. Louis XIV was a virtuoso of that semiotics of behavior. "No one had ever," Saint-Simon says of him, "sold his own words, even his smile and his very glances, at a better price" (4:1001). Saint-Simon delineates the political function of this mechanism with remarkable precision:

> He felt that he did not have enough favors to spread about to produce a sustained effect. He therefore substituted imaginary favors for actual ones, for the sake of jealousy, and showed minor preferences, which thanks to his skill he was able to come up with daily, or even, one might say, by the moment. . . . [One such distinction was] the right to hold a candlestick at his bedtime, a right that every evening he granted to a courtier whom he wanted to single out, and always one of the most highly placed among those he found there, loudly calling out his name after coming out after prayers. . . . Another invention of this kind was the mantle conferred by letter patent. . . . The secretary of state, having the household of the king in his department, issued the patent for the mantle and no one else was allowed to wear it. (4:996–997)

All this is not without a certain resemblance to the protocol of Eastern courts (even to the mantle "from the royal shoulder"), but there is an essential difference. Louis XIV was a confirmed despot and not infrequently a cruel one, but not in the Asiatic mold. This highly complex and nuanced gradation of favors was only possible in an atmosphere of courtesy. Courtesy itself thus became a method of control.

> Never was there anyone possessed of a more natural courtesy, or one who measured out that courtesy by such strict degrees, or better distinguished

differences of age, merit, or rank. . . . These different stages were precisely
marked by his manner of greeting and of responding to bows whenever he
departed or arrived. He was wonderful in the various ways he acknowledged
salutes while reviewing the ranks or at muster. But with the ladies he was
incomparable. He never passed by any lesser woman's cap without tipping
his own hat, even if it was the cap of a chambermaid, and he knew that it
was, as often happened at Marly. For ladies he removed his hat entirely, but
at a greater or lesser distance; for titled personages he removed it halfway
and held it in the air or by his ear for a few moments more or less, measuring
the time; with respect to the untitled, . . . he was content merely to touch his
hat brim; for princes of the blood, he removed it entirely, just as he did for
the ladies; and if he entered into conversation with the ladies, he replaced his
hat only after taking leave of them. (4:1001–1002)

Courtesy was at once carefully elaborated and formal. It got on remarkably well in that magnificent court with the vestiges of medieval grossness.

One may find in Saint-Simon and in the other memoirs and documents
of his time numerous examples attesting to the savage customs and sordid
behavior of that whole society, however imbued with etiquette it was.[20]
Yet even in that context, Saint-Simon's accounts of the princesse d'Harcourt are extraordinarily naturalistic. This former beauty and heroine
of gallant adventures beat her servants (who incidentally responded
in kind), openly stole money, played cards at court, and amused high-
ranking personages with her repulsive buffoonery. Once the duc de Bourgogne put a petard under a chair in her living room where she was playing
piquet. He was about to light it, when feelings of compassion restrained
him, warning him that the thing "might maim" the princesse d'Harcourt
(2:134).

Another butt of the insults of the future heir to the throne and his wife
was the voluntary buffoon Madame Panache. They once teased her so
much that she lost her temper while sitting at dinner, which "gave even
more amusement to the princes and princesses, who filled her pockets
with meat and stew, so that the sauce ran down her skirts; some of them
gave her a pistole or an ecu, others a flick of the finger or a tap of the foot,
which sent her into a rage, since her eyes were so filled with rheum that
she could not see in front of her nose and did not know who was striking
her, and this was how the court passed the time" (1:372).

In a letter written in 1695, the duchesse d'Orléans (the mother of the
future regent) describes a card game at court: "They play for terribly high
stakes here, and the gamblers are like madmen; one howls, another
pounds the table so hard with his fist that the whole hall echoes, a third
blasphemes in a way that makes your hair stand on end, and all are so
beside themselves that it is terrible to look at them."[21] Yet these howling
card players and pranksters stuffing stew into the pockets of their table

companion could the very next instant raise their hats with balletic elegance and make low bows in doses precisely measured by the rules of etiquette. There was the raw material of the life of these people, and there were the purposeful, politically and aesthetically organized forms, the behavioral molds into which that material was poured, only to break free again once the momentary ceremonial constraint had passed. Saint-Simon depicts with exceptional power the two aspects of that existence—its ritualism and its natural license.

In his preface to the *Mémoires*, Saint-Simon declares that "it pleased the Holy Spirit to conceal and represent the greatest things in the guise of actual historical and natural events" (1:2). Thus, even history has its place in the divine allegory. Saint-Simon extended the deciphering of allegories to everything, from the great to the small, even to particular actions, objects, and gestures. "While reading the *Mémoires*," writes a student of Saint-Simon's art, "one sometimes has the distinct impression that the papal nuncio is not really a wealthy and respectable civil servant of the head of the Catholic church, but merely a man who does not give his *hand* to the dukes. The canon of Toledo is a being in whose presence, by an effect as mysterious as the laws of physics, a *white flag* appears on the steeple of the Toledo Cathedral. . . . A prince of the blood is not so much a relation of the king . . . , more or less likely to succeed to the throne, as he is . . . someone who is permitted to walk across the *floor of Parlement*."[22]

The unity of Saint-Simon's political and aesthetic thought is revealed with exceptional clarity in the symbolic meaning of each individual trait. The very contradictions of his characterology are rooted in the initial duality of his social position. Saint-Simon's respect for the principle of monarchical power, indeed for all titles and ranks, never implies the least respect for its actual bearer. Although judging him harshly, Saint-Simon does recognize some virtues in Louis XIV, but he speaks with a complete lack of restraint about the "stupidity" of the queen or about the insignificance of the king's nephew, the duc de Chartres, who was installed on the throne of Spain. Louis' son and heir apparent (the first dauphin) is described as feebleminded and sunk in "apathy and obesity." And many pages of the *Mémoires* are devoted to the dullness, brutality, and depravity of the princes of the blood, which of course in no way prevents Saint-Simon from regarding them as the highest caste, the one to which not only the aristocracy and *Parlement* (the urban bourgeoisie and peasantry are left entirely out of account) but even the dukes and peers must render tokens of respect. It is from his regard for function and social attribute that Saint-Simon's ritual symbolism derives, just as his contempt for individuals is the source for his satirical concreteness.

All who have written about Saint-Simon have noted that concreteness. Taine held that Saint-Simon was concerned with what was individual, and he opposed him to the classical literature of his time, which proceeded from general ideas and abstractions. Generality and abstraction, however, were more typical of the high classical genres (tragedy and the epic). The low genres (comedy, satire, and the fable), which unquestionably influenced Saint-Simon, were quite receptive to the particular and the concrete. And the "documentary" writing of the period (memoirs and letters), standing as it did outside the boundaries of poetic art, was even more receptive. Seventeenth- and eighteenth-century memoiristic and epistolary characterization and portraits were acquainted with both concreteness and naturalism. There are numerous exact empirical observations in the celebrated letters of Madame de Sévigné and in the *Souvenirs* of Madame de Caylus, which, although published after Saint-Simon's death, were written before his *Mémoires* (Caylus died in 1729).

Bussy-Rabutin's *Histoire amoreuse des Gaules* belongs to an even earlier period (the 1660s). This is a special variety of memoir, the chronicle of court and society scandals. Yet for all of Bussy-Rabutin's fondness for gossip and anecdote, he sometimes produces portraits that permit one to regard him as a precursor of Saint-Simon. One such is his portrait of the Grand Condé, who appears under the name "Tyridate," and it is a portrait that is full of concrete and individual detail. It depicts the personal qualities of the military commander and includes the observations that the prince had "uneven and dirty teeth" and that "he laughed a lot and very unpleasantly."[23]

Similarly interesting material is provided by the prodigious correspondence of the regent's mother, the duchesse d'Orléans (who as the wife of the king's brother was, in keeping with French custom, simply called "Madame"). A former German princess, Madame could not endure the French court, and she poured out her indignation in letters written to German relatives from the 1670s through 1722. The "Saint-Simonian" features of that correspondence have already been noted by others. Saint-Simon could not, of course, have known her letters, excerpts of which were first published only at the end of the eighteenth century, and the duchesse d'Orléans could not have known his *Mémoires* either. It was the era that brought them together.

Here, for example, is an epistolary portrait of de Riom, the lover of the duchesse de Berry, the regent's daughter and Madame's granddaughter: "I do not understand how one can love such a clown: he has neither looks nor figure. With his green and yellow face, he looks like a water sprite, and his mouth, nose, and eyes are like those of a Chinaman. He is a Gasconer, but you would more likely take him for an ape. He is a fop and completely lacking in sense. He has a large head sunk between broad shoulders. You can tell from his eyes that his vision is poor. In short, he is an extremely ugly clown, although they say that he has the stamina of a jackass, which pleases all the loose women" (2:146–47).

Although her German and French were full of solecisms, Madame had a gift for writing, and her naturalistic burlesque occasionally gives way to incisive psychological characterization. Of the duchesse du Maine (the wife of one of Louis' bastards), who had been conspiring against the regent, she writes, for example, "His [the duc du Maine's] wife, though she is a little toad, is much more ferocious than he is. He is a great coward, and fear often holds him back, while his wife mixes something heroic into her comedies" (2:354).[24]

The individual and the concrete were not, of course, suddenly revealed to Saint-Simon in an utter desert of classical abstraction. Like every other great writer, he had precursors, traditions, and his own contemporary milieu to draw upon, particularly as regarded the important area of the physical and psychological portrait. Saint-Simon's uniqueness among the memoirists of his day is thus not to be found in his concreteness per se, but in the fact that he incorporated everything empirical and individual into a vast but coherent system of patterns and interactions. With regard to a characterization of the king's bastards, Saint-Simon remarks that it is necessary "for the clarification and laying bare of everything yet to be reported. Those persons instigated a great many events that may not be understood without this key" (2:831).

Saint-Simon strives to reveal the essence of his characters in features that are at once material and symbolic. But his task does not end there. He explains the mainsprings and mechanisms that have set those characters in motion. Individuals, court parties, social groups, armies, and even states are all subject to the laws of self-interest and passion, which are played out in the vast epical reachs of the *Mémoires*, thus producing the inimitable Saint-Simonian world.

Saint-Simon shared the view of his time that human beings are made up of qualities and governed by passions. The components of his analysis were mechanisms (*les machines*), mainsprings, and capacities. He was unable to depart from that analysis, but the juxtaposition of its abstracting and formal schemata with the powerful empiricism of his own memories produced extraordinary effects.

In his preface to the *Mémoires*, Saint-Simon propounds his conception of the nature of historical process, a conception that presumes a direct relationship between cause and effect:

> But history is of a kind entirely different from all the other forms of knowledge. . . . All the public and private events constituting it are the causes of each other, and everything in it is held together by such an extraordinary concatenation that the rupture of even one link would bring to a halt, or at least alter, the event issuing from it. . . . Thus, if it is to be useful, it is essential that a factual narrative reveal the origin of those facts, their causes, their consequences, and their relationship to each other. . . .

> To write a history of his country and his time, a person must reflect at
> length on all that he has seen, felt, or known . . . of what has happened on
> the world's stage, as well as reflect on the various mechanisms, at first glance
> insignificant, that motivated the events that had the greatest consequences
> and that formed other events. (1:3, 4, 13)

Saint-Simon understood such cause-and-effect relations mechanistically,
which, one may observe in passing, is reflected in his inability to distinguish between the great and the small, and in his naive explanations of the
significant events of his day in terms of the trivial happenstances of court
life. A classic example (one mentioned by all the students of the
Mémoires) is Saint-Simon's belief that the War of 1688 was caused by a
crooked window frame. The king had reprimanded Louvois, the minister
of war and superintendent of palace construction, for a poorly hewn window in Le Trianon, which was under construction at the time. Louvois,
according to Saint-Simon, decided that only a war could return him to
favor, since he would then be irreplaceable. He therefore provoked a conflict with the powerful European Alliance. The explanation is of course
naïve, but it is more than just the substitution of a court anecdote for a
serious explanation. It is a demonstration of Saint-Simon's theory of
mechanisms and linkages: a small mainspring had been tripped, and it
ultimately resulted in the unfolding of massive sequences of event.

Connected with this mechanistic orientation was yet another characteristic of rationalist thought: its division of life into closed hierarchical
spheres. Unlike romanticism with its metaphysically based conception of
the unity of the human soul, rationalism viewed man as simultaneously
residing in religious, political, courtly, and domestic spheres, and living
and acting in accordance with the appropriate laws of each.

The sphere of Christian morality was obviously higher than that of
courtly life, but, on the other hand, it was remote from actual behavior
and hardly influenced it at all. Any attempt to conduct oneself at court, in
the army, or in society according to the precepts of Christian morality
would only have provoked the laughter and contempt of one's peers, even
though they were people who sincerely regarded themselves as devout
Catholics.

This whole system of social and moral values is reflected in the classical
system of literary genres, each of which was assigned to a specific, hierar-
chically correlated sphere of objective reality. The literary character,
whether that of tragedy, comedy, epic, pastoral, or satire, was likewise
assigned together with its genre to a definite sphere, although actual
human beings were, under certain circumstances, permitted to move from
one sphere to another. It is because of this mobility in actual life that
criteria deriving from different spheres of value could, however paradox-
ically, converge in a single memoir character. That character could be

simultaneously judged from the point of view of religion and Christian morality, of practical life (whether bureaucratic, diplomatic, or military), of society and "courtly" qualities, and of conventional, "respectable" morality. Such motives as ambition, vanity, and self-interest, without which the mechanism of the court world could not have functioned, were then added in. All of this had decisive significance for the understanding and depiction of the individual human being.

Saint-Simon was a man of austere religious views, with a tendency toward Jansenism, the ecclesiastic movement of ascetic and moral-rigorist persuasion (whose membership included Pascal and Nicole, both authors of religious-moralistic *pensées* and men whom Saint-Simon held in the highest regard). Saint-Simon speaks in a Pascalian spirit and in the spirit of the "Ecclesiast" of the "insignificance of the world, and of its fears, desires, hopes, failures, successes, and labors," adding that "if people could tell what their troubles, their labors by the sweat of their brows, their efforts, and their intrigues would in the end be crowned with, all of them, with the exception of a mere dozen perhaps, would stop at the threshold of life and renounce all their intentions and their fondest hopes." All is vanity. . . Nonetheless, the vainest of all vanities, the life of the court, acquires epic sweep in the *Mémoires*, and trifles become exceptionally weighty and significant. The *Mémoires* are devoted to life at its most transitory and sinful, and they judge it according to its own laws. They do not even have to touch on the other, sacred sphere. After reporting the death of his spiritual guide, the head of the Trappist order (who died on straw and ashes in keeping with the requirements of his discipline), Saint-Simon adds, "These *Mémoires* are too profane to recount in them anything of a life so sublimely holy and of a death so majestic and so precious in the sight of God" (1:771). Saint-Simon did not, however, hold the vain life in contempt (as a romantic would have done); it fascinated him, and he gave it his most assiduous attention.

This hierarchical arrangement was entirely in the spirit of Saint-Simon's age and milieu. The majority of the society people of his day were zealous Catholics, but the ideal society model consisted of qualities that were diametrically opposed to the doctrines of the Christian church. Murder (war, dueling), adultery, slander, lust for power, and extravagance were not so much sins, not so much forgivable human weaknesses (the Catholic church practiced the remission of sins to an extraordinary degree), as they were positive qualities and values, identified in court and society usage under different names: extraordinary valor, gallantry, wit, generosity.

The sphere of ecclesiastical values was always kept in reserve, however. Madame has some caustic words to say on this subject: "Many French women, especially those who have been coquettes or libertines, as soon as they grow old and can no longer have lovers, become religious, or at any rate give themselves out to be; but they are usually very dangerous, since they are envious and can tolerate no one" (1:80).

In her famous novel *La Princesse de Clèves*, Madame de la Fayette investigates the questions of passion and duty, of honor and probity, and her heroine sacrifices passion for the sake of rational duty. La Fayette also wrote the *Mémoires de la cour de France* as well as a memoir of Henriette d'Angleterre, the first wife of the brother of Louis XIV. In comparison with her moral-psychological novel, the memoir presents an entirely different world. There is very little here in the way of politics and war, but there is a great deal of court gossip and wayward adventure, which are judged exclusively in terms of society norms. The author shares, as it were, the moral level of her characters, whose standards of behavior would have horrified the princesse de Clèves and her virtuous mother.

In Madame de la Fayette's portrayal of her, Henriette d'Angleterre shines with intellect, charm, and beauty. She is a source of delight to the memoirist, even though her conduct is in fact the antithesis of that of the princesse de Clèves: she betrays her husband, engages in dalliance and deceit, and is a participant in dark intrigues. Ethical choice is, so to speak, excluded from the sphere of practical society relations in which she moves.

While still enjoying the king's special favor (which provoked rumor), Henriette d'Angleterre suddenly died at the age of twenty-six after the performance of secret diplomatic missions for him. According to a habit of the day, her death was attributed to poisoning, although it was probably natural. Appended to Madame de la Fayette's memoir of Henriette is a work called "Relation de la mort de Madame." Not only does the whole atmosphere of the narrative change in the appendix (which is understandable), but there also emerges what in essence is a new character with a new set of qualities and characteristics. Whereas questionable amatory adventures are recounted in the memoir of this "best of all possible princesses," in the appendix she is described as a woman of extraordinary practical and diplomatic gifts and of Roman fortitude. Profoundly Christian feelings are also displayed.

This last feature is typical as well of the numerous other deaths transcribed by Saint-Simon. The most superficial of these Catholics at once repudiates all his earthly concerns and affairs in the hour of his death, gives his full attention to the choice between heaven and hell, and hastens to observe all the forms of Christian death (confession, remission of sins, communion), which assure him of salvation. "Her mind never again turned toward thoughts of life," Madame de la Fayette writes of her heroine.[25] In rationalistic literature, certain qualities were suitable for gallant adventures (the society sphere), others for diplomatic intrigues (the political sphere), and still others for the hour of death. The author felt no need to draw them all together into a consistent whole.

Saint-Simon was not at all reluctant to stress his own religious rigorism and his stern ideals of old-fashioned valor and honor. Yet he too recognized different spheres of value, and he made concessions to them, both as an artist and as a courtier. Even when satirizing and exposing court life in the *Mémoires*, he uses its criteria, employing such well-established honorific phrases as *l'homme gallant*, denoting the genteelly courteous person who is successful in amorous adventures, or *l'esprit de Mortemar*, identifying the particular stamp of mind that was characteristic of the king's favorite, Montespan, and her brother and sisters, as well as of their manner of speech, which was unaffected, mercilessly witty, and ruthless in its pursuit of the ridiculous.

Saint-Simon repeatedly stigmatizes as "a scandalous double adultery" the king's open liaison with Madame de Montespan, a woman whom the king had alienated from her husband. Yet Saint-Simon's portrait of her old age is written with unconcealed admiration. Denied the king's love and dismissed from Versailles, Madame de Montespan atoned for her sins through prayer, devoted herself to charity, and even wore a belt with iron nails. Saint-Simon notes all this with approval, but he admires something else—the fact that Montespan was "as fair as the day until the end of her life" (that is, until she was sixty-six).

> She was never able to rid herself of the regal demeanor . . . that she retained even in solitude. . . . Her armchair stood at the foot of her bed; there was no point in seeking another in her room, not even for her illegitimate children—Mme la duchesse d'Orléans no less than the others. Monsieur and the Grande Mademoiselle [his daughter] had not ceased to love her and visited her often: armchairs were brought for them, just as one was brought for the princesse [de Bourbon-Condé]; but even then she never dreamed of troubling herself, never accompanied her guests to the door. . . .

Following this is a depiction of the genuinely "Christian death" of the Marquise de Montespan. Calling her servants, even the "lowliest of them," she confessed her sins before them all and "begged forgiveness for the shameful example she had given them for so long" (2:863–866). Two sets of criteria are in continual conflict in this portrait. One involves the edifying penitence of the sinner, and the other, the attributes of the society beauty. Those brilliant attributes were the cause of Madame de Montespan's sins, while the "regal demeanor" that she retained until her final hour was their consequence.

Rationalist characteristics and abilities could not be derived from observation of individual human beings; they required a preestablished social and moral typology. The literary character had its own typological framework, by which it was "identified" and referred to a specific rubric. It was in fact on the basis of psychological conceptions of this kind that the genres of the *caractère* and *portrait*, with their selections of internal and external features, emerged as means for the rationalist modeling of human beings. Gustave Lanson writes that *portraits* and *maximes* were in a sense created "by the period's taste for moral analysis." He points out that *portraits* had traditional schemata, both satirical and approbatory, which included physical appearance (figure, degree of portliness, complexion, eyes, hair, and teeth), physical abilities (skill in weaponry or in dancing and singing), intellectual capabilities and defects, and faculties of the heart (a capacity for love and friendship, pride, phlegm, passion, and so forth). Lanson observes that "the era was inclined, even in the individual specimen, to accentuate the least individual features, and whenever possible to reduce them to a general type."[26]

The greatest achievement of seventeenth-century social and moral typology, its highest level of cultivation, is the famous *Caractères* of La Bruyère (first published in 1688). La Bruyère was an early forerunner of the bourgeois Enlightenment, and his characterizations have an intensely social tinge, and moreover an antiaristocratic one. He is already well acquainted with the influence of milieu and upbringing and with the variability and even contradictoriness of character. Yet the unit of analysis in his investigations is always the discrete attribute, and the sum of those attributes, the typical social and moral structure.

La Bruyère juxtaposes typological structures of different scope (ranging from large social groups to individual masks) formed on the basis of features having no necessary logical connection to each other (the chapter titles are symptomatic in this respect: "On the City," "On the Court," "On the Great," and then, "On Man" and "On Women").

"The great despise the intelligent if they have nothing but intelligence; the intelligent are contemptuous of the great if they have nothing but rank. The virtuous pity both if their sole merit is rank or intelligence without virtue."[27] This is an odd crossing of general social (class) and moral categories. The "great" constitute a class category based on a preconceived set of attributes (negative from La Bruyère's point of view). The "intelligent" are a general category of ability, but one that is also essentially social: it consists of bourgeois intellectuals who, like La Bruyère himself, were employed in the service of the court and the aristocracy. And the "virtuous" are the savants, the highest moral category, whose essence is that it is independent of the social. It is a pure abstraction, but as such entirely in keeping with the nature of rationalist thought: the higher the category, the more abstract it is.

Facts of a social, moral, or psychological order can, for La Bruyère, stand on equal footing. Such typological rubrics (with their characteristic qualities) as courtiers, aristocrats, the haute bourgeoisie, women in general, and all coquettes who deceive their husbands are fully commensurate. Phenomena of different origin and quality, as well as different features of character and different modes of behavior, are all fixed by a single, monosemantic term of qualification. "Miserly," "brave," "modest," "judicious," "magnanimous," "courteous," and "depraved" are all qualities; "gambler" and "coquette" are qualities as well.

> If, *Hermas*, I marry a miserly woman, at least she will not ruin me; if a gambler, she may make us wealthy; if a scholar, she will instruct me; if a prude, she will not be short-tempered, and if she is short-tempered, then she will exercise my patience; if a coquette, she will want to please me; if a loose woman, she will, perhaps, love even me; if a devout woman. . . . Tell me, Hermas, what should I expect of a woman who wants to deceive God but in fact only deceives herself? (119)

Saint-Simon, with his unremitting interest in individual character and his complex typology, learned a great deal from La Bruyère, and in the *Mémoires* he calls the latter's manner of portraiture "inimitable." La Bruyère, however, created literary characters, that is, purified, ideal characters with explicit schemata that absorbed the empirical observation of real prototypes. In a famous speech given at the French Academy in 1693, La Bruyère protested against the deliberate search for clues to the prototypes of his characters, declaring that he had not sought to paint portraits of specific individuals, portraits "that are faithful and lifelike, out of the fear that they might sometimes be unbelievable and would seem false or made-up." Rather, he selected and combined traits that "could have converged in a single person, [and] . . . created verisimilar images from them," offering the reader not a satire of individuals per se, but "faults to be avoided, and exemplars to be followed" (488).

The requirement of verisimilitude, a basic one in classical poetics, is applied here to *caractères* and *portraits*, with a curious result. An accurate portrait of an individual could, from the rationalist point of view, seem "implausible." It was just this that Saint-Simon was not afraid of.

La Bruyère did of course have prototypes in mind for his *Caractères*, just as his better-informed readers recognized. But those prototypes were relegated to a place outside the artistic structure and were not necessary for its comprehension. The solution to the problem of finding clues was for La Bruyère's contemporaries something on the order of gossip or a society diversion, whereas for Saint-Simon the type was equivalent to the prototype. His characters are called by their own names and are laden with a variety of biographical and characterological information. If La Bruyère dissolves actual empirical observation in the schema, then Saint-Simon superimposes the schema on actual, refractory experience. The whole of Saint-Simon is to be found in the tension between these two principles—the typological schema and what actually existed. Saint-Simon cannot do without the schema, for without it his world would collapse into chaos, since as a rationalist he has no other means of organization. But he cannot fit everything into the schema, and what remains unassimilated becomes a dynamic principle that transforms the context.

Fluidity of consciousness is still unknown to Saint-Simon. He is fond of contradictions, but he sees them as a conflict between opposing qualities that remain separate from and impervious to each other. He is true to his assumptions even when he is speaking of the influence of milieu and upbringing, or of the variability of individual character. If someone changes, it is because certain of his qualities have been supplanted by others. A good example is the story of the moral conversion of the duc de Bourgogne. The prince "was born ill-tempered": choleric to the highest degree, unable to tolerate even the slightest opposition, obstinate, and sybaritic. He "yielded to all his passions and was carried away by his pleasures; often savage, he was naturally inclined to cruelty," but wise tutors and God, who wished "to make of this prince the work of his right hand," triumphed in the end. "Out of that abyss emerged a prince who was affable, gentle, humane, temperate, patient, modest, penitent, . . . humble, and strict with himself" (3:1170–1173).

La Bruyère would say that Saint-Simon's combinations of qualities lack verisimilitude because of their concrete singularity. But they are in fact altered and enriched by virtue of their combination, so that complex and unexpected new relationships emerge between them and their corresponding typological formulas.

Saint-Simon's social typology is fundamentally different from La Bruyère's. La Bruyère observes the aristocracy, courtiers, and high-ranking officials externally, from off to the side, and he first of all types them. He assigns his courtiers, independently of their prototypes, to generalized categories—adventurers, the supercilious, the obsequious, the superficial, or those greedy for fame. Saint-Simon, however, regards his characters from within; he penetrates to their essence. He is not writing a moral tract but history, and he thinks in terms not merely of social typology but also of "social mechanisms"—the struggle of parties, the play of actual political passions, cabals, and intrigues. His noblemen are diverse; they include friends and enemies, companions-at-arms and rivals. La Bruyère's society women are a generalized category with a traditional selection of vices. In the world depicted by Saint-Simon, however, to be a woman of the court and high society is to perform a kind of duty, to play a part in a political drama, and his female characters are accordingly no less varied than his male.

Saint-Simon's sphere of observation was largely restricted to the life of the court, but he made his observations at a time when absolutism was at its zenith and when the court was the center of political life in France and therefore of particular importance. Within the limits imposed on his understanding by his time and his vantage, Saint-Simon investigates in the *Mémoires* the "mechanisms" of distinct social groups, endeavoring to make careful distinctions among them. He creates a variety of caste models for the courtiers and the military, the public servants, and the clergy. These models are combined with personal attributes, themselves divisible into practical qualities (capacities), society qualities, and moral qualities—the three basic components of individual character. Their artful juxtaposition sometimes yields surprising results, especially when it is accompanied by that precious "residue" of unmediated observation that cannot be fit into any schema.

Saint-Simon's social definitions are always sharply judgmental and in essence moralistic. At the same time, his criteria, both positive and negative, frankly depend on the disposition of political power and on his own relationship to the contending court parties. His positive criteria are derived from the aristocracy, which was struggling to retain its rights and its self-respect, and his negative criteria are variously derived from the king and his retainers, who were implementing a bourgeois leveling policy, from the king's bastards with their disruptive pretensions, and from their patroness, Louis' morganatic wife, the marquise de Maintenon.

The aristocracy attracted to the court is thus by no means homogeneous. There is a smaller group engaged in reestablishing its once high traditions. This group primarily consists of old friends of Saint-Simon's father, or of people belonging to the circle of his father-in-law, the maréchal de Lorge, but it also includes people close to the future heir apparent, the duc de Bourgogne, in whom such people hoped to find an adversary of the new bureaucratic nobility and a defender of aristocratic prerogatives. The other, larger group of hereditary aristocrats is sunk in court obsequiousness or in idleness, debauchery, and association with riffraff of every sort. The criteria of judgment are thus straightforward and clear-cut.

The king's officials represent, in terms of the distribution of valuative accents, a more complex group for Saint-Simon. The bourgeois bureaucracy created by Louis was hateful to Saint-Simon, but the schema he applies to it still permits variation. There are the parvenus, who are distinguished by modesty and a sense of their place; these merit condescension. There are the ministers Saint-Simon has befriended and from whom he seeks support. And finally there are the people of outstanding practical qualities, and these deserve respect. Moral and society criteria may thus be combined with practical criteria in a single character.

Saint-Simon offers several models for this bureaucratic caste, each time enriching the model through the admixture of individual traits. Take, for example, the nonsociety official of the old type, who is loyal to the traditions of his class (the *gentilhommes de la manche*). This type includes several subvarieties. There is Pussort, a relative of the hated Colbert. His characteristics are honesty, severity, and great practical abilities. He is in the Colbertian mold and, as Saint-Simon observes, "very dangerous." There is Rouillé, another severe official of the old school, but one with an individual trait: he likes to pass the time debauching in the company of people of the basest sort. He combines excellent practical abilities, cruelty, and vulgar tastes. And there is Rose, another official of the old variety, although, unlike the other two, he is gay and affable. These men, however, are all holdovers from the past. Much more threatening and relevant to Saint-Simon is the new model created by Louis XIV. This consists of ministers of bureaucratic (the *gentilhommes de la manche*) or bourgeois provenance to whom Louis has thrown open the doors of Versailles. They have been made marquises and counts and, whenever possible, they marry off their daughters to the dukes.

Two powerful bureaucrats of this new, society type are depicted in the *Mémoires*: the ministers Pontchartrain and Chamillart. They belong to an extremely negative category in the Saint-Simonian disposition of social forces, but since it was impossible to live and act at court without reckoning to some extent with the spirit of the times, Saint-Simon maintained the very best relations with both ministers, and each rendered services to him. A sympathetic tone therefore predominates in his characterizations of them, however negative it may ultimately be. Despite the fact that he is a bourgeois, Pontchartrain possesses positive practical and even society qualities (a society mind and gallantry). His moral qualities are also entirely satisfactory: he is respectable, honest, a philanthropist, and, most importantly, he knows his place when consorting with the dukes and peers. Chamillart is of the same stamp, but with a difference. Where Pontchartrain is an able official of the new type, Chamillart lacks ability. He owes his career to virtuoso skill at billiards (the king was in fact a passionate billiard player) and to the fact that the king preferred men of little talent, whom he gladly instructed. Pomponne is a minister of a different social class. Even though he is a *gentilhomme de la manche*, he comes from an old aristocratic family. He is a true man of society, unlike Pontchartrain and Chamillart, for all their titles and good manners. Yet he is still a hereditary professional, a fact that distinguishes him from Beauvillier, who was the only duke admitted to Louis' council of ministers.

It is usually possible to distinguish in each of Saint-Simon's large-scale characterizations features that are differentiating and others that are more or less standard or obligatory for a given rubric. The standard features allow for typological identification, for the assignment of the character to a definite social-moral category. Saint-Simon pays a great deal of attention to the type of the predatory aristocrat, of the intensely ambitious person and court intriguer. Harcourt, La Feuillade, Foucquet, and many others fit under this rubric. In enumerating their qualities, Saint-Simon sometimes uses formulas that are either repeated verbatim or that are varied only slightly. All of these figures possess outstanding practical abilities (in statecraft or military command) and exceptional intelligence. Harcourt has a "sharp mind," La Feuillade is "very intelligent," and Foucquet is "inexhaustibly intelligent." In society, Harcourt and La Feuillade are "courteous" and "charming." At the same time, they are ambitious, hypocritical, and "depraved"—these are their moral-psychological attributes. Harcourt is "depraved," La Feuillade and Foucquet have "depraved hearts," La Feuillade has a "gutter soul," and Foucquet has a "spiteful soul." These are their basic qualities according to the three basic components of individual character, and they are accompanied by corresponding sets of supplementary qualities.

At the same time, each of Saint-Simon's figures has its own individual coloration. Sometimes this is achieved by the artful crossing of two or even several typological schemata. Harcourt is a man of unalloyed ambition, utterly preoccupied with his "fortune." But of La Feuillade, Saint-Simon says that "that passion [ambition] and the passion for pleasure took possession of him by turns." The attributes of the sybarite are combined with those of the man of ambition. La Feuillade is extravagant, magnanimous, gallant, a libertine, a womanizer, and a great gambler. He is therefore neglectful of his duty, although he is a talented and courageous soldier. Of course, the qualities associated with the courtly seeker of pleasure are traditional ones too. It is the continual conflict between ambition and sensuality, however, that gives La Feuillade his individuality. The finishing touch is provided by features that are his alone and that are quite unpredictable, since they are the result of empirical observation: the captivating La Feuillade is ugly; his sallow face is covered with disgusting pimples.

Foucquet is individual too. His main passion is malice. If for Harcourt and La Feuillade evil is merely a means employed in the service of their ambition, then for Foucquet it is an end in itself (evil for its own sake). Saint-Simon recounts how Foucquet, for various reasons, destroyed armies entrusted to him and lost battles.

The type of the predatory aristocrat finds particularly vivid expression in the *Mémoires* in the image of the duc d'Harcourt (whom Saint-Simon hated). Harcourt is an odd and relatively rare version of this type. He is a hereditary aristocrat who is trying to make a bureaucratic career. His dream is to join the king's Council of State (his council of ministers), even though during the reign of Louis XIV this was almost impossible for someone of his provenance. There are general formulas that unite the character of Harcourt with those of the aristocrats La Feuillade and

Foucquet, although on the other hand he also has affinities with the "new man" Barbezieux.

Louis XIV gave the old aristocracy the opportunity of a court and partly military career, but he obtained his ministers from among the bourgeoisie or from the hereditary bureaucracy (the *gentilhommes de la manche*). The minister of war during the 1690s, the marquis de Barbezieux, came from this second group. He inherited the war ministry at the age of twenty-two from his father, the renowned Louvois, and he died at the age of thirty-three, weakened by debauchery and the king's impending disfavor.

Louvois was a statesman of the golden age of French absolutism and, with his antiaristocratic forms, hostile to Saint-Simon. Saint-Simon appreciated his value, however. In his "addenda" to Dangeau's journal, he sketched Louvois's portrait with great power and concision, although for some reason he failed to include it in the final version of the *Mémoires*, perhaps because he had already used a number of Louvois's traits in the portrait of his son.

The monumental figure of Barbezieux is one of Saint-Simon's most astonishing creations. Barbezieux too is a man of predatory ambition on a grand scale. He is titled and colossally rich. He is a courtier and a nobleman, generous, extravagant, and magnificent, although at the same time he is grasping and unscrupulous in the way he acquires his wealth. Combined in him are the traditional qualities of the man of state, the man of high society, and the debauchee. He is of a piece both with Harcourt and La Feuillade—ambition struggles with sensuality in him too—but everything in him is carried to an extreme, especially with regard to those features that constitute his personal "residue," or that part of him that is not assimilable to any typological schema—his violent temper, his audacity, his prodigality, and his debauchery.

Saint-Simon's Barbezieux has his own typological formula—the great official of the new, society stamp—but that formula is subtly differentiated. The essence of his character is duality, the fact that Barbezieux is both a nobleman and a parvenu. Saint-Simon is unable to explain this fact in social terms, but he does succeed in portraying a man of the new social stratum, someone belonging to the emerging bourgeoisie with its lust for power and pleasure. Barbezieux's aristocratism and courtly manners are a mask concealing forces that Saint-Simon finds disturbing. He observes that Barbezieux "could have become a great minister, although a curiously dangerous one" (1:818). Barbezieux's untimely death was, as Saint-Simon remarks, perhaps no loss to the state, since his ambition was boundless. Barbezieux's "athlete's constitution" inspired fear in Saint-Simon, as did the fact that he was rude and violent and insolent with his visitors, whom he would keep waiting while he played with his dogs, and that he was insolent with the king, to whom he would send word that he was sick and could not make an expected report, when in fact he was about to go on a drinking spree or was still recovering from the previous one (and the king knew it). The characterizations of Harcourt and Barbezieux abound in shared formulas, some of them following each other verbatim, others very closely. Saint-Simon says of Harcourt that his mind was "balanced, wide-ranging, easy, capable of assuming any shape, above all captivating, with much *charm*. His most ordinary conversation was *delightful*. . . . He *spoke of affairs with a facility and an eloquence that were natural and simple*. . . . Force and nobility always accompanied [his speech]. . . . Naturally cheerful and able to work easily, [he was] never . . . impatient, never boastful, and he never complained; always busy, he always seemed to have nothing to do" (2:16–17). Of Barbezieux, Saint-Simon says that he had "much intelligence, insight, energy, soundness of judgment, and an unbelievable *facility in work*, on which he relied in order to enjoy his pleasures, and he could do more in two hours, and do it better, than another could in a day. His own person, his speech, his manners, and his expression were easy, balanced, polished, but *natural*, with *force* and *eloquence*—all were *charming*. No one had so much the air of the man of the world and the manners of a great nobleman, which is what he would like to have been, . . . and, when it pleased him, he was most courteous, with a gallantry that was of the most natural and delicate kind, and his *charm* was evident in everything. And so, when he wanted to please, he *delighted*" (1:817–818).[28]

Harcourt's basic moral-psychological qualities—hypocrisy, ambition, and self-interest—tend toward seventeenth-century models worked out by La Rochefoucauld, La Bruyère, and Molière. Barbezieux fits those models less well, with a far greater residue of the unassimilated, and indeed the vices of the duc d'Harcourt seem inconsequential in comparison with the violent passions and lusts of this parvenu engaged in a giddily dangerous game with the king and hostile court forces.

The application of uniform typological formulas to different kinds of characters is typical of Saint-Simon; at the same time, however, the images of the two noblemen are each marked by precise social particularity. Both men work easily and succeed in accomplishing a great deal, but only of Harcourt is it said that although he was "always busy, he always seemed to have nothing to do." This is an attribute of the true man of society, who carefully conceals his labors and concerns. Both men belong to the *grand monde*, and both are charming, gallant, courteous, and so forth. Yet of Barbezieux it is said that he had "the manners of a great nobleman, which is what he would like to have been," and that says it all. Harcourt is that nobleman that Barbezieux would like to have been. Harcourt is a hypocrite, and virtue for him is merely a cover for ruthless

self-aggrandizement and careerism. Society courtesy is merely an outward show (*écorce*), a mechanism he puts into operation whenever he
needs to. Barbezieux has yet another specifically social trait: he is not
merely vindictive but offended by "the merest trifle." His is the suspiciousness of the upstart who secretly knows that he is not a "true" nobleman. Saint-Simon very rarely explains the underlying causes of such behavior (as later psychological literature would do), but he does select and
arrange the attributes of his characters in such a way that the very correlation of those attributes contains, as it were, an implicit explanation of
them.

The construction of the Saint-Simonian literary character is multileveled: somewhere at its foundation lies the most general social-moral typology of the age, then comes the "social machinery" that Saint-Simon investigated at the French court and that he regarded as the main subject of
history, and last is individual character, in which particular, sometimes
whimsical features are woven into a fabric of recurrent formulas. The
stable typological schema and its undercutting by continual differentiation—that is Saint-Simon's method.

Saint-Simon enumerates the qualities of the reborn dauphin (the duc de
Bourgogne), both negative ones (those belonging to the past) and positive
ones (those belonging to the present). These two sets of qualities are arrayed in precise opposition to each other, and yet something alien, something quite heterogeneous, obtrudes on their structure. Saint-Simon recounts how a hump gradually developed on one side of the dauphin's
back, in consequence of which he started to limp. "What is surprising is
that for all his perceptiveness and high intelligence, and for all of the
extraordinary virtue and steadfast and conspicuous piety he had
achieved, that prince could never see his physical deformity for what it
was, could never accustom himself to it" (3:1172). The hunchbacked heir
to the magnificent throne who hides his defect even from himself, the
ascetic who compels his own valets to conceal with a shudder the fact that
they have noticed the deformity that they themselves must disguise—that
detail is instantly engraved on the magnificent picture of the dauphin's
miraculous moral rebirth, and it at once transforms its structure (whatever the author's intentions). The one-dimensional picture becomes complex, leaving the door slightly ajar to certain still dimly glimpsed psychological possibilities in the hero.

La Bruyère frequently introduces contradictions into his *caractères*,
but he selects the *most suitable* ones, those that give direct expression to
his design. "Don Fernando is an idle, ignorant, slanderous, quarrelsome,
double-dealing, intemperate, and insolent provincial, but he draws his
sword against his neighbors, and risks his life for nothing; he has killed
men and will himself be killed" (333). Courage is of course a positive

quality, and therefore contradicts the whole set of Don Fernando's characteristic attributes. That contradiction, however, is the most advantageous for creating the typical mask of the provincial swashbuckler.

Saint-Simon proceeds differently, as can be seen, for example, in his
portrayal of Monsieur, the king's brother Philippe, duc d'Orléans.
"There never was a person more flaccid in body and mind, weaker, more
timid, more easily deceived, more easily led, or held in greater contempt
by his favorites or more often mistreated by them; pestering, incapable of
keeping a secret, suspicious, mistrustful, he spread gossip in the court in
order to provoke quarrels, to find out what he wanted to know, and often
merely to amuse himself, and he repeated it from one person to the next"
(1:914).

The essence of Monsieur's character is in his effeminacy. He "was a
small, potbellied man mounted on stilts, so high were his heels, who was
always dressed up like a woman, all in rings, bracelets, and jewels of
every kind . . . , and with ribbons everywhere it was possible to put them,
and with every kind of perfume. . . . He was accused of using rouge in
secret. . . . Looking at him, I was irritated to recall that he was the son of
Louis XIII, [whom], except for his courage, he in no way resembled."
Saint-Simon insists on that courage: "Monsieur, who with great valor
had won the battle of Cassel, and who always showed innate courage in
all the sieges in which he played a part, otherwise had only the bad qualities of women" (1:917, 914).

Unlike the courage of La Bruyère's Don Fernando, that of Monsieur is
not at all a *suitable* contradiction. It is a differentiating feature that gives
the character an unexpected twist. The king's insignificant brother is a
man of society; that is the sole content of his character. Courage is one of
the qualities conventionally ascribed to the seventeenth-century courtier
and man of society. Monsieur obviously exposed his life to danger in
battle just as thoughtlessly as he danced at balls, went hunting, stood at
mass in the royal chapel, and so forth.

Enumerated as well are the "outstanding courtly talents" of the maréchal de Noailles: courtesy, consideration, eloquence, elegance of manners, wide knowledge (although superficial), and so on. Yet behind that
charming exterior lie hidden depths—hypocrisy, falseness, treachery, a
black heart, contempt for goodness, and a capacity for crime.

The character of Noailles is not exhausted by these linear contrasts,
however: "The mainspring of so rare a depravity is unlimited ambition."
In addition, the maréchal possesses "an imagination that is wide-reach-
ing, fertile, and unruly in equal measure; that embraces everything, that
goes everywhere astray, that hampers and crosses itself, so that it is easily
his tormentor; and that is at once urged on by his unrestrained audacity
and held back by his even greater timidity; and under the burden of this
conflict he groans, he vacillates, he withdraws into himself, he does not

know what to do or where to turn, and yet that rarely saves him from his crimes" (3:1121).

Both Noailles's society and his criminal attributes correspond to sets of traditional characteristics that are persistently employed by Saint-Simon. "Imagination," however, is a neutral idea; it does not by itself belong to either a positive or a negative category. This *unpredetermined* feature lying outside the schema takes possession of the context and is dynamically conjoined with the standard attributes of ambition, audacity, and timidity. An unbridled and confused imagination thenceforth defines the behavior of Noailles, the military commander and man of state.

The Saint-Simonian depiction of external appearance also involves a conjoining of the empirically observed and the schematic (those individual features selected in accordance with the preestablished *portrait* schemata that Lanson spoke of). An attractive exterior is usually described in terms that remain unelaborated: a physiognomy may be pleasant, majestic, intelligent, and so forth; women may be called lovely, fair, or fair as the day. Ugliness is described in much more detail. That was characteristic of an era that associated the concrete with the satiric and the comic. Attractiveness and ugliness are expressive of the person's inner essence, sometimes directly and sometimes by way of contrast. Attractiveness may thus conceal a black heart or, conversely, it may be outward evidence of nobility (the celebrated Vauban, for example). There are more complex correlations as well. The dauphin's face is divided into two parts—a beautiful one (the upper) and a repellent one (the lower)—which reflect the struggle in him of divine and base principles.

His wife, the duchesse de Bourgogne, "was pleasing to the highest degree. Charms came into being of their own accord at her every step, in her manners, and in her speech" (3:1160). Nevertheless, this charmer is decidedly ugly, with an unattractiveness marked by thoroughly naturalistic features: she has jowls, thick sensual lips, and what teeth she still possesses are rotten. This is a typical example of Saint-Simon's mechanistic approach to the depiction of external appearance, which he understands as the sum of individual features. A general impression or consistent image is thus not always able to emerge, as in the present case, where the charm of the duchesse de Bourgogne is undercut by her jowls and her missing teeth.

On the other hand, it may sometimes happen that a single feature will dominate. The younger Pontchartrain is a villain with a set of qualities of the blackest sort that entirely correspond to his exterior. He is "heavy-jowled, thick-lipped, repulsive, and deformed by small pox, which claimed one of his eyes. He replaced it with another made of glass that wept constantly, and this gave him an expression that was false, hard, and sullen, and that instantly inspired fear" (3:1003). The weeping glass eye is one of those "accidents" from life beyond the reach of the seventeenth-century *literary* portrait; in the structural unity of Saint-Simon's image, however, it has become symbolic—the false eye, the unreal tears of the false man.

Saint-Simon is a sharply judgmental writer, something that is attributable both to his own fierce temperament and to the tradition of French moralism he adopted. Authorial judgment in the *Mémoires* becomes a means of formal organization. The criteria used by Saint-Simon do derive from different spheres of life, but beyond that, each character has, particularly if he is a principal one, a certain general valuational tone, a certain coloration that is expressive of the author's attitude toward him and that largely determines the method used in his depiction, since in Saint-Simon that method is always heterogeneous.

The judgment consists of several elements. The first is what might be called the individual's historical function (insofar as Saint-Simon's position is that of historian), his place in the array of forces that define the Saint-Simonian world, in the basic conflicts of that vast yet self-enclosed arena where positive principles (the great aristocracy) are disposed against negative ones (the bourgeois upstarts, the king's ministers, the overweening membership of *Parlement*, and the king's bastards, who are threatening to usurp the rights of the princes of the blood).

The second element is the most subjective, and it involves those bonds of friendship and enmity, of sympathy and antipathy, that exist between a given character and the author, and that play such an immense role in his book. The third element concerns the character's own attributes, each of which inevitably contains a moral valuation. These elements of character structure—historical function, personal connection, and individual attribute—may be consistently positive or consistently negative, or they may enter into conflict with one another.

Complete congruence naturally yields the simplest structures, and then one finds single-dimensional characters who are absolutely virtuous (Saint-Simon's father; his father-in-law, the maréchal de Lorge; his spiritual guide Rancé, the abbé of the Trappist monastery; and so on) or absolutely criminal.

Here, for example, is a brief characterization of Saint-Simon's uncle: "He was an extremely large man, very well-built, of magnificent appearance, who abounded in intellect, wisdom, courage, and integrity" (1:56). As regards the villains, the maréchal de Noailles and the oldest of the king's bastards, the duc du Maine, stand out in particular. Saint-Simon observes of the latter that he resembled a demon

in his spitefulness, heinousness, and perversity of soul, in the harm done to all and the good rendered to none, in his elaborate schemes, overbearing arrogance, and exquisite mendacity, in his innumerable stratagems and pre-

tenses without measure, and even in his charm, in his skill at amusing, di-
verting, and delighting whenever he wished to please; he was a consummate
coward in both heart and mind, and, for all that, a coward of the most
dangerous and resourceful kind, even if that only meant seeking refuge underground, or taking the most extreme measures to avoid whatever it was
that he was afraid of—a coward who was capable of the most despicable
tricks and baseness, in none of which he yielded anything to the devil.
(2:830)

The division of people into ideal heroes and villains, however, was not
at all required by seventeenth-century literary thought (it was actually
more typical of later Enlightenment literature), and of course Saint-Simon
does take another approach to the portrayal of individual human beings,
one that emerges from his complication of the relationships among those
individuals' attributes, their historical function, and their personal connection with the author. Saint-Simon betrays a certain indulgence toward
those people with whom he has had good relations, even though they may
be adversaries by virtue of their place in the overall distribution of power.
He is, for example, kindly disposed to the youngest of the king's bastards,
the compte de Toulouse, who though intellectually limited is "the very
soul of honor, virtue, probity, truth, and fairness" (2:830). The compte
de Toulouse's historical function as a legitimized prince is a mark against
him, but on the other hand his moral qualities and Saint-Simon's personal
ties to him are marks in his favor.

The portrait of the minister Chamillart presents precisely the same
kind of correlation of valuative elements; the portrait of the princesse des
Ursins, however, is somewhat different. She was a political protégée of
the "villainess" Madame de Maintenon, and her moral qualities are consistent with that role—quite enough, it would seem, for her to be classi-
fied with Saint-Simon's blacker demons. Yet Saint-Simon was linked to
her by mutual sympathy—he was even her confidant—and although his
final portrait of her is that of a political adventuress and unscrupulous
intriguer, it is one in which things are not called by their real names. The
valuational tone is mitigated and somehow elusive.

Yet another variant is the portrayal of the duchesse de Bourgogne. She
was the wife of Saint-Simon's idolized dauphin and was herself very fa-
vorably disposed to Saint-Simon and especially to his wife, whom she
singled out from among all the other ladies at court. Saint-Simon had
invested all of his political hopes in the young ducal couple. Their almost
simultaneous premature deaths were a blow from which he never fully
recovered. And so in consequence of her place in the Saint-Simonian
world, the dauphine is a phenomenon of the most positive kind. But
Saint-Simon was not writing a novel, and he could not therefore create at
his discretion the ideal figures he needed. He had to overcome the resis-

tance of actual life, which broke up the straight line of individual character by introducing undesirable qualities.

The dauphine was "good to the point of being afraid to cause anyone the slightest pain. . . . Complaisance was natural to her." It turns out, however, that she strove to please everyone at court. "One was tempted to believe that she was completely and exclusively devoted to whomever she happened to be with." It is clear at this point that the description concerns the behavior of a dissembler. Reality takes Saint-Simon even further, however: "Her amicability was the consequence of commerce, amusement, habit, or need; the only exception I saw was Madame de Saint-Simon; she herself acknowledged this with a charm and naïveté that made that strange shortcoming of hers almost tolerable" (3:1159–1165). This last sentence is already an attempt to obscure the import of the analysis. Saint-Simon has no wish to judge the dauphine, and he is assisted in this by the existence of diverse valuational spheres.

Brought together in the portrait of the dauphine are the attributes of the professional charmer, the dissembler and intriguer, and the woman of great political prospects who has been able, thanks to skillful play at childish naïveté and jealousy, to captivate the king and even the cunning Maintenon. The language used in her characterization, however, is not the moralistic language so common in Saint-Simon, but the language of *society*. The portrait has been removed to another valuational sphere, the gallant and courtly one, and it is constructed according to the criteria of that sphere. The dauphine is gracious, charming, courteous, and lighthearted, although the real motives for her behavior show through her mask. The morally rigorist and censorious Saint-Simon even recounts in a tone of society gossip the fact that she deceived her own ascetic husband: "She wished, as has been said, to please everyone; but neither would she prevent anyone from pleasing her" (3:1165).

Madame de Maintenon is a fiend from hell, yet her attributes, when taken by themselves, are oddly similar to those of the charming dauphine. Madame de Maintenon too was a "flatterer, ingratiating, complaisant, and always seeking to please. . . . Incomparable charm in everything, and an easy, but reserved and respectful manner grown natural through long experience of social inferiority wonderfully aided her talents" (4:1023). "Social inferiority" and the habits of the dependent as the real source of her exquisite courtesy—these are of course something quite different. On the one side is a princess by birth, and on the other, a woman with a questionable past, someone who was the widow of the crippled poet Scarron, but who had become, through an incredible sequence of events, the morganatic wife of Louis *le Grand*. It is not, however, merely the difference that is important here; it is also the fact that the criteria used to judge Madame de Maintenon have been transferred from the societal sphere to the moral one, where she is ruthlessly condemned. Although the attributes of Madame de Maintenon are analogous to those of the duchesse de Bourgogne, the resulting tone is entirely different.

What then is the place of the author himself in the conflicts and alliances of the world he has created? Saint-Simon is undoubtedly one of the most positive characters in the *Mémoires*, although his positive status derives less from his own personal attributes than it does from his affiliation with a particular group or caste. He conceives of himself as an ideal representative of his group and party, and ideal precisely because in the hopeless struggle for the "just cause" of the dukes and peers he stands virtually alone, receiving what he regards as inadequate assistance from the other dukes. The author reserves the right of judgment over everything that happens in his book, since he is the most "faithful" to his caste and is endowed with all the qualities necessary for that role: noble birth, a sense of his own dignity and honor, a clear mind, perspicacity, and so on. In his relations with the king, the ministers, and influential ladies of the court, however, he is prepared to compromise, since, for him, such compromise is a self-evident condition of life and of effective action at court.

In the *Mémoires* the author is not so much an individual character as he is a function of an irreproachable caste position. Saint-Simon was not seeking to know himself, as Montaigne had done, nor to know man in general through his own inner world, as Pascal had done. He was writing not a confession but a history, as he himself makes clear: "These memoirs are not intended for the expression of my own feelings."

Taken as a whole, Saint-Simon is an analytical writer (and as such a true son of his age), inasmuch as the task he has consciously set himself is that of a "moral anatomy"—the uncovering of mainsprings and of cause-and-effect relationships. He analyzes behavior in terms of the articulations of the social mechanism he is depicting, and that analysis does not always penetrate to the character's inner self. Complete congruence among all the levels of judgment leads to one-dimensional depictions (whether positive or negative) of the individual—leads, in other words, to praise or satire.

Pure praise and pure satire are synthetic methods, yet there are also characters in the *Mémoires* who are constructed by more analytical means, and it is in their depiction that Saint-Simon's "moral anatomy" reaches particular intensity. These characters are in fact the ones whose judgment breaks down into incongruent elements.

Analysis always operates by means of the juxtaposition of elements from different levels. One finds in La Rochefoucauld, for example, such straightforward aphorisms as "Self-love is the greatest of all flatterers," and so on. Yet La Rochefoucauld is acquainted with contradiction, and in the greatest of his achievements he is a brilliant analyst: "We are ashamed to acknowledge our jealousy, but proud that we have been jealous and that we were capable of being so." This contains not only a paradox but also a psychological dialectic. "Many people hold wealth in contempt, but few know how to share it." A more straightforward formulation of this idea might yield the statement, "All strive for wealth, and no one is capable of sharing it."

La Rochefoucauld explains in other maxims that the contempt for wealth is just as self-serving as the wish to attain it, and is therefore entirely consistent with a reluctance to share it: "Moderation is the fear of the envy and disdain that befall all those who exult in their own good fortune; it is an empty show of the strength of our minds, and in those who have achieved the greatest success, it is a desire to seem superior to the benevolence of fate."[29] The basic passions in La Rochefoucauld (vanity, self-esteem, pride, and self-interest), although they remain discrete and impermeable to each other, may in different situations lead to different consequences.

The analytical tendencies of La Rochefoucauld, La Bruyère, and Pascal underwent complex and extensive development in Saint-Simon. The individual characters of the people he describes emerge in the struggle between the typological schema and its individual embodiment. They move from the schema to its particular instance, breaking free of that schema at the same time that they retain a connection to it. In some figures it is the typological principle, in others, the differentiating principle that predominates. There are in Saint-Simon two main kinds of departure from typological schemata. The first is his interest in cranks, eccentrics, and those of unusual destiny. These people too have their own sets of discrete qualities, although those qualities are "not typical."

Saint-Simon sometimes begins a characterization with an explicit reference to the character's eccentricity. Of the duchesse d'Aiguillon, for example, he says that "she was one of the most unusual people in the world, and possessed great intelligence. She was a mixture of vanity and humility" (2:415). He concludes his characterization of the famous courtesan Ninon de Lanclos as follows: "The singular eccentricity of this personage has compelled me to elaborate on her" (2:516). And he observes of the old maréchale de Clérambault, "Her eccentricities have caused my pen to flow" (7:281). Saint-Simon's portraits of cranks and eccentrics have their own literary tradition and generic typology: they are constructed on the basis of the anecdote. In the seventeenth and eighteenth centuries, the anecdote was conceived as a brief, entertaining story, such as Saint-Simon's account of the maréchal d'Estrées, who all his life bought books and valuable objects, and not only never used them but did not even unwrap them. Once the maréchal promised a substantial reward to anyone who could find him a bust of the Jupiter Ammon, something he coveted very much, although it had in fact long been lying in his own storeroom. Saint-Simon's stories of the absent-minded Brancas or of the insufferably polite duc de Coislin are in the same spirit. The latter, while accompanying a certain caller to the door, so exasperated him with his endless civilities that the visitor, upon leaving the room, locked his host inside, whereupon the duc de Coislin leaped without a thought through a window and met his guest at the door to his coach, to the latter's complete consternation.

There is, however, a more serious and interesting departure from typological schemata in the *Mémoires* than Saint-Simon's portrayal of cranks and eccentrics. This is his especially acute and penetrating analysis of figures who are contradictory and multileveled. Authorial judgment in these instances is ambivalent and variable, advancing first a dark and then a light principle in varying relations and proportions.

The younger duc d'Orléans, regent after the death of Louis XIV, is a good example of this kind of analysis. Saint-Simon was devoted to this prince from the latter's youth until his death, after which Saint-Simon was himself compelled to retire from court. Nevertheless, Saint-Simon's judgment of the duc d'Orléans is severe, without any substitution of society criteria for morally rigorist ones. And that is because the vices that Saint-Simon enumerates—lack of will, silliness, atheism, debauchery, indifference to rank, and a predilection for low company—have in his opinion irreparably damaged the political interests of the regent's own party (to which Saint-Simon himself belonged). Yet the duc d'Orléans, with his wide-ranging mind, his talents, education, courage, and magnanimity, is by no means a negative character. Saint-Simon likes him, and his analysis of his conduct is, so to speak, defensive in nature.

The duc d'Orléans is a libertine. But Saint-Simon is not content merely to identify that quality; he explains it and adduces its contributory causes. The king, from envy of his nephew's talents and military valor, kept the latter away from the army and in enforced and destructive idleness. As if that were not enough, he also forced him into a disgraceful marriage with his illegitimate daughter. The prince agreed to this detestable marriage in the hope that it would lead to a place at court and to glory. That hope was deceived. He then abandoned himself to the most scandalous and flagrant debauchery in order to make his position less ridiculous, since, as the faithful husband of a woman thrust upon him by the king, he would have looked like a fool. That dissipation became habitual with him, and the mask of the libertine therefore so customary, that he never again succeeded in discarding it. For Saint-Simon, with his whole gallery of hypocrites, the image of the regent is thus an unusual solution to the problem of "being" versus "seeming."[30] Philippe d'Orléans is in fact the antithesis of the hypocrite; he is actually better than he appears to be.

The image of the renowned Fénelon, the tutor of the duc de Bourgogne and the author of *Télémaque*, is an even more complex and ambiguous solution to the same problem. Saint-Simon's attitude toward Fénelon, whom he barely knew personally, is one of concealed and extremely guarded antagonism. The prelate's physiognomy is magnificent: "I never saw anything like it, and it was impossible to forget, even if seen only once. It was all of a piece, and its contrasts did not conflict with each other. It had gravity and gallantry, seriousness and gaiety, and it expressed equally the doctor of the church, the bishop, and the nobleman" (4:606). Here the usual discrete qualities and typological models used by Saint-Simon (church doctor, bishop, nobleman) are deliberately multidimensional and contrastive, and arranged in such a way that from their convergence a new entity is derived, one that is complex and not reducible to a single formula. Saint-Simon speaks with respect of the virtue and "Christian humility" evinced by Fénelon after his fall from the king's favor and his forced retirement to his own archdiocese of Cambray. Yet in everything that is said of him there are glimpses of a different Fénelon, the man of great political prospects. Saint-Simon observes in connection with Fénelon's earlier elevation to the archbishopric that "he had refrained from seeking Cambray: the smallest spark of ambition would have destroyed the whole edifice he was constructing, especially since it was not Cambray that he desired" (1:259). This last sentence is a hint that Fénelon and his circle wanted him to be appointed archbishop of Paris.

Does this mean that Fénelon must take his place with those ambition-concealing hypocrites who are so numerous in Saint-Simon? No, his case is more complex and subtle than that. A life constructed in such a way that it may be utterly destroyed by a single flaring spark of ambition is based not on hypocrisy but on a carefully worked-out and committed attitude that is capable of coexisting both with genuine virtue and with a hidden desire for power.

The regent and Fénelon are men of great talent and complex spiritual constitution. A special and in its own way curious departure from typology is the analytic depiction of the individual character of the nonentity. I have in mind the portrait of the king's son, Monseigneur, or the so-called Grand Dauphin. In the play of court forces, Monseigneur belongs to a party that is hostile to Saint-Simon. Yet this heir to the most magnificent of thrones is virtually an idiot, and Saint-Simon therefore takes a kindly view of him, or rather he regards him with an investigatory interest that impels him to a "moral dissection" of the dauphin's character. "Of character [*caractère*], he had none." From this initial negative formula issues the whole subsequent and very precise logic of nonexistent character that follows, the logic of the character of someone who lived and died "sunk in fat and intellectual obscurantism."

The Grand Dauphin "was haughty and dignified in nature and appearance and from imitation of the king; he was inordinately stubborn, and his whole life a tissue of organized triviality; he was gentle from laziness and a sort of stupidity, but callous at heart, although with an appearance of kindliness that extended merely to his subalterns and valets and that was manifest only in the basest things; his conduct with such people was extraordinarily familiar, while he remained indifferent to the miseries and sorrows of others, although that was perhaps more from carelessness and imitation [of the king] than from innate wickedness" (3:827–828).

The individual character of the nonentity is rich in detail and fully elaborated; it consists entirely of form and is devoid of any substance whatever: callousness and an outward gentleness that are the consequences of dullness and indolence, and instead of amorous adventures, promiscuous and base liaisons. A strict upbringing and nervousness in the presence of his father have developed a timidity in the prince that verges on cowardice. On horseback, that cowardice is offset by his splendid appearance, but the dauphin has a large, stout body on legs that are too short and thin, so that he walks with a certain instability: "He always moved carefully when walking, placing his feet in two separate movements" (3:827). This feature is at once symbolic and physically observed; it belongs to the "not made-up," or to what Herzen called the "accidental."

Serving as a counterweight to the heir apparent's more pathetic qualities are his vanity, his petty concern with receiving his due, and his attraction to luxury—in spite of great stinginess, so characteristic of those governed by fear. He "himself wrote down everything that was spent on his behalf; he knew what the least little thing cost him, although he spent lavishly on buildings, furniture, and jewels of every kind, . . . and on hounds for wolf hunting, as soon as he had persuaded himself that he enjoyed it" (3:828). Monseigneur is a conceited fool, a figure fully consistent with classical typology. Yet even though Saint-Simon retains the typological schema, he renders it individual by adding concrete details to the portrait's standard hyperbole. The qualities that Saint-Simon ascribes to his one-dimensional characters have a linear arrangement that is gradually compressed. Multidimensional and contradictory qualities, however, require a different principle of organization. Certain initial, key elements are needed to draw the others together and set them in motion. The shell devoid of substance serves as the initial organizing formula for the individual character of the insignificant dauphin. What takes ridiculous and vulgarized form in the character of the insignificant son, however, is repeated on a higher level in the image of his father, the "Sun King," Louis *le Grand*.

The figure of Louis XIV has a special significance in the *Mémoires*. No single character is given so much attention or so much space. Following the detailed account of his last illness and his death is an extended critical examination of his reign and character.[31] Yet Louis is in fact one of the prime movers of the *Mémoires* as a whole, one of those who sets in motion its whole world of passions, desires, and interests. Because of his historical function as the embodiment of the leveling policies of bureaucratic absolutism, the king was profoundly hostile to Saint-Simon, who, for his part, neither liked the king nor enjoyed his favor, although he was impressed by him—so impressed, in fact, that he was compelled to avoid one-dimensional solutions to the problem of his characterization. The individual character of Louis XIV is thus one of Saint-Simon's most complex analytical constructions.

Is the king, however, an appropriate subject for social typology? By virtue of his position, he is of course unique. Yet at the same time he possesses the very same traditional and typical qualities that La Bruyère ascribes to the "powerful of this world"—to the nobility (*les grands*). As observers, La Bruyère and Saint-Simon occupy very different positions. La Bruyère judges the nobility from below, from a bourgeois standpoint, whereas Saint-Simon regards himself as standing at the very apex of the social pyramid. For him, only the king stands higher, and the characteristics of the king are the classic attributes of the "powerful of this world": egoism, ingratitude, callousness, ambition, despotism, and a love of flattery.

In the present instance the possessor of these qualities is an absolute monarch, and as a result both these qualities and others like them are enormously exaggerated, so that the customary self-glorification of the nobleman is transformed in Louis' case into self-deification and a demand for adoration from those around him. "If he had had no fear of the devil, which God preserved in him even in times of the greatest licentiousness, he would have made others worship him and would even have found worshipers; the monuments erected to him are evidence of this, . . . [as is] the statue in the Place des Victoires and the pagan ceremony at its unveiling . . . , in which he took such exquisite pleasure" (4:957–958). Louis' initial typological formula consists of the typical attributes of the aristocrat carried to their extreme, even to the point of absurdity. Later on the king is simultaneously regarded in terms of several other typological perspectives: the personal (moral-psychological), the practical (state), and the society. Each of these categories has its own characteristic attributes. On the moral-psychological plane, Saint-Simon's Louis is an average man (or, for a king, even "below average"), who is endowed with perceptiveness, common sense, and good moral instincts, but who has been spoiled, first by a bad upbringing and then by universal flattery and servility. Saint-Simon also applies to Louis the conventional formula of the *honnête homme*. The king is a "decent man" who prides himself on the fact that he keeps in the strictest confidence private secrets that have been entrusted to him.

The king's practical qualities are also entirely in keeping with the type of the average decent man. Although Saint-Simon does not hold Louis' intellect in very high regard, even emphasizing his complete ignorance, he does grant him industriousness, scrupulousness, and conscientious concern for what he himself took to be his responsibilities. Without such qualities, the king would not in fact have been able to create and maintain his system of government.

Saint-Simon's typological formulas and the qualities associated with them are, as always, discrete, but he is able to juxtapose them skillfully in a single character. Thus in the portrait of Louis XIV a new psychological effect is produced through a conflict between the formula of the average person of moderate practical abilities and that of the self-deifying seeker of glory. It is this conflict that is the basis of the king's hostility to everything superior, whether intellect, education, the independence of the hereditary aristocracy, or military valor and talent. "He wanted only such greatness as emanated from himself" (4:954). Such is the logic of his individual character.

Yet the king is not only an *honnête homme*; he is also an *homme galant*. In this typological aspect—the society one—he possesses all the qualities of the ideal seventeenth-century man of society: sensuality, a love of pleasure, courtesy, and exquisite manners with women. "One might say that he was created for [that greatness], . . . and his stature, carriage, elegance, beauty, and the imposing demeanor that later replaced that beauty, indeed everything, from the timbre of his voice and his gracefulness, to the inborn and stately elegance of his whole bearing, distinguished him from the rest like a king bee until the day of his death" (4:942).

This gift of "semiotic behavior" is the only one that Saint-Simon is willing to grant the king without reservation: "No prince had so perfect a command of the art of ruling as he did" (4:981). As Saint-Simon conceives him, it is indeed this that is the true essence of the king, the dominant feature of his character that organizes all the other elements.

When Saint-Simon speaks of the "art of ruling," however, he means neither strength of will nor wisdom in matters of state, but merely extraordinary virtuosity in the precise manipulation of the symbolic trappings of absolute power—virtuosity in a formal skill, that is. It is this mechanistic and formalistic bent that is the real key to Saint-Simon's Louis XIV. Louis' existence was "a succession of days and hours so arranged that it was sufficient to know the day and the hour in order to know what the king was doing, wherever he happened to be. . . . This precision contributed extraordinarily to the brilliance of his court and to the convenience of his courtiers."

But of course the mechanism set in motion by the king was hardly intended merely for the convenience of his entourage: "During the times

of his most ardent love for his mistresses, no indisposition, if it occurred
during a journey or a formal court occasion, . . . excused them from the
observance of etiquette. . . . Whether they were pregnant, ill, had given
birth less than six weeks before, or were otherwise afflicted, they were
expected to ride out in formal apparel, to dress up, to gird their waists, to
set off for Flanders or even farther, to dance, to stay awake, to take part
in feasts, to eat, to be gay and sociable, . . . to seem content, to brave the
heat, cold, open air, and dust, and to do all this at strictly appointed
hours, without disrupting anything by even a minute" (4:1046). This
same discipline was extended to the king's daughters and to the wives of
his son and grandsons. Even Madame de Maintenon, in the words of
Saint-Simon, "had more than once to go to Marly in the sort of condition
that would have excused even a servant girl from getting out of bed"
(4:1048). The king's excessive egoism, a basic quality of the "great of this
world," is combined here with his sense of etiquette. The Versailles machine must work unceasingly, for without it the "art of governing" cannot exist. Even the deaths of the king's relatives—of his son or his beloved
brother—interrupt its operation for only a moment and then are forgotten
as quickly as possible.[32] The creator of this mechanism is no less subject
to its exacting demands—his own death is just as circumscribed by etiquette as the rest. Louis XIV dies in accordance with all the rules of Catholic and courtly ritual—dies, that is, just as he believed a king should die.

Saint-Simon, however, depicts Louis' formalism as a tragedy—as the
tragedy of France, which the "Sun King" left oppressed, ravaged, and
exhausted by pointless wars, by the criminal extravagance of his court, by
heavy taxation, and by savage reprisals against the Huguenots. Saint-
Simon speaks of all this from the viewpoint of his own caste, but with
extraordinary denunciatory power nonetheless.

The fact is that the king's brilliant formalism is devoid of content.
Saint-Simon examines the various aspects of the king's character and actions one after another, each time revealing a fatal inconsistency between
form and content. This inconsistency is in every case a logical consequence of the initial structural opposition between the man of average
abilities and the self-deifying despot. "His mind, by nature inclined to
trifles, yielded to every sort of detail. . . . He effectively ruled in small
things, but he failed to do so in large ones. . . . His ministers, generals,
mistresses, and courtiers very soon noticed after he became ruler that
vanity was much stronger in him than a true love of glory" (4:952, 942,
951). Saint-Simon even denies Louis bravery, the nobleman's basic, elemental quality. Henri IV was fond of battles; his grandson likes parades.
The king's religious sentiments are also open to doubt. "The king became
devout, but with a devoutness extreme in its ignorance" (4:1027). In his
political views, Louis is controlled by the Jesuits. They enticed the king

"with the temptation of easy penance at the expense of others, which they assured him would gain him happiness in the next world" (4:1027). "Penance at the expense of others" refers to Louis' brutal persecution of the Huguenots, which Saint-Simon speaks of with loathing.

"Being" versus "seeming" was a basic moral-psychological problem for the seventeenth century. The playwrights, satirists, and moralists of the age devoted many great pages to the portrayal of hypocrites. Hypocrisy concealing baseness or villainy is also a persistent motif for Saint-Simon, yet the contradiction between "being" and "seeming" is resolved in the image of Louis XIV in a more subtle fashion. Louis is not a hypocrite (he is after all an *honnête homme*) but someone who always seems to himself to be other than "what he actually is."

A whole series of such self-delusions passes before the reader. It seems to the king that he is the most absolute of monarchs, although he in fact rules only in trifles and is himself ruled by cunning ministers who operate behind a mask of servility. The idea has been instilled in Louis that he is a great commander, although he is in fact only a "king of parades" (as his enemies dubbed him). Instead of valor, there is vanity; instead of piety, the formal implementation of the precepts of his Jesuit confessors; and instead of human feeling, tears that cost him nothing. "Nothing was easier," says Saint-Simon, "than to make the king weep, and nothing more difficult than to touch him in earnest." Even the king's courageous death is imbued with that same formalism. Saint-Simon summarizes all that burdened that "sinful soul at the moment when it was ready to stand before God, and weighed down moreover with the fifty-six years of its reign, a reign in consequence of whose arrogance, extravagance, building projects, prodigality of every kind, interminable warfare, and the vanity that engendered them, so much blood was spilled and so many billions squandered . . . , so many conflagrations started all over Europe, and all the procedures, regulations, and laws of the State so confounded and undermined, that the kingdom was reduced to irreversible poverty, almost to the verge of ruin, from which it was rescued only by the intercession of the Almighty" (4:1072). Saint-Simon is dismayed by the certainty with which "so sinful a soul" prepares to pass on to the next world. There is, however, an explanation for this too: "Penance made at the expense of others, at the expense of the Huguenots, the Jansenists, and the Jesuits' enemies and those not devoted to them . . . , and a pharisaical attachment to the letter of the law and the trappings of religion gave the king an astonishing tranquillity in those terrible moments when even that tranquility founded on a clear conscience and genuine repentance is usually in jeopardy" (4:1076). The letter of the law, the trappings of religion—appearance and form celebrate their victory over the essence of things even in the king's final hour.

Just as the king's formalism is reflected in the crooked mirror of the individual character of his insignificant son and heir apparent, so the structure of his own character finds a kind of reflection in the image of his morganatic wife, Madame de Maintenon, a woman who had a decisive effect on the last three decades of his reign.

In Saint-Simon's interpretation of her (very biased, to be sure), Maintenon, the patroness of the wicked duc du Maine, is herself a villainess, someone who is capable of murder or any other crime. One would therefore expect her to be portrayed in one-dimensional terms, like the duc du Maine himself, or the duc de Noailles. The image of Madame de Maintenon, however, is in fact another of Saint-Simon's most complicated and interesting constructions. Everything in her image receives a negative valuation, yet her depravity is complex, deriving from several interrelated typological formulas. These formulas emerge as it were in Saint-Simon's rather detailed account of Maintenon's biography. It is a biography that is confused and obscure and replete with questionable adventures and humiliating circumstances.

In Saint-Simon's portrayal of her, Madame de Maintenon belongs by nature to the category of the predatory intriguer, although she is someone who has passed through a series of transformations: the dependent of aristocratic households, the brilliant conversationalist of midcentury salons at a time when the "affected creatures" (les précieuses) immortalized by Molière held sway, the heroine of numerous gallant adventures, the governess of the children of the king and of the marquise de Montespan, and all this before becoming the lawful, though not officially proclaimed, wife of Louis XIV. This checkered career is, in Saint-Simon's image of Maintenon, parceled out among separate strata, so that by the time of her ascendancy she has accumulated the qualities of the dependent ("flattery, complaisance, and a constant seeking to please"), the affectation and prudishness of the précieuse, the pedantry of the "learned lady" of the salons of her youth, and even the frivolousness and fickleness of the heroine of gallant adventures. The different sets of qualities associated with the ambitious harpy, the dependent, the précieuse, and the libertine enter into startling combinations that are justified through analysis of the personal destiny that has brought them into being, and that are drawn together in her dominant, key characteristic, her sanctimoniousness. "Her best time, since she was three or four years older than the king, had been that of elegant conversation and elegant civilities. . . . Affectation and stiltedness, in combination with the spirit of the age, of which they were somewhat characteristic, were later laid over with a veneer of self-importance, and then augmented by the sanctimoniousness that became her dominant characteristic, and that, it seemed, absorbed everything else; that sanctimoniousness was essential to her for retaining the place to which she had been elevated, and no less essential to her for ruling. It became the very essence of her nature" (4:1023). If the purpose of Madame de Maintenon's life as Saint-Simon sees it was to acquire power, then sanctimoniousness was its all-pervading method.

Saint-Simon's Louis XIV is not a hypocrite but a man of vast self-deception. Nevertheless, in addition to his formal existence, another life shows through, one that is just as formal and that is governed by conscious hypocrisy. The life of Madame de Maintenon in her private chambers, in the disposition of her daily existence (described in detail in the *Mémoires*), is also a ceaselessly functioning machine. As one knowledgeable in such matters, the king could not fail to appreciate her industry and meticulousness, her highly developed sense of form, and the regularity of her habits.[33]

Everything in Madame de Maintenon's world is false, including her religious sentiments and her feelings for the king, everything, beginning with the initial falseness of her position as provisional queen. "In the inner life of the court, she was queen, . . . but outside it she was a very simple private lady of the court, and always occupied the last place" (4:1039). The life of Madame de Maintenon is an empty simulacrum of the empty life of the king. In depicting the character of Maintenon, Saint-Simon duplicates with amazing art the psychological structure of the king's own character(or rather he provides a third version of it, the character of the Grand Dauphin being the second). At the same time, however, the social and personal differentiations are kept very clear, as is usually the case with Saint-Simon. Madame de Maintenon, with her flexibility, adaptability, and pettiness, is a woman who has raised herself to unheard-of heights from poverty, a disorderly life, and humiliation.

Documentary literature, including the memoiristic variety, does not simply transplant already existing individual character from life; it constructs it, just as any other form of literature does. Combining sets of qualities (the practical, the societal, and the moral) that had been worked out by the rationalist view of the human being, Saint-Simon created his images in the political and aesthetic forms provided by his age.

It was impossible for him to escape either the psychological ideas of his century (the individual conceived as the sum of mechanistically understood qualities) or its literary usages (the conventional typology of classicism), but it was possible to subordinate both to a special documentary task. The unique and inimitable found expression in Saint-Simon in his unexpected conjoining of discrete qualities, in his bold crossing of typological formulas with empirical reality. There are great works that are long denied their true historical place, only to find it many years later when they suddenly reveal their relevance and their connection to underlying trends in the literary process. So it was with Saint-Simon's *Mémoires* in the second half of the nineteenth century, more than a hundred years after their creation. Their relevance has increased in the twentieth century. It is no accident that Saint-Simon has most often been compared to Balzac and Proust.

Part Two

ROUSSEAU'S *CONFESSIONS* AND
THE MODIFICATIONS OF PERSONALITY

THE CHRONOLOGICAL gap between Saint-Simon's *Mémoires* and the writings of Rousseau is actually not very great. It has been established that Saint-Simon wrote the *Mémoires* for the most part in the 1740s (finishing them at the end of the decade). Rousseau's creative activity was already flourishing by the 1750s, and he began work on the *Confessions* in 1765. The fundamental differences between the two figures are therefore that much more striking. Saint-Simon still rests on the culture of the eighteenth century; Rousseau anticipates the future. Saint-Simon is still mechanistic; he still operates on the basis of discrete human qualities (albeit in combinations of remarkable boldness), whereas it was in fact Rousseau who was able to reveal simultaneously both the fluidity of consciousness and the absolute unity of personality [*lichnost'*].

There is an immense quantity of literature devoted to Rousseau's role as the founder of the culture of the new age in all its multiform and contradictory manifestations—revolutionary ideology, the democratic idea of equality, utopian socialism, romantic irrationalism and individualism, the doctrine of the natural man, the cult of feeling and nature, and the pedagogical ideas of the nineteenth century. And Rousseau brought this whole multifaceted complex of new orientations in the spheres of politics, social thought, morality, psychology, and aesthetics into existence in the process of creating his model of the new man. This was someone of the third estate whose mind was free of the stereotypes of the old society, an intellectual commoner who proclaimed his own uniqueness. Properly speaking, it was Rousseau's entire oeuvre that served to elaborate his image of the new man, but it was in the *Confessions* that that image reached its fullest development. Sentimentalism and romanticism found their inspirations in *Émile* and *La Nouvelle Héloïse*. For nineteenth-century psychologism, it was the *Confessions* that proved the much more important and seminal work. Indeed, it retains its relevance and poignancy even today.

Like Saint-Simon, Rousseau has often been "exposed" in deliberate and inadvertent departures from the truth, beginning with mistakes in chronology and ending with errors in the interpretation of personalities, actions, and relationships. J. Guéhenno's two-volume study is expressly devoted to a comparison of the *Confessions* with Rousseau's correspondence and the other materials pertaining to his biography.[1] Guéhenno's work has interest as a practical commentary on the *Confessions*, but it fails to give a fundamentally new view of their creative history. The fact is that Rousseau himself anticipated all later observations about his errors and inaccuracies, especially in regard to the role of imagination and invention in the process of the book's creation. Beginning part 2 of the *Confessions*, he wrote:

> My first part has been entirely written from memory, and I must have made many mistakes in it. Being compelled to write the second part from memory also, I shall now probably make still more. . . .
>
> . . . I have only one faithful guide on which I can count; the succession of feelings which have marked the development of my being, and thereby recall the events that have acted upon it as cause or effect. . . . I may omit or transpose facts, or make mistakes in dates; but I cannot go wrong about what I have felt, or about what my feelings have made me do; and these are the chief subjects of my story. . . . It is the history of my soul that I have promised to recount, and to write it faithfully I have need of no other memories; it is enough if I enter again into my inner self, as I have done till now.[2]

Rousseau formulates the orientations of the *Confessions* with complete clarity here, at the same time sketching the movement from internal states to their external stimuli—from feelings to events. By studying the impulses of the soul, he reconstructs, on the basis of their psychological consequences, the factual circumstances that gave rise to them. And he realizes that such a reconstruction can be only approximate. The *Confessions* were intended to solve specific problems; whatever proved irrelevant was discarded.

Rousseau was concerned to the highest degree with the problem of memory. In this, as in much else, he is a true precursor of the writers of the twentieth century, especially of Proust. For Rousseau, the question of memory was one of the relationship of recollection to experienced reality and, at the same time, to invention and imagination. Rousseau conceived of these relationships as a very complex kind of interaction:

> I have studied men, and I think I am a fairly good observer. But all the same I do not know how to see what is before my eyes; I can only see clearly in retrospect, it is only in my memories that my mind can work [a key theme for Proust]. I have neither feeling nor understanding for anything that is said or done or that happens before my eyes. All that strikes me is the external manifestation. But afterwards it all comes back to me, I remember the place and the time, the tone of voice and look, the gesture and situation; nothing

escapes me. Then from what a man has done or said I can read his thoughts, and I am rarely mistaken. (114–115; 114)

Thus in the one instance Rousseau asserts that on the basis of their indelible traces he has reconstructed the events that gave rise to his feelings and inner experiences, and in the other he asserts the converse: the internal process has been reestablished by means of external manifestations and actions. This contradiction may be resolved if one conceives of remembering as a creative process—one that cannot, for the artist at any rate, be anything else.

In the now famous first lines of the *Confessions*, Rousseau himself announced in unique fashion the central image on which his creative memory was to be focused: "I have resolved on an enterprise which has no precedent, and which, once complete, will have no imitator. My purpose is to display to my kind a portrait in every way true to nature, and the man I shall portray is myself. Simply myself. I know my own heart and understand my fellow man. But I am unlike anyone I have ever met; I will even venture to say that I am like no one in the whole world. I may be no better, but at least I am different. Whether Nature did well or ill in breaking the mold in which she formed me, is a question which can only be resolved after the reading of my book" (5; 17).

For Rousseau, who stood at the threshold of both individualism and a new, revolutionary civic spirit, this sense of his own uniqueness was essential. Uniqueness sanctioned the audacity of his psychological revelations, the replacement of typological schemata with personality. But the great significance of the *Confessions*, of course, is not that they depicted someone who was "not like anyone else," but that they provided mankind with a majestic new generalization of the laws of spiritual life by which people have been measuring themselves for two centuries.

A tradition of self-knowledge had, to be sure, existed since the writers of antiquity. Montaigne, whom Rousseau jealously refers to more than once as his predecessor, wrote in the *Essais* that "to follow a movement so wandering as that of our mind, to penetrate the opaque depths of its innermost folds, to pick out and immobilize the innumerable flutterings that agitate it," is no easy matter. "It is many years now that I have had only myself as object of my thoughts, that I have been examining and studying only myself; and if I study anything else, it is in order promptly to apply it to myself, or rather within myself."[3] Even so, Rousseau did have the right, Montaigne notwithstanding, to declare that he had undertaken "an enterprise that has no precedent." The great psychological discoveries of Montaigne were still arrayed in the rather archaic form of allusions to ancient sources and of historical exempla and "anecdotes." But more to the point is the fact that Montaigne was deliberately fragmentary, and not merely in the form of his *Essais* but also in the very essence of his approach to the human being, whom he studied in diverse aspects and diverse relations to the surrounding world.

"In modeling this figure upon myself, I have had to fashion and compose myself so often to bring myself out, that the model itself has to some extent grown firm and taken shape. Painting myself for others, I have painted my inward self with colors clearer than my original ones. I have no more made my book than my book has made me" (647–648; 504). In the course of this self-modeling, this self-rendering in "clearer colors," Montaigne persistently measured himself against the models of the savant who held the vanity of the Epicurean in contempt, and of the man of "ordinary" common sense who was earthy and physical "from head to toe." Yet for all the boldness and innovation of the issues addressed by Montaigne, he still largely employed the legacy of antiquity for his models, thereby aligning himself with a hallowed philosophical and literary tradition. Rousseau, by contrast, insisted that nature had "broken the mold" in which he was formed.

If Montaigne does employ traditional schemata, he nevertheless shades them in with information that is frequently of the most homespun and empirically concrete variety. In the chapter called "De l'experience," he complains that over the years he has become a creature of habit: "I would feel as uncomfortable without my gloves as without my shirt, or without washing when I leave the table or get up in the morning, or without canopy and curtains for my bed. . . . I could dine without a tablecloth; but very uncomfortably without a clean napkin, German fashion; I soil napkins more than they or the Italians do, and make little use of spoon or fork" (1062; 830). This is the Renaissance appetite for observation, the Renaissance curiosity about any human manifestation, even the most personal and corporeal.

There is in addition to this another kind of observation in Montaigne, one that moves in the opposite direction toward the universal laws of spiritual experience. Transitions from the description of personal sensation and feeling to the establishment of their general principles, and vice versa, are thus very characteristic of him. Take, for example, the chapter entitled "Nous ne goustons rien de pur," where the argument concerns the consanguineous relationship between "pleasures . . . and discomfort" (655; 510), or the famous description of the fall from a horse that left Montaigne close to death: "It seemed to me that my life was hanging only by the tip of my lips; I closed my eyes in order, it seemed to me, to help push it out, and took pleasure in growing languid and letting myself go." While still in a semiconscious state, Montaigne considered ordering that a horse be given to his wife, who was having difficulty reaching him:

It would seem that this consideration must have proceeded from a wide-awake soul; yet the fact is that I was not there at all. These were idle thoughts, in the clouds, set in motion by the sensations of the eyes and ears; they did not come from within me. I did not know, for all that, where I was coming from or where I was going, nor could I weigh and consider what I was asked. These are slight effects which the senses produce of themselves, as if by habit; what the soul contributed was in a dream, touched very lightly, and merely licked and sprinkled, as it were, by the soft impression of the senses.

. . . For in truth, in order to get used to the idea of death, I find there is nothing like coming close to it. Now, as Pliny says, each man is a good education to himself, provided he has the capacity to spy on himself from close up. (354, 356–357; 269, 271–272)

Thus a universal principle is revealed in a personal experience.

Montaigne's departures from the personally experienced vary in degree, sometimes even reaching the point where the author disappears in reflections on the most diverse themes and in the depiction of actual phenomena of the most varied kind—disappears and yet remains continually present, thanks to his vividly expressed attitude toward whatever he is depicting.

Montaigne's method is illustrative. His judgments are accompanied by examples—historical, literary, or drawn from everyday life. He is illustrative and deliberately fragmentary. He continually alters the scope and angle of vision. Different points of view reveal different objects of knowledge to him: empirical details, general laws of behavior, material drawn from the historical tradition, or facts of contemporary life. Rousseau discovered something else—the absolute unity of personality, the continuous operation of an integrated spiritual mechanism that is consistent both in its development and in its explained contradictions. The appropriate form for that discovery was not reflections, fragments, or aphorisms, but a coherent narrative of purposefully linked events.

Rousseau's conception of the human being was based on the premises of contemporary philosophy, in particular on Lockean sensationalism as it was apprehended and elaborated by the Encyclopédistes. In book 9 of the *Confessions*, Rousseau speaks of his intention to write a work called the *Morale sensitive, ou le matérialisme du sage*,[4] the basic idea of which was as follows:

It has been observed that the majority of men are often in the course of their lives quite unlike themselves; they seem to be changed into quite different people. . . .

Looking within myself and seeking in others for the cause upon which these different states of being depended, I discovered that they had a great deal to do with our previous impressions from external objects, and that, being continually modified through the agency of our senses and our organs, we were unconsciously affected in our thoughts, our feelings, and even our actions by the impact of these slight modifications upon us. Numerous striking examples that I had collected . . . , thanks to their physical basis . . . seemed to me capable of providing an external code which, varied according to circumstances, could put or keep the spirit in the state most conducive to virtue. . . . Climates, seasons, sounds, colors, darkness, light, the elements, food, noise, silence, movement, repose: they all act on our machines, and consequently upon our souls, and they all offer us innumerable and almost certain opportunities for controlling those feelings which we allow to dominate us at their very onset. (408–409; 380–381)

This conception is characteristic of eighteenth-century sensationalism and has affinities with the teachings of both Helvétius and Diderot. Rousseau, however, never wrote his treatise on psychology, and he never worked out the regimen that he had planned for maintaining virtue. He did something else. As a great artist, he applied his conception to the understanding of a concrete personality, emphasizing the transformations or "modifications" [*modifications*] of its spiritual states under the pressure of ceaselessly changing impressions. Thus, in speaking of his removal to the Hermitage, he observes, "Before I record the effect of this unprecedented state of things upon my heart I must recapitulate and tell once more of my secret desires, so that the effect of my new change of circumstances may be traced to its source" (413; 384–385).

The sensationalist doctrine of Helvétius stressed the homogeneity of human sense impressions, arguing that it was that homogeneity that in fact made social relations possible in the first place: "People . . . apprehend the same relationships among objects"; otherwise, "they would not be able to communicate their knowledge, or perfect their reason, or work together on the vast edifice of art and science."[5]

Rousseau did not deny the universality of sense experience, but as a practical psychologist he sought a dynamic in sensationalism. He found "modification," impulse, and the variable functions of external sense impressions, and he not only saw contradictions; he also explained them— by introducing cause and effect. In Rousseau, qualitatively different psychological phenomena intersect, and one phenomenon frequently imparts its features to another. Thus he shows how moral attributes may emerge from physical influences and, conversely, how emotional and other spiritual states may affect physiology. He also shows how analogous events may, depending on the circumstances, have different or even diametrically opposed psychological consequences. "When I trace my nature back in this way to its earliest manifestations, I find features which may appear incompatible, but which have nevertheless combined to form a strong, simple, and uniform whole. I find other features, however, which though similar in appearance, have formed by a concatenation of circumstances combinations so different that one could never suppose them to be in any way related to one another" (18; 28).

Discrete qualities and closed-off feelings have been replaced here by continuous modification and transformation and their transitional states. The power of situation, which alters the effects of external stimuli and of internal reactions to them, has been discovered. Good and evil have ceased to be precisely defined polar opposites, even when they are present in a single individual. The transitions between good and evil are so subtle that the individual himself often does not know which of them has led him to a certain action—"a good lesson for honest souls," Rousseau observes, "whom vice never attacks openly, but whom it finds [the] means of surprising by hiding itself always beneath the mask of some sophistry, and sometimes beneath that of some virtue" (442; 411–412). This statement occurs in a discussion of the ethical rationalizations employed by the conscious mind to conceal its unconscious desires. Rousseau investigates the particular mechanism of this "moral sophistry" in connection with the account of his conversion to Catholicism, at the same time looking at the mechanism by which associations come to dominate the feeble will.

Driven to despair by the cruel treatment of the engraver to whom he had been apprenticed, the sixteen-year-old Rousseau fled Protestant Geneva for Catholic Savoy, where he at once fell into the hands of clerics engaged in the conversion of heretics. The young Rousseau resolved to accept their ministrations, seeing in a change of religion the only means of securing his future existence. But once in the asylum for catechumens, he was overcome by doubts and regrets; he had been brought up to despise Catholic priests. "This point of view was so strong in my case that in my childhood I had never peeped inside a Catholic church, never met a priest in his vestments, and never heard a processional bell, without a shiver of terror and alarm. . . . These impressions contrasted strangely, it is true, with memories of the kindness with which priests all around Geneva spontaneously treated the children of the city. Whereas the viaticum bell struck me with fear, the bells for mass and vespers reminded me of a breakfast with good fare, fresh butter, fruit, and milk" (63; 67–68).

Despite these associations, which accustomed Rousseau to consider "popery only in relation to feasting and good cheer," he was still determined to make his escape from the asylum. But the idea

could not prevail. There were too many secret desires working against it. What is more, there was my stubborn resolve not to go back to Geneva; the

shame, and the difficulty too, of returning across the mountains; the embarrassment of being poor and friendless in a strange land; all these combined
to make me feel that my scruples of conscience were but repentance too late.
I affected to reproach myself for what I had done in order to excuse what I
was going to do. By exaggerating my past sins, I accepted the future as their
inevitable consequence. I did not say to myself: "Nothing is done yet. You
can retain your innocence if you wish." What I did say was, "Sigh for the
crime of which you have incurred the guilt, and which you cannot help carrying out now." . . .

The sophistry that undid me is common to the majority of men, who
deplore their lack of strength when it is already too late to make use of it.
(63–64; 68–69)

Rousseau carefully scrutinizes the "secret desires," the repressed and confused egoistic longings and self-interest that are obscure even to the person himself, at the moment when the conscious mind refashions and conceals them behind a mask of moral sophistry. Rousseau comes close here
to the psychological conceptions of the second half of the nineteenth century and the beginning of the twentieth (by means, obviously, of unsys-
tematic conjecture). The fluidity of consciousness instead of stable qualities, the complex interplay of external stimuli and internal reactions, the
dynamics of association (the sounds of the viaticum bell and the bell for
mass or vespers in the above passage, for example)—Rousseau was already acquainted with these. And he was already acquainted with the
unconscious as well (though Leibniz had spoken of it too). In *Les Rêveries
du promeneur solitaire*, Rousseau recounts how, in order to avoid a beg-
gar boy who had been annoying him, he "unconsciously acquired the
habit of making a detour as often as possible, whenever I approached that
crossing. . . . That observation brought successively to mind numerous
other [habits] which confirmed that the true and primary motives of most
of my actions were not as clear to me as I had long imagined."[6]

Psychologists regularly allude to Rousseau's descriptions of childhood
traumas and complexes. And Rousseau really is close to modern psychoanalysis in his conception of "displacement." His father made an attempt
to track down the boy after he had fled Geneva for Savoy. Rousseau mentions his father's irreproachable honesty and the fact that the latter, because he was growing old, very much needed the revenue from the small
estate that had been left to Jean-Jacques by his mother. "That, I think, is
the reason why, having traced me as far as Annecy, he did not pursue me
to Chambéry, where he was morally certain to catch up with me. . . . This
behavior of a father of whose goodness and affection I am convinced, has
caused me to reflect on my own conduct; and my reflections have had no
small share in preserving the integrity of my conduct. They have taught

me one great maxim of morality . . . , to avoid situations which place our duties in opposition to our interests" (55–56; 61–62).

The dialectic of spiritual life, the fluidity of its psychic elements, the correlation of the conscious and the unconscious—whatever Rousseau's insight into these matters, he was of course still unable to put them on a scientific basis or to draw them together in a unified system. But with regard to psychology realized by *literary* means, his discoveries were truly momentous. In comparison with the spiritual dialectics of the *Confessions*, the psychological notions not only of sentimentalism but also of romanticism seem naive. And even the realistic novel was at first unable to cope with the tasks set forth in the *Confessions*. In essence, it was only the genius of Tolstoi that proved capable of finding solutions to those tasks and of penetrating still further into the depths of the human mind.

The author of memoirs, or indeed of any other work in the memoiristic and autobiographical genre, is always a kind of positive hero, since everything that is depicted in the work is judged from his point of view, and he necessarily retains the *right* to judge and evaluate. Obviously, there are a great many gradations here. That positive quality may be straightforward, even to the point of frank self-praise, or it may be complex, oblique, and underplayed. Nobility, if it is to be seen as the bedrock of a mind, can shine through only if it is accompanied by the admission of its own sins and errors, the very capacity for such admission then becoming a basic feature of the lofty nature.

The Montaigne of the *Essais* is essentially a positive figure of the straightforward variety: he has shortcomings, but they are the characteristic ones of the normal person. Rousseau's attitude toward this issue in the *Confessions* is much more complex. Moreover, the role of self-affirmation and self-revelation in the *Confessions* is, in contrast to the *Essais*, a crucial one, since it is what determines the work's inner structure.

The *Confessions* are the astonishing fruit of two conflicting tasks undertaken by Rousseau in the course of his work. He wanted to reveal *everything* about himself, to lay himself bare without reservation, and he wanted to disgrace his enemies, justify himself, and mount a defense against the slanders with which he was convinced the Encyclopédistes, Hume, and many others were persecuting him.

> I decided to make [the *Confessions*] a work unique and unparalleled in its truthfulness, so that for once at least the world might behold a man as he was within. I had always been amused at Montaigne's false ingenuousness, and at his pretense of confessing his faults while taking good care only to admit to likeable ones; whereas I, who believe, and have always believed, that I am on the whole the best of men, felt that there is no human heart, however pure, that does not conceal some odious vice. I knew that I was represented

in the world under features so unlike my own and at times so distorted, that
notwithstanding my faults, none of which I intended to pass over, I could not
help gaining by showing myself as I was. (516; 478–479)

Rousseau attempted in this way to reconcile the contrary tendencies of
his autobiography. All men, to one degree or another, are corrupt. He is
the best of men, and the best precisely because he dares to admit his vices,
although they are entirely different ones than those attributed to him by
his slanderers. But the equilibrium of self-affirmation and self-revelation
proved unstable. In the years he was working on the *Confessions* (1765–
1770), the atmosphere of hostility surrounding Rousseau became increasingly intense. His suspiciousness grew, eventually turning into a persecution mania. Part 2 of the *Confessions* is essentially an exercise in self-
justification, verging from time to time on personal apologetic and impas-
sioned denunciation of real and imagined enemies. Part 1 (the first six
books), on the other hand, is governed by the author's desire to speak
about himself as no one had ever done before. Rousseau's creative joy in
the solution of that artistic and moral task counterbalanced the humiliating admissions. He could therefore take pride in them and speak of them
with the fervor of a prophet.

These declarations are especially fervent in Rousseau's preface to the
first edition of the *Confessions* (which he omitted from the later versions):

> How many nothings, how many trifles shall I have to expose, into what
> details, shocking, unseemly, childish, and often ridiculous, shall I have to go
> in order to follow the thread of my hidden tendencies, in order to show how
> each impression that has left its trace on my soul first came into it? . . . I tell
> of myself the most sordid things, which I do not in the least wish to jus-
> tify. . . . I am ready for . . . the severity of public judgment. . . . But let every
> reader do as I have done, let each descend into himself . . . and in the depths
> of his own conscience say to himself, if he dare, *at least I am better than this
> man.*[7]

Rousseau actually does tell much about himself in the first books of the
Confessions that is "unseemly," humiliating, and even ridiculous—
much, in short, that even those who are ready to acknowledge their greatest vices would scrupulously conceal. He recounts how he stole, cheated,
served as a lackey, and lived at the expense of benefactors; he speaks in
detail of the psychological consequences of a bladder defect, and in even
more detail of his sexual difficulties and of experiences that would inevitably make him ridiculous in the eyes of those of his contemporaries who
lived according to the erotic code of high society. These difficult admissions had a variety of purposes. Some were prompted and made for tactical reasons, so to speak. A number of facts pertaining to Rousseau's

youth, and indeed to his past as a whole, had already been used by his enemies. He wanted to translate what had become the subject of innuendo and gossip into the language of feeling and moral inquiry, and to trace the tortuous inner path by which he had each time come to his faults and misdeeds. Besides these tactical admissions, however, there were others that Rousseau was impelled to by the need to solve the creative task he had set himself. Many sordid episodes would have been forgotten forever, had not Rousseau himself rescued them from oblivion. And it is here that we see a second Rousseau—not the paranoid tortured by suspicion, compulsively defending himself and settling accounts with his slanderers, but the genius utterly absorbed in the process of realizing an unprecedented psychological endeavor.

One of the most important problems for that endeavor was the problem of the *range of the depictable*. In order to understand the idea embodied in an autobiographical hero, it is necessary to determine the range of what has been included from his life and the extent of his inner experience of it—to determine what the writer has selected and what he has omitted, or what he is himself aware of and what he cannot, or will not, admit into his purview, and that therefore remains unrealized.

Rousseau was in essence the first to admit into consciousness the full range of human experience (Montaigne's efforts in this regard still had not been raised to the level of a systematic and thoroughgoing investigation of human personality and destiny). In this lies the great significance of the *Confessions* for the whole subsequent development of psychological literature. For Rousseau, there was theoretically nothing, not even the most trivial and "obscure" psychological detail, that could not be fully and consciously integrated into the unity of personality. But it would be naive to suppose that this comprehensiveness was *indiscriminate*. Like any other memoirist, Rousseau as a practical matter selected and omitted, pointed up or played down the facts of his life according to the programmatic conception of the formation and development of his personality that he wished to present to his readers. And it should not be forgotten that that conception was ideological. One of Rousseau's principal discoveries was that of an unprecedented new relationship between the author's creative work and his personality, a relationship in which that personality came to define the author's work, to be perceived as the source of its identity.

Rousseau's personality as it is depicted in the *Confessions* is the same one that was responsible for the *Discours* on the origin of inequality and *Du contrat social*, and for *Émile* and *La Nouvelle Héloïse*. The doctrine of the natural man's instinct for good and the pernicious effects of his encounter with the artificiality of civilization, the democratic opposing of the man of the people to a corrupt aristocracy, the primacy of feeling over reason, and Rousseau's sensationalist philosophy all found their place in the structuring of that personality. The motives for the selection and omission of what was to be included in it were therefore varied. Sometimes it is easy to understand them, and sometimes difficult. Rousseau constantly says humiliating and even shameful things about himself, at the same time concealing others that would seem easier to talk about. There is, for example, the account of his relations with Madame de Warens, one of the most important episodes of his youth. Rousseau conceals nothing of the fact that she had simultaneously been both his lover and that of her servant Claude Anet, nor that she later came to prefer a third member of her household to Rousseau. But then he immediately departs from the truth in describing his serene life with Madame de Warens at her country house *Les Charmettes*. There was no such life. Documentary evidence has shown that even though Rousseau did reside at *Les Charmettes*, he in fact did so only after the period of his intimacy with Madame de Warens was over, and that while living there he managed the estate and was almost always alone.

Rousseau needed to recall his rivals for Madame de Warens's affection for the sake of his brilliant analysis of her personality (I shall come back to this). He likewise needed to forget his true situation at *Les Charmettes* in order to portray a love idyll in all its charm—a utopia of simple love in the bosom of bucolic nature. There was, nevertheless, an authentic basis for the inner experience that is his subject here (the cultivation of feeling that transformed an uncouth adolescent into a man of refined emotions), even if that experience did in fact occur a little earlier, in other places, and under somewhat different circumstances.

These considerations may to a certain extent be applied to the *Confessions* as a whole. Guéhenno in his two massive volumes traces the narrative of the *Confessions* step by step, checking their accuracy and summarizing earlier investigations of the same kind. A number of factual errors, suppressions, distortions, and the like have been found. Yet it is remarkable that for all their detection of inaccuracy and falsehood, the documentary investigators have, in everything that pertains to the psychological atmosphere and the meaning and tenor of Rousseau's relations with others, ultimately reached essentially the same conclusions as the *Confessions* themselves. If Rousseau does not always dot his *i*'s, he does do everything possible so that the reader may dot them for him. The lofty psychological truth of his book triumphs over every possible distortion.[8]

Psychologism has from antiquity to Tolstoi been closely linked with moralism. Self-knowledge has typically been a twofold act of analysis and valuation. Rousseau is an eloquent example of this. He constructs his personality in the *Confessions* as an object both of psychological investigation and of moral judgment. The two objects explain each other. That is why Rousseau the moralist is reticent whenever he is afraid of interfering with Rousseau the psychologist.

Rousseau did not talk about everything, and he did not say everything there was to say. But what he did say was sufficient for centuries. I am clearly not pursuing biographical goals of any kind in the present work. I want to talk about the means that Rousseau used to portray himself and others in the *Confessions*, rather than about what he and they were actually like.

What then were the basic principles and means used by Rousseau to construct his autobiographical image in the *Confessions*?

There is a tendency in contemporary literary scholarship to emphasize as much as possible the connection between sentimentalism and the late Enlightenment, a connection so close that it is hard to find a boundary. This applies in equal measure to Rousseau, the prophet of sentimentalism. The Rousseau who proclaimed the primacy of feeling over reason was nonetheless a true son of the Enlightenment. He is rationalistic and even didactic not merely in *Émile* and *Du contrat social* but also in *La nouvelle Héloïse*, that Bible of sensitive hearts. Although the correspondence between Julie and Saint-Preux concerns their tender and ardent feelings, the method used to examine and give expression to them is of the most rationalistic kind. The jesting comparison of the style of Julie's love letters to that of the sermons of Bossuet is hardly gratuitous.

Rousseau also applied his rationalistic method to the work on the *Confessions*, but here the fundamental difference between creating ideal literary images and reproducing something that had actually taken place, however transformed it was by imagination, proved decisive. In his fictional work, Rousseau created ideal schemata based on general ideas. In the *Confessions*, he set himself the task of investigating a unique phenomenon in a unique way, one that would, by virtue of its very uniqueness, necessarily become a new human standard. His rationalism was thus transformed in the *Confessions* into the book's brilliant analyses of psychic life.

There are especially clear-cut formulations of the consciously analytical treatment of inner life in two of Rousseau's late works intended as supplements to the *Confessions*: *Rousseau juge de Jean Jaques, Dialogues* (1772–1776) and *Les Rêveries du promeneur solitaire* (1776–1778). In the second of the *Dialogues*, Rousseau makes the following observation in regard to his autobiographical hero: "The causes arising from the events of his life would alone have been sufficient to make him flee the crowd and search for solitude. The innate causes arising from his constitution would alone have produced the same effect. Judge if he could, given the combination of those two different causes, have escaped becoming what he is today. In order to have a better sense of that necessity, let us discard all the external facts for a moment, assuming that we know only the temperament I have described to you, and look at what would have to be the natural result in any fictional being about whom we have no other idea."⁹The analytical approach is taken here to the point of a program for the experimental investigation of the individual. It is, to be sure, still not a physiological experiment, but a logical one.

In the later *Rêveries*, however, Rousseau is already reaching for an experiment of the natural-science variety: "I shall, in a certain regard, perform those operations on myself that natural scientists perform on air in order to ascertain its daily state. I shall attach a barometer to my soul, and these operations, carefully regulated and repeated for a long time, may furnish results just as reliable as theirs" (1000–1001). The barometer of the soul, however, is still a metaphor. In practical terms, Rousseau had to use the methods not of "natural science," but of literature—artistic synthesis and artistic analysis. And artistic analysis simultaneously breaks the phenomenon down into its constituent parts and, on a new, higher level of cognition, reconstitutes it in a new, integrated structure.

Rousseau himself spoke of the theatricality he introduced into his life in the 1750s at the apogee of his fame and success. Having decided that it was necessary to act "in keeping with his principles," he adopted "an unusual mode of behavior," and cultivated in his everyday life the image of the "savage," "bear," and "stern citizen." This was a completely "synthetic" image, and one moreover that lacked any inconsistent features that might have undermined it from within or at least complicated it. It was in fact a polemical image directed at the false civilization he had condemned in his first *Discours*. The author of the *Discours* had refused the profitable office of treasurer offered him by the tax farmer and Maecenas Francueil, and he had likewise renounced the dress of the privileged classes—white stockings, watch, and sword—and proclaimed that he would henceforth earn his daily bread copying music.

It is curious, however, that Rousseau's account of that self-image in the *Confessions* is ironical: "People wanted to meet this odd man who sought no acquaintances and only wanted to pursue his freedom and happiness in his own way—which was enough to make it impossible for him to do so. My room was never empty of the people who came on various excuses to take up my time. The ladies employed countless ruses to get me to dine with them.The ruder I was to people, the more they persisted. . . . The next thing would have been to show myself like Punch, at so much a head" (367; 342). The irony soon turns into analysis, however:

> Precipitated against my will into the world without possessing its manners, and in no state to learn them or conform to them, I decided to adopt manners of my own which would excuse me from the necessity. Since my foolish and

tiresome silence, which I could not overcome, arose from my fear of making social blunders I elected, in order to give myself courage, to trample all courtesies underfoot. I became cynical and sarcastic out of awkwardness, and affected to despise the manners I did not know how to practice. . . . However, despite the misanthropic reputation which my appearance and a few happy phrases gained for me in the world, in private I always sustained the part badly. Certainly my friends and acquaintances led this unsociable bear around like a lamb. I limited my sarcasms to unwelcome but general truths, and never could say an unkind word to anybody. (368–369; 343–344)

It is obvious here how one image of personality has been supplanted by another. The first image, formed in life itself, is impervious to irony, contradiction, and analysis; it consists of a restricted number of monotypal features looked at from the outside. The second image is a literary revision of the first. The range of awareness has been considerably enlarged, and in essence has completely absorbed the first image, which is no longer apprehended directly but as a mask or role (albeit one of great ideological significance). The second image retains the element of social protest contained in the first—its civic and plebeian essence—but it adds the hidden motives of pride and embarrassment, and of an awkwardness that attempts to compensate for itself by rudeness and contempt. In other words, the second image adds psychological analysis.

Even though Rousseau as a man of his time was still unable to refashion philosophical sensationalism into a consistent dialectic, his concrete psychological vision was nonetheless astonishingly dialectical in nature. He saw the fluidity of human consciousness, its modifications and changing elements, yet at the same time he had in the *Confessions* a definite *object* of analysis—the personality, which he logically derived from a few primary characteristics, and whose reactions to continually changing influences he traced. "There is," Rousseau says in the *Confessions*, "a certain sequence of impressions and ideas which modify those that follow them, and it is necessary to know the original set before passing any judgments. I endeavor in all cases to explain the [first] causes, in order to convey the interrelation of results" (174–175; 169). This is reiterated in the *Dialogues*: "This conflict among the primary elements [*premiers éléments*] of his constitution is evident in most of the qualities that derive from them, and in his conduct as a whole" (811). The correlation of those primary psychic elements with their derivatives was thus a fully conscious analytical procedure for Rousseau. The *Confessions* are not a novel, and analysis in them therefore takes the form of direct investigation by the author. This is of course not a rejection of the task of art, but a unique solution to it.

Rousseau's autobiographical image in the *Confessions* is constructed with all the logic of rationalism, a fact entirely in keeping both with his sensationalist conception of the personality's vital reactions and with that image's Rousseauean quiddity. Rousseau makes a conscious effort in the *Confessions* to show that the ideas of the primacy of feeling over thought and of the opposition between the states of nature and of civilization that had so impressed European society were both grounded in their author's nature, in that contradiction between his emotional and intellectual constitution that he regarded as the key to his personality.

Rousseau seeks the primary elements of that personality in such categories as will, reason, feeling, sensuality, imagination, and so on. These are no longer discrete characteristics but features entering into sharply dialectical relations with each other. He speaks (to translate a few of his observations into the language of modern psychology) of external stimuli and reflex reactions and of the processes of impulse and inhibition. Rousseau describes himself as a weak-willed person who is slow to act and who does so with difficulty, and as someone whose mind is as if clouded, but who possesses a strong imagination, highly developed sensibilities, and easily aroused feelings. These characteristics are, in fact, his "primary elements," and they are reducible to predispositions of an essentially physiological order.

Rousseau considered the contradiction between his "passionate" temperament and his sluggish mind to be the fundamental contradiction of his personality and the source of his positive and negative qualities: "In me are united two almost irreconcilable characteristics, though in what way I cannot imagine. I have a passionate temperament, and lively and headstrong emotions. Yet my thoughts arise slowly and confusedly, and are never ready till too late. It is as if my heart and brain did not belong to the same person" (113; 112–113). Speaking of himself in the third person in the second *Dialogue* of *Rousseau juge de Jean Jaques*, Rousseau gives a kind of condensed version of his personality as it is elaborated in the *Confessions*:

> Here is a summary of the observations from which I have derived my knowledge of his physical constitution and . . . true personality. These observations . . . yield a mixed temperament formed of apparently contradictory elements: a sensitive, passionate, and easily inflamed heart, and a dense and sluggish brain whose solid and massive parts can only be put in motion by a prolonged and lively agitation of the blood. I have not at all sought as a student of natural science to eliminate these apparent conflicts. . . . The important thing to me was to assure myself of their reality. . . . But that result, if it is to appear before you in its full light, needs the explanations I shall endeavor to add. (804)

Following as explanation is a theoretical digression on *sensibilité*, which is divided into physical and moral sensibility, with moral sensibility in its turn divided into positive and negative sensibility (attraction and repulsion). Jean-Jacques is endowed to an extraordinary degree with both moral and physical sensibility (a heightened reaction to external stimuli), and he also possesses a highly developed sensuality.[10] That sensuality, however, is by no means direct or crude. In order for Jean-Jacques to experience sensual pleasure, it must be distilled through feeling and imagination. This "modification" is one of the most characteristic for Rousseau's psychological system. An analogous demand is made of thought as well. Thought that has not passed through the heart leaves Jean-Jacques indifferent and sunk in the apathy that is his natural condition when his passions and feelings have not been aroused. This is the source both of his aversion to enlightened and fashionable conversation, various in theme and requiring deft intellectual reactions, and of the labored quality of his speech during such conversation, as well as of his dullness, his absentmindedness (sunk in apathy, he does not listen to his interlocutor), and even his awkward chatter, which is the result of his embarrassment and his desire to conceal it.

Evident here are very concrete and well-defined features deriving from Rousseau's "primary elements": a sluggish mind and a temperament that although passionate is quick to cool. More general qualities are also derived from the same elements: "The same conflict that obtains among the elements of his constitution is found in his propensities, manners, and behavior. . . . He passes from one extreme to another with incredible rapidity. . . ." He is active, eager, diligent, tireless, proud, and audacious, and he is apathetic, indolent, ineffectual, timid, self-conscious, and awkward. If one should "trace these various effects back to their first causes [*causes primitives*], then he is timorous and languid whenever he is aroused only by reason, and he bursts into flame as soon as he is animated by any passion" (*Dialogues*, 817–818).

The "primary elements" we have been speaking of are those organic, natural elements that are to a certain extent reducible to physiological characteristics. Their subsequent modifications are related to the pressure of milieu and circumstance, and to the susceptibility to its distortions of the personality caught up in the mechanism of a false civilization.

Book 1 of the *Confessions* is an account of those first impressions that shape a person for life. Rousseau anticipated the views of modern psychology on the significance of childhood traumas and complexes. Many have written about this, and I shall not go into this specialized matter.

In addition to its physiologism, there is also in book 1 of the *Confessions* a very strong sense of the social principle. In his account of what he calls his "degeneration," Rousseau painstakingly traces the modification of his primary qualities under the pressure of circumstance and milieu. He was apprenticed to an engraver, and the cruel treatment he received in the home and shop of his master quickly reduced him to a state of spiritual wildness and turned an essentially good boy into a thief, a liar, and an idler. Rousseau depicts both the social conditions themselves and the psychic mechanism that was subject to their influence. It was in fact the primary qualities of his psyche that made him so vulnerable to the destructive effects of the circumstances in which he found himself: "I must have had a strong inclination toward degeneracy; for I degenerated very rapidly, and without the least difficulty" (30–31; 39).

The preconditions of that degeneration were weakness of will and introversion, an almost pathological receptivity to external stimuli, strong momentary impulses and appetites, and a consequent lack of self-restraint. Rousseau thinks in terms of processes rather than qualities. Depending on the situation and their particular correlation, impressionability, lack of will, and impulsiveness could yield quite different results. The favorable circumstances of Jean-Jacques's early childhood produced a personality that was mild, affectionate, and dreamy. Brutalizing pressure from without transformed that mildness and complaisance into a fear of the external world and its coarseness. The weak-willed person takes refuge under such circumstances in a defensive timidity and egoism. In an atmosphere of social injustice and the moral stagnation of those around him, the lack of strong inner constraints in the individual leads the way to the immediate satisfaction of his desires by whatever means are available. Hence Jean-Jacques's irresponsibility and mendacity and especially his thievery.

The problem of childhood theft is one of the most important in this study of the maturation, or rather, the temporary degeneration of Jean-Jacques's personality. Rousseau admitted that once he had acquired the "habit" of theft, he could never afterward quite rid himself of it. That "habit" is, however, presented as a modified form of behavior that is fully consistent with the psychological makeup of the hero as it is depicted in the *Confessions*. Jean-Jacques's thefts are neither planned nor practical; they are rather impulsive acts intended to satisfy momentary and for the most part childish desires.

"Jean-Jacques was undoubtedly weak," Rousseau says in the *Dialogues*, "and incapable of overcoming his passions! But he could have only those passions that corresponded to his character" (897). And, in fact, even when he is analyzing and taking things apart, Rousseau loses sight neither of the integrated system of personality that he has created, nor of the importance of context in modifying that personality's constituent elements. It is this fact that permits us to speak of the analytical structuring of a synthetic image of personality. The later "larcenous" episodes in the *Confessions* are just as impulsive and infantile as the first ones. The most characteristic of these concerns the young Rousseau's short-lived and unhappy sojourn in Lyons as a tutor in the family of the city's chief magistrate, Monsieur de Mably. "At Mamma's [that is, at Madame de

Warens's] I had completely lost my habit of petty thieving; since everything was mine, I had nothing to steal. Moreover the lofty principles I had adopted ought to have made me superior to such meannesses; indeed from that time I have generally been so. But that is not so much because I have learned to conquer my temptations as that I have cut them down at the root; and I should be in some danger of stealing as I did in my childhood, were I subject to the same greeds as I was in those days." A certain "white wine from Arbois" presented just such a temptation. Rousseau could have had the wine while at table, but he nevertheless pilfered several bottles. "But when I had once secured my coveted little cake I went to get my bottle from the back of the cupboard. And what pleasant swigs I enjoyed there on my own, while reading a few pages of a novel! For it has always been a fancy of mine to read as I eat when I am on my own; it makes up for the lack of society. I devour a page and a mouthful alternately, and it is as if my book were dining with me" (268–269; 254–255). Here we find not only theft in its individual psychological aspect, but also, and even more importantly for Rousseau's system of self-knowledge, an individual modification of the predisposition to sensual pleasure. In another passage of the *Confessions*, Rousseau says, "Without being greedy, I like my food. I am a sensualist but not a glutton" (35; 43). This is the peculiarly Rousseauean variety of sensual receptivity, which must undergo emotional and intellectual transformation so that the attributes of sensual pleasure may become the symbolic reflection of values of a higher order. Wine is pleasant to the taste, but if it is to afford genuine pleasure, it must signify amicable relations or the solitary enjoyment of a book.

Whatever the case, the problem of childhood theft is a compelling autobiographical issue for Rousseau. He goes into it thoroughly, depicting in book 1 of the *Confessions* the socially conditioned degeneration of a child. His psychological analysis is especially painstaking and discriminating in this section, although it is also didactic. One senses the author of *Émile* with his faith in the essential goodness of people and his belief in the futility of severe punishment. "I reckoned that to be beaten like a rogue justified my being one. I found that thieving and being beaten belonged together, and were in a sense a single state, and that if I fulfilled my share in the bargain by doing my part I could leave the responsibility for the rest to my master" (34–35; 43).

In exposing the injustices and cruelties and the temptations and fantasies that together have led to him to steal, Rousseau demonstrates the perfection of his psychological dialectic. In the classical view, theft was a *quality*. For Rousseau, it is a mode of behavior that may have any number of different first causes, and that may manifest itself in any number of different functions, to the degree that it is combined with other elements of the individual psyche.

Rousseau recounts that he pilfered not only food but also paper, fine tools, and drawings that his employer had hidden from him (and which he used, incidentally, in his employer's service), but that he never touched money or valuables. Rousseau indicates several motives for this latter restraint, including an aversion to theft of this kind instilled in him by his upbringing and by "secret broodings upon disgrace, punishment, prison, and the scaffold" (35; 43). These are general motives, valid for anyone. For Rousseau, however, the main thing as always is his individual "primary elements," in relation to which any feature of his behavior and personality remains secondary. And because it is secondary, it may be logically deduced and explained.

> A single sheet of drawing paper tempted me more than the money to buy a ream. This strange desire is connected with one of the principal facets in my character, which has had considerable influence on my conduct and which it is important to explain.
>
> My passions are extremely strong, and while I am under their sway nothing can equal my impetuosity. I am amenable to no restraint, respect, fear, or decorum. I am cynical, bold, violent, and daring. No shame can stop me, no fear of danger alarm me. Except for the one object in my mind the universe for me is nonexistent. But all this lasts only a moment; and the next moment plunges me into complete annihilation. Catch me in a calm mood, I am all indolence and timidity. Everything alarms me, everything discourages me. I am frightened by a buzzing fly. I am too lazy to speak a word or make a gesture. (36; 43–44)

Rousseau's behavior is always defined by the same "primary elements" of his impulsive nature. The forbidden apple or the sheets of paper are merely the objects of momentary desires; to engage in obtaining money to purchase them, however, would lead only to a condition of apathy. Money "has no value in itself and must be transformed to be enjoyed. One must bargain and purchase and often be cheated, paying dear for poor services. . . . I am less tempted by money than by things, because between money and the desired object there is always an intermediary, whereas between a thing and its enjoyment there is none. If I see something, it tempts me. But if all I see is the way of acquiring it, I am not tempted" (36–38; 44–46). Indolence, timidity, and apathy oppose temptation. A behavioral mechanism is derived here from a first cause with the paradoxicality and undeniable logic that are so characteristic of the *Confessions*. If we understand Rousseau's complex attitude toward money, then, as he points out, we "will have no difficulty in understanding one of the apparent contradictions of my personality: the combination of an almost sordid avarice with the greatest contempt for money. . . . Money in one's possession is the instrument of liberty; money one pursues is the symbol of servitude. That is why I hold fast to what I have, but covet no more. My lack of interest, therefore, is a sign of indolence; the pleasure of possession is not worth the trouble involved in acquisition. And my mad spending is a sign of indolence too; when the occasion for spending agreeably arises, too much use cannot be made of it" (37–38; 45–46). Indolence is not a discrete quality, but a variable condition that may have, depending on the circumstances, different or even diametrically opposed meanings. This particular line of psychological analysis is brought to a conclusion in the account of one final paradoxical episode. During the period of his apprenticeship to the engraver, Rousseau became passionately fond of reading. Everything he owned, including even his shirts and cravats, now passed into the hands of a woman who lent books for reading. "There, it may be said, is a case where money became necessary. That is true, but it was at a moment when reading had cut down every activity. Given over entirely to my new craze, I did nothing but read; I gave up stealing. This is another of my characteristic contradictions. When I am in a certain mood a trifle distracts me, changes me, captures me, and becomes a passion. Then I forget everything, and think only of the new subject of interest" (39–40; 47).

Rousseau promised to show the reader the "modifications" of his spiritual states. And he really did reveal how they occurred in an impulsive mind governed by imagination and ideal conceptions. Rousseau studied himself with the curiosity and even the astonishment of an investigator faced with an unexpected natural phenomenon. Frequently encountered in the pages devoted to the story of the youthful Rousseau's moral degeneration and in many other pages of the *Confessions* and the *Dialogues* are the words "oddity" (*bizarrerie*), "peculiarity" (*singularité*), and "contradiction," all of which denote the "characteristic features" of the autobiographical hero. But Rousseau's contradictions are not so much a way of thought as a striking form for the exposition of an idea. On close inspection, one finds concealed behind the contradiction a syllogism that correlates the primary elements of his personality with their derived features. Rousseau's first application to himself of the idea of psychological contradiction is to be found in his 1762 letters to Malesherbes, which are usually regarded as a kind of first draft for the *Confessions*: "An indolent soul which is afraid of every effort and a temperament that is passionate, irritable, easily stimulated, and inordinately sensitive to all that affects it would seem to be incapable of being united in the same personality, yet those two contraries are nevertheless the foundation of my own."[11]

Rousseau was still unable to explain contradiction scientifically, as physiology would later be able to do. Thus, Pavlov, classifying the different types of nervous activity and temperament on the basis of "excitability" and "inhibition," identifies the type of person who is productive "only when he has much that is interesting to do, that is, only when he is continually stimulated. But when he has nothing to do, he becomes bored and lethargic, exactly like our sanguine dogs (as we usually call them) that are lively and energetic to the highest degree whenever circumstances arouse them, but then immediately doze off and sleep, once those stimuli are lacking."[12] Although the theory of reflexes and inhibitions was unknown to Rousseau, he was, thanks to observation, experience, and a brilliant intuition, still able to appreciate their interrelations, and he invariably provides the reader of the *Confessions* with explanations to his contradictions that are at the same time logical keys to psychological puzzles: "Here, sir, is a great discovery in which I take much joy, since I regard it as the key to the other peculiarities of this man," and "I can even say that the more I examined him, the more unusual his ordinary exterior and all that was most commonplace in him seemed to me. This contradiction will become clear in due course as you listen to me" (*Dialogues*, 817, 800).

The contradictions are systematically explained, thereby becoming only "apparent contradictions." Let me recall the sentence that prefaces Rousseau's investigation of his attitude toward money: the reader "will have no difficulty in understanding one of the apparent contradictions of my personality: the combination of an almost sordid avarice with the greatest contempt for money." The great writer's system was obviously unacquainted with chance. Contradiction was not the essence of Rousseau's thought, but it was necessary to him, and not merely to astonish and entertain the reader. Contradiction was the relevant form for Rousseau's dynamic, for his interest in paradox, modifications, and the variable functions of things. Rousseau offers that contradiction to the reader as a riddle whose solution he himself already knows, and once having given the solution, he announces that the riddle was merely "apparent."

Psychologism could not sustain itself on a one-dimensional selection of features. It required contradiction as the starting point for its separation of things into their constituent elements, and for its analysis and new correlation of those elements. It is in the contradiction that is not only capable of being explained but that actually *is* explained that the kernel of the psychological method is to be found. To be sure, one may also find in psychological prose contradictions that remain unresolved—riddles that remain riddles (a device that was abused, incidentally, in the late psychological novel). This is the dangerous path of a disappointing glibness, wherein the writer makes whatever psychological moves he wishes, without ever actually coming to terms with the resistance of his material.

One of the most brilliant "apparent contradictions" in the *Confessions* is the meticulously described personality of Madame de Warens. Rousseau declared that the task of the *Confessions* was the portrayal of his own personality, the only one that he could know completely and from within. He does depict in various ways the life of his time in the *Confessions*, but it is his mind alone that is the subject of the book's great psychological experiment. Its numerous other characters, even its principal ones, are treated differently, with a method that relies more on summary definition than on the analysis of their "primary elements" and conditioned psychological mechanisms. Madame de Warens, however, is the exception to this. Rousseau applies to her the same method that he applies to himself—the method of internal analysis. The privileged position of Madame de Warens in the artistic system of the *Confessions* is of course not accidental. She played an extremely important role in the initial formation of Rousseau's personality, and therefore also in his future activity and destiny.

Françoise-Louise de la Tour (de Warens was her married name) was the descendent of an old Swiss family and the wife of a man who had occupied a prominent place in Swiss life. For various reasons, she abandoned her husband and fled to Catholic Savoy, where, as a reward for her conversion to Catholicism, she received a generous pension from the king of Sardinia.[13] This pension required her to assist in the conversion of Swiss Calvinists who turned up in Savoy. One of those newly converted through the good offices of Madame de Warens was the sixteen-year-old Geneva apprentice Jean-Jacques Rousseau, who had fled the beatings of his master. When they first met (in 1728), Madame de Warens was about thirty. She was beautiful, fashionable, and at the same time natural, and she had a lively mind and a personality that was cheerful, easy, and affable. Her charm, according to the testimony of a number of her contemporaries, was difficult to resist. Madame de Warens gave refuge to the fugitive, and for the next fourteen years he lived with her, sometimes leaving her house for long periods, but always returning to it. The youth grown wild in the engraving shop was a still undiscovered genius, and Madame de Warens, merely an ordinary woman (although undoubtedly a gifted one). Yet Rousseau remained convinced until the end of his life that it was indeed she who had first revealed to him the world of love, nature, and culture. That world was the one in which his feelings were first nurtured, and the very last thing that he wrote, the broken off *Rêveries du promeneur solitaire*, is dedicated to its memory. "Without that short, but precious time, I would perhaps have remained unsure of myself." The passage concludes, "I thought that laying by a stock of talents was the surest expedient against misery, and I resolved to employ my leisure in putting myself in a position, if possible, of one day returning to the best of women the help that I had received from her" (1099). This was written in 1778 on the fiftieth anniversary of Rousseau's first acquaintance with Madame de Warens and just a few months before his death.

Madame de Warens is a positive principle in Rousseau's autobiography. Nevertheless, her image is at the same time antagonistic to his, opposing it on the level of Rousseauean ideas. If the autobiographical hero embodies the supremacy of sensibility and feeling over reason, with all the joys and torments issuing therefrom, then Madame de Warens exemplifies the misfortunes and errors to which the sway of reason and "false philosophy" over an excellent human heart may lead. The Madame de Warens of the *Confessions* is, however, no mere schema devised for the illustration of authorial ideas and intentions. On the contrary, it is rather the Julie of *La Nouvelle Héloïse* or the Sophie of *Émile* that are schemata. Those women were invented by Rousseau. Madame de Warens actually existed. He interpreted her personality, and contained in that interpretation is an astonishing amalgam of analysis and lyricism.

It really did require the audacity of a genius to justify that personality poetically. It is a personality that ought to have offended Rousseau with his moralism, and therefore the reader as well. The woman portrayed in the *Confessions* is coldly amoral. She enters into liaisons with whomever she needs (providing they are unfortunate), in order to bind them more securely to herself. Relations of this kind with her servant Claude Anet[14] do not keep her from tempting the youth who has become her ward and establishing a ménage à trois, and then betraying that youth (after Claude Anet's death) with another servant or barber described in the *Confessions* as "vain and stupid, ignorant and insolent" (262; 248) and once again offering Jean-Jacques a ménage, which this time he refuses. And yet Rousseau created out of this quite thankless material an image marked by exceptional charm, an image that is in fact one of the most brilliant female images in world literature.

Rousseau's success here is once again attributable to his characteristic system of modifications. Madame de Warens's actions do not exist in isolation, but only in terms of their correlation with the "primary elements" of her personality—with those qualities of temperament, mind, sincere kindness, and generosity from which everything else derives. That personality is therefore justified ethically and even aesthetically, if only because it is *explained*. It is constructed analytically.

A student of Rousseau's writings has justly observed that we know incomparably more about Madame de Warens today than Rousseau did. There is a significant body of literature about this woman he made famous, and numerous documents have been collected and published that throw considerable light on her life. Almost all her biographers have noted her intelligence, her appetite for activity, her immense self-esteem, and her lack of scruples. It may well be that concealed in Madame de Warens were the instincts of a brilliant political and court intriguer (on the order of Saint-Simon's Madame des Ursins), but that her social opportunities proved too confining. She sought an outlet for her energy, ambition, and need to be in control in doubtful commercial ventures—despite a complete lack of business sense and of scrupulousness in business affairs. This propensity, in combination with her extravagance, generosity, and faith in every kind of rascal, ruined her and by the end of her life reduced her to poverty. A few biographers, regarding her from the viewpoint of psychopathology or psychoanalysis, have found either narcissism or symptoms of hysteria in her, and however idealized the portrait of her left to us by Rousseau, these features are still contained within it. For him, however, the most important thing in that portrait was something else.

Rousseau wanted to share with the reader one of his most beautiful and tormenting memories, and he wanted to set his own idea of life against a different one, to show two solutions to the alternatives of reason and the heart. He proceeded with Madame de Warens much as he had done with himself: he investigated the primary elements of her personality and their consequences.

The personalities of Madame de Warens and the young Rousseau are alike in many respects. Both of them are kind, sympathetic, and able to delight in nature and enjoy life. Both love virtue and rarely keep to it in practice. Why? It is here that the basic difference between their two natures comes into play, eventually emerging as a polarity of ideological significance. The autobiographical hero is weak-willed, impulsive, and incapable of self-restraint and resistance. From these characteristics come not only all his errors and vices, but also all that is best in him, thanks to the dominance of feeling over reason. Madame de Warens is an example of the fatal (especially for a woman) sway of reason. In contrast to Rousseau, she is characterized by will, activity, systematic intelligence, and an "ice-cold temperament."

The exclusive rule of reason is fraught with error and misfortune, in the same way that the exclusive rule of passion and feeling would be. Yet the person of sensibility still retains loftiness of mind, whereas the merely rational person is inevitably reduced to ultimate degradation. Rousseau is a moralist, and such is indeed the moral of the different fates of the autobiographical hero and his first beloved. Both Rousseauean ideology and moralism shaped the structure of Madame de Warens as a character. "Her errors arose from an inexhaustible fund of activity, which perpetually demanded employment. A woman's intrigues did not satisfy her; what she required were enterprises to carry out and direct. She was born for affairs of state. In her place Madame de Longueville[15] would have been a mere intriguer; in Madame de Longueville's place, she would have ruled France. Her talents were misplaced. What might have won her glory in a more exalted station worked her ruin in the position in which she lived" (51; 57). Depending on the situation, virtues may become defects, and strengths, weaknesses. One of the "first causes" of Madame de Warens's personality—her organic energy—came up against the circumscribed opportunities of her social position, which immediately deflected it.

Madame de Warens's unsuccessful business ventures resulted from the crossing of her desire to be in control with yet another of her first causes. This was her "systematic intelligence," which Rousseau mentions frequently. Rationality was also a primary attribute, but in her case, it had developed in the atmosphere of the age of Enlightenment. Madame de Warens was interested in medicine, botany, philosophy (particularly moral philosophy), and even in religious dogma. The teachings of the German Pietists imbibed in her youth later assisted her in devising her own religion, which was quite unorthodox and based entirely on the idea of universal love and forgiveness.[16] "Since she always reduced things to a system," Rousseau remarks, "she had not failed to treat religion in this way" (228; 218). But the systematic and even pedantic mind of Madame de Warens was by no means a practical one. It fed on abstractions and fantasies, and for that reason got on very well with irrationality, which, in combination with her frustrated energy, gave rise to a predilection for wild schemes.

Rousseau is concerned less with Madame de Warens's business and social conduct, however, than he is with her intimate behavior. This is understandable, inasmuch as it was in fact she who first acquainted him with love. With the audacity of a genius and the ruthlessness of a detective, he portrays facts that are unseemly from his own point of view, and he justifies them on the basis of the first causes from which they are logically derived.

All her faults ... came from her lack of judgment, never from her passions. . . . She was born for an elegant way of life which she always loved but never followed, because instead of listening to her heart, which gave her good counsel, she listened to her reason which gave her bad. When false principles led her astray, her true feelings always gave them the lie. But unfortunately she prided herself on her philosophy, and the morality she invented for herself corrupted that which her heart dictated.

Monsieur de Tavel, her first lover, was her master in philosophy, and the principles which he taught her were those he required in order to seduce her. . . . Thus the wretch achieved his purpose by corrupting the mind of a child whose heart he could not corrupt. . . . This young woman's coldness, which should have protected her from that way of life, was just what prevented her afterward from giving it up. She could not imagine that so much importance could be attached to something which had none for her; and never dignified with the name of virture an abstinence which cost her so little.

She would have been loath to take advantage of this false philosophy for her own ends; but she did so for others, and this by virtue of a rule almost equally false but more consonant with the kindness of her heart. She always believed that nothing attaches a man to a woman so much as possession; and though her feeling for her men friends was one of pure friendship, it was of such a tender friendship that she used every means in her power to attach them more closely to herself. . . . She only bestowed her favors on the unfortunate. Persons of distinction all wasted their labors on her. (197–198; 190–191)

Madame de Warens's behavior is thus derivable from a few primary elements. Sincere kindness, a rationality that verged on excess (the soundly mastered lessons of skeptical philosophy), and sexual coldness all combined to produce an attitude toward life that Rousseau condemns, but that he recognizes as the inevitable consequence of her nature and social milieu. Madame de Warens's thirst for activity may also be added to these first causes, since it is obvious from Rousseau's narrative that she regarded those "unfortunates" on whom she bestowed her favors as helpers in her domestic and business enterprises.

It is curious that in creating this flawlessly functioning psychological mechanism, Rousseau involuntarily ascribed to this woman whose memory he so cherished faults that she was not even guilty of. Thus, Madame deWarens's biographers have questioned Rousseau's account of the amorous affairs that preceded her separation from her husband and her escape to Savoy. Most likely, that account was based on nothing more than local rumors that had reached Rousseau. But he was prepared to credit them, inasmuch as the edifice he was constructing very much required the figure of the libertine de Tavel who had poisoned the "systematic mind" of a young woman with a fashionably amoral philosophy. Concealed here was a polemic with Voltaire and the Encyclopédistes (especially Grimm and Diderot), whom at the time he was writing the *Confessions* Rousseau regarded as his mortal enemies, both ideological and personal.

Students of Rousseau have been dismayed by the lack of accord among the qualities of Madame de Warens as she is portrayed in the *Confessions*. As one of them writes, "For the youthful Rousseau, fresh from Puritanic Geneva, she could not but be at once not only a revelation but also an enigma. He never quite unraveled it, and she never aided him to do so. That is why his picture of her is so incoherent and contradictory. So that he represents her as at once the 'best of women' and the victim of vulgar tastes."[17] Rousseau's construction of Madame de Warens's personality as a contradiction was fully conscious. It is, however, one of his "apparent contradictions" that are ultimately resolved through the explanation of their mechanisms. The erotic "permissiveness" of her personality turns out to be derived from her coldness, and the dubious liaisons, from her generosity and sincere kindness. The logic of her personality is very precise. Rousseau himself says in this regard, "By ascribing to her a sensitive character and a cold nature, I know in advance that I shall be accused, as usual, of being contradictory, and with no more reason than usual. It is possible that Nature was at fault, and that such a combination should not have existed; I only know that it did exist. . . . My function is to tell the truth, not to make people believe it" (199; 191–192). The schemata of Julie (in *La Nouvelle Héloïse*) or Sophie (in *Émile*) consist only of *what ought to be*—of what expresses the idea of the author in the most direct way. The personality of Madame de Warens in the *Confessions* is also a product of Rousseau's ideas, but retained in it is the living tissue of *what actually was*—the charm of contradiction and the unexpected. And therein is its great anticipation of the future possibilities of psychological literature.

Human spiritual life in the *Confessions* is presented in a variety of different aspects. The experience of love and the cultivation of feeling are the most important among them, a fact that is entirely in keeping with Rousseau's basic conception of life and with his philosophy of the man of sensibility. Madame de Warens is a key figure in this regard. The investigation of feeling gave Rousseau particularly broad license to display his system of psychological modifications. The autobiographical hero experiences several kinds of love, each in its own way a product of the same primary elements of his personality. Each of his principal infatuations embodies one or another modification of love. Present here once again are paradox and the "apparent contradictions" that are so characteristic of Rousseau, especially the contradiction involving the relation between sensuality and imagination (already discussed above). Strong sensual propensities and a heightened reaction to external impressions are at once subject to imagination, intellect, and symbolic representation. The opposition between the sensuality of the dreamer and the sensibility of the intellectual serves as the initial contradiction, one that is completely explainable since it is rooted in the "first causes" of the psyche in question. The intellectual principle was in fact a far more important part of Rousseau's spiritual life than he supposed, or at least than he was willing to admit.

Rousseau maintained that neither nature nor people could surpass the richness of his imagination. That imagination is fertile, endlessly creating over and above the real world its own world of dreams. "If I want to describe the spring it must be in winter; if I want to describe a fine landscape I must be within doors; and as I have said a hundred times, if ever I were confined in the Bastille, there I would draw the picture of liberty" (172; 166–167).

Rousseau also brought his dreamer's temperament to the realm of love. Of Madame de Warens he writes: "Sometimes I left her, to give myself over to her there and think of her with greater pleasure. . . . I remember Madame de Luxembourg once telling me with a laugh about a man who left his mistress in order to write to her. I answered that I could easily have been that man, and I might have added that I sometimes was" (181; 176).

Twentieth-century French critics have tried repeatedly to draw analogies between Rousseau and Proust. The image of the man whose beloved's presence interferes with his thinking about her does indeed anticipate the Proustian conception of love. One may speak of Rousseau and Proust, however, only in terms of affinities that are temporally remote and separated by numerous intermediate links. On the other hand, there can be no doubt that the Rousseau of the *Confessions* was the direct precursor of the idea of love worked out by the sentimentalists and especially by the romantics. This above all concerns his conception of the split between sensual and ideal, or "mundane" and "celestial" love. The symbolists inherited that conception from the romantics. Russian symbolist poetry presented it in a version given new vitality by the philosophical ideas of Vladimir Solov'ev, as may be seen, for example, in Blok's *Verses on a Beautiful Lady* [1904].

Rousseau discusses his sexual complexes in the *Confessions* with a pointedly programmatic candor. This has all been sufficiently elucidated in the biographical literature, and there are even specialized psychological investigations devoted to this theme. But more important than the individual aberrations is the historically generalized in Rousseau—that model of feeling that he gave to succeeding generations and that found its ultimate expression in the idea of romantic love. The dualism inherent in that feeling, the fact that sensual and ideal love may have different objects, is delineated very clearly in the *Confessions*. For Rousseau, however, that dualism had not yet become standardized and obligatory, as it would for the romantics.[18] In the *Confessions* that dualism is still the concrete experience of a particular individual, and it is conditioned by his constitution, both spiritual and physiological.

Rousseau traces his erotic dualism back to the level of his childhood infatuations. "I know two very distinct sorts of love, both real but with practically nothing in common except that they are both extremely violent and different in every way from a mere friendly affection. The whole course of my life has been divided between these two quite separate emotions, and I have experienced them both simultaneously" (27; 36). Rousseau then recounts how, as an eleven-year-old boy, he nourished both an intellectual and a sensual love for the already adult Mademoiselle de Vulson, and at the same time indulged in sensual delights with another girl only a few years his senior.

Mentioned in the sentence just quoted is yet another modification of love: tender friendship. It was this in fact that Rousseau regarded as the basis of his deep and steadfast attachment to Madame de Warens. Madame de Warens at first gave their relations the form of a risqué game of mother and son; they called each other "Mamma" [*maman*] and "Little One" [*mon petit*]. Several years later she herself suggested that she become Rousseau's lover (something he had not even dared to dream about), accompanying that suggestion with edifying reflections and a characteristically practical motivation: she wanted to protect him from other, possibly baser temptations. There are, once again, numerous peculiarities and contradictions in this on both sides. Rousseau tells how an "invincible sadness poisoned" the charm of their new relations, but he at once deciphers the apparent contradiction: "I felt as if I had committed incest." The key to it all is the formula of his dualistic conception of love: "I loved her too much to desire her" (197; 189).

Sensuality repressed by tenderness sought other outlets, however. Such were the impulses that led the young Rousseau to an affair during a journey with a certain Madame de Larnage. Those pleasures "were the first and the last I have ever savored in that way. I may say, indeed, that I owe it to Madame de Larnarge that I shall not die without ever having known sensual delight" (253; 240–241). Yet Rousseau does not, in recalling his youth, speak only of the unalloyed pleasure he experienced with Madame de Larnage, a pleasure that was in such contrast to the one he had known with Madame de Warens, which "was always troubled by a feeling of sadness, by a secret oppression at the heart that I had difficulty in overcoming" (254; 241). Rousseau also mentions other sensual reactions that are more complex, and for him much more characteristic, inasmuch as they are governed by imagination. In these instances, the keenness of his reactions and the stimulation of his feelings are in inverse proportion, so to speak, to the material or carnal content of the experience in question.

The first episode of this kind concerns a very early period (1728) and involves Rousseau's encounter in Turin with a young Italian woman, the proprietor of a shop where he worked for a few days as an engraver. "None of the feelings I have had from the possession of women have been equal to those two minutes spent at her feet without even the courage to touch her dress. No, there are no pleasures like those one gets from a modest woman whom one loves. Everything is a favor with her. A beckoning finger and a hand lightly pressed against my lips—these are all the favors I ever received from Madame Basile, and the memory of them, slight though they were, still moves me when I think of them" (76–77; 80).

The same theme occurs in the story of a day spent in the country with two girls from respectable families:

> We dined in the farm, the two friends sitting on benches on either side of the long table and their guest between them on a three-legged stool. What a dinner! What a most charming memory! Why, when one can enjoy such pure and genuine pleasures so cheaply, must one try to find others? Never could a supper at any little place in Paris compare with that meal. I do not mean only for its gaiety and its charm and joy; I mean also for its sensuous pleasure [*pour la sensualité*]. . . .
>
> Anyone reading this will not fail to laugh at my amorous adventures, and observe that after lengthy preliminaries the most advanced of them concluded with a kiss of the hand. Make no mistake, my readers. I probably had more pleasure from this affair which ended with a kiss of the hand than you will ever have from yours which, at the very least, begin there. (137, 139; 134–136)

This is yet another modification of sensuality, one accessible only to the intellectual dreamer who thrives on the symbolism of love. The person depicted here by Rousseau lingers at love's distant approaches. Little is given him, but little is required. And that is the reason why that experience, though focused on so little, could assume such incredible intensity.

Rousseau's relations with Thérèse Le Vasseur, an ugly, almost illiterate servant at the hotel where he stayed after his arrival in Paris, are of a special variety. He maintained a household with her for a quarter of a century, eventually marrying her. Rousseau says in the *Confessions* that he felt neither love nor even sensual attraction for this woman he could not live without. His relations with Thérèse were also a contradiction since they consisted of two apparently incompatible elements—on the one hand, relations of the coldest variety, "purely sexual [that] had nothing to do with her as an individual" (414; 386); and on the other, of the warmest kind, an indomitable need for a heartfelt attachment. "I have always regarded the day which united me to my Thérèse as the one that determined my moral being. I needed an attachment, for the one that should have sufficed me had been so cruelly broken [the allusion is to Madame de Warens]. . . . The first, the greatest, the strongest, the most inextinguishable of all my needs was entirely one of the heart. It was the need for intimate companionship, for a companionship as intimate as possible, which was the chief reason why I needed a woman rather than a man, a woman friend rather than a man friend" (413; 385–386). Rousseau then adds the following observation about his relationships with Madame de Warens and Thérèse: the reader "will believe that I was not made like other men, and that I was incapable of feeling love, since love did not enter into the feelings that attached me to the woman who has been dearest to me. Patience, my dear reader, the fatal moment is approaching when you will be only too rudely undeceived" (414; 386). The last sentence refers to the comtesse d'Houdetot. Rousseau's passion for her was one of the causes of the fatal crisis that initiated the final period of his life, a period full of torments and wandering overshadowed by real and imagined persecutions. Rousseau regarded his relationship with Madame d'Houdetot as a synthesis. Combined in it were all those feelings that he had until then experienced only separately with different women: tender friendship, ideal impulses, sensual attraction, affection, but above all that particular feeling that he terms love, the only time in his life that he felt it. "This time it was love, love with all its strength and all its violence" (445; 414). Yet once again it is not passionate love in general that is portrayed, but a love that is very precisely and individually differentiated. And once more that love is derived from the primary elements of the hero's personality, so that all of his characteristics find expression in it: excitability and inhibition, sensuality and dreaminess, sensibility and intellectuality.

Rousseau wanted to be a natural man, but what actually set that catastrophic love in motion was intellectual and even literary. He was working on *La Nouvelle Héloïse* and was "intoxicated with love that lacked an object" (440; 410) at the time that the comtesse d'Houdetot entered his life. She was the lover of the poet Saint-Lambert, Rousseau's friend and a collaborator on the *Encyclopédie*. If Rousseau had written a significant part of *La Nouvelle Héloïse* under the influence of youthful recollections—of Madame de Warens, that is—then the emotional center of the novel now shifted. "My object became identified with her; I saw my Julie in Madame d'Houdetot, and soon I saw only Madame d'Houdetot, but endowed with all the perfections with which I had just embellished the idol of my heart" (440; 410). After this literary beginning, the contradictions follow. Rousseau fell passionately in love with Madame d'Houdetot precisely because her "heart was already in the possession of another":

> To complete my undoing, she talked to me of Saint-Lambert like a passionate lover. . . . I imagined that I was only sympathizing with her feelings, when really I was beginning to feel as she did. I swallowed the poisoned cup in long drafts, and at first only tasted its sweetness. . . .
>
> But I am wrong to speak of an unrequited love, for mine was in a sense returned. There was equal love on both sides, though it was never mutual. We were both intoxicated with love—hers for her lover, and mine for her; our sighs and our delicious tears mingled together. We confided tenderly in one another, and our feelings were so closely in tune that it was impossible for them not to have united in something. (440, 443–444; 410, 413)

This is the initial contradiction from which the subsequent contradictory development of their relationship *logically* followed. There was for several months the greatest of intimacies between Rousseau and Madame d'Houdetot. Recounting their kisses and embraces in the *Confessions*, Rousseau takes great comfort in the fact that she did not deceive her lover, and that he himself did not betray (or rather completely betray) the trust of his then absent friend. "Yet even when our intoxication was at its most dangerous height she never forgot herself for a moment. As for myself, I protest, I swear, that if ever I was betrayed by my senses and tried to make her unfaithful, I never truly desired it. The vehemence of my passion of itself kept it within bounds. . . . The light of every virtue adorned in my eyes the idol of my heart; to have soiled that divine image would have been to destroy it. . . . I loved her too well to wish to possess her" (444; 413).

The conception of love depicted here is by no means simply Rousseau's latest illusion, nor is it merely an arbitrary reconstruction of his and Madame D'Houdetot's relationship. Its psychological reality is fully confirmed, even to the point of virtual textual coincidence, by an extant draft of a letter (dated June 1757) from Rousseau to Madame d'Houdetot (who as a precaution destroyed almost all of his letters to her). At work in the letter, although to be sure with incomparably greater force, is the very same psychic mechanism governed by intellect and imagination alluded to in relation to the idyllic meal taken with the two girls of good family, where Rousseau mockingly addresses his reader with the words, "I probably had more pleasure from this affair which ended with a kiss of the hand than you will ever have from yours which, at the very least, begin there." In Rousseau's conception, that mechanism entails not a rejection of sensuality, but a constraint that heightens his responsiveness to it.

It is generally agreed that Rousseau is the writer who revealed new forms of love to mankind, just as he revealed new ways of apprehending nature and a new conception of personality. That is why the depiction of the experience of love in all its varieties is such an important part of the *Confessions*. That experience is so highly differentiated that each encounter with it is tantamount to the presentation of a new facet. Each female image in the *Confessions* (Madame de Warens, Madame de Larnage, Thérèse, Madame d'Houdetot, and so on) embodies but one of the many diverse modifications of the hero's experience of love.

In the autobiographical material of the *Confessions*, Rousseau enlarges on two aspects of personality that would later become basic to psychologism. They are the infinite differentiation of spiritual impulses within the personality, and at the same time their compatibility, their contradictory coexistence.

In comparison with Rousseau's conception of spiritual life, that of the romantics was reductive. Romanticism operated not on the basis of mod-

ifications or transformations, but of contrasts and antitheses (a method
that reached its limit in the novels of Hugo). Personalities stood in direct
opposition to each other, and contrasts clashed within a single personality. Yet romanticism had no interest in explaining the mechanism by
which the mundane and the celestial, the ideal and the base, or the beautiful and the ugly could be combined in a single soul; it merely stated the
existence of the duality it had derived from its philosophical premises. For
Rousseau, the author of the *Confessions*, the human being was a complex, intricate mechanism that reacted continually to the full gamut of
external stimuli, and that adapted continually to its surroundings as it
sought to satisfy its needs and desires. For him, the individual human
being was subject to many different influences simultaneously, from the
purely physiological to the loftily spiritual, inasmuch as that individual's
ideals and moral values were just as inalienably a part of him as his desire
to eat and drink. Spiritual life for Rousseau was thus a simultaneous
blending of different levels, and it was this blending that produced the
"apparent contradictions" that interested him so much. This conception
of the human being brought him to the initial discovery of the psychic
mechanism that Dostoevskii would eventually call "dual thoughts."

Claude Anet, Jean-Jacques's friend and rival, has died. "Next day I was
talking of him to Mamma, in the deepest and sincerest of grief, when
suddenly, in the middle of our conversation, the vile and unworthy
thought came to me that I should inherit his clothes, and particularly a
fine black coat which had caught my fancy. No sooner did it occur to me
than I gave utterance to my thought; for in her presence thought and
speech were to me as one. Nothing made her more conscious of her loss
than those mean and odious words, for disinterestedness and nobility had
been outstanding qualities in the dead man" (205–206; 197).

In the Part 2 of *The Idiot*, the degenerate and dissolute Keller says to
Prince Myshkin:

> "... I wanted, after making my complete and sincere confession to you, so
> to speak, ... to further my own development; with that idea I fell asleep
> after three, my eyes welling with tears. . . . But just as I was falling asleep,
> . . . a diabolical thought occurred to me: 'Why not, after my little confession,
> borrow some money from him?' . . . Is that not despicable, in your opinion?"
>
> "Oh well, it probably was not like that, but just two thoughts converging
> with each other. Two thoughts converged; it happens a lot. It happens to me
> all the time. . . . It is as if you were telling me about myself just now. It has
> sometimes even occurred to me," the Prince went on very seriously, as he
> was now deeply and genuinely interested, "that everybody is like that, so
> that I had almost started to accept it in myself, since it is terribly difficult to
> struggle against these *dual thoughts*. . . ." (Chap. 9)

Rousseau was already aware of this phenomenon. A man mourns his friend, but lodged somewhere in his mind is an impression of a beautiful coat that he has taken a fancy to; the coat becomes his property, and the impression is revived.

In the *Confessions* we frequently encounter depictions of a multitude of simultaneous motives for one action or another, motives of the most varied kind. Rousseau has promised to go with Madame de Larnage to her estate, but then suddenly decides to break off this traveler's liaison and return to "Mamma" at Chambéry. The explanations for his decision are numerous: he is afraid that he will be found out (he has for some reason pretended to be an Englishman), that the family of his lover will meet him with hostility, and that he will fall in love with her fifteen-year-old daughter and have to struggle against the temptation to seduce her. He is also aware that his passion for Madame de Larnage has cooled. But working at the same time on another level of consciousness are those ideal moral conceptions that satisfy a person's need to take pride in himself. "I kept to my resolution courageously, with a few sighs I admit. But I also had the inward satisfaction of saying to myself, for the first time in my life: 'I have a right to think well of myself. I am capable of putting duty before pleasure. . . .' Perhaps pride played as large a part in my resolution as virtue. But if pride is not itself a virtue, it has such similar effects that it is pardonable to confuse them" (260; 246–247). Thus, both ideal motives and their antitheses operate side by side, brought into being by different impulses. There is another thing here that is also very characteristic of Rousseau's psychology. Both pride and virtue are seen as fluid and therefore as capable of replacing each other. And there are different kinds of pride as well—from base conceit to satisfaction in the finest possibilities of one's spirit.

In 1752 Rousseau's opera *Le Devin du village* was successfully performed before Louis XV. Although financially distressed, Rousseau decided after much doubt and vacillation costing him a sleepless night to refuse an audience with the king and thereby a royal pension. He offers the reader a number of different reasons for this decision. He had suffered all his life from an infirmity of the bladder, which caused him much inconvenience and embarrassment in society. It is impossible to suppose, however, that the consequences of that infirmity could actually manifest themselves during an audience at the royal palace, and this consideration is therefore replaced by another reason—his "cursed timidity." Rousseau by 1752 had already adopted the manners and appearance of the "stern citizen": "I wished, without abandoning the severe air and tone I had adopted, to show myself sensible of the honor paid me by so great a monarch. It was necessary to clothe some great and useful truth in the form of a choice and well-deserved eulogy. . . . What would become of me at that moment, beneath the eyes of the whole Court, if in my confusion one of my usual inanities were to escape my lips?" (380; 354).

And then, without the least transition, yet another reason is adduced, one of a completely different moral quality. Accepting the pension would have been the same thing as saying: "Farewell truth, liberty, and courage! How should I be able ever to speak again of independence and disinterestedness? So long as I took that pension I should have to flatter or be silent. Besides, what assurance had I that it would be paid? What steps should I have to take to obtain it? How many people should I have to petition? It would cost me more trouble, and far more unpleasant trouble, to keep it than to do without it" (380; 354). This is once again Rousseau's fear of any outward effort, his desire to have money in order to live independently and his aversion to the inevitable difficulties of acquiring it and even spending it. Thus, his bladder affliction, his awkwardness and confusion in society, his love of liberty, and his dread of taking trouble all stand, simultaneously, as reasons for his decision. Rousseau revealed the presence of a multiplicity of coexisting impulses deriving simultaneously from different sources—the physiological, the psychological, and the social— inasmuch as the individual is subject to the influence of all these spheres at once. Though not yet formulating it theoretically, he exhibited a kind of "stream of consciousness," albeit one worked up in rationalist form. Of course, that form is ultimately just as conventional as any other, since the true stream of consciousness cannot in fact be expressed in words.

Contained in the decisions both to renounce sensual love for the sake of a more durable attachment and to refuse the king's pension are motives that not only operate simultaneously but that also quite clearly belong to different levels of spiritual life—from physiological impulses and the demands of everyday existence to the loftiest principles and ideals. Rousseau was, after all, a moralist. He could not conceive of a person's behavior merely as a system of reactions to external stimuli since to do so would have meant disregarding the dependence of that behavior on a hierarchical system of values. The problem of the simultaneity of the different levels of spiritual life was for Rousseau also the problem of the simultaneity of good and evil in human spiritual experience, but above all in his own spiritual experience, since that was the principal subject of his investigation.

Arthur Chuquet in a once-famous book on Rousseau summed him up this way:

> Extreme in everything and the next moment contradicting himself, timid and insolent, abashed and cynical, as difficult to get started as to restrain . . . , given to enthusiasms and soon drooping in torpor, contending with and flattering of his age, cursing his literary fame and concerned only with how

to preserve and enhance it, seeking solitude and wanting to be known by the whole world, fleeing all attentions and vexed at not receiving them, disparaging of the great and residing among them, extolling the pleasures of independence and continually accepting hospitality for which he must pay with his wit, dreaming only of cottages and living in castles, attached to a hotel maid and caring only for women of the highest class, extolling the joys of the family and failing in his duties as father, covering the children of others with caresses and putting his own in an orphanage, effusively praising the celestial feeling of friendship and experiencing it for no one, giving of himself and at once reserved, at first expansive and warm and then suspicious and morose—that is Rousseau.[19]

Chuquet's book was written at the end of the nineteenth century, when the psychological methods of Taine dominated literary biography, but the essential thing is that Chuquet, like many of his contemporaries, was still unable to dispense with the romantic antithesis, so striking in its unexplained contradictoriness. Yet Rousseau knew over a hundred years before Chuquet how to *explain*, and he would have traced the greater part of the contradictions enumerated by Chuquet back to his own "primary elements." Rousseau the moralist had a very firm grasp of what was good and what was evil, categories that were defined for him by the morality of the natural man and the antidogmatic religion of love whose principles he had expounded in the *Profession de foi du vicaire savoyard*, and by ideas of civic virtue and republican moral purity (*Du contrat social*). For Rousseau the problem was not what a person ought to do (that was clear), but what he in fact did—the relationship between his obligations and his conduct.

For the hero of the *Confessions*, the nature of that relationship derives from the primary elements of his nature. He is kind and compassionate (he cannot bear the sight of the sufferings of others). He is capable of love and for that reason he seeks what is good. Yet there is also an inexhaustible source of evil in him—weakness, lack of will, vulnerability to momentary impulses, lack of self-restraint. Observing himself with curiosity, Rousseau recounts a series of episodes that demonstrate his susceptibility to a kind of lapse during which the power of momentary impulses completely overwhelms any thought about their consequences (and not merely those that will inevitably come later, but even those that will immediately follow upon the action itself) and he ceases to be in control of himself. He reports how once in his youth he dined, spent the night, and took breakfast at an inn without a sou to pay for it, nor any idea that he was cheating the innkeeper. He also reports how, despite the fact that he could not read music, he publicly conducted an orchestra he had asked to perform a piece of his own composition. And there are other instances too, many not in the least funny. Thus, Rousseau, bitterly judging himself, tells how he once abandoned on the street in a strange city a friend who had fallen down in an epileptic fit—abandoned him because he was weary of visiting Lyons and wanted to return to Annecy and Madame de Warens as quickly as possible. Rousseau calls these instances "moments of incomprehensible folly," although in constructing his image in the *Confessions*, he explains them very well.

A great deal is said about that folly in the *Confessions*, and it is said even more clearly in the *Dialogues*, which abound in summary formulations. "There is nothing great, beautiful, or generous that he would not be capable of on impulse, but he very quickly tires and falls again into torpor: it is in vain that beautiful and noble actions are for a few moments within the reach of his courage; the laziness and timidity that soon follow stifle and annihilate it, and that is why, although his feelings are sometimes lofty and noble, he has always been mean and worthless in his conduct" (811). Rousseau returned to this theme with the relentlessness of a detective. Several years later in *Les Rêveries du promeneur solitaire* he wrote, "Innately sensitive and good, pitying to a fault, and sensing that my soul was elevated by everything that contained generosity, I was humane, charitable, and helpful by inclination and even by passion, so long as only my heart was engaged. . . . As soon as my duty and my heart were opposed, it was rarely the former that was the victor . . . , [for] to act contrary to my inclinations was always impossible for me" (1053). Rousseau explains the mechanism of good and evil that the individual carries within himself in terms of the primary, organic features of that individual's nature. The source of evil in his own case is to be found in his ungovernable passions and desires and in his apathy. The correlation is possible because rapid transitions from enthusiasm to apathy are characteristic of impulsive natures.

But the greatest psychological discovery here is the simultaneity of ethically shaped experiences and spontaneous desires, and the operation of spiritual processes on several different planes at once. Someone may take pleasure in "the great, the true, and the noble" and in the fact that he is capable of experiencing and advocating such values; if at the same time he yields to the sensual needs active within himself, then he is guilty of weakness, or of a lack of moral discipline, but not necessarily of hypocrisy. Rousseau would never have accepted the reproach of hypocrisy for himself. The hypocrite is someone who does not really care about goodness; he just pretends to.

Consciousness is fluid. Rousseau's moral dogma knows the difference between good and evil, but psychological practice cannot always be so sure. A love of goodness and a true ethical sense prompt one to be ashamed of evil and to conceal it with other evil—with falsehood and deceit. Rousseau meticulously analyzes the spiritual condition that he calls "false shame"[*mauvaise honte*] as the constant and principal source of his own reprehensible actions. "The only thing that was able to lead him to evil was false shame, against which he struggled all his life with efforts that were as great as they were futile, since that shame was linked to his timid disposition, which confounded the ardent desires of his heart and compelled him to resort to a multitude of circuitous paths that were often blameworthy" (*Dialogues*, 897). False shame is thus derived from the initial contradiction between Rousseau's ardent passions and his timid disposition.

One of the most profound achievements of Rousseau's psychological analysis in the *Confessions* is connected with this theme of false shame. It is the story of the action that he considered the most criminal in his life. While employed as a servant in the home of Madame de Vercellis (in 1728), the sixteen-year-old Rousseau stole an old pink and white ribbon. When the theft was discovered, he accused a peasant girl, the servant Marion, of having given the ribbon to him, and thereby of having stolen it. He continued to insist on his story in the presence of Marion, who had denied her guilt. Both he and Marion were dismissed. Rousseau declares that he was tormented for the rest of his life by the thought of the subsequent fate of that girl, who, suspected of theft, could hardly have been expected to find a decent position, and who might have died of privation, or in despair have taken the path of degradation.

> No one will accuse me, I am certain, of palliating the heinousness of my offense. But I should not fulfill the aim of this book if I did not at the same time reveal my inner feelings. . . . Never was deliberate wickedness further from my intention than at that cruel moment. When I accused that poor girl, it is strange but true that my friendship for her was the cause. She was present in my thoughts, and I threw the blame on the first person who occurred to me. I accused her of having done what I intended to do myself. I said that she had given the ribbon to me because I meant to give it to her. When afterwards I saw her in the flesh my heart was torn. But the presence of all those people prevailed over my repentance. I was not much afraid of punishment, I was only afraid of disgrace. But that I feared more than death, more than crime, more than anything in the world. . . . It was my shame that made me impudent, and the more wickedly I behaved, the bolder my fear of confession made me. I saw nothing but the horror of being found out, of being publicly proclaimed, to my face, as a thief, a liar, and a slanderer. . . . If Monsieur de la Roque had taken me aside and said, "Do not ruin that poor girl. If you are guilty tell me so," I should immediately have thrown myself at his feet, I am perfectly sure. But all they did was to frighten me, when what I needed was encouragement. (86–87; 88–89)

Rousseau's psychological method takes its most concentrated form in this episode. The first causes of his behavior are weakness of will and impressionability, powerful reactions to external influences, and helplessness and terror in the face of the external world. Contradictions appear and are at once logically resolved: evil as the result of affection and attraction, shamelessness as the result of shame. And finally there are psychological gambits that the literature of the nineteenth and twentieth centuries might envy: the unconscious imputation of one's guilt to the object of one's innermost concerns, and the tranference of one's intention (to make a gift of the ribbon) to the victim of one's calumny. Revealed here as well is the logic of the simultaneous action of diametrically opposed impulses: compassion, love, and egoistical self-defense. At the same time, that self-defense has a social tinge—the sense of helplessness before those of high station who find it so easy to humiliate and trample another person.

In the *Confessions* and in the *Dialogues* and *Rêveries*, which continue its themes, Rousseau constructed a system of personality that is at once contradictory and consistent and that has a clearly defined dialectic of polar elements.

This system is embodied in the "sensitive" person, with his refined understanding of truth and goodness and his complete lack of those psychic mechanisms that control self-governance. He takes pleasure in the lofty and the good, and in moral values and the eloquence with which he proclaims them, but in every situation his conduct is subject to spontaneous emotions, passions, and desires, or to apathy, indolence, and aversion to constraint and external effort. He has all the necessary features for the explanation of that action taken by Rousseau which his contemporaries and posterity have condemned most harshly—the rejection of his own children. Rousseau did not feel spontaneous emotion for them (which might have been decisive), since the newborns were not shown to him. Instead, he felt fear at the increased hardship they might bring to a life that was already sufficiently difficult and unstable. He saw, that is, a threat to what was most important to him—his creative work—and he defended himself with a reaction of impulsive egoism.

It was no simple thing to admit, however. Rousseau kept silent until he learned in 1764 from an anonymous pamphlet called "*Le sentiment des citoyens*" (attributed to Voltaire) that his secret had been mercilessly exposed. He then proceeded to talk about it in the *Confessions*. Rousseau excoriates himself for the betrayal he was responsible for as a sixteen-year-old waif, a crime that may not have had anything like the disastrous consequences for his victim that he imagined. He speaks differently about his children, however. He discreetly admits that he made a mistake and indicates that he is repentant, although he immediately adduces reasons and justifications of every kind, and not merely ordinary domestic ones, but what is more astonishing, moral ones as well. "In handing my children over for the State to educate, for lack of means to bring them up myself, by destining them to become workers and peasants instead of adventurers and fortune hunters, I thought I was acting as a citizen and a father, and looked upon myself as a member of Plato's Republic" (357; 333).[20] The issue of his children has here become an ideological issue. The question is no longer the behavior of a frightened boy, but the conduct of an ideologue, the same one who brought about a revolution in pedagogical ideas and taught women to be mothers, as a contemporary lady put it.[21] A few lines before this declaration of membership in the republic of Plato, Rousseau observes, "My burning love for the great, the true, the beautiful, and the just; my horror of evil in every form . . . : is it possible that all these can ever dwell in the same soul along with depravity which, quite unscrupulously, tramples the dearest of obligations underfoot?" (356; 333). This last question is largely rhetorical, of course, since the whole thrust of Rousseau's brilliant psychological analysis has already shown the typically multilayered character of human consciousness.

But the essential thing here involved something else—the right of a weak man full of shortcomings to be an ideologue and a teacher of life. Rousseau's enemies wished to deprive him of that right and to dismiss him as a hypocrite. And he fought back passionately, because for him it was not ultimately a matter of hypocrisy at all but of the simultaneity of the different levels of spiritual life, and because virtue stood for him on the highest creative level, inasmuch as he was the energetic champion who had brought its lessons to humanity.

With regard to the period during which he adopted the position of the "stern citizen," Rousseau says in the *Confessions*, "Until then I had been good; from that moment I became virtuous, or at least intoxicated with virtue," and he declares that for four years he actually "became what" he "appeared" to be (416; 388). In the *Dialogues* he judges himself more severely, although he reaches the same conclusion:

> . . . Weak and governed by his inclinations, how could he have been [virtuous], having as his guide only his own heart and never his duty or his reason? How could virtue, which is always an effort and a struggle, have ruled in the bosom of weakness and pleasant idleness? He was good, because it was his nature to be so, and he did what was good, because it pleased him to do it; but if doing it meant going against his most cherished desires and slandering his heart in order to fulfill his duty, would he still have done it? I doubt it. The law of nature, or its voice at least, does not extend that far. Another voice would have had to command him then, and nature become silent. . . .
>
> Our man will not be virtuous because he is weak and virtue has belonged only to souls that are strong. But who, unable to attain that virtue, could

have admired, cherished, and adored it more than he? Who is there whose imagination could have depicted its divine image better and more vividly? (823–824)

From Rousseau's point of view, the psychological mechanism depicted here is not hypocrisy, but creative idealization. But this advocacy of a virtue that has not been realized in practice may become an objective part of cultural life only when it corresponds to an authentic inner experience that is ready to pay for its thought and its creative activity in full measure. And Rousseau did satisfy that condition. His creative life tolerated neither lack of will, nor timidity, nor indolence. In his writing he was relentless, indefatigable, and bold. The fearful, maniacally suspicious, egoistical person was, in this regard at least, wholly uncompromising. The press persecuted him and the church reviled him. His works were burned in Paris by the hand of the executioner and a warrant was signed for his arrest. His native Switzerland drove him from its borders, and local fanatics stoned the little house that served as his refuge. But Rousseau kept on writing and, when he could, he published whatever he thought needed to be said.

At the end of the nineteenth century and the beginning of the twentieth, Tolstoi approached the same question that had concerned Rousseau, although from the opposite direction. He asked whether a moralist could in his own life fall short of his moral teaching. His answer was that he could not. From this came the drama of Tolstoi's final years, a drama whose ground had been prepared by the whole development of his creative life and by that Russian tradition of total moral responsibility whose claims had been so insistently stated by Stankevich and Belinskii.

Part Three

HERZEN'S *MY PAST AND THOUGHTS* AND HISTORICAL IDENTITY

MY PAST AND THOUGHTS occupies a special place among the great works of world memoir literature. This memoir epic emerged from the same powerful ideological impulses as did the nineteenth-century Russian novel.[1]

Herzen passed through the Russian revolutionary romanticism of the 1830s and the natural school of the 1840s. His youthful autobiographical experiments are remarkable documents of post-Decembrist Russian romanticism, of the romantic mind's gradual mastery of the ideas of utopian socialism. While constructing his new, realistic worldview in the 1840s, Herzen sought objective forms for the expression of his own and his contemporaries' experience of life. Hence his interest in fiction (*Who Is to Blame?*, "The Thieving Magpie," "Doctor Krupov," and so on), which at other stages in his development he did not regard as his true vocation. In the creative work of the Herzen of the 1840s, the autobiographical hero deferred for a time to an authorial identity that embraced the philosophical, publicistic, and artistic works of the period.

Even though Herzen did depart in the 1840s from the directly autobiographical, both an unmediated yet generalized revelation of the self and a direct authorial judgment of life remained inseparable features of his creative thought. At the end of the decade, impelled by the momentous political events of the period, the Herzenian hero was, so to speak, reborn in the authorial image of the last *Letters from France and Italy* and the cycle *From the Other Shore*, which gave personal and passionate voice to the historical drama of the Russian revolutionary shaken by the revolution's collapse in Europe. That authorial image, the immediate antecedent of the autobiographical hero of *My Past and Thoughts*, was already far removed from the subjectivity of the romantic fragments of the 1830s, reflecting as it did a conflation of the earlier lyrical principle with a sharp sense of history.

Herzen brought to the conception of his autobiography philosophical, political, and moral criteria he had worked out in the 1840s. The sources for the method of *My Past and Thoughts*, however, are to be found not only in the early autobiographical sketches and in the lyrical journalism written at the end of that decade and the beginning of the 1850s. Of considerable importance too was Herzen's experience of the natural school (especially the work on *Who Is to Blame?*), as is apparent in the autobiography's first four parts with their characteristically broad spectrum of Russian life. In *My Past and Thoughts* Herzen returned to the autobiographical principle that had been such an organic part of his artistic thought, although he did so on a new, realistic basis. The autobiographical hero now became the focal point through which the immense, infinitely variegated world of objective reality was refracted. In working on *My Past and Thoughts* after 1852, Herzen was, for all the specificity of his creative method, engaged in the solution of problems that the life of that period had set before all Russian literature. Broached again in his book were numerous themes that had already been touched on by Pushkin and Lermontov in the 1820s and 1830s, and that would later become key issues for the Russian sociopsychological novel in the second half of the 1850s.

My Past and Thoughts is about the place and role of the thinking person in an unjustly organized social reality, about the relationship of the individual personality to society and to shared interests. That theme was prompted by the acute contradictions of Russian life in an era when the issue of the hero, of the Russian ideologue as the bearer of an active social consciousness, had acquired decisive significance for literature. The fate of that hero in the world around him was a theme of the Russian ideological novel, and it became a basic theme of *My Past and Thoughts*.

Herzen invested the central autobiographical hero of his epic with such a conscious relation to historical problems, and with such power of artistic generalization, that we do indeed have the right to speak of the *hero* of *My Past and Thoughts*, thereby linking him to heroes of the nineteenth-century Russian novel from Onegin and Pechorin to Bazarov and [Chernyshevskii's] Rakhmetov. Herzen's generalizing attitude toward himself is clearly stated in a letter he wrote to [his friend] Maria Reikhel' (on November 5, 1852) about the initial plan for *My Past and Thoughts*: "The position of the Russian revolutionary in relation to the European infidels should also be addressed, and nobody has thought about it yet" (24:359).

Herzen was free of the prohibitions of censorship, and in his writing the thinking hero or Russian ideologue appears undisguised as the revolutionary. But the theme of revolution is no less pervasive in censored nineteenth-century Russian literature. Herzen began speaking out loud about issues that the opposing thought of Dostoevskii would also be unwaveringly concerned with, that Turgenev would touch on in most of his novels (*Rudin*, *On the Eve*, *Fathers and Sons*, and *Virgin Soil*), and that Chernyshevskii would approach in *What Is to Be Done?* and "The Prologue" with all the directness of revolutionary thought breaking through the dissimulation imposed by the censorship. In the process of talking about himself in *My Past and Thoughts*, Herzen created a generalized image of the Russian revolutionary moving from Decembrism toward a revolutionary-democratic worldview. For the mature Herzen, the positive hero was above all an *active participant* (or potential participant) in the liberation movement, someone bent on transforming theory into practice.

The artistic system of *My Past and Thoughts* was the culmination of Herzen's entire previous development. At the same time, it was also conditioned by general historical and literary trends—it responded to the pressing demands of contemporary life.

The first half of the 1850s, the period when the plan for *My Past and Thoughts* had not only taken shape but was also largely realized, was a period of transition, a time when energy and materials were being accumulated for the great novel of the second half of the century. This was true of both Russian and French literature (Herzen was in those years involved in French cultural life in the most direct way).

After the death of Belinskii and the crushing of the Petrashevskii circle in Russia toward the end of the 1840s, the first period in the development of the Gogolian movement (the flowering of the natural school) came to a close. In France the 1840s and 1850s saw the end of the activity of Stendhal and Balzac. The events of 1848 placed a limit on the development of the prose of radical French romantics who had been closely linked to the ideology of utopian socialism. A transitional period followed, which ended in 1856 with the appearance of Flaubert's *Madame Bovary*, a book that opened the way for the French novel of the second half of the century. In Russian literature a similar role was played by *Rudin*, which appeared in 1856, a year after the completion of the initial version of the first five parts of *My Past and Thoughts*.

The transitional period of the end of the 1840s and the first half of the 1850s saw in both Russia and the West a heightened interest in memoirs, autobiographies, notes, and essays—indeed, in every kind of documentary genre. The historically conditioned and thus quite natural character of that interest is clear enough. After 1848–1849 it had become necessary to summarize what had taken place, to analyze the lessons of the revolution on the basis of prerevolutionary and revolutionary experience. World literature had already entered the age of realism as a theoretically proclaimed movement with its own aesthetic principles. And realism insisted in particular on the cognitive possibilities of literature. The search in the first half of the 1850s for analytical incisiveness and scientific reliability in the comprehension of reality still had not discovered the form of the large-scale sociopsychological novel, and it therefore frequently turned to the distinctive possibilities of the intermediate genres.

In 1857, when the first five parts of *My Past and Thoughts* were nearly finished, Herzen described the decade following 1848 in a survey article called "Western Books" (in the sixth issue of *The Bell*):

> Externally, the willfulness of power, concordats, and executions. Internally, the uncertainty of someone who, having come halfway, begins to suspect that he was mistaken, and as a consequence goes over his past, recent and remote, recollecting how it was, and comparing it to the present.
>
> In literature everything really has been taken over by the history and by the social novel. On the one hand, the life of particular eras, states, and individuals, and on the other, for the sake, so to speak, of comparison with the past, the confessions of contemporary man barely concealed in novelistic guise or directly in the form of memoirs and letters. . . .
>
> Together with an ever more alienated science whose only connection with life is through its applications, another, internal kind of work has been going on, one that we may may call social pathology. Proudhon and Dickens belong to it in equal degree. Proudhon's new vivisection seems to us the most remarkable development of the last two years—no scalpel has ever gone deeper. (13:92–93, 95)

Herzen had already been working on *My Past and Thoughts* for five years when he wrote that contemporary man was "going over his past, . . . recollecting how it was, and comparing it to the present."

However deeply immersed in western European scientific and literary interests Herzen became, Russian life remained a constant source of nourishment for his creative activity. In the 1850s the attention of Russia too was concentrated on memoir literature, as is evidenced by the appearance of such memoiristic works as Konstantin Aksakov's *Family Chronicle* and Dostoevskii's *Notes from the House of the Dead*. There was from the very beginning of the decade a heightened interest in confessions and autobiographies, especially those concerned with the depiction of childhood.[2] It was under these circumstances that Tolstoi's trilogy *Childhood, Boyhood, Youth*, was created.

Tolstoi finished *Childhood* in July 1852, and in October of the same year Herzen set to work on the first part of *My Past and Thoughts*, "Nursery and University." This fact is hardly accidental when regarded in a broad historical context, even though Herzen's memoirs in no way resemble Tolstoi's trilogy. For Tolstoi, *Childhood* was an early effort, whereas *My Past and Thoughts* was one of Herzen's greatest achievements in prose. The young Tolstoi created a tale of the autobiographical type (although its material is rather more autopsychological than autobiographical). Herzen created a work without precedent, one imbued with the same issues that the Russian novel would address in the following decades, but one that remained a "human document," that still contained unmediated evidence about life.

What is *My Past and Thoughts*—memoirs, an autobiographical novel, a unique historical chronicle? The question of the genre of *My Past and Thoughts* is of the utmost importance, inasmuch as our concern here is the specific cognitive nature of the book, the underlying principles of its reflection or refraction of reality. It is precisely this that the problem of genre pertains to, providing it is not understood in merely formal terms.

On the basis of its external, formal features, one might be inclined to assign *My Past and Thoughts* to the category of the artistic memoir. It is only too obvious, however, that Herzen's work does not fit under that rubric, that it exceeds it both in the reach of its historical conception and in the newness of the artistic problems it addresses.

Herzen's creative thinking about *My Past and Thoughts* began in October 1852, soon after the family drama that ended in the death of his wife. At first he wanted to write an account of the catastrophic events of his private life, a "memoir about my own affairs" (letter to Maria Reikhel' of November 5)—wanted, that is, to discredit [his adversary] Georg Herwegh and to fix the image of the woman he loved. But that initial plan grew irrepressibly under Herzen's pen, drawing in diverse social material and turning into a very complex structure that verged on the history, the memoir, and the novel, but that became neither novel nor historical chronicle.

It is characteristic that Herzen himself avoided precise definitions of *My Past and Thoughts*. In his letters, prefaces, and commentaries, he most often called the book "notes" [*zapiski*], but that was merely a provisional term for him, convenient precisely because of its vagueness, its lack of definite generic content.

One sometimes finds in the literature on Herzen a tendency to interpret *My Past and Thoughts* as a special variety of autobiographical novel. In taking this path, however, the investigator risks losing sight of the essence of Herzen's method, of its particular mode of cognition. Generic nomenclature is not important in itself, after all, but only to the extent that it assists in clarifying, in making more precise for us the underlying principles of a particular creative apprehension of reality.

Herzen's historical, publicistic, philosophical, and memoiristic book belongs within the province of art, inasmuch as it cognizes reality in terms of concrete, individual manifestations that have been symbolically extended to the point of becoming expressions of the general patterns of life.

The material depicted in *My Past and Thoughts* does, however, have a special quality that serves to define the methodology of the work. That quality is *authenticity*, since Herzen, like a historian, portrays what has actually taken place. The reader of the book is thus simultaneously subject to the influence of two powerful forces—the authenticity of real life and the expressiveness of art.

Generically, *My Past and Thoughts* is not a novel. The reason for this is not, of course, that it is insufficiently artistic but that it is based on a different cognitive principle, on a different kind of relationship between reality and its creative refraction. I have already discussed the cognitive specificity of the documentary genres in the introduction to the present book.

My Past and Thoughts also differs fundamentally from those artistic works that are based on the *material* of actual events. The factual or documentary character of a novel or tale is usually an extra-aesthetic fact (except in the historical novel). The reader may or may not be aware, for example, of the source of what is portayed in the actual personal experience of the author. That source material is vital for an understanding of the psychology of the writer's art, but as far as the work itself is concerned, it is not the origin of a fact that is important but its subsequent function in a specific artistic unity. The "genetic" approach to such questions blurs the difference, say, between *My Past and Thoughts* and the works of Tolstoi. Tolstoi reproduced actual events not only in their general outlines but frequently in their most concrete and insignificant details, whereas Herzen in *My Past and Thoughts* does not particularly excel in factual accuracy. And yet *Anna Karenina* is unquestionably a novel, while *My Past and Thoughts* is not a novel but rather, as Herzen put it, "the reflection of history in someone" (10:9).

The nonfictitiousness of what is depicted in *My Past and Thoughts* is thus not an accidental feature but one that is necessary, even essential to the reader—essential for a proper reading, that is. One may fully understand *Anna Karenina* without, for example, having any idea that the scene in which Levin proposes to Kitty is autobiographical, that Tolstoi in his own proposal to Sophia Andreevna Bers wrote the initials of the appropriate words on a card table with a piece of chalk.[3] It would, however, by no means be unimportant for an understanding or apprehension of *My Past and Thoughts* if it suddenly turned out that Herzen did not in fact elope with his bride, did not come to her in secret from Vladimir, and so on. To be sure, there is a variety of novel in which the issue of factual reliability is important, and that is the historical novel (which may sometimes be based on material that is contemporary or virtually contemporary to the author himself). The historical novel, however, remains open to aesthetic invention—indeed, remains wide open, and does so on principle. It is no accident that invented characters no different from the characters of any other novel usually stand at the center of the nineteenth-century historical novel.

There are two features linked to the "orientation toward authenticity" in *My Past and Thoughts* that ultimately determine the book's artistic system: the paramount importance of theoretical, generalizing thought, and the depiction of reality in terms that remain unmediated by the invented world of the artist. In creating a reflected, "second reality," the artist in the novel or tale reveals within it and through it his own conception of actual reality. The narrative of *My Past and Thoughts* is characterized by vast, epical sweep, but there is no plot in the work that stands like a partition between authorial consciousness and objective reality. Instead of a "second reality" with the author concealed at its heart, there is a direct discussion of life, with frank authorial judgments applied directly to real-life material.

The nineteenth-century novel is obviously no stranger to direct authorial commentary (one need only recall *War and Peace*, where the author's reflections take up whole chapters). This is a phenomenon of a different order, however. Authorial reflections in the classic sociopsychological novel are digressive, and authorial analysis is always accompanied by a figurative recreation of reality. Such is not the case with the documentary genres. Analytical thought in *My Past and Thoughts* is the living tissue of the artistic work, the medium that sustains the real-life material encompassed within it. A theoretical element may of course remain unassimilated in the literary work, sometimes exposing thereby the author's artistic impotence. But the theoretical element woven into the artistic unity of Herzen's autobiography acquires a special aesthetic quality. His thought is not a scientific syllogism, valuable only for its final result or its conclusion. What is important in Herzen is rather the very movement of his thought processes, the very fabric of his conceptual combinations and unique associations securing a new vision of reality. The "thoughts" in *My Past and Thoughts* have as much aesthetic import as do the scenes, dialogue, and portrait sketches.

Herzen maintains a continual awareness in the reader of the authenticity of what is being depicted. But the authentic reality of *My Past and Thoughts* is nonetheless a reality that has been purposefully organized both in its most general outlines and in its concrete details. Herzen examines that reality from a definite point of view, interpreting everything that reflects the general patterns that interest him. From the infinite multiplicity of the facts provided by life itself, he selects those that are best able to express the philosophical, historical, and moral significance of what has actually taken place. It is in this way that artistic symbolism comes into being in *My Past and Thoughts*.

The reader's certainty that the concrete details of *My Past and Thoughts* are not invented imparts a special quality to them. At the same time, the structural organization of the book is so important to Herzen that it gives him the right to rework creatively the factual material that has been included in it. He not only depicts scenes and recreates dialogue that he could not have witnessed; he also polishes, arranges, and edits for style the authentic documents (letters and diaries) that he has introduced into the text of his book, as a result not infrequently giving the events of the past a new valuation or emotional tonality, and sometimes even deviating when necessary from accurate communication of the facts. It is for these reasons that *My Past and Thoughts*, though it is an exceedingly important document in the history of Russian social thought and of the European liberation movement, cannot be used as a primary documentary source in the strict sense of the word. It would be a mistake to accept the book uncritically as factual material, or to use it without scrupulous verification. Yet even when Herzen does intentionally reshape reality, he still does not, even for a moment, break loose from it. He may alter a document, but that document is still necessary to him. In his system, the writer's choice between fact and fiction is not arbitrary.

Herzen was intensely interested in contemporary historiography, particularly in those representatives of the new historical school who were attempting to combine scientific research with artistic representation of the past. Herzen had great admiration for Thierry, Carlyle, and Michelet. In regard to Michelet's *Histoire de France au seizième siècle: La Renaissance*, Herzen wrote to him, "It is a poem; it is history turned into art and philosophy" (25:241), a formulation that was no less programmatic for Herzen himself. Michelet's *Renaissance* appeared in 1855, after Herzen had already written the first version of the first five chapters of *My Past and Thoughts*. Herzen responded with such interest to Michelet's artistic historicism precisely because it was in harmony with his own just-completed creative experiment.

Boris Reizov, in characterizing the method of French historians of the 1810s and 1820s in his book *French Romantic Historiography*, speaks of Michelet's characteristic mastery of the "two-dimensional" portrait:

> Michelet's whole intellectual development, as well as the tendencies of the science and literature of his day, impelled him toward a method that might, with a certain approximateness, be termed "symbolical." And Michelet himself in a letter to Charles Manion defined his method in this way: "The pictorialist school (and the materialist school: Barante et al.) was concerned with form; the analytical school (Mignet et al.) wanted to capture the spirit. It was left to the translator of Vico [that is, Michelet] to found the symbolical school, which tried to reveal the idea behind the transparent form."[4]

The purposeful selection of what is to be portrayed, the organization of actual events in a structural unity, the constructing of personalities, individual and yet at the same time historically generalized, the historical symbolism of expressive details—all this brought the author of *My Past and Thoughts* closer to his older contemporaries, the representatives of the new historical school.

Comparison of *My Past and Thoughts* with the works of historians is obviously possible only on the level of a few general tendencies, since Herzen's book takes a different cross section of reality than histories do, and it draws its material from a different kind of human experience than they do. Herzen himself put it very clearly in the 1866 preface to part 5: "*My Past and Thoughts* is not a historical monograph but the reflection of history in someone who *accidentally* got in its way." This formulation defines *My Past and Thoughts* as a distinctive amalgam of historiography and autobiography and memoir, but to the extent that one regards the book as a special form of the "reflection of history," it also sets it apart from the memoir. Indeed, it is unlikely that there is another memoir so imbued with *conscious historicism* or so governed by the conception of the clash and struggle of different historical stages, a conception that Herzen took from the Russian Hegelianism of the 1840s and reworked in terms of his own revolutionary dialectic. It is in the first five parts of *My Past and Thoughts* that that conception finds its most cogent and finished expression.

The first five parts of *My Past and Thoughts* and the three subsequent parts (which survive in fragmentary or unfinished form) reflect different phases in the development of Herzen's worldview, and therefore different ways of embodying authorial consciousness. The last three parts have neither the precise construction, the distinctive "unity of action," of the first five, nor their markedly lyrical authorial stance. The episodically essayistic form of the last three parts and the completely purposeful and systematic arrangement of the first five are methodologically heterogeneous phenomena. When Herzen set about publishing the first five parts of *My Past and Thoughts* in London in 1860, he regarded them as a finished work (despite the fact that he had already been working on part 6 for a long time), as the culmination of a plan that had first taken shape during the political and personal catastrophes of 1852. Herzen is quite explicit about this in his preface to the London edition of *My Past and Thoughts*: "Many of my friends advised me to begin complete publication of *My Past and Thoughts*. . . . Rereading my last notebooks to an old friend of my youth last summer, I myself *recognized familiar* features and stopped. My work was done!" (8:9–11).

The first five parts of *My Past and Thoughts* recount the story of the maturation of an ideologue of the Russian revolutionary movement in the light of Herzen's favorite idea of a clash between two worlds—the old and the new. The theme of two worlds is pervasive in Herzen's writing (beginning with the romantic sketches of the 1830s). In *My Past and Thoughts* it receives a realistic and dialectical treatment.

Part 1, "Nursery and University," involves the hero's "learning years." He spares no effort to find a way out of the old world of gentry life into a world of new human relationships. Part 2, "Prison and Exile," describes his confrontation with cruel reality (the old world of serfdom and Nicholas's bureaucracy). Part 3, "Vladimir-on-the-Kliaz'ma," concerns the maturation of the heroine, of the new woman, as well as the hero's development under the salutary influence of a great love and the reality of family life. The main theme of part 4, "Moscow, Petersburg, and Novgorod," is the formation of a new worldview (Herzen himself called it "realistic") and, from its perspective, a structured history of Russian social thought in the 1840s. Part 5, "Paris—Italy—Paris," reengages the themes of the *Letters from France and Italy* and *From the Other Shore*: the bourgeois revolution, the capitalist system, and Western philistinism. Presented in the first half of part 5 is the sociopolitical dimension of the clash between the Russian revolutionary and the old world of the bourgeois West. In the second half, that political theme is combined with the story of Herzen's family drama.

The most recent attempt (in 1848) to change the world had come to nought, as had the hero's own efforts to base his personal happiness on the principles of a morality that was both rational and free. But neither the first failure nor the second altered the meaning of the struggle or Herzen's conviction that the old would ultimately give way to the new. Such is the subject matter of the first five parts of *My Past and Thoughts*.

In order to portray someone in a novel, tale, memoir, or *portrait*, it is necessary not merely to identify certain elements of his spiritual life, but also to establish the correlation among those elements, to find the structural principle of their interrelation. For a writer this also means finding an *object of depiction* [*predmet izobrazheniia*]. For Herzen, that structural principle was the individual's historical identity.

The origins of *My Past and Thoughts* go back to the 1840s, an era that was fascinated with historicism and imbued with philosophical dialectics. Herzen sought to understand not so much the individual's psychological features as he did his historical ones. This did not mean that sociohistorical and psychological analysis were opposed to each other. On the contrary, they were part of a continuum in which individual sociohistorical conditionality was perceived as essential to psychological analysis and as the basis of the psychological novel. In delineating cause-and-effect relationships, nineteenth-century realism moved beyond the general understanding of the conditioning of human beings by epoch, milieu, and circumstance toward an understanding that was ever more detailed and precise, even to the point of apprehending the complex determinations of individual spiritual impulses.

The plan for *My Past and Thoughts* took shape in the early 1850s, when the sociopsychological novel of the second half of the nineteenth century was still in a nascent stage. As a consequence, there is nothing in *My Past and Thoughts* like the psychologism that eventually found realization in the novel, nor could there be. Every original artistic system comes into being by way of a *selection* of the means that are most necessary to the author's cognitive purposes. Herzen, in portraying those people who were characteristic of the Russian reality of his day, called them "filament conductors of historical currents."

Although an older contemporary of the great novelists of the second half of the century and a witness of their quests (Tolstoi's *War and Peace*, Dostoevskii's *Crime and Punishment* and *The Idiot*, Flaubert's *Madame Bovary* and *L'Éducation sentimentale*, and all of Turgenev's novels except for *Virgin Soil* were published during his lifetime), Herzen continued to follow his own path. Neither Turgenev's detailed examination of inner life, nor Tolstoi's dialectic of the soul, nor Dostoevskii's psychological "abysses" affected his own treatment of the individual human being.

Heightened interest in the contradictions of spiritual life and concern with the details of psychic processes were two essential features of nineteenth-century realism. In *My Past and Thoughts*, however, experiences are related directly, in very clear and rather traditional outlines, without any attempt to reveal either the contradictoriness or the multidimensionality of spiritual life. And this is true in the book's depiction of even the sharpest conflicts and spiritual traumas.

Portrayed in the chapter "A Year Later (1851)" in part 5 is Herzen's decisive and catastrophic final confrontation with his wife. There is nothing unforeseen, paradoxical, or contradictory about the hero's behavior. All his reactions follow each other in a predictable sequence and are fully in keeping with the psychological norm. At first there are "impulses of vengefulness, jealousy, and outraged pride." Even their external expression remains traditional: "I stood in front of the large table in the living room with my arms folded—my face, very likely, was completely distorted." Then, upon seeing his wife's suffering, the hero is overcome with pity and remorse, and the external expression of these feelings too is of the most straightforward and ordinary kind: "That look of infinite suffering, of mute anguish, at once stilled the ferment of my passion. I began to pity her, tears ran down my cheeks, and I was ready to throw myself at her feet and beg her forgiveness" (10: 261).

At the end of the 1830s in his portrait of the spiritual life of Pechorin, Lermontov had introduced into Russian literature an element of psychological contradiction. Herzen therefore contented himself with summary depictions of spiritual states not because he neither knew nor understood

the possibilities of their detailed elaboration and complication, but because they were not what he required. The nineteeenth-century psychological novel showed the individual as historically and socially conditioned. His particular cast of mind was regarded as a product of that
conditionality. Herzen, however, was primarily interested in analyzing
the nature of historical conditionality itself and in its spontaneous manifestation in human material.

The novelist usually presents his characters in terms of their actions,
reflections, and conversations, and it is only in passing that he explains
from his own vantage what is being portrayed. But a generalized unity of
character, event, and subject may be constructed not only by means of
figurative synthesis; explanation and analysis may also be employed. This
is possible because elements that have been analytically separated in an
artistic context at once reassemble themselves in a new structural unity. It
is this path, the opposite as it were, that Herzen takes in his autobiography, a work in which things that have actually happened are recounted by
a biographically concrete author who remains unmediated in a conventional narrator or storyteller and whose own voice is therefore necessarily
audible. Dialogue, scenes, and the concrete depiction of feelings and
events are used by Herzen to *reinforce* his conception of the individual
personalities that he has already subjected to explicit authorial judgment,
and whose historical and social essence he has already explained theoretically. He may also project his own historically generalized personality
into this context.

A number of monumental characters embodying Herzen's understanding of historical processes are constructed in this analytical fashion in
My Past and Thoughts. Such, for example, is his image of Vladimir
Engel'son. Herzen revealed in Engel'son, whom he had known for a long
time, the same psychic type to which Dostoevskii was to give his attention. In Herzen's view, his own and Engel'son's generations belonged to
two different psychological stages—before the reign of Nikolai I and during it (even though Engel'son and his contemporaries had as children
been exposed to Decembrism). Herzen's image of Engel'son is derived
deductively from this premise:

> In Engel'son I studied the difference between that generation and our own.
> Later on I met many people who were not so talented, not so developed, but
> who had the *species' same morbid flaw* in all their parts. A terrible sin lies
> upon the reign of Nikolai for that moral destruction of a generation, for that
> wrecking of the souls of its children. . . . They were all infected with a pas-
> sion for introspection, self-analysis, and self-criticism; they scrupulously
> confided their psychic phenomena and were fond of endless confessions and
> accounts of the nervous events of their lives. (10:344–345)

This characterization reminds one of Dostoevskii's theory of the "hysterical display" [*nadryv*] as it is expounded in his *Notes from Underground*. Herzen's essay on the "Engel'son" type, however, was written in 1858 for the most part, whereas *Notes from Underground* was not published until 1864. Herzen reached an understanding of that new variety of egocentric person on the basis of his own experience and independently of Dostoevskii.

One of the most remarkable pieces of writing in *My Past and Thoughts* is the image of Herzen's father, Ivan Alekseevich Iakovlev. The monumental image of the Russian Voltairean rotting away in isolation from the life of the people at once takes on vast historical significance. The features of his father's personality were for Herzen the "consequence of the encounter of two things so opposed to each other as the eighteenth century and Russian life through the agency of a third that was highly conducive to the development of capricious behavior: the idleness of the manor" (8:86). The key to this formulation is Herzen's conception of the eighteenth century as an age of enlightenment and revolution. Eighteenth-century Russian aristocratic freethinking was a combination of skepticism, gentry arrogance, feudal habits, and a disdain for Russian culture. Here the mechanism of the theoretical explanation of personality is not kept outside the confines of the text as it usually is in the mid-nineteenth-century novel but is frankly and directly introduced into it. The depiction of Ivan Alekseevich Iakovlev's peculiar spiritual stamp is preceded by an analysis of the conditions that engendered it. The most basic of those conditions was his irreparable social isolation, which led to his contempt for others, his cult of superficial decorum, his bitterness and suspiciousness, and even his miserliness as a manifestation of his fear of life, of his distrust of the external world.

The theoretical explanation of personality in *My Past and Thoughts* is, however, always surrounded by a living tissue of concrete, uniquely individual details: "The old man read the *Moscow Gazette* and the *Journal de St. Pétersbourg* over his coffee; it would not hurt to note that he gave orders for the *Moscow Gazette* to be warmed so that his hands would not be chilled by the dampness of the pages, and that he read the political news in the French text, finding the Russian obscure" (8:93).

Squeezed into this close-up is a wealth of social content. The old man's suspiciousness has reached the point it reaches only in the misanthrope, and his misanthropy is intimately linked to the isolation of his circle from Russian culture and from the Russian people. There is therefore an internal connection between the warmed pages of the *Moscow Gazette* and the fact that Iakovlev read the political news in French.

Annenkov praised Turgenev in 1854 for the fact that in his writing "the idea . . . is always concealed deep inside the work": "the work must carry everything that is required within itself and not permit the author's interference. The latter's observations always make an unpleasant impression, recalling to mind the sign with the pointing finger."[5] The pointing finger of the writer's thought is met with at every step in *My Past and Thoughts*. Herzen takes someone who actually existed as his character, depicts him in the circumstances in which he actually lived, and then theoretically explains the general patterns that governed the acts, gestures, and words of that character, whom he regards as a concretely individual representative of a particular social stratum.

The Tolstoi and Volkonskii family chronicles were used extensively in *War and Peace*, where among others Tolstoi's own grandfather, Nikolai Sergeevich Volkonskii, is portrayed—in the guise of the old Prince Bolkonskii, an artistic symbol of the old-fashioned Russian aristocracy.[6] Herzen in *My Past and Thoughts* also needed to generalize about the historical fate of the eighteenth-century Russian aristocracy. His own father served him as a living resource for that purpose. But in Herzen's system, the original real-life experience has not been left outside the text, nor is there in the text any "second reality" or any mediating link of invented character. Rather it is the original real-life experience itself that has become the object of analysis and that directly embodies the artist's idea. Herzen's act is a fully creative one, inasmuch as it involves drawing the disparate empirical manifestations of personality together into a system, identifying what is dominant in those manifestations, correlating what until then has been left uncorrelated, and generalizing the particular. It involves, in other words, cognizing the interconnections of individual spiritual life. As applied to the characters of *My Past and Thoughts*, the author's analytical investigations are also in every instance acts that serve to create aesthetic unity and concrete artistic form.

All this pertains not merely to those people who have taken their place in history (of whom there are so many in *My Past and Thoughts*), or to those who have been clearly shaped by historical events and circumstances, but also to personalities of the most private kind. There is, for example, the story of the intimacy of Herzen's and Ogarev's friend [the translator] Nikolai Ketscher with the poor orphan Serafima. Ketscher was about to leave Serafima, but then, moved by her devotion to him, he married her.

> She completely ruined Ketscher's life. . . . Between Ketscher and Serafima, and between Serafima and our circle, there was a vast and terrible chasm. . . . We belonged to different ages of man, to different geological formations, to different volumes in the history of the world. We were the children of the new Russia educated at the university and the academy; we were fascinated then by the political brilliance of the West, and we adhered

religiously to our lack of faith, . . . while she, having been brought up in a schismatic monastery, still belonged to the world of pre-Petrine Russia and possessed all the prejudices of esoteric religion and all the fantastic notions of old Russian society. (9:236–37)

The conflict between Ketscher and Serafima is not the psychological conflict of two lovers from different social backgrounds but the clash of two different cultural stages, of two different "ages of man."

Serafima's whole psyche with its "stuck understanding" and its backwardness is derived from its connection to the pre-Petrine stage of Russian life. Ketscher's circle accepted Serafima wholeheartedly and utterly destroyed her, turning her backwardness into a pose by suggesting to her that it was "a good thing": "But she herself did not want to remain *merely* what she had been. What then was the result? We—revolutionaries, socialists, and champions of the emancipation of women—turned that naive, devoted, simple creature into a Muscovite petite bourgeoise! And did not the Convention, the Jacobins, and the Commune itself turn France into a petit bourgeois and Paris into an *épicier*?" (9:242). The shift from the socially displaced and disoriented Serafima to the Western petty bourgeoisie, which Herzen saw as the historical consequence of "unsuccessful revolution," is in the system of his thought a perfectly natural one, however abrupt it may be.

In the memoiristic and autobiographical genres the principle of authorial self-expression has special importance, although the absence of an explicit authorial personality may also be just as fundamental.

The tasks and methods of the merely factual memoir were alien to Herzen, but so too was its contrary, the psychological memoir, whose eternal model and prototype is Rousseau's *Confessions. My Past and Thoughts*, after all, is concerned less with psychological self-revelation than with the historical self-definition of an individual human being. The autobiographical hero of *My Past and Thoughts* is, like the whole structure of the work as a whole, fundamentally defined by a conscious historicism. In this sense, the basic orientations of *My Past and Thoughts* are even opposed to those of the *Confessions*. Rousseau was to the highest degree a product of his time, although subjectively he conceived of himself as an unprecedented and unique phenomenon. Herzen, however, for all the intensity of his self-consciousness, always viewed himself as the representative of a generation, of a particular historical stratum. And it is this that conditions both the scope and the selection of the elements that constitute the personality of the central hero of *My Past and Thoughts*.

The Rousseauean tradition had extraordinary significance for the formation of the psychological method in nineteenth-century literature. It was combined in a distinctive way with an interest in physiology and biology, and with efforts to use them as the basis of psychological analysis. Ogarev, the person closest to Herzen, was especially active in efforts of this kind. Fragments of Ogarev's *My Confession,* a work intended as an answer to *My Past and Thoughts,* have survived (Militsa Nechkina dates the beginning of Ogarev's work on this project from 1856). Addressing Herzen in the very first lines of his *Confession,* Ogarev emphasizes the nature of his own orientation, deliberately contrasting it with Herzen's:

> Confessing merely for the sake of repentance is hard for us to comprehend; to do that you need a genuine feeling of repentance and of responsibility to some higher judge. Our repentance is understanding. And understanding is both our delight and our punishment. I want to look at myself and my story, which is after all better known to me than it is to anyone else, from the point of view of a naturalist. I want to see how this animal called N[ikolai] Ogarev turned out the way he did and not otherwise; I want to see what his physiopathological development consists of, from what kind of features, both internal and external, it has been shaped and will continue to be shaped for a certain time. You realize that great candor is needed for this, certainly no less than is required by repentance? Nowhere may one ascribe an effect to some other, inauthentic cause; nowhere may one be intimidated by the word "shame"! Thought and passion, health and sickness—all must be readily apparent, all must point to a logic, not *my own* but the *logic* of nature, of necessity, the one that the ancients called *fatum,* and that for him who observes and understands is the process of life. My confession must be a fragment of the physiological pathology of a human personality.[7]

Ogarev's letters, especially those written to Herzen, are consistent with *My Confession.* They contain authentic nineteenth-century psychological analysis; they are tortuous and precise, but by no means are they always prepared to explain spiritual life completely or to break it down into its simpler elements. In an 1861 letter to Herzen, Ogarev examines in merciless detail the story of his break with Natal'ia Ogareva:

> Well then, what if my consent and my blessing at that time merely crowned a growing indifference and weariness? That is frightening! And what if my enthusiasm, self-analysis, and confused egoism had all got so mixed up together that they were the cause of an irrational act that one moment seemed elegant and the next made one ask oneself: did I not put up with it all out of indifference, did I not have in myself a dark craving for personal freedom? And suddenly I am overcome with horror. Am I delirious now, am I losing my mind, or was I an unconscious mixture of elegance and meanness? . . . It is obvious that I still have not got over the vile habit of doing to myself what

Ketscher does to everybody else—root around, that is, until one digs up either an imaginary or a genuine meanness. . . . A human being, if he is not merely something unknown, is a machine so complicated that all its wheels are suspect to me, yet not to know how to take an objective view of oneself would also be cowardice and blind man's buff. . . . And what if there is a literary requirement in all this agitation—that I say how agitated I am and that it be well written too.[8]

The accomplishments of contemporary natural science, the philosophical problem of the relationship between nature and history, and the physiologically conditioned nature of human behavior were all important to Herzen. Nevertheless, the strongest element in his creative thought remained the historicism that he had mastered so thoroughly in the 1840s. It was not at all his intention in constructing his autobiographical image in *My Past and Thoughts* to unveil every secret. On the contrary, he was convinced that there were facts concerning a person's internal and external life that there was no reason to expose to the light of analysis and artistic depiction. He *omitted* those facts, as may easily be demonstrated by comparing the autobiography with the available documentary and biographical materials.

The family drama presented in part 5 of *My Past and Thoughts* had an ideological and consequently a historical meaning for Herzen. But in none of his works did he ever refer to the painful situation that developed between him and Natal'ia Ogareva in the 1860s (although it found extensive reflection in his letters). From Herzen's point of view, that situation lacked general significance and interest. Moreover, he saw himself as a champion of enlightenment, and a pathology humiliating to the rational person therefore had no place in his approach to the examination of spiritual life.

Yet another example is chapter 21 of part 3. After recounting the denouement of his affair with Praskov'ia Medvedeva in Viatka, Herzen concludes: "Sobbing, I read her letter over and over. *Qual cuor tradisti!* Later on I saw her again; she gave me her hand amicably, but it was awkward for both of us; each left something unsaid, each avoided referring to something" (8:350). This contains no misrepresentation of the facts, but much has been suppressed. Herzen had found Medvedeva a position in Vladimir as governess in the family of Governor Kuruta. In 1840 he wrote from Vladimir to [the architect and his fellow exile] Aleksandr Vitberg that she had moved to Moscow with the children:

I know about her bad luck, and I have long known about her complaints against me. Here are the facts from the beginning. . . . Kuruta decided not to keep her on since Prask[ov'ia] Petr[ovna] had turned up knowing no French or German whatsoever and had not the slightest inkling of what her duties

were. . . . Nikolen'ka had been placed, Soniuta had applied to school . . . ,
Liudin'ka was already in a pension, and payment for six months had already
been made, and *not by Praskov'ia Petrovna*. . . . Until last month she lived
in her apartment free of charge, her firewood was given to her, and now she
has just been offered a well-paying position. What is she complaining about?
. . . She is upset because I did not visit her very much. . . . Except for losing
her subsidy, which of course was not my fault, her affairs are in fact in very
good shape. (22:75)

It is not difficult to imagine a nineteenth-century psychological novel in
which the whole banal cruelty of this conflict would have been fully exploited. For Herzen, however, it was merely a lamentable but marginal
episode in his private life, the sort of thing, in fact, that ought to be *omitted*. The *limits of the depictable* in Herzen's writing were in part established by the aesthetic habits of the romantic era that had formed him and
by the cult of the beautiful and the harmonious that had been combined
as early as the 1830s with utopian dreams of a harmonious social order.
In *My Past and Thoughts*, however, those limits were above all determined by the book's historical task—its portrayal of the maturation of a
positive hero, of a Russian ideologue and revolutionary activist.

The criteria of judgment used in *My Past and Thoughts* were derived
from the ethics of revolutionary activism (I shall look at this in more
detail later on). Herzen's political and moral views and their mutual influence on each other conditioned both the underlying principle governing
the expression of authorial personality in his works and the evolution of
that principle from the romantic hero in the 1830s, through the search for
objective knowledge in the 1840s, to the realistic autobiography of *My
Past and Thoughts*, in which the hero is regarded as a phenomenon of the
objective world, and finally to the departure from autobiography in the
book's final sections, which were written at a time when populist criteria
were assuming crucial significance for Herzen.

The positive hero of *My Past and Thoughts* is by no means an "elect
personality" in the old romantic sense. Instead, he is conceived as a *representative*, as the best representative, of the "educated minority" that has
been called upon to lead the Russian liberation movement. The life of this
representative of the best forces in Russian society must therefore be exemplary, since the individual whose life it is bears a responsibility for it to
the people of the new world.

If in part 1 of *My Past and Thoughts* the hero enters the life of a circle
of excellent young people very much like himself, then in part 2 he stands
opposed to the terrible and immoral world of serfdom and the tsarist
bureaucracy. Depicted in part 3 is his triumphant struggle for a great
love. In part 4 he is a member of a Moscow circle of advanced Russians

of the 1840s, where he is portrayed as the most sober-minded and right-thinking among them, the one who has reached the highest level of inner freedom, since that is in fact how Herzen's relationship with Granovskii and the other Moscow liberals is interpreted. In part 5, as the representative of young Russia, the hero comes into conflict with Western philistinism and bourgeois corruption, and as the rigorously consistent revolutionary he clashes with "incomplete revolutionaries" and ultimately with Herwegh.

The elements constituting the autobiographical hero's image in *My Past and Thoughts* are almost entirely devoid of individual psychological coloration, especially in the first chapters. Instead, they are qualities that by their very nature are measured quantitatively, that express the intensity of the individual's inner sense of the world around him, his energy, and the degree of his enthusiasm and vigor. Somehow we imagine Herzen's creative work, ultimate destiny, and individual identity for ourselves, and it is on this basis that we project his personality as we read *My Past and Thoughts*. Yet what do we actually know about that personality from the text itself (irrespective of our preconceived ideas)? A characterization frequently encountered in part 1 is "lively boy." Associated with it are such qualities as "playfulness," "impulsiveness," "enthusiasm," and even "impressionability" and "responsiveness" [*udobodvizhimost'*] (in part 3). These attributes, which are indicative of the intensity of the hero's apprehension of life, would be almost physiological were they not subsumed in a kind of historical and ideological system—were they not imbued, that is, with the values characteristic of that system. The criteria for these values have been derived from the ideal of the Russian revolutionary activist and, more broadly, from the harmonious man of utopian socialism who is receptive both to a higher spiritual life and to more mundane pleasures and passions. Sometimes explicit moral values are applied to the hero of *My Past and Thoughts*—sincerity, truthfulness, and hatred of falsehood and duplicity. The criteria for these values may be found in the same ideal of the struggling, life-affirming, and self-affirming personality, since falsehood and duplicity degrade and diminish that personality and cause it to shrivel up.

"The new world was knocking at the door, and our hearts and souls opened themselves to it. . . . Impressionable, sincerely youthful, we were easily carried away by its powerful current" (8:162). Taken by itself, the phrase "sincerely youthful" is an odd collocation, but in the light of the historical meaning that Herzen ascribed to all phenomena, including the biological, it is completely predictable. The contrast between old age and youth, or rather between senescence and youth, in part 1 of *My Past and Thoughts* is neither biological nor based on signs of age. The point is not that Ivan Alekseevich Iakovlev is old, but that he embodies the idea of decrepitude, obsolescence, and death. He is old and infirm as a matter of principle. Health is offensive to him. Youthfulness, on the other hand, is a forward movement; it is love and revolution. Beginning with chapter 6 ("Moscow University"), Herzen's autobiography is inseparably linked with the history of Russian culture and Russian social thought. The maturation of the hero merges with the political education of Russian youth. Youthfulness becomes the youthfulness of a generation. And it is quite clear here that Herzen is interpreting youthfulness as the historically formed mode of behavior of definite social groups at a definite period of time. "I regard as a great misfortune the situation of a people whose younger generation has no youthfulness...; mere youngness is not enough." "Youngness" in this context is a physiological concept, whereas "youthfulness" is a historical or even political concept. That this is so is fully apparent in Herzen's discussion of the fact that the French Revolution "was made by young people," but that "the last youth in France were the Saint-Simonists and the phalanstery" (8:151). There thus emerges a historical and even an ideological meaning for such apparently ahistorical qualities as "vitality," "playfulness," "impulsiveness," "impressionability," and so on.

The contrasting in part 5 of My Past and Thoughts of the positive hero with a negative one (Herwegh) also finds expression in the contrasting of psychic perversity and hysterical display with spiritual health and the ideal of "simple" behavior: "It may be that the uninhibited truthfulness, inordinate self-confidence, and rich simplicity of my behavior—its *laisser aller*—came from vanity too; it may be that I brought down misfortune on myself because of it, but so be it. . . . With strong muscles and nerves I stood independent and unique, passionately ready to offer my hand to another, but for myself accepting, like alms, neither help nor support" (10:251).

The hero of My Past and Thoughts bears a responsibility for Russian culture and the Russian revolutionary movement; it is for this reason that everything dubious, everything casting a shadow, must be stripped from him. He must be neither guilty nor degraded.

When touching, in the Viatka letters to his betrothed, on his relations with Medvedeva, Herzen was repentant and judged himself harshly. In My Past and Thoughts he speaks merely in passing of the "pitiful weakness" with which he "prolonged the half-truth" that he had "ruined" the existence of R. (the initial by which Medvedeva is referred to in the book). And behind all this is the certainty that in making the choice between a great love and a momentary attraction, it would not have been possible to act otherwise than he did.

In chapter 28, where the family conflict of 1842–1843 is recounted, there is a similar relationship between the text of My Past and Thoughts and a document contemporary to the events it describes. In his journal for 1843 Herzen reproached himself with extraordinary severity for a casual infatuation that resulted in his wife's humiliation. In *My Past and Thoughts* the same episode is turned against the hypocrisy of conventional morality and those religio-ascetic views that brought about a woman's mental breakdown.

It would be naive to suppose that Herzen's moral sense was less rigorous in the 1850s than it had been in the 1840s and 1830s. He did in fact continue to take full responsibility for the conduct of his life. But as the author of *My Past and Thoughts*, he was faced with a special task. He was less interested in delving into the details of his own and others' spiritual life than in showing the maturation of a man of the new world. The valuational accent in *My Past and Thoughts* is different than in Herzen's journal because in the former the family conflict of 1843 has been transferred from the psychological plane to the historical and the philosophical—to that of the struggle against the "Christian phantoms" of the old world. The moral-psychological problem of guilt has accordingly been pushed into the background.

In his judgment in *My Past and Thoughts* of the episodes concerning Medvedeva and the servant girl Katerina, Herzen remains true to himself. As a utopian socialist who in his youth had espoused Saint-Simon's "rehabilitation of the flesh" and Fourier's doctrine of the passions, he is unable to regard either passion or pleasure as evil. That evil is rather to be found in falsehood, which degrades and circumscribes the individual, and in the suffering and wrong that are inflicted on or that bring harm to others. Such is the historical logic of Herzen's moral judgments and self-judgments in the book.

Without the historical conception from which *My Past and Thoughts* takes its departure, neither the juxtaposition of Herzen and Herwegh that constitutes the basis of part 5 and its family drama nor the moral judgment of Herwegh that was so essential to Herzen would have been possible. What was it that Herwegh was actually guilty of? Egoism? But Herzen, like every other revolutionary democrat of the 1840s, 1850s, and 1860s was steadfast in defending "lofty" egoism from conventional and religio-ascetic morality. Was it Herwegh's unrestrained passion and desire for pleasure? But Herzen himself acknowledged the human right to pleasure. Was it his deception of a friend? But Natal'ia Aleksandrovna, the model heroine of *My Past and Thoughts*, was just as guilty of deception and falsehood as Herwegh himself. Nevertheless, in his account of the family drama Herzen still draws a clear line between good and evil, turning that line into the historical boundary between the old world and the new. He remembers a French novel called *Arminius* that he had read in his youth:

We all know from the history of the first centuries of the encounter and collision of two different worlds: the old one—classical, educated, but corrupt and obsolete, and the new one—savage as a forest animal, but full of slumbering strength and chaotic striving; we know, that is, the *official*, journalistic side of the collision, but not the side that resides in insignificant details and in the mute life of the hearth. We know the events in their large-scale aspect, but nothing of the fates of those who were directly dependent on those events, and whose lives were broken and quietly destroyed by them. Here blood is replaced by tears, ravaged cities by devastated families, and battlefields by forgotten tombs. The author of *Arminius* . . . tried to reproduce the clash of the two worlds in the family hearth—one world entering history from the forest, and the other departing it for the grave.

. . . It never occurred to me that I too would fall victim to the same kind of collision, that my own hearth would be devastated and crushed in the meeting of two different tracks of world history. (10:238)

Self-affirmation in *My Past and Thoughts* never becomes self-admiration, since it is oriented not toward an individual as a particular, self-contained entity, but rather to that individual's historical function—his political and social activism. Herzen transforms those involved in the family drama into the representatives of two different historical formations—young Russia and the bourgeois West. It is on this basis, rather than on that of proscriptions and prohibitions derived from prevailing standards of morality, that the guilt of the one and the righteousness of the other are determined. The page devoted to the novel *Arminius* is a splendid example of Herzen's historicism. The individual human being is answerable to history not only for his participation in "large-scale" events, but also for his "domestic life" and for the life of his soul. As Herzen puts it, "Whoever could survive had to have the strength to remember."

There is a concealed, barely perceptible theme of remorse in part 5 of *My Past and Thoughts* (a section that had particular importance for its author). Herzen was tormented until the end of his life by the knowledge that he had been unable to shield his sick wife from the shocks that were destroying her, and that he himself had been unpitying. In his journal for 1866 he wrote of his relations with Natal'ia Ogareva, "*Then* I wanted to save a woman and murdered her. *Now* I want to save another one, and shall not do so" (20, 2:608).

Herzen's depiction of his wife's death in the last chapter of part 5 is a kind of self-torment by delayed memory. Herzen forces himself to take a close look at a continually shifting sequence of painful details, so that their reconstruction and reexperiencing becomes a kind of moral duty, a creative expiation of guilt. "Strewn on the floor and stairs were a great many reddish-yellow geraniums. Even now their fragrance hits me like an electric shock . . . , and I remember all the details, moment by moment, and I see the room draped in white and the veiled mirrors; and beside *her*, covered in flowers too, is the yellow body of the infant who fell asleep and never woke up; and her cold, terribly cold forehead" (10:302).

The theme of remorse remains outside the text of *My Past and Thoughts* (since self-recrimination would have weakened the blow against the enemy). Indeed, it is not even so much a theme as a psychological impulse, and the compulsion to remember that is engendered by it is not presented as such but is generalized in the idea of creative memory. "The past . . . remains as though cast in metal, detailed, unchanged, as dark as bronze. . . . One does not need to be a Macbeth in order to see the ghost of Banquo. Ghosts are neither criminal judges nor the gnawings of conscience, but the *ineradicable events of memory*" (10:274, "Oceano Nox").

It is through knowledge and action that suffering, guilt, and failure are expiated. It was from this conviction that the initial plan for *My Past and Thoughts* emerged (subsequently evolving into the book's enormous canvas of social life). The book as planned was not, however, intended merely as vengeance and atonement, but also as an act of artistic cognition that would recover the past for the future, that would transform that past into history and art. That sense of the past as something the creative person *does not have the right* to allow to disappear without a trace, that historicism in its most particular and personal manifestation, is correlated in *My Past and Thoughts* with Herzen's sense of history as the shared awareness of a common past.

Problems of the
Psychological Novel

Part One

CAUSAL CONDITIONALITY

THE IDEAS about the psychological novel (mainly of the nineteenth century) set forth in this third part of the present book are not only not a history of the novel (which is obvious enough); they are not even a theory of the novel regarded as a particular form of verbal art. Instead, the subject here involves only certain problems of the novel, problems that are moreover viewed in terms of a single aspect—the artistic cognition of individual spiritual life and behavior. I shall therefore discuss here primarily those authors whose writings have evinced with particular clarity the changing principles and successive stages of that artistic cognition.

In one way or another, the themes of this section all lead to Tolstoi. That is as it should be. The writings of Tolstoi are the high point of nineteenth-century analytical, *explanatory* psychologism (the writings of Dostoevskii being based on other principles), and all its possibilities are manifest in him with a power and a consistency that represent not so much an outgrowth or development of what preceded them, as they do a fundamental change in its direction. The creations of Tolstoi are thus a unique resource for formulation of the theoretical issues involved in artistic psychologism. One of Tolstoi's ground-breaking discoveries was of a new relationship between the fluid and the stable elements of spiritual life. What psychologists call the "stereotyping" of psychic processes may in a sense also be applied to artistic cognition of the individual human being. The naming of phenomena—their identification in words—by its very nature involves their generalization, abstraction, and fixation, so that a special effort entailing additional verbal work is required if even a part of their original uniqueness and dynamism is to be restored.

Representation of the individual human being became more dynamic as artistic psychologism developed, but that dynamism did not merely replace stereotyping; it transformed it. Without the "stereotypes" of aspirations and passions, without such components, however called, of the individual image as qualities, characteristics, or features of personality (even if those qualities and passions were no longer the same ones that the literature of the seventeenth and eighteenth centuries endowed its characters with), it would have been impossible not only in the nineteenth, but even in the twentieth century to portray individual human beings and their behavior.

To be sure, attempts have been made in the twentieth century to abandon psychological generalization. A demoting of personality is apparent in numerous areas of twentieth-century Western prose. If Tolstoi detached psychological processes from individuals, making those processes themselves the subject of his artistic investigations (as even Chernyshevskii said), then recent writers have attempted to reduce the individual to those processes. The French *nouveau roman* of the 1950s and 1960s wanted, in theoretical terms at least, to depict more or less pure processes, processes that were, so to speak, deprived of individuation, that were something like an ideal of pure fluidity—an impossible task, of course, since it was opposed to the very nature of art as meaningful and generalizing form. Discourse itself is already a suspension of flux and a mastering of chaos.

In a discussion of the *nouveau roman* in 1959, several participants asserted that the device of identifying literary characters by name betrayed an obsolete statistical conception of the human being. That naming device was regarded as inconsistent with the striving to depict, not literary character, but those states that fluctuate on the borderline between consciousness and the subconscious. What was their solution, then? To replace those names with the pronouns "he" and "she."[1] But pronouns are defined as that part of speech that designates an object (although without naming it). Here is a remarkably clear confirmation of the fact that whenever one structural link is destroyed in art, another at once emerges to take its place. Literary character may in fact be reduced to a minimum, may be stripped of any number of distinctive features, but whenever that happens those structural features inevitably attach themselves to the process itself, to the extent that it becomes an object of depiction.

The literary character is a series of consistent manifestations of a single individual or of references to him. The depiction of that individual's words, actions, external features, and internal conditions, the narration of events connected to him, and the authorial analysis of it all gradually accumulate to the point where they coalesce into a definite entity capable of functioning in a variety of narrative situations. The formal sign of that entity is the character's name. His structural unity, the *principle of connection* underlying his separate but consistent manifestations, is established in the exposition, in the typological model presented there as the indispensable basis of the reader's initial orientation (as has already been discussed in the introduction to the present book).

So long as the literary character remained a mask, an ideal image, or a social-moral type, his unity could be established by repetition, by the reiteration of stable traits and characteristics, whether homogeneous or contrastive. But then that character became a personality, a dynamic, multidimensional system in which derived features emerged in complex fashion from initial social, biological, and psychological premises. The *relationship* among those different elements was the personality, and the principle of their interconnection therefore acquired new and decisive significance. There are, even within the limits of the novel of the second half of the nineteenth century, several such principles of interconnection. It would, for example, be impossible to understand and interpret the structural unity of the behavior of the heroes of Zola without the mechanism of biological continuity, of heredity, or that of the heroes of Turgenev without the historically specific self-consciousness of the successive generations of the Russian intelligentsia, or that of the heroes of Dostoevskii without the idea, the moral-philosophical problem, that each of them endeavors to resolve. The writer may himself explain the principles underlying his characters, or he may entrust that explanation to the reader.

In depicting the relationship between the individual and the external-world, rationalist poetics treated the latter as the object of individual desires. Those desires and their objects could be lofty (the hero of the ode or that of the epic exhibiting valor and achieving the glory he craves), or they could be "base," as a consequence of which fact the actual material of life was distributed among a variety of different genres. Dominant characteristics were something like an aggregate of those desires. Such were the misers, the ambitious people, the hypocrites, and the libertines of classical comedy and satire and of the *caractère* and memoir. The characteristics constituting a caste and moral type in comedy and satire tended to be discrete and to gravitate toward one-dimensional typological combinations. The classical type was frequently formed from a single characteristic, and it then became something like that characteristic extended in space. In the tragedy, the relationship of the individual to the object of his desires took the form of a fatal passion that was destructive of the norm. To be sure, the investigation of passion by the great dramatists of classicism was complex and subtle, complete with transitions and full of shadings, but it nevertheless remained an analysis of passion itself rather than of individual human beings, since the latter were regarded as simpler, as more elementary than the passions that governed them.

Characteristics and qualities remained important structural units in the romantic conception of personality as well. Indeed, as G. A. Gukovskii has noted, they acquired a certain repetitiveness, whereas rationalistic literature endowed its characters with considerable typological variety (however circumscribed it ultimately was).[2] Romanticism could not dispense with separate elements, with the stereotypes of spiritual life, but it did radically change the principle of their interconnection. Romanticism was concerned not with typological sums of qualities, not with the mechanisms and mainsprings of behavior, but with the metaphysically conceived integrity of the soul. Separate elements were fused into a unity of personality that had been unknown to rationalism with its careful disposition of discrete characteristics. The idea of "contradiction" accordingly acquired new meaning in the romantic system.

The nineteenth century with its psychological novel was not of course the first to discover the contradictions of spiritual life; they had been known since antiquity and had only changed their form and function. The work of verbal art exists in time. The structures it creates must as a consequence be set in motion, and that motion necessarily entails contradiction and conflict. In classical poetics, the contradictions of spiritual life had a formal, logical basis; they involved the clash of differently directed but still separate units. Those units might alternate, thereby displacing or replacing each other and forming a variety of new configurations, but in so doing they lost neither their impermeability nor their definite outlines. Classical tragedy brought into conflict in a single person either two differently directed passions or passion and duty. By means of its continual iteration, that conflict produced a zigzag-like development of spiritual states—the object of subtle artistic investigations, to be sure, but one that was invariably based on the clash of two opposing principles.

A similar "binary" quality was characteristic of the romantic conflict too, although in the romantic system that conflict had an entirely different meaning. The romantic contradiction was philosophically conceived as a polarity (a cornerstone idea for Schelling and for all romantic *Naturphilosophie*)—conceived, that is, as the coexistence of diametrically opposed yet inseparably linked principles. That polarity was manifest on the level of spiritual life in the contradictory unity of personality, which although finite was at the same time characterized by a striving toward the infinite and the transcendental. Although early German romanticism did rehabilitate the flesh and accept the material world in mystically illumined terms, the very act of doing so presupposed the duality of the infinite and the finite, a duality that could only be overcome through spiritualization of the finite.

Late romanticism, with its open split between dream and reality, between the ideal and the material, transformed contrasts and antitheses into one of its most important structural principles, wherein those polarities were comprised in the integrated image of the romantic soul. The poetics of contrast was in different ways equally essential to the late German romantics and to Byron and Hugo.

The doctrine of the early German romantics (the Jena school) with respect to romantic irony did not, of course, presuppose linear contrasts. On the contrary, romantic irony involved a complex philosophical game of affirmation and negation, of creation and destruction, and of the displacement and blending of the serious and the comic, and of the sublime and the mundane. Yet that game remained a game of polarities. Moreover, the irony of the early romantics existed rather by virtue of the philosophical and a esthetic position of the author. This position colored the work as a whole but hardly ever penetrated the inner structure of the literary character itself. It had not yet become a psychology,[3] although the romantic conjoining of different levels of consciousness and of different aesthetic levels did in fact lay the groundwork for the subsequent psychologism of the realistic novel.[4]

Much has been written about the genetic link between romanticism and realism. Continual reference has been made as well to another source of realistic psychologism—the tradition of the analytical novel reaching back to the seventeenth century. Madame de la Fayette's *La Princesse de Clèves* is usually regarded as the first analytical novel, as the prototype of the nineteenth-century psychological novel, although that role has sometimes been assigned to *Manon Lescaut*. N. A. Rykova in an article on Choderlos de Laclos's *Les Liaisons dangereuses* has written that that work "anticipated the novel of the nineteenth century and foreshadowed Balzac and Stendhal."[5] The honor of first discovery has thus been attributed to at least three different works, one appearing in 1678, and the other two in 1731 and 1782—which is not to say that the attributions are unjustified. Elements and preconditions for one movement or another may exist for a long time and be periodically renewed, reemerging in different connections and correlations, before they ultimately take shape in a consciously formulated system. *La Princesse de Clèves*, with its skepticism and rigorous analysis of the "mainsprings" of human behavior, has been compared both to classical tragedy and to the *Maximes* of La Rochefoucauld.[6] Yet however complex it may sometimes be, the psychological framework of La Fayette's book still takes its form from two basic and opposed elements, in the same way that the framework of classical tragedy does. And just as in classical tragedy, that duality is not necessarily always reducible to the neat formula of passion and duty. Present in the spiritual conflict of the princesse de Clèves is not merely duty but also egoistic caution and a rationally inspired mistrust of the idea that it is possible to find lasting happiness by giving in to one's passions. The widowed heroine speaks of this with great logic and clarity to de Nemours, who is in love with her: "I distrust my own strength, despite all my justifications. What I believe I owe to the memory of M. de Clèves would be inadequate, were it not sustained by concern for my own peace of mind."[7] The mechanism is the same, however: passion comes up against another internal or external force that is opposed to it. In their different ways, both classicism and romanticism understood the spiritual conflict as a clash between two elements. This applies to the analytical novel as well—and not just to *La Princesse de Clèves*, but also to the form it took a hundred or so years later at the beginning of the nineteenth century.

Benjamin Constant's *Adolphe* (written in 1807 and published in 1815) has even more right to be regarded as the undisputed "father of the psychological novel." *Adolphe*, a book that delighted both Pushkin and

Stendhal, is striking for its penetrating analysis, the accuracy of which long remained unsurpassed. It was for its time a novel of genuine psychological discoveries, the tenor of which Constant himself formulated in identifying "that part of us which is, so to speak, the observer of the other."[8] I shall confine myself here to a single extended example of the depiction of spiritual processes in *Adolphe*. The hero's father and his father's friends have demanded that he break off relations with a certain "fallen woman," since his liaison with her jeopardizes his whole future. Adolphe, however, firmly and nobly refuses to abandon Ellénore, who has sacrificed everything for his sake. "Ending with those words I left; but who will explain to me the fickleness of that feeling, which though it had dictated the words to me, had expired even before I had finished speaking them!" (56).

Tormented by thoughts of the futility of his passing youth, Adolphe wanders all night on the outskirts of the city. "I felt an access of rage against [Ellénore], and by a strange mixture that rage did not at all diminish the fear that the idea of distressing her inspired in me" (57). The immensity and calm of approaching night awaken in Adolphe a yearning for thoughts of a loftier nature. "I was interested merely in Ellénore and in myself—in Ellénore who inspired in me only pity mingled with weariness, and in myself, for whom I no longer had any respect. I was reduced, so to speak, to a new kind of egoism, one that was disheartened, discontented, and humiliated. I was glad to return to thoughts of another kind and once again find the ability to forget myself and to give myself over to unselfish musings" (59–60). Finally, influenced by thoughts about the futility of life and the inevitability of death, Adolphe's excitement abates. "All my irritation disappeared, and there remained of the night's delirium only a mild, almost peaceful feeling; perhaps the physical weariness I was experiencing contributed to that tranquillity" (60). A series of spiritual states whose modifications are examined in detail is ultimately resolved in a tranquillity for which the author suggests a physiological explanation. This is hardly accidental, inasmuch as Constant was trained in the school of French sensationalism, although later on (in the 1800s), he too would struggle against the ideas of Enlightenment philosophy.

In addition to the physiological impulses underlying actions and spiritual states, Constant was also acquainted with the unconscious.[9] With regard to those things that someone may conceal not only from others but also from himself, he observes, "but that which remains unsaid still exists, and all that exists may be divined" (32). There is in another passage an even more explicit reference to the way in which unconscious thoughts may enter consciousness. Ellénore reproves her lover during one of their encounters for the fact that he does not love her but only pities her. "Why had she spoken those fatal words? Why had she revealed to me that secret which I wanted to ignore? I made an effort to reassure her, and perhaps I even succeeded, but the truth had found its way into my soul; the mood was broken" (47).

Benjamin Constant's analysis is on occasion reminiscent of the twentieth-century novel. Thus, the conflict between the hero's eternal longing for the unattainable and elusive, and his instantaneous indifference toward whatever has been achieved, is invested in psychological forms that seem quite Proustian. "I desired [that meeting] with such ardor that it seemed impossible to me. . . . At last I heard the chiming of the hour when I had to take myself to the count's. My impatience was at once replaced by timidity. I dressed slowly; I no longer felt in a hurry to arrive: I was so frightened that my hopes would be deceived, I felt so vividly the pain that I was likely to experience, that I would gladly have agreed to any postponement" (25). And once more: "We calmly make resolutions in advance to break [things] off, and we impatiently await the moment when we shall do so, but when that moment arrives, we are overcome with fear; and such are the peculiarities of our pitiful hearts that we suffer cruelly in departing those with whom we have passed the time without pleasure" (43).[10] *Adolphe*'s own unique tonality, however, is really to be found in the fact that shining through its convoluted psychological movement and "Proustian" complexes is a clear-cut analytical schema.

Pushkin perceived *Adolphe* as a pre-Byronic novel. "Benj. Constant was the first to bring on stage that character that was later to be popularized by the the genius of Lord Byron," he wrote in a note to Viazemskii's translation of the novel. In *Adolphe*, however, "that character" still remains within the rationalist tradition and is still investigated by rationalist means. We immediately recognize the novel's classical "mainsprings" when we read at its very beginning "that it takes time to get used to the human species and to what self-interest, affectation, vanity, and fear have made of it" (17). And the narrative itself is constructed in such a way that the direct authorial analysis (presented through the narrator) sometimes takes the concentrated form of sharply drawn aphorisms: "Fools make of their morality a compact and indivisible mass, so that it will touch on their actions as little as possible and leave them unencumbered in all the details" (16). Sometimes maxims reminiscent of La Rochefoucauld slice into the narrative like the edge of a slowly unfolding psychological process: "I wanted to awaken her sense of generosity, as if love were not the most egoistical of all emotions, and, whenever it is wounded, therefore the least generous" (52).

But *Adolphe* is most closely linked to rationalist poetics by the fact that its hero's psychological structure is based on a set of logically clear binary oppositions (which, moreover, are still remote from the romantic antinomies of the infinite and the finite). Adolphe's most delicate spiritual processes are governed by a mechanism consisting of two basic elements. In classical tragedy and in *La Princesse de Clèves* those elements were passion and duty, or passion and the arguments of reason, or a second passion in conflict with the first. In *Adolphe* passion (for Ellénore) stands in opposition to egoism, indifference, and a mind that has grown cold—the characteristics of Adolphe as a "contemporary man." All the varieties of feeling in *Adolphe*, all of its manifold psychological transitions, are invariably transitions from passion, and then from suffering to "egoism" and back again. Contained in the "Lettre à l'éditeur" that concludes the novel is a summary of this binary logic of personality: "You will see him in the most varied circumstances, and always as the victim of a mixture of egoism and sensibility, which have been combined in him to his own unhappiness and that of others" (82).

And yet *Adolphe* really does anticipate the novel's future, for its subject matter is no longer passion in the pure, almost disembodied form that it had in eighteenth-century literature. Rather, the clash of two principles with all their variations has become a personality,[11] a model of the "contemporary man" with that set of new, "egoistical" qualities that Pushkin fixes with such precision in the famous lines from chapter 7 of *Onegin* where he speaks of novels "that reflect the age."

Constant's book already belongs to the nineteenth century, and his hero may indeed be regarded in the same terms as those of Byron or Chateaubriand, despite the fact that that hero is based on different analytical principles than theirs are.

Stendhal too has been justifiably included in the tradition of the analytical novel, especially with regard to *Le Rouge et le noir*. But *Le Rouge et le noir*, which was written at the very end of the 1820s, already represents an entirely different stage of the novel in comparison with the 1807 *Adolphe*. *Adolphe* is in its own way historical, inasmuch as it is a novel about a contemporary man, and the concepts of contemporaneity and history are in fact correlative. To be sure, the novelists of the seventeenth and eighteenth centuries, the authors of *La Princesse de Clèves* and *Manon Lescaut* and *Les Liaisons dangereuses*, also depicted contemporary feelings and customs, but a consciously historical orientation was still beyond their reach. By Benjamin Constant's time that orientation had emerged, although the historicism of *Adolphe* is covert, so to speak. It is a consequence of the theme of a melancholy young man who is conceived as a product of the Revolution and of postrevolutionary disillusionment, although these conditioning historical forces are neither named nor exhibited. Stendhal's historicism, on the other hand, is already fully conscious and loudly self-proclaiming. It is indeed Stendhal, raised in the traditions of the French revolution and of sensationalism, and attracted in the 1810s to the new romantic ideas (just as Pushkin was), who was the true discoverer of the nineteenth-century realistic method, and it was therefore in his work that the central realistic problem of causal conditionality received a new solution.

In conformity with the dominant scientific, philosophical, and sociological ideas of the nineteenth century, realism opened up to artistic cognition a concrete, unified, and monistically conceived reality. That reality was subject to exposure and judgment, and yet it was also the source of the highest values. As a result, any one of its phenomena could potentially have aesthetic significance. For nineteenth-century realism, objective reality was no longer broken down into opposed spheres of the lofty and the base, or the ideal and the material, and there was thus no longer any philosophical justification for the existence of a distinctive means of artistic expression or of a special language of poetry. The linguistic material of realistic prose was in principle the same material as that of colloquial, business, scientific, and journalistic discourse.

Gukovskii defines nineteenth-century realism in a number of his works as an attempt at the historical and social *explanation* of the human being (explanation in artistic terms, obviously). Gukovskii's idea also bears on the more general issue of the new understanding of causal conditionality that followed from the new conception of reality. Any work of literary art, whatever its period or its school, depicts or at least presupposes certain motivations for the actions of its characters—that is inevitable. In prerealistic literature, the variations on those motivations could be bold or subtle, but the principles initially setting them in motion remained predetermined, since they were based not on the infinitely various and unforeseeable possibilities of concrete reality, but on ideal qualities of reason or soul that were defined in advance. Nineteenth-century artistic determinism, on the other hand, was compelled to seek out for itself the laws that govern reality and the individual human being. And that is the reason for its explanatory zeal. The underlying principle governing the correlation of the elements contained in the artistic structures created by realism was the relationship between cause and effect, and the cognition of that relationship was therefore aesthetic in nature. For all of its artistic specificity, however, that cognition was impelled by a desire to ground itself in the same laws that served as the foundation of the era's scientific thought. Conditionality, whether conceived in the broadest historical and social terms or in relation to the most minute spiritual impulses, as was the case in the late psychological novel, had become an *object of depiction*, at once individual and generalized, like any aesthetic object. As the novel developed, that depiction grew ever more discriminating and multifaceted. The causal relationships of realism were individualized to the utmost degree, inasmuch as the artist was each time discovering them anew as he applied them to the infinitely various and unpredictable phenomena of concrete reality.

Le Rouge et le noir represents an early stage of realism, and the system of causal conditionality worked out in it is fundamentally different from the realistic systems of later works. Reflected in all of Julien Sorel's thoughts and actions is his social and historical nature, that of a man of the third estate attempting to make his way in the world, of a young plebeian of the 1820s captivated by images of the Revolution and the Empire. Julien's characteristics—his plebeian pride and hatred of those in power, his ardent temperament and calculating intelligence, his ambition, and his hypocrisy forced upon him by circumstances—are defined and colored by his historical situation. Yet for all the book's historicism, Stendhal is still unable and unwilling to abandon rationalist polarity in his depiction of the individual human being; he still cannot dispense with the conception of behavior as a continuous operation of two elements, one or the other of which may prevail for a time, only to be replaced by its contrary. History and social circumstances have set the hero and his "mainsprings" in motion, mainsprings that, as it were, have been inherited by history from the seventeenth century and adapted to other times and temperaments.

The conflict in Adolphe is between passion and "egoism" (indifference, spiritual coldness); in the active Julien it is between two passions—love and ambition. Each of these passions brings its own appropriate qualities to the character's structure. On the one side are ardor, excitability, and refinement of feeling, and on the other, strength of will, arrogance, dissimulation, calculation, contempt for the "mob," and so on. Julien's opposing aspirations are embodied in the two objects he strives for, the haughty Mathilde and the tender Madame de Rênal. They are the emotional poles between which Julien oscillates, approaching first one and then the other in accordance with his changing spiritual state. The famous portrayal of Julien's first night with Mathilde at the Hôtel de la Mole is based entirely on the contrast between true love (his relationship with Madame de Rênal) and a bookish imitation of romantic distraction.

> Mathilde made an effort to use the more intimate form; she was evidently more attentive to this unusual way of speaking than she was to what she was saying. This use of the singular form, stripped of the tone of affection, ceased, after a moment, to afford Julien any pleasure; he was astonished at the absence of happiness; finally, in order to feel it, he had recourse to his reason. He saw himself highly esteemed by this girl who was so proud, and who never bestowed unrestricted praise; by this line of reasoning he arrived at a gratification of his self-esteem.
>
> This was not, it is true, that spiritual ecstasy which he had found at imes in the company of Madame de Rênal.[12]

Offended self-esteem provokes Julien into an attempt on the life of Madame de Rênal, who has tried to come between him and Mathilde. But the crime itself and prison instantly put an end to his ambitious dreams and thus hurl him back toward the other pole. Awaiting execution, he is "worn out by the heroism" of Mademoiselle de la Môle. "Ambition was dead in his heart, another passion had risen from its ashes; he called it remorse for having [attempted the murder of] Madame de Rênal. As a matter of fact, he was hopelessly in love with her" (664; 2: 305).

Thus with emphatic clarity does Stendhal reveal the structure of his hero's behavior—a classic alternation and conflict between two passions (ambition and love), in which the extinguishing of one immediately brings the other back to life.

Le Rouge et le noir is a unique amalgam of literary processes that were both rooted in the past and linked to the future. Julien Sorel's is a romantic personality that has been subsumed in a system of strict social and historical conditionality. At the same time, the investigation of that hero's spiritual life involves the familiar traits of the rationalist-analytical novel with its binomial disposition of the forces governing human behavior.

In the mature writings of Balzac, social causal conditionality (milieu and the predictable patterns of social life) has already become a decisive feature, a true object of depiction. A great deal has been written about the representation of milieu in Balzac's novels and about the power of his social generalizations, and there is no need to repeat it here. Embodied to an exaggerated degree in the characters of *La Comédie humaine* are the motive forces of bourgeois society. Yet there are also characters in Balzac whose spiritual life is examined from within, and whose treatment therefore involves the solution of problems of a psychological order. This above all pertains to the era's inevitable theme of the young contemporary and to such figures as Rastignac and Lucien de Rubempré. In these instances too we again encounter the mechanism of the clash and alternation of two opposing principles, although Rastignac and Lucien are certainly no less socially conditioned than the other characters of *La Comédie humaine*. The pettily ambitious Rastignac of *Le Père Goriot* (pettily ambitious in comparison with Julien Sorel), the seeker after social success who is prepared to do anything, is still a budding, still a vacillating Rastignac. His ambition, however, is in conflict not with a great human feeling (as in Julien's love for Madame de Rênal), but merely with the patriarchal habits and predisposition to goodness that were instilled in him by the provincial family in which he grew up.

It is characteristic of Balzac's social method that he brings into conflict in the image of Rastignac two milieus, so to speak, which are the sources of two opposed sets of qualities: those of the sensitive man and those of the society predator (ambition, egoism, envy, thirst for pleasure). The first set of qualities is destined to disappear and the second to develop, but in *Le Père Goriot* Rastignac for the time being still experiences repentance and shame at the thought of his mother and sisters who are sacrificing their last possessions for the sake of his success in society. Rastignac also remains faithful to his strange friendship with the old man Goriot. He defends him from the coarseness of those around him, looks after him as he is dying, and pawns his own watch in order to obtain money to give the old man a pauper's funeral.

The same model of personality and behavior may be found in the character of Lucien de Rubempré in *Illusions perdues*, with the difference that whereas Rastignac is strong, Lucien is a weak variety of the type, someone doomed to perish in a world dominated by the struggle for power, success, and wealth. Lucien's family is even more modest than Rastignac's, but it too is a nest of provincial patriarchal virtues that this time are embodied in the persons of his mother and his sister, who are no less prepared to sacrifice themselves for the sake of their son and brother. Lucien's personality is also formed on the basis of a combination of and clash between two sets of qualities: those of a patriarchal sentimentalist provenance and those of the young egoist and ambitious person resolved to conquer Paris. This duality is retained until the very end of the novel, even when it appears that evil has irrevocably triumphed after Lucien becomes the thrall of the demonic convict Vautrin in order to rescue his sister's family from utter ruin. The repetition of the psychological formula is marked by textual coincidence as well. Rastignac is moved to tears by thoughts of the sacrifice his mother and sisters will make on his behalf, tears that were "the last grains of incense hurled on the sacred altar of his family."[13] Lucien is placed in the same situation: "'My God, my sister is to be married the day after tomorrow!' That cry was the last gasp of pure and noble youth."[14]

Balzac's attention was indeed focused on the spiritual life of Rastignac and Lucien, but one should not confuse mere interest in the inner lives of fictional characters with the methods of the psychological novel. Hugo, George Sand, Alfred de Musset in *La Confession d'un enfant de siècle*, Sainte-Beuve in his novel *Volupté*, and many other writers of the age gave considerable attention to the individual spiritual lives of their characters. The term "psychological novel," however, designates phenomena of a later period. It refers to the fundamentally new methods of analysis that emerged at midcentury.

Rationalist poetics constructed the spiritual life of its characters as an alternation between aspirations and those forces (both external and internal) that were opposed to them. Romanticism turned its attention away from the contradictions of passion conceived in abstract, disembodied form to the contradictions of the integral personality. Hugo raised contrast to the level of an aesthetic theory and then applied it in hyperbolic fashion. Rationalist and romantic contradictions followed from different philosophical premises and as a consequence assumed different forms, although they did share duality, polarity, and the stable mechanism of thesis and antithesis. That is why early realism, as an offshoot of romanticism but still under the powerful sway of Enlightenment thought, was in a way able to combine both traditions. With the passage of time, however, the principle of realized sociohistorical conditionality introduced ever more profound changes into the structure of spiritual contradiction.

Early realism conceived of sociohistorical conditionality in very broad terms (thus producing Balzac's epic) and applied it intensively, but it was still unable to abandon the binary mechanism of passions and aspirations, although that mechanism was subordinated to conditionality. As realism developed, it became ever more imbued with historicism, which entered the very fabric of the phenomena depicted by literature—its experiences, events, and personalities. History no longer merely set the mainsprings of classical passions in motion; it engendered in the contemporary man completely new *historical* qualities that entered into new and unprecedented relations with each other. This was the path taken by Turgenev.

At the same time, the idea of conditionality, whether historical, physiological, or social, became increasingly more differentiated and particularized, more multifaceted and variegated. Analysis that was both explicit and implicit, both direct and oblique, was applied to those riddles of human behavior that only it was capable of comprehending, and applied in particular to the disjunction [*nesovpadenie*] between conduct and feeling. Such analysis became the dominant method of the novel that acquired the name "psychological."

Literary psychologism thus began with disjunction and the unpredictable nature of the hero's behavior. But it is the essence of analysis to search for logic, for causal relationships. How were the two principles reconciled? The fact is that the analytical character of the psychological novel canceled out its apparent contradictoriness. Direct, unilateral conditionality gave way to multilateral conditionality. The resultant actual behavior was now the consequence of a multitude of contradictory influences of differing quality. From one point of view, the behavior of a character might seem contradictory, but the next facet at once suggested a logical solution. The psychological novel as a combination of the unexpected (or paradoxical) with the predictable was taken to its farthest limit by Tolstoi. In the pre-Tolstoian novel (in terms of stages), this was the path taken by Flaubert.

The problem of causal conditionality assumed special significance in the Flaubertian system, but more to the point it acquired an unprecedentedly clear theoretical realization. That realization was of course connected to Flaubert's whole aesthetic system—to his conception of art as a profoundly cognitive activity resting on science and to his celebrated demand for objectivity. "The artist must depict," writes a student of Flaubert's work, "not separate objects or even essences, but essences in their tightly bound and enduring interconnections with each other, in their unity and their necessity. In Flaubert's view, anything accidental or independent of the totality of other things was something that had not yet been cognized."[15] The science from which Flaubert took his inspiration was above all contemporary physiology and the physiologically oriented school of psychology of the second half of the nineteenth century. The unconscious and the irrational as the hidden regulators of individual behavior, consciousness as the "resultant of a number of contradictory impulses," and similar principles of physiological psychology were crucial for Flaubert.[16] His determinism had obviously come a long way from the clear-cut correlations of the rationalist investigation of passions.

These new principles of conditionality are already evident in *Madame Bovary*, but they are fully implemented in *L'Éducation sentimentale*, where "physiology" is crossed with history. Taken as a whole, the image of Frédéric Moreau is historical. It is another version of the "contemporary man," the young man of the first half of the century (one senses in the complex feelings of Frédéric the framework of qualities that are very close to those of Balzac's more primitive Lucien). But history, after giving birth to Frédéric Moreau, later on seems to lose sight of him, leaving him in the midst of the events of 1848–1852 to withdraw into his own private experience.

In Balzac, the hero enters the narrative accompanied by direct characterizations, whether those of the author himself or of the other characters. For Flaubert, with his doctrine of the concealed author and "impersonal" narration, that path was closed. Frédéric Moreau makes his appearance on the very first page of *L'Éducation sentimentale*. From the deck of a steamboat he admires the gardens and cottages along the bank. "Frédéric thought about his room at home, about the plot for a play, about subjects for paintings, about loves to come. He reflected that the happiness his nobility of soul warranted was a little slow in coming. He recited melancholy verse to himself."[17] Although presented without authorial comment, these few lines conveying Frédéric's thoughts in concentrated form reveal to the reader the familiar attributes of the romantic personality (and one, moreover, that is extremely dated): intensity of imagination, dreaminess, artiness (plans for a play, subjects for paintings), a melancholy temperament, and awareness of its own exceptional nature. These attributes are from outset viewed ironically.

The hero's attributes in *L'Éducation sentimentale* are merely the most general conditions for the development of a feeling whose grandiose image is constructed over the full course of the novel (it is not the feeling but its representation that is grandiose). The correlation of elements here is entirely different from that found in earlier novels, with their straightforward intensification of passion or the zigzag-like movement of that passion between aspiration and obstacle.[18] In Flaubert, the structure of passion derives its form from a contradictory multiplicity of qualitatively different influences and reactions that are distributed among the various levels of psychic life. It is this kind of conditionality that was discovered by the psychological novel of the second half of the century.

The method is already present in *Madame Bovary*. Yet despite the subtle, frequently unexpected psychological twists of that novel, its basic conflict in essence still involves a clearcut functional mechanism. Emma Bovary's conflict with her first lover, Rodolphe, is conditioned by his foppishness and by his betrayal of her, while that with her second lover, Léon, is conditioned by their mutual satiation and growing indifference. Emma's emotional disappointments and her hopeless domestic and financial circumstances (each of which aggravates the other) lead to catastrophe. In *L'Éducation sentimentale* the impulses governing passion can no longer be expressed unambiguously, since the link between circumstances and feelings has been mediated and concealed.

The idea of "binarity," of a logically clear opposition between aspiration and obstacle, is the first thing that has disappeared from Flaubert's system. In *L'Éducation sentimentale* there is only one obstacle, which is identified at the outset: the virtue and prudence of the heroine. Madame Arnoux is a kind of princesse de Clèves (in bourgeois form). She responds to Frédéric Moreau the same way that the princesse de Clèves does to the duc de Nemours: " 'So happiness is unattainable?' 'No! But it is never to be found in lies, anxiety, and remorse.' 'What does that matter, if it brings sublime joy?' 'The price is too high' " (231; 195). The Flaubertian treatment of the obstacle is quite different, however. In *La Princesse de Clèves* duty and prudence ultimately destroy the happiness and life of the three noble participants in the conflict. In *L'Éducation sentimentale* the obstacle turns out to be constructive; it shapes passion from within, giving it its form, its special quality. Unconsummated love torments Frédéric and at the same time creates that special erotic tonality in which he and Madame Arnoux both seek their own kind of happiness.

It was a vague beatitude, so intoxicating that he forgot even the possibility of an absolute happiness. Away from her he was devoured by furious lusts.

Soon their conversations were broken up by long intervals of silence. Sometimes a kind of sexual modesty made them blush when they were together. All the precautions they took to hide their love made it more evident; the stronger it grew the more reserved they became. Living a lie this way made their sensibility more acute. The scent of wet leaves caused them an exquisite pleasure; they suffered when the wind blew from the east, were the prey of groundless irritations and ominous presentiments; the sound of footsteps, the cracking of the woodwork terrified them as if they were guilty; they felt that they were being pushed toward an abyss. (304; 267)

Even before Flaubert, literature had regularly shown how obstacles may spur striving toward a goal or revive a dying passion. For him, however, the real issue lay elsewhere—in the particular emotional experience occasioned by that obstacle. In *L'Éducation sentimentale* the relationship between desire and the obstacle placed in its path has less in common with the rationally clearcut story of Julie and Saint-Preux than it does with Rousseau's account (in the *Confessions*) of his relations with the Comtesse d'Houdetot.

The depiction of social milieu and of political events is immensely important in *L'Éducation sentimentale*, yet as a psychological novel it remains uneventful. The primary and in essence the only obstacle is not logically opposed to feeling, and it therefore does not produce a stable conflict. The incessant modifications and shifts of that feeling are thus determined not so much by events, whether social or personal, as by impressions, sensations, and nervous impulses. Causal connection, though undeniably present, at the same time remains flexible and fragmented.

The young Frédéric Moreau meets Madame Arnoux for the first time on the steamboat. His dominant impression is of her membership in a mysteriously beautiful and inaccessible world that provokes "agonizing curiosity" in him. After several unsuccessful attempts to establish relations with her Frédéric begins to visit Madame Arnoux regularly at her home in Paris. "The contemplation of this woman enfeebled him like the use of too strong a perfume. Sinking into the depths of his character it became almost a general way of apprehending reality, a new mode of existence" (99–100; 70). This period in their relations reaches its culmination while Frédéric is riding in a carriage with Madame Arnoux and her young daughter. Madame Arnoux has by accident just discovered her husband's infidelity. She is weeping. "The carriage rolled on. . . . The many folds of her dress hid her feet. He seemed to himself to communicate with her whole person through the child stretched between them. He leaned over the little girl and, parting her pretty brown hair, kissed her gently on the forehead" (117; 87). Symbolically expressed in this contact through the body of the child lying on her mother's lap is the identity of a continually repressed feeling.

After returning from a trip to the provinces, Frédéric finds the Arnoux family in a new place. Their affairs have entered a period of decline, and mystery has disappeared from the new apartment, exposing the lineaments of everyday life. "But passions are enfeebled by a change of location and, not finding Madame Arnoux in the surroundings where he had originally known her, she seemed to him to have lost something, to be somehow degraded, in fact not to be the same. He was astounded at the calm of his emotions" (140; 108). Tied to these impressions is that produced by her indifferent reception of him, and taken together they are sufficient to alter the course of his feeling. Frédéric calls Madame Arnoux a "bourgeoise" to himself, and a long period of cooling affection follows.

Frédéric strives to win the favor of the courtesan Rosanette (whose sobriquet is "the Maréchale"). "He went out lightheartedly, convinced that the Maréchale would soon be his mistress. This desire awoke another and, in spite of the sort of rancor he felt for her, he was overcome by a longing to see Madame Arnoux" (164–165; 132). "This desire awoke another"—a shift that is elicited by an association—an impulse—that is completely unexpected but still strictly determined. And when Frédéric visits Madame Arnoux again, a number of distinct impressions—of the sun shining through the windowpane, of her children, and of the curls in her hair—converge in a picture of tranquillity and beauty. "He was seized once again by an immense love for her, stronger than ever" (165; 133).

Frédéric's and Madame Arnoux's relations become increasingly domestic: he witnesses a noisy argument between her and her husband, and she shares her family sorrows and financial difficulties with him. Frédéric arrives during breakfast at a moment that is particularly difficult for the Arnoux family, which is now facing ruin. "There were slippers lying about on the carpet and clothes on the chairs. Arnoux, in a pair of drawers and a knitted jacket, had red eyes and his hair was standing on end; little Eugène was crying because of his mumps as he nibbled at his slice of bread and jam; his sister was eating peacefully and Madame Arnoux, a little paler than usual, was waiting on all three of them" (204; 170). This time the unsightly circumstances are located within another context, one of deepened relations. They do not extinguish Frédéric's feeling but strengthen it. He is proud of his role as Madame Arnoux's defender against life's misfortunes. The next modification is elicited by an impression of Arnoux's abominable behavior. He fails to return to Frédéric some money borrowed for a short period and lies to him about it. But the main thing is the way he refers to his wife: "And Arnoux started on his eulogy again. She had no equal for intelligence, affection, or thrift; and he added in a lower voice, rolling his eyes: 'And a body!' 'Good-bye!' said Frédéric. Arnoux started: 'Why, what's wrong?' And, his hand half-extended, he examined Frédéric, disconcerted by the anger in his face" (215; 181). Frédéric's jealousy of Arnoux, combined with revulsion at his behavior, is so strong that that revulsion is transferred to the beloved woman as well, and Frédéric stops visiting her.

The succession of impulses and impressions that determine the modifications of Frédéric's feelings, the alternating rhythm of shifts between animosity and tenderness, and between sensual transport and voluntary repression, is maintained throughout the novel. Yet the book's sheer eventfulness has obviously increased by its end. A child's illness that has interfered with a tryst that was supposed to take place in an apartment that Frédéric had prepared for that purpose, Rosanette's appearance at the very instant that Frédéric kisses Madame Arnoux, Frédéric's plan to marry Madame Dambreuse, the widow of a wealthy financier, the ultimate ruin of the Arnoux family as a result of the latter's intrigues, the sale of their property during which the exultant Madame Dambreuse, making no attempt to conceal her feelings, buys a casket that had belonged to her defeated rival—all these plot effects are the very ones that Flaubert condemned in theory. But the novel required a denouement—a way out of the vicissitudes of passion. And having found that denouement, Flaubert brought the novel to a close in the famous last meeting of Frédéric Moreau and Madame Arnoux. After a separation that has lasted many years, she arrives in Paris and comes to Frédéric. They talk and then go outside together. "When they returned to the apartment, Madame Arnoux took off her hat. The lamp, standing on a console table, lit up her [gray] hair. It was like a blow full in his chest. To conceal his disillusionment he fell to his knees beside her and, taking her hands in his, spoke to her tenderly." He tells her of his extraordinary love. "Frédéric, intoxicated by his own words, began to believe what he was saying." He takes Madame Arnoux in his arms. She pushes him away, but says to him, "I should have liked to make you happy." The text continues:

> Frédéric suspected that Madame Arnoux had come to offer herself to him, and once again he was seized by a furious, ravening lust, stronger than any he had known before. But he felt something inexpressible, a repulsion, and something like the dread of incest. Another fear held him back, that of feeling disgust later. Besides, what a problem it would be! And impelled simultaneously by prudence and by the desire not to degrade his ideal, he turned on his heel and started to roll a cigarettte.
>
> She watched him, marveling.
>
> "How chivalrous you are! There's no one like you, no one!" (451–452; 414–416)

As is well known, Flaubert preferred concealed analysis to the explicit variety. He was opposed to the intrusion of authorial explanations into the objectivity of the depiction. One need not take the pronouncements of writers literally, however. The Flaubertian theory of "impersonality" does of course reflect the salient tendencies of his writing, but it hardly keeps him from intervening and explaining whenever he needs to, although it is also true that when he does intervene, he does not always explain the "incomprehensible" to the reader. The remarkable thing about the scene depicting Frédéric's last encounter with Madame Arnoux is that the authorial explanations do not simplify it but rather complicate it. They turn it into a psychological problem requiring solution. A man refuses physical intimacy with a woman whom he had once passionately loved but who has aged. The sight of her gray hair causes him pain and disillusionment. This is quite understandable to even the least quick-witted of readers, and Frédéric's action would therefore appear to follow directly from this premise. But in his analysis Flaubert refers the situation to a number of different cause-and-effect relations. There is the physiological relation—the eruption of a furious lust that has been repressed Frédéric's entire life and that is now suddenly free, and accompanying that lust, a premonition of disgust. There is the social relation—the bourgeois prudence of a man who has somehow managed to establish a certain equilibrium in his life. And following close upon this last relation is the idealization required by the former romantic: the fear of "degrading his ideal." And all of these differently valued relations are brought together in a single result, a single action that is reflected in a single gesture: "He turned on his heel and started to roll a cigarette." From this multileveled scene, during which Frédéric Moreau does not himself know whether he is lying or telling the truth, whether he is suffering or merely lapsing into nervous reactions, a harsh light is thrown on all that has gone before, on the story of a great love that now appears as the infinitely pointless, spiritually jejune impotence of a man whose basic characteristics are "idleness of thought" and "callousness of heart."

The multilateral (rather than binary) nature of the conflict and the diverse, fragmentary nature of the factors that actually condition behavior, factors that are distributed among a number of different levels yet that still function simultaneously and contradictorily, are the very essence of the psychological novel. Flaubert made conditionality, whether explained by the author or left for the reader himself to interpret, the basic connecting principle of his artistic structures. He employed, in other words, not a scientific syllogism, significant only for its result, but the actual material of cause-and-effect relations—their embodiment in individual phenomena and personalities. Flaubert was of course aware of the conditioning power of history. And yet the historical atmosphere surrounding the hero of *L'éducation sentimentale* does not penetrate very deeply into his spiritual experience. History as something capable of governing that experience and of structuring the personality from within defined a new type of psychological novel, the one created by Turgenev in response to the conditions of Russian social life.

The appearance of the new type of novel on Russian soil was entirely appropriate. As Turgenev himself put it in his 1879 "Introduction to the Novels": "The author of *Rudin*, written in 1855, and the author of *Virgin Soil*, written in 1876, are one and the same. During that whole period I tried to the full extent of my power and ability to render conscientiously and impartially and to embody in appropriate types both 'the form and pressure' of time, as Shakespeare called it, and the rapidly changing physiognomy of those Russians who belonged to the cultural stratum that served as the principal subject of my observations."[19]

Turgenev of course had in mind (although he could not say so directly) the liberation movement in whose atmosphere the intellectual life of successive generations of Russians reached such intensity. Turgenev had been prepared for the creation of historical novels concerned with contemporary life by means of association with those people who passed through the Russian ideological circles of the 1830s and 1840s. In his 1848 "Hamlet of the Shchigrov District," he spoke of the Moscow circles with extreme disapproval. The most powerful influence on the young Turgenev was Belinskii, who at the time was struggling to overcome his own past, and the attacks on the circles in "A Hamlet of the Shchigrov District" bear a close resemblance to what Belinskii was saying about them in his own articles and letters of the 1840s. Turgenev's most important associations, however, were with Bakunin, Stankevich, Herzen, and Granovskii—people who had in one way or another become aware of the problem of "historical personality."

Turgenev shared an all-pervasive historicism with Herzen, although the differences between the two men were no less fundamental than their similarities. Herzen had the mind of a thinker. He was quite willing to mix the theoretical with the "figurative"; indeed, he sought their connection. Turgenev, on the other hand, was, like Flaubert, fundamentally opposed to detailed authorial explanation. Herzen, moreover, did not at all strive for ideal typifications, typifications of the sort that Turgenev in fact required. Turgenev announced as much himself (if one may believe the [Norwegian-American] memoirist who quotes him): "I seldom find it suitable to my purpose to copy directly a person of my own acquaintance, because it is but rarely that one finds a pure type."[20]

L. V. Pumpianskii, in a prefatory article on Turgenev's novels, wrote that they "really are the most social kind of literature, since through them society engages in the process of self-reckoning, of coming to terms with the forces, kinds of people, and types and categories of public figure that it has at its disposal—of giving itself an account, in other words, of the human material of its movers, actors, and leaders."[21]

Turgenev really did want to create an "unalloyed," fixed model of historical personality in his novels. That is in fact the fundamental principle of organization to which the other elements of his artistic structures are subordinated. History imbues the literary character and works on it from within. Its characteristics are engendered by a given historical situation and have no meaning apart from it. What would be left, for example, if one were to abstract the set of "common human" features contained in Lezhnev's unmasking of Rudin? "He is a remarkably intelligent person, although essentially an empty one. . . . He is a tyrant at heart, lazy, and not particularly knowledgeable. . . . He likes living off other people, he plays a role, and so on. . . , all of which is in the order of things. But what is bad is that he is as cold as ice. . . . As cold as ice, and he knows it, although he pretends to be passionate. . . . He is playing a dangerous game—not for himself, obviously, since he does not risk a kopeck on his cards or a single strand of his own hair, whereas other people risk their souls. . . . He is eloquent, only his eloquence is not Russian." It is here that the characterization of Rudin comes closest to Bakunin, especially Bakunin as Belinskii saw him, and there are in the passage virtual textual coincidences with Belinskii's letters. Turgenev himself knew Bakunin well, but the Bakunin theme as such undoubtedly emerged in the course of discussions Turgenev had as a young man with Belinskii. If one sets these considerations aside, however, then just what sort of person is Lezhnev describing? A man who is intelligent, empty, cold, a tyrant, a phrasemonger, a poseur, unscrupulous about financial affairs, and so on. But these qualities do not by themselves describe Rudin. They do not even resemble him. They do not in the context of the novel come together as an image without their reference to Bakunin and the circles and intellectual life of the 1830s and the people of the 1840s. The characteristics ascribed to Rudin by Lezhnev are in fact characteristics of a special kind, one that is historical in its very fabric. Rudin's weakness of character and indecisiveness are the "introspectiveness" investigated by Belinskii; his phrasemongering is not merely that, but the "stiltedness" and "cant" that Stankevich struggled with; and his despotism is the kind of despotism that was engendered by the peculiar forms of circle social intercourse.

Rastignac's ambition differs in its historical nature from Julien Sorel's, just as Lucien de Rubempré's lack of character or the melancholy temperament of Frédéric Moreau both exhibit the pressure of time, which has left its indelible traces on them. Nevertheless, it is still possible to say of each of them: he is an "ambitious person" or he is a "melancholy person," and so on. But to say of Rudin that "he is a tyrant, a chatterer, and someone who enjoys living at the expense of others" still leaves us without a structure. His qualities have no independent existence outside his historical function as a Russian circle ideologue of the 1830s.

In *A Nest of Gentlefolk* Mikhalevich endeavors in the heat of a Russian all-night argument to formulate the nature of Lavretskii's historical personality: "I see what to call you now. . . . You are not a skeptic or disillusioned, and you are not a Voltairean; you are a loafer, and a malicious one, a loafer who is not naive but aware. Naive loafers lie on their stoves at home and do nothing, because that is all they know how to do; they do not think anything either, but you are a thinking person, a thinking person who just lies around. You could do something, but you do not; you lie around with your well-fed belly sticking out and talk, lie around just as you ought to, because whatever people do, it is all rubbish and non-sense that is not going anywhere" (chap. 25). The "skeptic," the "Voltairean," and the "disillusioned" person were all models of histori-cal personality having worldwide significance, and all were well-known in Russian society. In such a context the colloquial term "loafer" ac-quired a new semantic charge. It was no longer Oblomovism in the Gon-charovian domestic sense but that historical, ideological avatar of Oblo-movism that permitted [the radical critic] Dobroliubov [in his famous essay on Goncharov] to place Oblomov with all the other "superfluous men" of Russian literature.

From the very first moments of his arrival at the Kirsanov estate [in *Fathers and Sons*], Bazarov is insistently presented to the reader by Tur-genev in terms of his historical capacity. "Nikolai Petrovich . . . , after walking up to a man of tall stature dressed in a long loose peasant cloak with tassels . . . , firmly squeezed the bare red hand that the other had been slow in offering" (chap. 2). Bazarov introduces himself to Nikolai Petrovich as "Evgenii Vasil'ev" (instead of Vasil'evich). Nikolai Petrovich later suggests some food: " 'The main thing now is to have some supper and a rest.' 'Having something to eat really would not be such a bad thing,' Bazarov observed, stretching and then flopping down on the couch. . . . 'But would you not like to go to your room first, Evgenii Vasil'ich?' 'No, much obliged, but there is no reason to. Just tell them to take my little bag up, and this rag too,' he added, taking off his cloak" (chap. 4).

The characteristic details are given in quick succession. Bazarov does not immediately give the master of the house his red hand, yawningly demands dinner, does not consider it necessary to wash after his journey, and so on. In the context of the novel, however, Bazarov's appearance and behavior take on historical meaning and are read not as rudeness and slovenliness but as signs of his "nihilism."

The main heroes of Turgenev's novels possess clearly defined personal-ities with very stable characteristics that are apparent in every one of their utterances, actions, and gestures. Turgenev's identity as a novelist, how-ever, lies in his desire to understand the individual human being in all of his manifestations, to understand him not merely as conditioned but also as a direct expression of that which conditions him—as an expression of historical energy itself.[22]

In what sense are Flaubert's novels "pre-Tolstoian"? Not in a chronologi-cal sense, obviously, but rather in the sense that they represent a different stage of development. *Madame Bovary* was first published in 1856, and *L'Éducation sentimentale* in 1869, the same year that Tolstoi completed work on the first separate edition of *War and Peace*. Flaubert made his artistic discoveries independently of Tolstoi (he read *War and Peace* at Turgenev's suggestion only in the 1870s). Working at the same time as Flaubert, Tolstoi mastered dimensions of spiritual life that until then had not been fully grasped by anyone. He entered the future. His works are full of astonishing artistic anticipations of that future (as has often been observed in the critical literature). One may find in him the seed of everything that twentieth-century literature would later elaborate to its full extent and come to regard as most characteristic of itself: "stream of consciousness" (its classic prototype is Anna's inner monologue on the way to the station where she throws herself under a train), the unconscious, the subterranean currents of conversation, and the use of extended, vividly marked details. Tolstoi did not, given his immense productivity, concentrate on any one of these innovations. Each of them, however, was subsequently raised to the level of a system.

From all that has been said in this regard, I shall confine myself to some words of André Maurois:

> One already finds in him everything that is viewed as innovation today. The person who sees himself as a stranger in the world? Anguish? Who feels it more than Levin who, while working all day long with his peasants, repeats over and over to himself, "Who am I? Where am I? And for what purpose am I here?" Freud? Bungled actions? Read for yourself: "Stepan Arkad'evich picked up his hat and then stopped, trying to remember whether he had forgotten anything. It turned out that he had forgotten nothing except the one thing that he wanted to forget—his wife." Proust? The blossoming girls? The little band? Recall the atmosphere of mystery that, for Levin, surrounds the three Shcherbatskii sisters and that is enough to captivate him. Truly, everything we have come to love was already present in Tolstoi.[23]

There is another Western attitude toward Tolstoi (as opposed to Dostoevskii), the view that he is a classic who belongs irrevocably to the past. But that is rather like forgetting the existence of the very air we breathe. Tolstoi discovered the first principles of the shared spiritual experience of the contemporary human being, and that human being is not even aware that he conceives of himself in Tolstoian terms, and that in fact he has no other choice. To be sure, he finds it more *interesting* to conceive of himself in Dostoevskiian terms, since doing so allows him to focus his attention on himself.

Tolstoi liberated the depiction of the individual human being from the strict constraints of an ideal artistic model. The ideal model absorbed what was most expressive and typical and excluded everything else as either superfluous or accidental. The work of art had always involved a selection and correlation of the elements contained in it—and not just a selection, but a conscious one. To be sure, no one had ever believed that human beings actually consisted of single qualities, yet that was how individuals were portrayed—by typification. Unconcealed selection ruled in literature—from the masks of old-fashioned comedy to the novels of Turgenev and his need for "unalloyed types." Selection is of course one of the laws of art and fundamental to its nature, and Tolstoi obviously could not escape it entirely; he therefore transformed it, bringing the individuals he depicted closer to the models of documentary literature, models that were less constraining, that concealed in themselves "what the anatomist did not know," as Herzen put it.

Tolstoi wrote neither autobiographies nor memoirs (except for the unfinished *Recollections of Childhood* begun in 1903), and the reason may well be that the autobiographical principle was already a pervasive part of his writing. His diaries served as the raw material for his moral maturation. The novels absorbed the detailed self-analysis, the introspection of the diaries, although that self-analysis was always summary in nature—a starting point for the work of self-improvement. That is why the diaries contain not investigations of Tolstoi's whole personality or character, but rather separate features, passions, and events as tests of that personality.[24] It is common knowledge that Tolstoi used the circumstances of his own life extensively in his literary works, yet in portraying Levin or Nikolen'ka Irten'ev he was just as willing to invent. (*Childhood, Boyhood,* and *Youth* are, as was observed above, in fact more autopsychological than autobiographical.) The "documentary" quality of Tolstoi's writing is no mere external fact, however. Its true essence is to be found in the direct and unconcealed link that exists between Tolstoi's own moral concerns and the concerns that occupy his heroes. For Tolstoi, achieving an understanding of life's purposes and values was never simply an abstract activity of the spirit. It also found practical reflection in his life and artistic reflection in his creative work. From early youth to the end, Tolstoi worked unremittingly, even daily, on that life, on realizing the nature of his own experience, whether that of an army officer, a landowner, a family man, a pedagogue, or a thinker. And for him as a subjective matter, the writing of tales and novels was merely one of the manifestations of that incessant reworking of his life (hence the need to record that life in his diaries).

Every true work of art unquestionably derives from the inner experience of the artist as a consequence of his reworking of objective reality. Yet the distance between that experience and its creative reworking varies considerably from one writer to the next, just as the nature of the correlation between the two may also vary. Rousseau believed that he had portrayed himself in the character of Saint-Preux. But that character is an ideal, artificial model that reflects only certain elements of the spiritual and emotional life of its creator. Saint-Preux and the hero of the *Confes-*

sions are different forms involving different utilizations of Rousseau's own inner experience. It is the principle of the *Confessions* that was closer to Tolstoi.

The "documentary" character of Tolstoi's psychological and ethical investigations is especially clear if one compares him to his contemporaries Flaubert, Goncharov, and Turgenev. Their private spiritual experience is undoubtedly present in everything they wrote, but that experience is mediated and circumscribed by the aesthetic doctrine of objectivity. Tolstoi had no such problem. With enormous freedom he created whole worlds, simultaneously introducing into them his own personality and his own experience, both spiritual and domestic. And he did so frankly, in a way that was apparent to the reader, thereby transforming that private experience into one of the structural principles of his fiction.

It was different with Dostoevskii, who left very little direct evidence of his own inner life in his works. The complex link between Dostoevskii and his characters remained concealed not only from his readers, but also from those who were close to him and who regularly corresponded with him. In his letters to [the poet] Apollon Maikov and [the critic] Nikolai Strakhov and to [his niece] Sof'ia Ivanova written in the 1860s and 1870s, Dostoevskii speaks of the emergence of the plans for his works, something that for him always involves discussion of the Russian social phenomena that have engaged his attention.[25] If the autobiographical ever does break through into the novels of Dostoevskii, then it does so in isolated features or episodes (the description in *The Idiot*, for example, of the state of mind that a person experiences before his execution or before succumbing to an epileptic seizure). *Taken as a whole*, however, neither Raskol'nikov, nor Svidrigailov, nor Stavrogin, nor Ivan Karamazov may be regarded as projections of Dostoevskii's own personality, if for no other reason than that the protagonist of a novel of ideas cannot by its very nature be the projection of an empirical personality.

The documentary character of Tolstoi's writing consists of the fact that his heroes not only address the same problems of existence that he addressed, but that they address them in the *same psychological form* and in relation to virtually the same everyday circumstances that he himself was faced with. As is well known, Tolstoi found it necessary even in *War and Peace* to use as prototypes not only his own experience of the Sevastopol' campaign but also the chronicles of the Tolstoi, Volkonskii, and Bers families. The vast system of the Tolstoi novel was set in motion by the inclusion in it of the author's personal experience, the experience of addressing the problems that had accumulated at that point in his life. Such was also the case in *Anna Karenina* with regard to the Levin theme, one that had not originally been intended but that acquired increasing importance as work on the novel progressed. Those plans lacking a close connection to the themes of Tolstoi's own private life more often than not fell by the wayside. One such abortive effort involving the expense of a great deal of time and energy between the work on *War and Peace* and *Anna Karenina* was an attempt to write a novel about the age of Peter I. The novel was eventually abandoned, having been supplanted by *Anna Karenina*. According to P. L. Biriukov, Tolstoi said that he was unable to "bring that period to life in his imagination."[26] It may be that the decisive factor here was the absence of any autobiographical connection.

The documentary nature of Tolstoi's psychological inquiries freed his heroes from the strict laws governing artistic modeling of the individual human being. The Tolstoian hero is not indivisibly attached to his particular personality nor is the novel itself indivisibly attached to its hero. The greatest representatives of European realism in the middle of the nineteenth century had all passed through the romantic school. This was true of Balzac, Flaubert, Turgenev, and even of their younger contemporary Zola. These writers suppressed romantic individualism in themselves, but they could not entirely dispense with its characteristic set of problems, even if only on the level of polemic and negation. Balzac revealed the social conditionality of the "Byronic hero," Turgenev debunked that hero's moral pretensions, and Flaubert, in his Frédéric Moreau, reduced him to utter insignificance. Yet even though the romantic hero was subjected to a thorough reevaluation, he still remained at the center of attention. Tolstoi was the first of the great writers of his time who had not passed through the romantic school. This is most profoundly evident in his attitude toward the personal and the general. Although Tolstoi understood the individual human being as no one had before him, artistic cognition for him did not stop there, but extended over the full range of that part of human experience that transcends the merely personal. Tolstoi was a great master of individual personality, but he went beyond that personality in order to see and reveal the nature of "life in general" [*obshchaia zhizn'*], and not merely in the sense that what was characteristic of a given human being was also characteristic of human nature but also in the sense that the very processes of life itself—of objective reality as such—had become for him an object of depiction.[27] It is Tolstoi's discovery of "life in general" (before him the European novel had depicted only personality or milieu) that undoubtedly explains the inimitable illusion of authenticity, of "real life," that captivated and that still captivates his readers.

The individual human being in Tolstoi is not restricted to his personality. In the pre-Tolstoian novel, it was considered a great achievement if absolutely everything that was said about a literary character contributed to the definition of his personality. It was a writer's highest praise. But the Tolstoian hero exceeds the dimensions of his personality; that is, he functions not merely as a personality but also as someone in whom the laws and forms of life in general are manifest, and through whom they may be cognized. This is the source of those psychological features that transcend the merely personal and that seemed superfluous, that seemed to be mere luxuries of observation, to those people who had been raised on the pre-Tolstoian novel. Such was Turgenev's opinion. And Konstantin Leont'ev, one of Tolstoi's more discerning admirers, wrote of it as well.

In regard to Pierre Bezukhov's semidrowsy state in *War and Peace* (vol. 4, pt. 3, chap. 9) and the way in which the words "unite" [*sopriagat'*] and "harness" [*zapriagat'*] flow together in his mind, Leont'ev observed: "'Unite-harness' depicts nothing whatever of *Pierre's* character *as such*; it is merely a fairly accurate representation of an accidental physiological fact. But the *age-old* rules of aesthetics direct us to discard everything accidental and superfluous, everything that is not germane to the central issue. And I would gladly discard this superfluous physiological observation as well. . . . Even the magnificent depiction of Andrei Bolkonskii's semidelirium and the lofty scene of his quiet death are merely excellent *in and of themselves*. These *states of his soul* do not involve any *subsequent actions*, for he dies immediately afterward."[28] The "age-old rules of aesthetics" alluded to here by Leont'ev are less important, however, than the fact that for people of the nineteenth century the measure of literary psychology remained the hero, the distinct personality with his fate that begins and ends within the confines of the novel. Such people were not always able to grasp the higher connection present in the Tolstoian novel, the connection that transcends mere individuality and links the phenomena of perceived reality.

When Prince Andrei dies, it is of course the death of a hero, but at the same time, and to an even greater extent, it is also the death of a human being. In *The Death of Ivan Il'ich* it is merely the death of a human being. Ivan Il'ich has no individualized personality; he possesses only those qualities that are typical of the middle-level reformed bureaucrat, and they are enough for the horror of his meaningless middle-level bureaucratic life to shine through in the portrayal of his death.

The truest expressions of Tolstoi's genius are his depictions of certain general psychic states that transcend the limits of individual consciousness and unite people in a shared experience of life. There are a number of such scenes involving military, national, and family experience in *War and Peace*—the hunt, Christmastide at Otradnoe, the Rostovs' departure from Moscow, the gathering for the ball, Nikolai's arrival on his first leave home, and so forth. Whether in battle, during the hunt, or at the moment when the family greets its son returning on leave, the behavior of Tolstoi's characters follows consistently from their personalities. For us, however, the most important thing in these scenes is the battle itself or the hunt or the return of the young officer to his home as psychological cross sections of life in general.

Christmastide at Otradnoe with its mummers and drive to the neighbors' is merely part of Nikolai Rostov's spiritual state, although his perception of it is extended to everyone experiencing that "enchanting evening," and despite its fantastical quality, that perception is utterly real. This is not because the scene of the Christmas drive contains anything like a graphic description (on the contrary, instead of the village and the manor house, the mummers see "an enchanted forest with black flickering shadows, glittering diamonds, and a flight of marble steps, and then the silver roofs of enchanted buildings" [vol. 2, pt. 4, chap. 10]), but because the object of depiction here is not isolated individuals or nature or the particular situation itself, but in fact a shared sense of life. Tolstoi conceived of life in general in its concrete sense as the life of the people, as national life. *War and Peace*, in both its wartime and its peacetime scenes, is therefore especially responsive to that artistic conception. The elements of Tolstoi's artistic system are tightly interwoven, and one requirement engenders another. The depiction of life in general is necessarily also a depiction of its processes. And processes presuppose the fluidity of consciousness. A great deal has been said about Tolstoian "fluidity," and he himself spoke about it all his life, from his youthful diaries, to *Resurrection*, to the diary for 1898 containing the following entry (dated March 19): "One of our greatest errors in judging a person is to call or define him as intelligent, foolish, good, evil, strong, or weak, for he is all of these— all possibilities—since he is a fluid substance."

Let me reiterate: the statements made by writers are very important, but they do not relieve us of the obligation to investigate the facts independently of them. After all, the writer is "fluid" too; he is engaged in the solution of a variety of problems, and his theoretical pronouncements serve a variety of tasks as well. Tolstoi thought not only in terms of processes but also of qualities. The initial plans and drafts of *War and Peace* are evidence enough of that:

> The older brother Arkadii has died, leaving behind a widow, intelligent and priggish, and a son—Boris, a pure, rather stupid, but handsome young knight. The other brother was a minister in 1811 and had two sons: Ivan, arrogant (*mordant*) and a diplomat, and Petr, a drunkard, but strong, audacious, decisive, fickle, erratic, yet honest. . . . Volkonskii is a proud, practical, and rational nobleman (?); his daughter is an old maid who is saved by selflessness, a gifted musician, a poetical and intelligent aristocrat above the vulgarity of everyday life. Arkadii's widow is a cousin and childhood friend of the kind and stupid Count Tolstoi. . . . He has a son, Nikolai, gifted but narrow-minded, and three daughters: the eldest, Liza, is blond, intelligent,

pretty, *disgracieuse*, listless; the second, Aleksandra, is cheerful, light-hearted, and affectionate; and the third, Nataliia, is a graceful, poetical imp. Anatole, the son of the Countess T.'s sister, is a young rascal. (13:13)

Anticipated here are the qualities of a number of the novel's characters: Pierre Bezukhov, the old count Bolkonskii, Princess Mary, Count Il'ia Andreevich, Vera and Natasha Rostova, and Anatole Kuragin. Apparent in these notes is the very same method of characterization that Tolstoi condemned in his diaries, both early and late, but a method that he practiced in all his novels, although in a form that in comparison with the notes is certainly much more complex and flexible. In the midst of all the processes and modifications, Tolstoi needed to arrest and fix personality as a mobile, changeable, yet *identifiable* structure. It was impossible to do this without stable components—without qualities, that is. The apperception of personality is moreover assured in Tolstoi by the presence of certain sociotypological frameworks. The literary character is, so to speak, invested with a schema that has been complicated to the utmost degree and then concealed under an accumulation of individual traits. The reader recognizes the bureaucrat in Karenin, the brilliant guards' officer in Vronskii, the thinking landowner of his day in Levin, and the unthinking landowner in Nikolai Rostov. But Tolstoi, although using the schema, at the same time calls it into question by removing any possibility for the schematic application of that schema, so that to treat Karenin, say, as a mere heartless bureaucratic machine (as has been done on occasion), or Vronskii as a mere society vulgarian, is to see the sociotypological formula suggested by Tolstoi, but fail to notice the dynamic Tolstoian solution to it.

Yet how are stability and fluidity actually combined in Tolstoi's system? The fluidity of the Tolstoian character is not an absence of personality but a special relationship obtaining among the characteristics of that personality and among the motives underlying the character's actions and the actions themselves. In prerealistic literature the predominant relationship among those elements was a simple one. Characteristics gave rise to definite motives of behavior, and actions followed directly from those motives. Nineteenth-century realism, with its keen interest in the conditionality of behavior, demonstrated that analogous actions might indeed have different motives, that one and the same impulse could, depending on the circumstances, have entirely different consequences. Tolstoi was in fact the first to address these questions, since they were for him the ones whose answer involved the very possibility of depicting the fluidity of consciousness (while still retaining personality), and he addressed them with unprecedented insight (both theoretical and practical). Tolstoi's characters may be intelligent, brave, and decent, but that does not mean that all the impulses they are aware of are necessarily consistent with those qualities. The personality with its stable characteristics is merely one element in the multilayered situation that each time determines behavior. The processes investigated by Tolstoi are in fact the ones involved in the ceaseless alternation and interrelation of such situations.

Seventeenth-century rationalism worked out an elegant system of human qualities. Earlier Renaissance thinking had been more flexible, more individualistic, and more empirical in its approach to man. There are astonishing psychological insights and anticipations of the future in Montaigne, particularly as regards the issue at hand, since he was one of the most important writers for Tolstoi and also one of his favorites.

Even though he does not employ the term, the idea of the fluidity of the individual human being is pervasive in Montaigne's *Essais*. To a certain extent, the idea of the changeable nature of everything real was suggested to Montaigne by the authors of antiquity—he could not fail to acquire information about the teachings of Heraclitus and his school from the works of Plato, Aristotle, and Plutarch, which he knew well. That idea was also rooted in the philosophical premises of Montaigne's own worldview, in his empiricism and skepticism and in the sensationalism that prompted him to seek a material, sense-oriented basis for the conditioning of individual reactions to the external world. Brilliant powers of observation gave those conceptions extraordinary psychological concreteness. The very names of the separate chapters in the *Essais* are symptomatic: "Par divers moyens on arrive à pareille fin" (this chapter concerns the way in which the actions of the same people may be cruel or noble, depending on the effect of different influences), "Divers evenements de mesme conseil," "Comme nous pleurons et rions d'une mesme chose," "De l'inconstance de nos actions," and so on.

Montaigne already knew that people do not have stable characteristics, that actions are determined by circumstances, and that the value of things depends to a certain extent on their place in the context of a given subjective consciousness. Pain, said Montaigne, "occupies in us only as much room as we give it" (58; 39). And he spoke directly of the "fluidity" of consciousness: "In our soul, though various impulses stir it, there must be one that remains master of the field. Its advantage is not complete, however; because of the volatility and pliancy of our soul, the weaker ones on occasion regain the lost ground and make a brief attack in their turn. Hence we see children, who quite spontaneously follow nature, often cry and laugh at the same thing" (230; 173).

The idea of fluidity broke down the identification of action and motive. Actions "that wear virtue's appearance do not for all that have its essence; for profit, glory, fear, habit, and other such extraneous causes lead us to perform them. The justice, the valor, the good nature that we then exercise may be so called in consideration of others and of the appearance they bear in public, but in the doer this is not virtue at all; there is another end proposed, another motivating cause" (226; 170).

And here is a concrete example to accompany these theoretical reflections: "Fear expresses its utmost power when, in its own service, it throws us back upon the courage that it has snatched away from our sense of duty and honor. In the first pitched battle that the Romans lost against Hannibal under the consul Sempronious, a body of at least ten thousand infantrymen, having taken fright and seeing no other way out for their cowardice, threw themselves into the main body of the enemy, which by a marvelous effort they pierced, slaughtering a great many of the Carthaginians and purchasing a shameful flight at the same price they would have paid for a glorious victory" (76; 53). "Can a horse be called brave, which fearing the whip, hurls itself itself down a slope . . . ?" the young Tolstoi wrote in his 1852 story "The Raid" devoted to the the problem of bravery, which was of such concern to him.

In rejecting the formal unity of an action, the unity of its motives and its ethical value (a unity that would later be characteristic of classical rationalism), Montaigne at the same time denied the legitimacy of one-dimensional definitions of behavior: "Not only do I find it hard to link our actions with one another, but each one separately I find hard to designate properly by some principal characteristic, so two-sided and motley do they seem in different lights" (1054; 824–825). Montaigne, however, saw man not only in terms of his fluidity, of the variability of his reactions and sensations, but also in terms of something like the stability of his biological and social features. Both approaches are clearly set forth in the chapter entitled "De repentir": "I cannot keep my subject still. . . . I take it in this condition, just as it is at the moment I give my attention to it. . . . I portray passing. . . . My history needs to be adapted to the moment. I may presently change, not only by chance, but also by intention" (782; 610–611). Yet later on in the same chapter Montaigne reflects on the "stable condition" of men: "There is no one who, if he listens to himself, does not discover in himself a pattern all his own, which struggles against education and against the tempest of the passions that oppose it" (789; 615). Montaigne did not try to reconcile the contradiction between the fluidity and stability of consciousness. But the possibility of a reconciliation is hinted at by the tenor of his thought: Montaigne recognized the stability of certain primary elements of personality that are capable, as the situation varies, of producing entirely different forms of behavior.

Montaigne, along with Rousseau, was one of the most important sources for the Tolstoian understanding of life. Tolstoi did not, needless to say, repeat Montaigne. Three hundred years of human experience, both scientific and artistic, and the vast genius of Tolstoi were needed for

Montaigne's fluidity to be turned into the realistic dialectic of the soul. Montaigne's penetrating grasp of the laws of spiritual life was abstracted from the experience of a single, concrete individual, or from the separate states and features of that individual. Tolstoi, however, understood the interrelationship of the fluid and the stable in personality from the vantage of the until then undiscerned plenitude and concreteness of its spiritual, physical, social, and domestic existence.

The Tolstoian character is a complex, multidimensional structure. In comparison with the mask or type of classical comedy or the ideal image of romanticism, the pre-Tolstoian realistic personality was already a mutual interaction of a variety of elements, contradictory in their multilateral conditionality. And yet that personality was always goal-oriented, was always intended for the solution of a particular task, whether the depiction of the personality's social nature, or of a particular variety of psychological complex (as in L'Éducation sentimentale), or of a new kind of historical typology (as in Turgenev), and so on. This cannot be said of Tolstoi's main characters. Each is universal in its own way, and each performs a variety of functions and fulfills a variety of tasks. The multidimensionality of Tolstoi's individual characters produces, in the same way that his depiction of life in general does, that powerful illusion of authenticity that has possessed his readers to the present day.

By means of one and the same character, Tolstoi is able to investigate the different realms of existence in their different aspects. It is to this that the character's complex nature corresponds. Distinguishable in it are primary organic qualities that have not yet been ethically developed, qualities that have been socially developed, and even social and typological schemata that have been given a pointedly Tolstoian interpretation. The character is the focal point of a variety of processes. On the one hand, it is a personality—that is, an interaction of psychological elements. On the other hand, it is an embodiment of life in general, and in that capacity its behavior may be broken down and related to a multitude of different situations, each of which represents a kind of structural unity. Tolstoi's paradoxicality is thus merely a mask for the dynamic inner logic of his fictional personalities, a logic in which the character's derived characteristics emerge sequentially from his basic biological and social features.

The universality of the tasks and the multiplicity of the functions and constituent elements of the Tolstoian character are well exemplified by Pierre Bezukhov. Pierre has certain organic qualities (beginning with his great physical size and strength)—sensuality and weak-willed gentleness, goodness (a heightened capacity, that is, for pity and sympathy), and from his father an inherited propensity to devastating outbursts of rage (indignant at Hélène's baseness, Pierre "felt the infatuation and delight of rage" [vol. 2, pt. 1, chap. 6]). These primary qualities are the matrices of

Pierre's organic, spontaneous reactions to the surrounding world, and Tolstoi has no doubt about their stability. They interact with the character's secondary sociohistorical attributes: Pierre is an educated Russian nobleman of the pre-Decembrist period who has been brought up abroad, a son of the Enlightenment, and a future Decembrist.

Pierre has not only a firm social framework but also a typological one—an image subsumed in the traditional category of the absent-minded eccentric but included at the same time in another category, that of Tolstoi's truth seekers, with all the features of their peculiarly Tolstoian solutions to moral questions.

During the ceremony in which Pierre is inducted into the Masons, he is invited to disclose his chief "passion": "Pierre paused, searching for an answer. 'Wine? Gluttony? Idleness? Laziness? Rashness? Malice? Women?' He went over his vices, weighing them in his mind and not knowing which to give preference to" (vol. 2, pt. 2, chap. 3). In the company of Kuragin and Dolokhov, Pierre has led a dissolute and idle life. In Tolstoi's system, however, this does not mean that he is therefore a rake and a wastrel. His sins derive from the interaction of his organic sensuality and hereditary indiscipline with the habits of his aristocratic milieu.[29] The time with Kuragin and Dolokhov is a transitory situation. But the understanding reached by Pierre during his association with Platon Karataev is a transitory experience too, since in part 1 of the epilogue to *War and Peace* Pierre is once more an enlightened nobleman who dreams of giving "a new direction to all of Russian society and to the whole world" (chap. 16). He remembers Karataev, but he can no longer be the person he was when he marched at Karataev's side, barefoot, starving, and crawling with lice. That ordeal is over, and life, like a rubber band stretched to its limit and then released, has returned to its place. Tolstoi shows how in addition to the law of memory, the law of forgetfulness also operates in human beings, a law that is necessary to clear the way for the new conditions that subsequently take possession of them.

Pierre's personality emerges from the interrelation of the biological and the social, the stable and the fluid, the primary and the derived. Yet, as with every one of his other major characters, Tolstoi needs Pierre not merely as a given personality. Apprehended through Pierre are the processes of life itself, and moreover of life taken at its extremes. Pierre is one of the characters through whose eyes the war or a death sentence is rendered. He witnesses the execution of Russian prisoners of war, believing that he himself will be shot at any moment, but the artistic focus shifts from his particular spiritual state to the execution itself, to the very process of senselessly murdering defenseless and innocent people. Since it is intended to solve a variety of different problems of artistic cognition, the Tolstoian character passes through a number of such shifts in focus.

From his very first steps in literature, Tolstoi's method was regarded as exceptionally analytical. But the true essence of Tolstoi is his unique combination of analysis and synthesis. There is perhaps no more powerful depiction in world literature of the phenomena of life in their psychological integrity and their corporeal three-dimensionality, their materiality.

Tolstoi was completely under the sway of analytic interests in the trilogy *Childhood*, *Boyhood*, and *Youth*, and in the story "Sevastopol' in May." In *The Cossacks* and *War and Peace* it is the synthetic images that are most significant. This was required in *War and Peace* by the epical nature of the work itself, by its historical coloration. There are a number of figures in it whose historical characteristics are rendered primarily from the outside as unitary images—the old Prince Bolkonskii or Count Il'ia Andreevich Rostov, among many other examples. But even in those heroes who are examined from the inside, the irreducible integument of the historically and humanly characteristic is extraordinarily close fitting.

Tolstoi carried the combining of disjunctive and conjunctive principles to an extreme. As a general matter, the artistic combination of analysis and synthesis is above all possible because artistic analysis is itself synthetic in its own way. In the process of investigating personalities, behavior, and circumstances, the artist establishes sequences of cause and effect. He breaks the unitary phenomenon down into components unnoticed at first glance, then combines some of those components with others or brings about an exchange or a substitution, thereby revealing, for example, vanity or egoism in place of an apparently generous act. But in all these instances, the depiction is never merely the sum of its parts. The analytically separated components at once enter into new relationships among themselves, whether as cause-and-effect linkages, mutual interactions, or contradictions. New images thus emerge with their own aesthetic concreteness and symbolic meaning. The analytically depicted process may also be an image, a structure, or, as Tolstoi put it, a "focal point" of life.

Tolstoi's contemporaries thus did not fully grasp that for him the authorial discussion and explicitly stated idea were equally important elements in the "labyrinth of concatenations" that constituted art as he understood it. The historical-philosophical and military-theoretical digressions in *War and Peace* met with the unanimous exasperation of contemporary criticism. Even Strakhov, who unlike the others defended Tolstoi's philosophical views, still believed that "the one enterprise damages the other," and that it would have been better if Tolstoi had taken up his philosophical disquisitions "in another book."[30] For Tolstoi, however, it was as natural to reflect in a novel on the immense processes of life in general and on war and history as it was to reflect on the personalities and actions of the novel's heroes. Such reflection was merely a continuation of authorial analysis.

B. M. Eikhenbaum has already pointed out the structural and generic significance of the philosophical digressions in *War and Peace*, their link with the work's epical character, which distinguishes it from the traditional novel.[31] A. Saburov in his book on *War and Peace* has examined in detail the relationship of the digressions to the basic artistic text, and not only in ideological terms, but also in relation to the novel's plot.[32]

I shall only observe that even the novel's invented characters intrude into its philosophical digressions:

> Napoleon started the war with Russia because he could not help going to Dresden, could not help being confused by the honors he received, could not help putting on a Polish uniform or yielding to the invigorating influence of a June morning, and could not refrain from outbursts of rage in the presence of Kurakin and then Balashev.
>
> Aleksandr refused to negotiate at all because he felt he had been personally insulted. Barclay de Tolly tried to command the army in the best way he could in order to do his duty and to earn glory as a great commander. Rostov charged at the French because he could not resist the desire to gallop across a level field. And all the participants of the war acted in the same way, in keeping with their personal qualities, habits, circumstances, and goals. (vol. 3, pt. 2, chap. 1)

Nikolai Rostov turns up in the philosophical digression right along with the historical characters—with Napoleon, Aleksandr, Barclay, [the Russian ambassador] Kurakin, and [the peace emissary] Balashev. But the historical figures in *War and Peace* are characters too, and their images (and this is particularly true of Napoleon and Kutuzov) are developed both in the digressions and in the basic text, often by virtually the same means.

Tolstoi's practice denies the aesthetic incompatibility of depiction and discussion. If nineteenth-century realism is an art of *explanation*, then Tolstoi as its greatest exponent explains without concealment, confident that his explanation is an artistic fact. The investigatory tenacity of Tolstoian psychological analysis could hardly have been sustained without that explanation. In the process of seeking an explanatory, analytical style, Tolstoi availed himself of the tradition of eighteenth-century didactic literature that had attracted him in his youth, but of course it was merely a tradition, an impulse; Tolstoi worked out for himself the syntactic intensity of that style, which A. Chicherin has called "restlessly analytical."[33]

Tolstoi's attitude toward the aesthetic possibilities of authorial explanation undoubtedly has affinities with that of Herzen. It is hardly accidental that Tolstoi was probably the first to appreciate that Herzen was a great artist standing in the same rank with Pushkin, Lermontov, Gogol, and Dostoevskii, and that *My Past and Thoughts* is one of the most remarkable works of Russian literature, and moreover a work whose form is "utterly original," as Tolstoi said in remarks on Herzen recorded by [the pianist] Aleksandr Gol'denveizer in 1901–1902. In fact, however, the "utterly original" form of *My Past and Thoughts* would have to have attracted Tolstoi's attention as early as the first half of the 1860s, when he was working on his projected novel about a returned Decembrist and the plan for *War and Peace* was gradually taking shape. Tolstoi was at that time undoubtedly reading Herzen's *North Star* [*Poliarnaia zvezda*], where along with material on the Decembrists, chapters from *My Past and Thoughts* were being published from year to year. In March 1857 Herzen wrote to Turgenev (with whom Tolstoi was planning a trip from Paris to London), "I would be very, very pleased to make Tolstoi's acquaintance. . . . If he liked my notes, then when you are here I shall read the chapter about Viatka, which has just come out, and the one about Granovskii and Ketscher" (26:77).

Tolstoi in the 1850s and 1860s was an avid reader of the book in which the boundary between the past and the author's thoughts, and between depiction and analysis, had been erased. It would be superfluous to demonstrate that Tolstoi did not imitate Herzen, since the function of explanation in his system is entirely different. For Tolstoi that explanation is always commentary, always a sustained authorial accompaniment to what is taking place, whereas for Herzen it is the very fabric of the work into which everything else is woven. Herzen was not in fact writing a *novel*, whereas that is precisely what Tolstoi was doing, however much he disavowed it in his unrelenting struggle against literary convention. And yet *My Past and Thoughts* was very likely one of those books that Tolstoi apprehended in a writerly way—intimately, as something bearing on his own artistic experience.

Tolstoi's psychological analysis is a dissection of the infinitely differentiated conditionality of behavior. The determined nature of behavior and personality was of course a basic orientation of nineteenth-century realism, which began with the general conditionality of the individual by his time and milieu and then gradually refined that idea. Conditionality in Flaubert is already extraordinarily ramified and subtle; it pervades the individual situation and takes into account the variable, transitory influence of the external world. But what Tolstoi did was far from being merely a quantitative augmentation of the analytical character of earlier realism. Of this new quality in Tolstoian analysis, A. Skaftymov has written: "An alternation of states, thoughts, feelings, desires, and so on takes place. But what is it that elicits that alternation? What is it that motivates that world? What is it that awakens the sleeping potential that until then has been silent and unaware of itself? It is indeed here that Tolstoi's unprecedented actualization of the petty details of everyday life is born, details that no artist before him had known." According to Skaftymov, this actualization is based on Tolstoi's discovery of the "tonus of the individual's average, everyday state."[34]

Conditionality in Tolstoi passes through a number of different gradations—from the individual's most general historical and social definitions, including all that is derived from them, to the infinitesimally minute influences that govern his behavior. The source of these impulses is both the individual's inner nature and his external material surroundings. Rostov is happily on his way to his first attack: "He noticed a solitary tree out in front. That tree had been in the middle of the line that had seemed at first so terrible. But now they had crossed that line, and not only was there nothing terrible about it, but everything was becoming more enjoyable and lively." Rostov is knocked down by the concussion of an exploding shell and his horse is killed. He is left alone on the field. He is confused. But the fearful state he is in comes not from the increased danger, but from the fact that he can see the face of the first of the Frenchmen who are running toward him. "The Frenchman out in front with the hooked nose had come so close that the expression on his face was already visible. And the excited, alien face of that man who, while holding his breath, was running toward him with his bayonet extended, frightened Rostov" (vol. 1, pt. 2, chap. 19). Later on another cavalry attack is described, and Rostov, now a combat-seasoned officer unerringly in control of his nerves, once again sees the face of his enemy up close, but the function of this close-up is diametrically opposed to that of the first: "The French dragoon officer was hopping with one foot on the ground, the other having caught in his stirrup. Flinching in fear as if expecting another blow at any moment, he gazed up at Rostov with an expression of horror. His face, pale and spattered with mud, fair and young, with a dimple on the chin and light blue eyes, was not at all suited to the battlefield, was not the face of an enemy, but the simplest of indoor faces" (vol. 3, pt. 1, chap. 15). One face is hooknosed and alien, and the other fair and blue-eyed, even Slavic it would seem. And along with the momentary impression of the childish and domestic in the Frenchman's face, an unaccustomed thought begins to work in Rostov—doubt about the rightness of what he is doing and of what is being done around him.

What then does Tolstoi's psychological analysis consist of? It is the tracing of ever more precise cause-and-effect linkages within the net of conditionality that he casts over all that exists. It is the phenomenon that is derived from general formulas (the Tolstoian "generalization") and simultaneously broken down into its constituent parts, which, though variable and fluid, give rise to a sequence of situations, to a process. And it is the substitution, the exchange of certain constituents for others, as when,

for example, a great feat is revealed as egoism, or, on the contrary, a selfish act turns out to be the very one that is needed by a whole society or
people. Any one of these operations may be concerned not with logical
abstractions but with concrete and individualized artistic symbolism.

Nikolai Rostov loses forty-three thousand rubles to Dolokhov—a terrible blow for the Rostovs, who are on the verge of ruin. Both Nikolai and
Dolokhov are presented in terms of their conditionality, which extends
with increasing precision from the sociohistorical premises of their personalities and behavior to the particular situation that determines their
relationship (Sonia, who is in love with Nikolai, has just refused Dolokhov), and thence to the situation of the card game itself and the magnetic impression made by the reddish, big-boned, faro-dealing hands of
Dolokhov with "the hair visible beneath his shirt cuffs" (vol. 2, pt. 1,
chap. 13). These are all figurative structures of varying scope, and the
more precisely detailed structures are, so to speak, disposed within others
that are more comprehensive.

The card-playing scene in Pushkin's *The Queen of Spades* remains undifferentiated, as if it has been chiseled from a single piece. "Chekalinskii
gathered up the lost banknotes. Hermann stood motionless. When he
stepped away from the table, there was an uproar. 'Splendidly punted!'
the players said. Chekalinskii shuffled the cards again, and the game re-
sumed its course." In Dostoevskii's *The Gambler*, the psychology of des-
perate play is set forth in detail in the scene (in chapter 4) where Aleksei
Ivanovich wins two hundred thousand francs. The momentary fear, the
stupefaction, the fury, the lapses of memory, the flashes of conceit and the
thirst for risk, "the terrible pleasure of luck, victory, and power"—such
is the sequence of alternating states. But for all the complexity of its shifts,
this episode of *The Gambler* is entirely focused on the development of a
single passion, the very one that will destroy the person caught in its grip.

With Tolstoi it is different. For him the image of card playing, though
existing as an integral image, is at the same time broken down into its
constituent structures, each of which brings into the context of the novel
its own system of cause and effect. Thus, the gambling and losing Rostov
is conditioned by the contexts of his past relationships—by his whole
domestic, Rostovian principle, by his diminishing love for Sonia, and by
his residual admiration for Dolokhov. As a result of analytical verification, expected feelings are replaced by others of a different kind. Thus,
instead of unalloyed despair, we find in Rostov amazement or incompre-
hension, the agonizing impossibility of in fact grasping just when and just
how the misfortune has come about, or the impossibility of believing that
Dolokhov actually desires his destruction—the feeling of a young,
healthy, good-natured person that is rather like the feeling Rostov experienced in his first battle, when he could not believe that the French actually

wanted to kill him. And there is in Rostov as well a sense of guilt before Dolokhov (because of Sonia's rejection of him) and an awkwardness with him as a result of their recent "strange conversation." "Only fools rely on luck in cards," Dolokhov had said. All these impulses are arrayed at the various levels of spiritual experience and derive from different causes belonging to different spheres of life. Since they function simultaneously, they inevitably enter into conflict with one another.

In Tolstoi the principle of realistic contradiction reached its limit— the point where it was no longer polar but emerged from the manifold conditionality of the phenomenal world. What Tolstoi's contemporaries termed his paradoxicality was never anything more than an acute sense of the predictability of behavior. Nikolai does not want to play, but he begins to do so in spite of himself because Dolokhov has said to him, "Why aren't you playing?" The whole game takes place in the atmosphere of Dolokhov's hypnotic influence ("Sometimes he staked a high card, but Dolokhov refused to cover it and himself named a large sum. Nikolai submitted"), which is embodied in the symbol of the hands marking the cards: "Those hands, which he both loved and hated, held him in their power." Once it is broken down into its constituent parts, the paradoxical combination is explained: on the one side is the momentum of Nikolai's infatuation with Dolokhov (which has not yet run its course) and his habit of obeying him, and on the other, the situation of the game itself, with its feelings of hostility and fear.

Tolstoi not only refined conditionality and made it more detailed; he also created an extremely intense variety of it—something like a magnetic field within which his characters move. Tolstoi could leave nothing as it appeared to be, could permit nothing to remain untouched (which particularly irritated Turgenev). Everything was continually passed through the creative mechanism of his art, which transformed, explained, and verified it. Because of the intensity of this process, the novel itself was turned into something different, something quite unlike anything that had existed before.

The high intensity of Dostoevskii's novels is an entirely different kind of phenomenon, inasmuch as Dostoevskii found a different solution to the problem (the artistic problem, that is) of causality and conditionality. One of the most controversial issues in the Dostoevskii literature is whether his novels are psychological in the sense the nineteenth century gave that term. If psychologism means the investigation of spiritual life in all of its contradictions and depth, then it would be odd, to say the very least, to exclude Dostoevskii. Yet there can be no doubt that in creating his novel of ideas,[35] Dostoevskii departed from classical nineteenth-century psychologism, the basic principle of which was *explanation*, whether explicit or concealed. Dostoevskii, when he wished to, brilliantly controlled the methods of explanatory psychologism; *Notes from the House of the Dead*, with the carefully drawn personalities of its convicts and the precise analysis of their behavior, is sufficient evidence of that. There are also elements of classic psychologism in *Crime and Punishment*, where Raskol'nikov's behavior, his spiritual states, and the motives underlying his actions are examined from within. Later on, however, Dostoevskii undertook the solution of other tasks. He turned the ambiguity and equivocation of the mystery novel into a means for the psychological characterization of his heroes. The interpretation of the motives governing a character's behavior frequently changes in the course of the Dostoevskiian novel, and each new solution is by no means the final one. The views of N. M. Chirkov in this respect are certainly correct: "Dostoevskii," he writes, "continually introduces an unexplained residue in the course of explaining the actions of his characters."[36]

Dostoevskii did not attempt to solve the enigma of behavior and to tie up all the loose ends, and he therefore did not need the mechanism of all-pervasive conditionality that Tolstoi brought to such perfection. In a broad historical sense, Dostoevskii was concerned to the utmost with the conditionality of his characters. He constantly stressed his interest in the present moment—in the topic of the day and in current newspaper material. He regarded himself as called upon to depict the different types of contemporary consciousness, and especially the type of the new man that he called "the hero from an accidental family."[37] But Dostoevskii's primary concern remained the historical forces that engendered a particular type of consciousness. He did not know, nor did he wish to know, about the "tonus of the individual's average, everyday state." In comparison with the characters of the "explanatory" nineteenth-century novel, Dostoevskii's hero is extraordinarily free in his actions, inasmuch as the motives for those actions issue spontaneously from his dominant idea. For Tolstoi the individual is, apart from everything else, inevitably conditioned in his "average, everyday" behavior by the nature of his activities. He is an officer, a landowner, a bureaucrat, and so forth. The young heroes of Dostoevskii, on the other hand, all lack occupations; they do not work, or go to school, or manage households. For the most part they are poor, even to the point of privation; nevertheless, they neither sow, nor do they reap. The hero of *A Raw Youth* has fictitious employment with a prince, Raskol'nikov is a student who does not study, Rogozhin is a merchant who does not trade, Kirillov is an unemployed engineer, Dmitrii Karamazov is a former officer, Alesha is a former novice, and Ivan is a man of ill-defined activities. And all of them have unlimited time at their disposal for their ideological adventures.

Unlike the writings of Dostoevskii, those of Tolstoi belong to the explanatory and conditioning branch of nineteenth-century psychologism.

But conditionality in Tolstoi's hands is extraordinarily particularized, concentrated, and multivalent. The combining of contradictory elements is as a result the basic principle of connection in the Tolstoian artistic structure. Rousseau was aware in the *Confessions* of the multilayered and simultaneous nature of spiritual experience, but that awareness was the consequence of brilliant intuition and of conjectures that were far in advance of their time. For nineteenth-century realism, that simultaneity had already become a necessary result of the multiform conditionality of the individual by means of a myriad of concurrently operative causes.

What had been merely a tendency in the pre-Tolstoian novel became a conscious principle in Tolstoi's writing, another hypostasis of Tolstoian fluidity. Fluidity presupposes process—a conditioned alternation of psychic states. Tolstoi proceeded logically from alternation to combination. He showed that it is possible for a person to be both vainly egocentric and selfless, or to be both overcome with grief and worried about the impression he is making (as is the case with Nikolen'ka Irten'ev at his mother's coffin). He showed how Nikolai Rostov both loved Dolokhov and hated him, how Natasha both loved Prince Andrei (whom she in fact never stopped loving) and felt an irresistible attraction for Anatole, and how Aleksei Aleksandrovich Karenin both knew about his misfortune and did not want to know about it, how he wished to crush Anna with his contempt and was at the same time afraid of her, since he feared the pain she was capable of inflicting on him. External and internal stimuli distributed among the various levels of spiritual life and originating in the different realms of human experience operate simultaneously. Elements that are mutually exclusive from a logical point of view are shown to be compatible from a psychological one. If the personality is conceived as a soul that is always equivalent to itself alone, its contradictions can only be regarded as irrational or puzzling. Such was the romantic enigma, disturbing yet requiring no solution. But if consciousness is movement, if the individual human being is a dynamic entity that contains everything in itself—from physiological irritants to the loftiest spiritual activity—and an entity, moreover, that is capable of responding to every conceivable kind of stimulus, then contradictions in it are not only inevitable; they may also be explained.

Yet individual consciousness for Tolstoi was not merely a chaos of equivalent and contradictory impulses. Without the organization of inner experience, without a hierarchical disposition of the levels of spiritual life, there could be no such thing as *behavior*, let alone the stereotyping of that behavior in the categories of personality or character that were so important to him.

According to the momentary situation he is faced with, the individual selects and activates certain elements of his consciousness, setting those elements into motion and repressing others. Some of the latter are thrust completely into the subconscious, while others coexist in the conscious mind in varying degrees of distinctness and realization. Tolstoi (and even his contemporaries noted this) scrutinized those states located on the borderline between consciousness and the unconscious. Such are his famous depictions of dreams, deliriums, half-awake states, and so on. But it was a much more difficult thing to grasp the mechanics of completely sober, daytime consciousness with its different levels coexisting simultaneously and its combining of logically incompatible contents. Tolstoi investigated, for example, the mechanism by means of which someone may go on living as if he did not know what he in fact does know. In depicting phenomena of this kind, Tolstoi came near in his artistic practice to something like the modern psychological theory of "set" or "attitude"—the special readiness or predisposition with which an individual responds to a given situation. Of exceptional relevance to this theory are the writings of the Soviet school of psychology led by D. N. Unadze. Unadze in particular has elaborated the idea of the "fixed attitude" that emerges in the process of the personality's formation by means of the consolidation of those attitudes that are most characteristic of it. A change in conditions may of course bring about a change in fixed attitude.

Attitude, in Unadze's formulation, "consists of a peculiar regulation or predisposition of the subject, its readiness . . . to manifest precisely those psychic or motor acts that ensure a response in thought or action appropriate to the situation."[38] And again: "Only that which at any given moment already occupies a place in the established channel of the subject's relevant attitude penetrates from the surrounding milieu into the psyche of the subject operating in certain conditions, and is experienced by him with sufficient clarity."[39] The individual thus activates certain elements in his consciousness, while leaving the others inactive and in a sense outside the mechanism of the attitude in question.

Tolstoi willingly portrayed those defensive gambits to which the conscious mind resorts in order to avoid destructive impressions. Such gambits are particularly successful in people who lead artificial lives—Aleksei Karenin, for instance.

> It would have been too terrible for him to admit his true situation, and he had closed, locked, and sealed the drawer in his soul that contained his feelings for his family. . . . Aleksei Aleksandrovich did not want to think anything about his wife's conduct and feelings, and he really did not think anything about them. . . . He did not want to understand, and he did not understand why his wife particularly insisted on moving to Tsarskoe Selo, where Betsy lived and where Vronskii's regiment was stationed nearby. . . .
> Yet deep down in his soul, without ever betraying it to himself, or having for

it not merely evidence but even a suspicion, he knew without any doubt that he was a deceived husband, and that he was for that reason profoundly unhappy. (pt. 2, chap. 26)

Karenin does not think, does not see, does not betray to himself, and so on—all phrases that would appear to suggest that the subject here is the thrusting of the contents of spiritual life into the unconscious. But then it turns out that Karenin "knew without any doubt that he was a deceived husband." Tolstoi uses the metaphor of the "sealed drawer" and the everyday phrase "deep down in his soul," but what he really has in mind are the different levels of consciousness, with their differently conditioned but simultaneously operative processes. In regard to Karenin, some of those processes are conditioned by the brutal obviousness of what is taking place, while others are conditioned by his inextinguishable desire to hold on to the habitual external forms of existence and internal sense of himself that he has established. Thus, although he is aware that he is a wronged husband and a contemptible and ridiculous creature in the eyes of society, Karenin tries to his utmost (until Anna's confession) to retain in his life those forms of trust and dignity that are so essential to him.

A man knows what he does not wish to know, but he leaves that knowledge outside the boundaries of those images, those internal models, by which he organizes his personality and behavior. That knowledge exists in the same way that a more direct meaning may exist alongside a euphemism that is used to suppress the significance of an unattractive phenomenon. A handsome man knows that he has a physical defect, but he ignores that fact in order to regard himself as handsome; a decent man knows that he has done something dishonest, but both externally and internally he continues to live as a decent man, as if what happened did not in fact happen. But the situation may change at any moment, bringing about a shift in mental attitude and a rearrangement of its components. And then what a person did not wish to face may suddenly become painfully active.

Vronskii is ambitious. At first his career proceeds successfully, but then he blunders.

Wishing to show his independence and obtain a promotion, he refused a post that had been offered to him, hoping that his refusal would increase his value. But it turned out he had been too bold, and he was passed over. But having willy-nilly created for himself the position of the independent man, he accepted it, very skillfully and cleverly conducting himself as if he were not angry with anybody, did not consider himself offended in any way, and only wished to be left alone, since he was enjoying himself. In point of fact, however, he had ceased to enjoy himself the year before when he left for

Moscow. He felt that the independent position of the man who could do whatever he wanted, but wanted nothing, was already beginning to pall, and that many people were beginning to wonder whether he was really capable of being anything but an honest, decent fellow. (pt. 3, chap. 20)

Vronskii is aware of his insatiable, easily offended ambition, of his envy of Serpukhovskoi, a former comrade in the cadet corps, "who had just returned from Central Asia, where he had been promoted two grades and won a distinction rarely given to generals so young." But knowing all of this, he still maintains his image of the "independent man" (his passion for Anna introduces a new element into that image), and maintains it not as a mask contrived to hide his disappointment and envy, but as a form of self-affirmation that is necessary to his existence.

"Once he had decided for himself that he was happy in his love and had sacrificed his ambition for it, or at least had assumed that role, Vronskii could no longer feel envious of Serpukhovskoi or vexed with him for not having come to see him first after joining the regiment" (pt. 3, chap. 21). But the elements of consciousness that coexist with this position and that are in conflict with it ultimately render it unstable. The implication is that Vronskii's attitude may change the first time his ambition succeeds.

For Tolstoi, the person "assuming a role" is always someone belonging to the highest levels of society, the levels where the artificial life that Tolstoi opposes to the organic, natural life of the people takes place. Tolstoi's delineation of the mechanism of self-modeling is especially clearcut in his depictions of the apex of the artificial state pyramid. I have in mind chapter 15 of *Hadji Murat* with its political and moral dissection of Nikolai I. The Nikolai of *Hadji Murat* is an extreme embodiment of artificial life, someone who has been deranged by absolute power and by the servile mendacity that surrounds him. Combining the incompatible has become a spiritual habit with him, and against all common sense he includes whatever gives him pleasure in his model of "the great man"—the monarch and military leader. He sleeps on a hard, narrow bed (a historical fact, as are all the other details in this chapter of *Hadji Murat*) and covers himself with a military cloak "which he regarded as being just as famous as Napoleon's hat (and said so)." "Praise of his strategic abilities was particularly satisfying to Nikolai, because, although he took pride in those abilities, he knew deep down in his soul that he had none. And now he wanted to hear even more detailed praise of himself." The minister of war Chernyshev flatteringly praises Nikolai's orders in regard to a military campaign being undertaken in the Caucasus. "It would seem that in order to believe that the plan of slow movement, razing forests, and destroying provisions was indeed his own plan, it would have been necessary to conceal the fact that in 1845 he had insisted on an entirely different kind of military operation. But he did not conceal it from himself and was proud of both the plan for his 1845 expedition and the plan for slow advance, despite the fact that the two obviously contradicted one another."

By means of a similar psychological mechanism, Tolstoi also explains Nikolai's decision with regard to a Polish student who has committed some offense.

> He had done great evil to the Poles. In order to justify that evil he needed to assure himself that all Poles were scoundrels. And Nikolai regarded them as such and hated them: hated them to the same degree as the evil he had done them. . . . He took the report and in his large hand wrote in the margin: "Deserves capital punishment. But, thank goodness, we do not have capital punishment. And I have no intention of instituting it now. Let him run the gauntlet of a thousand men twelve times. Nikolai. . . ." Nikolai knew that twelve thousand rods not only meant certain and agonizing death, but that it was also exceptionally cruel, since five thousand blows would have been enough to kill even the strongest of men. But he enjoyed being implacably cruel, and he enjoyed thinking that we have no capital punishment.

For Tolstoi, the bloodthirsty and grotesque decision taken by Nikolai was not so much the result of hypocrisy as of his private play at being a great man. A great monarch is both terrible and magnanimous. In the present instance, it did not matter that the two were incompatible, as long as they gave him pleasure.

But even the most powerful psychological fictions are powerless to rid consciousness of whatever it is that contradicts them. The unwanted elements have their own conditionality and for that reason continue their independent existence. Tolstoi's Nikolai knows a great deal. He knows that he has done the Poles much evil and that he has no talent for strategy. He knows that he is no longer the magnificently handsome person he once was, but a flabby old man with an immense pot belly, and he knows that he has led a dissolute life. "Nikolai . . . walked on and began pronouncing the first words that came to mind. 'Kopervein, Kopervein,' he said, repeating the name of yesterday's maiden several times. 'It's bad, it's bad.' He did not think about what he was saying, but suppressed his feeling by listening to the words alone. 'Yes, what would Russia be without me,' he said to himself, once more sensing the approach of a dissatisfied feeling. 'Yes, and not only Russia, but Europe as well.'" There is the private attitude, the "persona" of the great man, and there is something amorphous enclosing that form of self-awareness, a form that permits the individual both to know and not to know, to live as if what has happened did not happen. And all the same the individual carries everything that he knows and everything that has happened to him within himself, and there is nowhere he can lay down his burden.

Literature assimilated the inquiries of science and at the same time entered on its own into new areas of spiritual life, leaving psychology behind. The artistic comprehension of the simultaneity of psychological processes was decisive for the Tolstoian system. And it was decisive precisely because it was not an isolated discovery, but was interconnected and interactive with all the other elements of that system—with dynamism and fluidity and a new level in the realistic understanding of conditionality and contradiction. At the end of the nineteenth century and the beginning of the twentieth, the artistic discoveries of Tolstoi were met on the one hand by the elaboration of the doctrine of the subconscious and the unconscious, and on the other, by the interpretation of behavior as a system of conditioned reflexes. What for him had been merely a feature of the personality regarded dynamically, subsequently grew in importance, on occasion acquiring exceptional significance for the depiction of the twentieth-century human being with his fragmented consciousness, but especially of the "turn-of-the-century" Russian intellectual in the grip of decadent trends.

A remarkable experiment in this regard is Gor'kii's *Life of Klim Samgin*. *Klim Samgin* is an extremely multifaceted work, and I shall touch on only one aspect of it here—the methods used by Gor'kii to investigate the novel's main hero, inasmuch as that hero is the only one who is regarded internally.

Gor'kii formulated the theme of *Klim Samgin* in a June 3, 1925, letter to Konstantin Fedin: "People who have made themselves up."[40] The theme cultivated by Tolstoi, among many others, of a person's work on his own image was apprehended by Gor'kii as a highly important node of moral and political issues. What does Klim Samgin actually consist of? He is a man of mediocre abilities and of immense conceit, egoism, and emptiness. Emptiness is in fact the most constructive element in his spiritual organization. Lofty individualism presupposes both the enrichment of the personality by extrapersonal, universally significant values and a particularly intense personal realization of those values. In this sense, egoism stands opposed to individualism, and Klim Samgin is devoid of universal values in the extreme. Yet he resides in a prerevolutionary intellectual milieu where, with a greater or lesser degree of authenticity or falseness, everyone speaks of universal values, and he must remain on that level. For Klim Samgin, then, "the individual is a system of phrases," although he is quite incapable of working out that system for himself. He is a sieve through which the streams of other phrases pass without leaving a trace. Self-assertion is possible for Samgin only in the milieu in which he exists, and possible therefore only in terms of the norms that are accepted in that milieu. And regarded formally, Samgin's behavior does for the most part correspond to the habits of the middle intelligentsia of his day. His private, spontaneous impulses are marked by self-interest, cowardice, and petty egoism, but he restrains them in accordance with the prevailing norm, and not just in his public behavior, since, as Gor'kii says of his hero, he sought for himself "a place in life where he could be comfortable both materially and internally" (19:542). Too large a gap between inner states and outward manifestations may also be uncomfortable.

Self-modeling is hard for Klim. He has not been able to find his "system of phrases," and he is therefore unable to fashion from the chaos of coexisting, intersecting psychic elements a "persona," a mask with which to organize his behavior. Gor'kii frequently depicts the very process of Klim's futile effort to fashion that persona, the makeshift solutions that quickly end in new frustration and emptiness. Klim is tormented at such moments by doubles that, although they do not resemble each other, do resemble him—doubles that emerge from different undesirable conjectures about himself. The undesirable conjectures are repressed in a number of ways. Samgin knows that his divorced wife must be dying in the hospital. "He awoke early in a very good mood, and rang for some coffee, but the bellboy came in and said, 'There's somebody from the undertaker's office waiting for you. . . . ' Samgin sat on the bed for a moment, listening to see what effect the news of Varvara's death would have on him. But unable to detect any, he frowned, dissatisfied with himself and reproachfully asking somebody, 'Am I really so heartless?' While getting dressed, he thought, 'The poor thing. So soon. So quickly.' And thinking in words, he tried to imagine the order and quantity of the unpleasant tasks awaiting him" (22:174–175). Klim represses the conjecture about his own callousness by means of words that formally correspond to the norms of propriety.

The conjecture about his own lack of talent is much more threatening to Klim, however.

> Klim Samgin dimly sensed that he needed to confess something to himself, but could not and was afraid to admit what it was: what was it in fact? . . . Klim wrapped the blanket around his head, suddenly thinking: "When it comes down to it, I have no talent at all." But that conjecture vanished without offending him, and once again he fell to listening, while vague and desolate thoughts coursed through him. . . . "When it comes down to it, all these clever fellows are really boring people. And hypocrites," Samgin forced himself to think. . . . "What's really on their minds beneath all those words, probably, is something quite simple. . . ." This was not the first time that Klim Samgin conceived of a multitude of equivalent, pointed thoughts

mechanically invading him from without. They were contradictory, and it was necessary to sort out from them the ones he was most comfortable with. . . . Sometimes he was terrified by a sense of himself as a void in which thoughts and words constantly seethed. . . . He even asked himself: "It isn't that I'm stupid, is it? . . . I'm getting upset over nothing. . . . Somewhere deep down in my soul the seed of my true faith is ripening! That faith is not yet clear to me, but its mysterious power is thrusting everything alien away from me, without allowing me to make it my own. There are ideas that are for me and ideas that are not. . . . I have not yet encountered the ideas that are 'chemically suited' to me. . . ." He smiled cautiously, cheered by his discovery, yet not quite sure of its value. (19:312–316)

Clearly shown here is the way someone may simultaneously know and as it were not know what he does not want to know about himself. From the multitude of his "equivalent thoughts" a person may, depending on his psychological "attitude," select and combine the most "comfortable" ones, tolerating the rest as unavoidable alogisms that must be circumvented if they cannot merely be swept aside. This is what Samgin does with the thought that he has no talent, that he is not on the same level as the "clever fellows." That knowledge exists in him, but without threatening the pleasant sense he has of his own value. The degree of clarity with which one and the same uncomfortable thought may be apprehended varies according to the circumstances. Gor'kii investigates this last mechanism primarily on the basis of material relating to the most threatening of his hero's undesirable conjectures about himself, that of his own uncontrollable propensity to betray other people. Klim has been raised to believe that informing on others is bad, that one ought not to do it, that the society by whose standards he lives ostracizes informers, and yet ever since his boyhood years he has somehow always been an informer. While a student at the gymnasium, he betrayed a comrade and, "realizing that he had betrayed Inokov, he began thinking fearfully about why he had done so. And thinking it over, he decided that the cartoonlike shadow of the inspector's head had inspired in him a sudden desire to do something unpleasant to the braggart Dronov. . . . Feeling guilty, Klim thought of how he might make amends for it, but unable to think of anything, he became firmer in his resolve to do something unpleasant to Dronov" (19:68). Next he betrays to his stepfather Varavka a secret about the latter's daughter. "This came out very easily, all by itself: two serious people who were intellectual equals were worriedly discussing people who were young and lacking in poise, and expressing concern about their future. It would even have been awkward to remain silent about the strange relations between Lydia and Makarov" (19:152). Klim Samgin betrays other people, but he is far from being able to translate his actions into the language of qualities. He informs, but he will not say of himself, "I am an informer." Gor'kii's Samgin wants to inform on others at the same time that he wants to regard himself as a decent person and condemn those who inform. Tolstoi's Nikolai I wants to sentence a person to a slow, agonizing death and at the same time believe that in Russia there is no such thing as capital punishment. Both the one and the other give him pleasure. And each of those desires is the consequence of its own cause-and-effect sequence.

During Samgin's contacts with the police, his thoughts about betrayal pass through a number of different levels—from complete displacement from consciousness to fully conscious realization. Klim has been told that his lover Nikonova is suspected of connections with the tsar's secret police. " 'That's impossible!' Samgin exclaimed *sincerely* [italics mine], even though he had already guessed that it was true. He even thought he had guessed it not today, not now, but long before, when he had read the note written in invisible ink. But it was necessary to conceal that fact not merely from Gogin, but also from himself" (20:481). And it was necessary to conceal it because he was still having relations with that woman and still wished to regard himself as a decent person. Samgin is earlier interrogated by a police officer and is invited by him to become an agent; he refuses.

> It now seemed to him that long before the officer had offered the work of spy to him, he had known that the suggestion would be made. . . . He stood up and went home, trying to persuade himself: "I've obviously been morally insulted, like any other decent person. Morally." But he dimly conjectured that the very necessity of persuading himself of that fact confirmed the opposite: the policeman's offer had not insulted him. Attempting to suppress that conjecture, he hastily reflected, "If theory must be put into practice, then Schopenhauer and Hartmann would have had to kill themselves. Lenau, Leopardi. . . ." But Samgin already understood: what frightened him was precisely the fact that he was not insulted by the offer to become a spy. That disturbed him and that was what he wanted to forget. "I'm slandering myself," he thought. "That colonel or captain is a fool. And brazen too. Sacrifice for the cause. . . Active struggle against Liubasha. The idiot." (20:199–200)

In *The Life of Klim Samgin* Gor'kii depicts potential betrayal waiting for the moment when the constraints imposed on it by social pressure will be removed. For the time being that pressure exists, forming in combination with a propensity for betrayal a dual conditionality. Although Samgin is aware that he has not been insulted by the offer to become an informer, he continues, even internally, to measure himself against the model of the morally engaged intellectual, of the decent person, that has been worked out by his milieu. Taking the method inherited from Tolstoi for examining the simultaneous operation of conditionality on different levels of spiritual life, Gor'kii adapted it and applied it to the moral and political issues of the prerevolutionary era.

Part Two

DIRECT DISCOURSE

PSYCHOLOGICAL analysis employs a variety of means. It may take the form of direct authorial reflection, it may be presented through the characters' self-analysis, or it may be indirect—may be expressed, that is, through the depiction of their gestures and actions, which must then be analytically interpreted by the reader after he has been prepared for that task by the author. Among these different means, a special place must be given to the representation of the characters' external and internal discourse. The writer translates the behavior and experiences of his characters into the language of words; in representing their discourse, however, he uses the same system of signs that the characters themselves use, so that the means of depiction and the object of depiction are identical. Concealed in the characters' direct discourse, therefore, are special possibilities for unmediated and as it were particularly reliable evidence about their psychological states. A character's words may reflect his personality, experiences, and impulses in the most highly concentrated way, becoming a sort of focal point for the artistic interpretation of his image. Before such possibilities of the word could be realized, however, a long period of development involving the work of many great artists was necessary.

The literary forms and functions of direct discourse have changed profoundly over the centuries—from the undifferentiated speech of the characters of medieval literature that was distinguishable from the narrative only formally, to the deliberately disjointed dialogue of twentieth-century prose with its undercurrents of meaning.

The stylistic and intonational uniformity of the direct discourse of medieval literature (whether Russian or Western European), its lack of contrast with authorial discourse, and its illustrative function were characteristic as well of the high rationalist prose genres and even of the analytical novel (although in altered form obviously). The characters of *La Princesse de Clèves* converse a great deal, but their conversations are a means rather than an object of analysis. The authorial narrative flows smoothly into direct discourse and reemerges from it without seeming to be aware of the difference. The discourse of the heroes retains its intellectual clarity and logical elegance regardless of the circumstances—whether spoken in the heat of a lover's declaration or on the deathbed (the prince de Clèves's last appeal to his wife whom he suspects of infidelity, for example). Even the direct discourse of the hero and heroine of *Adolphe* is no more than a neutral means for conveying the psychological struggle between them, although that book was written in the nineteenth century.

Sentimentalism, following hard upon the Enlightenment, retained in its depiction of direct discourse many of the features that had been characteristic of the rationalist approach, including logical clarity and stylistic uniformity in regard to the language of the author and his characters. There was, however, a new element. Sentimentalism, though still under the sway of rationalism, applied the latter's methods to a different kind of material, to passions and feelings of a different social quality. A clearly defined emotional tone emerged, a distinctive mode of expression of the sensitive soul that was shared by the discourse of the author and his hero.

All this applied only to that hero through whom literature apprehended the loftiest manifestations of spiritual life. The comic characters of sentimentalist-Enlightenment and of later romantic prose were based on other principles adopted from the tradition of the lower classical genres. The direct discourse of the comic heroes of prose, like that of the characters of classical comedy and of later bourgeois drama, was permeated with everyday reality and the socially characteristic. It was already possible by the middle of the eighteenth century for a phenomenon as complex as that of the language of Rameau's nephew in Diderot to crop up in the midst of domestic naturalism and satirical generalization. That language was not only investigated in relation to its social character but also represented in terms of a kind of dramatic interplay [*deistvo*] full of astonishing psychological insights and physical vividness.

The closeness of the discourse of the lofty hero of pre-realistic prose to that of the author was of course a logical consequence of the fact that the author and the character carrying the work's main ideological burden shared the same cultural assumptions and had the same spiritual makeup. Their discourse therefore acquired the same stylistic structure, and not merely externally but also internally, since the internal discourse was no less conventional than the external variety, was indeed its stylistic mirror image.

Until the advent of nineteenth-century psychological realism, the prevailing correlation between the character's inner motives and his external utterances remained direct. To be sure, the character might hide the truth, might lie, engage in intrigue, and so on, but even his falseness was an unambiguous expression of his intentions, which were already known to the reader, or soon would be. Corresponding to the direct relationship between the character's discourse and his motives was an "ideal" relationship between those utterances and the situation in which they occurred. An utterance took place not because in a given situation it was empirically possible in a particular form, but because it corresponded to the idea of the situation created by the artist. Although she is dying, Julie in *La Nouvelle Héloïse* makes over the course of several days a number of long, edifying speeches (even engaging in debate with her pastor about the dogma of the resurrection of the body) that are remarkable both for their logical structure and their elegant style. Rousseau had no interest in the empirical possibilities of such discourse; it was enough for him that it bore an ideal relation to the lofty, selfless death of his heroine.

An ideal relationship between situation and character discourse was typical of romanticism as well. This is obvious enough when applied to romantic emotionalism. Romantic irony, however, would seem to have been incompatible with direct disclosure of the hero's inner states. Yet romantic irony, from the Jena school to Byron's *Don Juan* and Heine's *Buch Le Grand*, was (as has already been observed above) essentially a stylistic device for revealing the presence of the author, who ruled over the world he had created, building it up and breaking it down by right of the arbitrary rule of genius. The romantic hero resided in that world, and his discourse was an ideal expression (in reference to the situation) of his consciousness, which was part of the universal romantic consciousness embracing all romantic heroes.

The elements of the new, realistic tendency crystallized in late romanticism, bringing with them new forms of direct discourse, forms that were characterized, differentiated, and historically and socially colored. The development of these new forms found fertile soil in the historical novel created by romanticism. Dialogue acquired vital significance in the novels of Walter Scott and in the historical novels of the French romantics. The dialogic fabric of Hugo's *Notre-Dame de Paris* (1831) is complex and multileveled, containing not only the differentiated and socially colored discourse of the tramps, beggars, bourgeoisie, judicial officers, and noblemen of the fifteenth century, but also the grotesquely and cruelly limned speech of King Louis XI and the deranged emotionalism of the monologues of the demonic hero Claude Frollo. The speeches of Claude Frollo, with his vocabulary of the Catholic priest and the student of alchemy, are historically colored, although they are interspersed with the historically neutral language of Esmeralda. Hers is an ideal style employed merely to give expression to those ideas of life-affirming beauty and national character that have been abstracted from her empirical traits. Frollo and Esmeralda represent romanticism in its purest form. Corresponding to the diverse dialogic strata of *Notre-Dame de Paris* is the deliberately motley discourse of the author himself. Emotionalism is combined in his extensive observations with the comic and the grotesque, just as colloquial language is crossed with the language of the professional historian, the archaeologist, and the publicist.

Accompanying the transition in the nineteenth century from romanticism to early realism was the appearance in the literary text of the more transitional forms of direct discourse. Emerging along with a heightened awareness of the social and psychological characteristics of individual speech was a desire to represent it more naturalistically, to include its solecisms, its pauses, its whole physical texture. The vast monologue spoken by the dying Goriot has a conventional, ideal relation to the situation of his death. But where the deathbed speeches of the prince de Clèves or of Julie in *La Nouvelle Héloïse* were constructed in complete accordance with the elegant rules of logic, and sometimes even of rhetoric, the romantically expressive speech of Balzac's Goriot is accompanied by gasping for breath, coughing, moaning, and complaints about his physical suffering.

The more nineteenth-century realistic psychologism developed, the less directly purposeful the discourse of its characters became. Their personalities, their inner motivations and external circumstances, their situations at any given instant, their fleeting impressions, and the momentary influences impinging on them were all combined in their dialogic speech, and combined moreover as factors. Characteristic of the direct discourse of nineteenth-century psychological prose is an empirical (as opposed to ideal) relationship to situation, and, by virtue of its multileveled conditionality, an indirect or disjunctive relationship between the utterance and its inner motivation.

Disjunctions of this kind are already apparent in Lermontov's *Hero of Our Time*, the immediate predecessor of the Russian psychological novel of the second half of the nineteenth century. Pechorin wears a mask in which cold contempt has been combined with a demonism moderated by the habits of polite society. This is common in Byronic literature, but what is not is that Pechorin himself scoffs at demonism of the mundane variety, regarding with aversion its reflection in the distorting mirror of Grushnitskii. What, then, is Grushnitskii? A model of the obsolescent historical personality of the 1830s. Demonism was no longer an adequate form for the new, realistic experience of the authorial consciousness, so that a romantic identification of author and main hero was impossible. Those of the hero's remarks falling under the shadow of Grushnitskii's outmoded phraseology are therefore suspect.

There are in early realistic prose numerous instances of this kind of convoluted or disjunctive relationship between the words of a character and his internal aspirations or states. Pride and passion in Julien Sorel's speeches are indivisibly fused with hypocrisy, falsehood, and a habitual concealment of his true state of mind. Rudin's speeches are the artificially inflated verbal passion with which a cold mind amuses itself. "As cold as ice," Lezhnev says of him, "and he knows it, although he pretends to be passionate." Rudin's speeches are neither truth nor falsehood; they are "cant" in the complex meaning given that term by the young ideologues of the 1830s and 1840s.

Psychologism required disjunctions. Nonetheless, the discourse of the characters in the pre-Tolstoian novel was still completely functional. Every monologue, every dialogue, every rejoinder given to a pre-Tolstoian character was in persistent fulfillment of a particular task, whether to provide evidence about the character's personality, his time and place, those who had raised him, or his experiences and thoughts, or whether to convey information about events or to advance the plot. Direct discourse in the Tolstoian novel performs the same functions, but it is not restricted to them. The Tolstoian revolution in the conception and depiction of human beings was also a revolution in the depiction of their language.[1] Although that language continues to fulfill tasks relating to plot and personality, it also moves beyond them. Tolstoi's new attitude toward the language of his characters was rooted in his endeavor to grasp life in general, life per se, in terms of those processes and patterns that transcend the merely personal. Conversation was one of those processes. And discourse as such—the different types and purposes of verbal utterance— therefore became for Tolstoi both an object of depiction and one of the areas in which he carried out his artistic investigations. Those investigations concerned both discourse as an externally conditioned medium of practical communication directed toward changing the external world and discourse as something conditioned by the individual's ineluctable need to give objective form in language to the full potential of his inner life (both emotional and intellectual) and to realize his own values, interests, and creative possibilities. Tolstoi gave particular attention to those verbal situations in which conversation is an end in itself, a ritualistic property of a given form of social intercourse (the small talk, soirees, and dinners of polite society, "hunting stories," the chitchat of traveling companions, and the like). Conversation in these instances is prescribed by the rules of social decorum, and silence is apprehended as a violation of the norm producing either awkwardness or affront.

Tolstoi also explored the function of conversation as a means of filling a void that someone may find intolerable. Discourse in such cases is induced by the inner need to act, to utilize one's energy. It may become the most accessible substitute for action, albeit a substitute that may on occasion lack an object. Sometimes anything at all will do as a defense against idleness, boredom, and emptiness, be it casual impressions, random recollections, free associations, or the casting up of fragments from the inexhaustible stream of internal speech.

I shall later try to demonstrate just how wide-ranging and variegated Tolstoi's depiction of the different functions and purposes of verbal intercourse is. These functions and purposes do not, of course, occur in Tolstoi in pure, abstracted guise, but rather in vital combinations involving interaction and transition among concrete, socially differentiated forms.

Tolstoi's interest in such forms took shape at the very beginning. In *Youth*, for example, that interest is apparent in the experimental clarity so characteristic of the book. There is one mode of conversation in the Nekhliudov family and another in the Irten'ev family.

> There is a private ability, more or less developed in different social circles and especially in families, an ability that I shall call "mutual understanding." . . . Two people of the same circle or family who possess this ability will always permit the expression of feeling up to a certain point, beyond which they both become aware of cant; and they see at the same time where praise ends and irony begins, where enthusiasm ends and pretense begins. . . . In order to facilitate this shared understanding, the people of a circle or family develop their own language, their own turns of phrase, and even their own words defining nuances of meaning that are nonexistent for other people. . . . The following words with their corresponding ideas came to have a special meaning, although God knows why, for Volodia and me: "raisins" meant a vain desire to show you had money; "cone" [*shishka*] (and here you had to join your fingers together and give particular stress to both *sh* sounds) meant something fresh, healthy, attractive, but not ostentatious; a noun used in the plural meant an unjustified passion for that object, and so forth and so on. (Chap. 29)

It should be noted that the family semantics of the Irten'evs is of a completely different variety than that of the Rostovs; it has none of the Rostovian warmth or subtle intuitiveness. On the contrary, it is based on distrust and even contempt for "sentimentality" of any kind.

Analyses of direct discourse in Tolstoi sometimes acquire a clear-cut social tinge, as happens, for example, in the chapter called "New Comrades" in *Youth*, where the hero's new acquaintance with students of plebeian intellectual provenance is described. A "feeling of contempt" is provoked in Nikolen'ka by their mode of life,

> and especially [by] their manner of speaking, the way they used and stressed certain words. For example, they used the word "silly" instead of "fool," "such as" instead of "like," "splendid" instead of "excellent," "motivational" instead of "motivating," and so on, which seemed bookish and offensively ungentlemanly to me. But what provoked my sense of comme il faut even more were the stresses they gave to certain Russian and especially certain foreign words: they said "máchine" instead of "machíne," "áctivity" instead of "actívity," "íntentionally" instead of "inténtionally," "in the firepláce" instead of "in the fíreplace," "Shakespéare" instead of "Shákespeare," and so forth and so on.

Tolstoi was also interested in the types of conversation that were characteristic of particular psychological situations. One of the chapters of

Youth is in fact called "An Intimate Conversation with My Friend." In the course of that conversation, each interlocutor strives to say what he himself wants to talk about, while responding rather indifferently to the declarations of the other. Nikolen'ka Irten'ev is embarrassed by the intimate direction the conversation has taken. "'And, really, what of it,' I thought, reassuring myself. 'It does not matter; we are *adults*, two friends riding in a phaeton and discussing our future lives. Anybody would enjoy listening to us and looking at us.'" Conversation as such—its very mechanism—becomes here an unmediated object of depiction, one of the "focal points" that Tolstoi mentioned in an 1857 note: "It is the business of art to seek out focal points and expose them to full view. Such focal points . . . are the personalities of people, but they may also be the personalities of scenes, peoples, or nature" (47:213).

The representation of the separate "focal points" of conversation was subordinated in Tolstoi to his philosophy of language, which was in turn derived from his classification of people into those who are artificial and those who are endowed with feeling—with an intuitive grasp of authentic life values. Tolstoi sought out unfeeling, artificial discourse at every level, whether in the professional discussions in *Anna Karenina* or in the conversation of Speranskii's intimates over dinner at his home in *War and Peace*. Prince Andrei is present at that dinner at the moment when his feelings for Natasha first take root, so that the banal chatter of the diners is especially unbearable to him. "He wanted to join in the conversation several times, but each time his words were thrust aside like a cork tossed out of the water" (vol. 2, pt. 3, chap. 18). Unfeeling discourse is exposed as well in the invariably rational speeches of Vera Rostova, who reacts to a letter from Nikolai containing the news that he has been slightly wounded but that he has been made an officer by remarking, "But what are you crying about, *maman*. From everything he says, you ought to be rejoicing instead of crying" (vol. 1, pt. 3, chap. 6). And everyone stares at her in astonishment and dismay.

Trivial, one-dimensional discourse in Tolstoi may express not merely narrowness of mind but also baseness of soul. In the scene in *A Nest of Gentlefolk* depicting Lavretskii's confrontation with his suddenly returned wife, Turgenev presents Varvara Pavlovna's speech in terms that are not only psychologically characteristic but that also contain a distinctive social tinge. That was enough for Turgenev. Tolstoi, however, in depicting Pierre Bezukhov's confrontation with Hélène, probes the actual forms of her speech and exposes their loathsome meaning. "He recalled the coarseness and bluntness of her thoughts and the vulgarity of the expressions that were characteristic of her, despite the fact that she had been brought up in the most aristocratic of circles. 'I am not some fool. . . . Why don't you just try it. . . . *Allez-vous promener*,' she would say. . . . Why did I ever get involved with her? Why did I say '*Je vous aime*' to her, which was a lie, and worse than a lie?" Pierre is distressed not only by Hélène's language, with its unembarrassed bluntness; he is tormented as well by the verbal clichés that he himself uses, which contain in themselves the mendacity of the artificial world. After Pierre's duel with Dolokhov, Hélène comes to her husband to have it out. "'You believe everything you are told, and they told you . . .'—Hélène started laughing—'that Dolokhov was my lover,' she said in French with her usual coarse exactitude, pronouncing the word 'lover' like any other, 'and you believed it! . . . Separate if you want, but only if you give me a living,' said Hélène. . . . 'Separate—what a thing to frighten me with!'" (vol. 2, pt. 1, chap. 6). After this Pierre rushes at her with a marble table-top in his hands, shouting, "I'll kill you!" The sudden access of fury is spontaneously provoked not by the obviousness of Hélène's betrayal of him, nor by her attempt to extort money from him (there was nothing new about that), but by the intolerable baseness of her phraseology. Attention to the individual words and phrases spoken by Hélène or Vera Rostova or by the Moscow professors in *Anna Karenina* is undoubtedly a kind of microcharacterology, but it is also a relation to the speech of others as one of the "focal points" of reality.

To the unfeeling word with its "coarse exactitude," Tolstoi opposed the intuitive, irrational word, revealing in it an infinite semantic perspective. Investigated in his works are such phenomena as internal discourse; the different functions of the word in semiconscious, delirious, and dying states; gestures that say more than words; and the richly significant, associative, and intuitive semantics of the Rostov family, whose true virtuoso is Natasha.

A great deal of attention has been paid in the Tolstoi literature to the internal discourse of his characters. This theme has been developed in a particularly extensive way by V. V. Vinogradov. Through the examination of discourse that is unusually associative, that demands a special, "family" apperception, Vinogradov shows how in the conversation of the Rostov children, in Natasha's exchanges with her mother, and in the epilogue to *War and Peace*, and so forth, an objectively logical semantics is replaced by an expressively symbolic one.[2] This feature of the domestic conversations brings them, in Vinogradov's opinion, close to Tolstoi's celebrated interior monologues. Vinogradov distinguishes two types of interior monologue: the irrational variety, which reproduces internal discourse (to the extent that its unformulated components may actually be fixed in words), and the more conventional, more purely logical variety. He regards the latter as an exception, as a deviation (albeit a very important one) from the basic Tolstoian mode of conveying internal speech.[3] It is the logical type of interior monologue, however, that actually predominates in Tolstoi. The more irrational forms of monologue usually accompany the depiction of special, confused states of mind, whether in the deathbed delirium of Prince Andrei or in the incoherent thoughts of Ensign Il'in in *Two Hussars* after he has gambled away state funds.

The two types of interior monologue reflect one of the most basic and productive contradictions in Tolstoi's point of view. The zealous analyst in him required "ratiocination" [*rassuditel'stvo*] as a reliable tool of analysis. Connected with this were his "archaistic" enthusiasms, especially his taste for the literature of eighteenth-century rationalism. Tolstoi's worldview, however, was antirationalistic. Using rational, analytical means, including a pointedly logical and sometimes even pedantic syntax, Tolstoi broke through the rational veneer of life, delving into what he regarded as its innate, natural essence. Tolstoi was, in the unique quality of this combination, quite close to his favorite thinker, Rousseau.

To be sure, depiction of the internal discourse of literary characters was widely practiced before Tolstoi (one need only recall the fevered interior monologues of Julien Sorel while in prison). Nonetheless, it is in fact with Tolstoi that the interior monologue is associated, as if he were its inventor. External discourse in pre-Tolstoian literature merged imperceptibly with internal discourse, remaining quite undifferentiated from it.[4] Tolstoi turned internal discourse into something highly distinctive, functionally setting it off from authorial discourse and from the colloquial speech of his characters. And this is true of both the logical and the nonlogical varieties of the Tolstoian interior monologue. Tolstoi really was the first to convey the uninterrupted yet disjointed stream of consciousness, and he transformed logical internal discourse into a special, unprecedentedly powerful means of analysis possessing a sort of unmediated authenticity: the individual analyzes himself, resorting for the sake of greater clarity to articulated formulations.

The French scholar Michel Aucouturier has argued in an interesting article devoted to internal discourse in Tolstoi that internal discourse of the logical variety is essentially the property of the ideological heroes, of Levin, Nekhliudov, and the rest.[5] That is not quite true. The interior monologues of Prince Andrei, Pierre, Levin, and Nekhliudov do indeed have special weight and significance, but monologues of the same kind may also be found in the discourse of the other primary characters, including the most intuitive among them. Thus Nikolai Rostov, despite his extreme perturbation at losing to Dolokhov, is nonetheless able to reason very coherently. "I was so happy and so free, and enjoying myself! And I did not realize then how happy I was! When did all that end and this new, terrible state begin? What marked the change? I was sitting in the very same place next to the table, and choosing and laying down the cards, and watching those large-boned, nimble hands. When did it happen, and what was it that happened?" (vol. 2, pt. 1, chap. 14).

A precisely articulated syntax is from time to time even characteristic of Natasha's monologues. "'If after that I could return his smile while saying goodbye to him, if I could permit it to come to that, then it means that I loved him from the very beginning. It means that he is kind, noble, and fine, and that it was impossible not to love him. But what am I to do if I love him and someone else?' she said to herself, unable to find answers to these terrible questions" (vol. 2, pt. 5, chap. 13). The logical interior monologue is necessary here as a means of delineating as clearly as possible the "terrible questions" confronting Natasha. This internal discourse with its surprisingly bookish tinge is quite unlike Natasha's conversation. And on the whole, the external, dialogic speech of Tolstoi's characters is much more disconnected, syntactically compressed, and associative than their interior monologues of the logical type. The difference between the two varieties is particularly clear when they occur in close proximity. On the eve of the Battle of Austerlitz Prince Andrei thinks, "Tomorrow, perhaps, everything will be finished for me! All these memories will be no more, will no longer have any meaning for me. Tomorrow, maybe—or even probably, since I have a presentiment—I shall for the first time finally have to show everything I am capable of" (vol. 1, pt. 3, chap. 12). And then, on the very next page, there is the internal discourse of Nikolai Rostov as he begins to nod off while on flanking patrol: "What was I thinking about then? Don't forget. What I will say to the sovereign? No, that's not right—that's tomorrow. Oh yes! A tack, attack. . . . At whom—at us? At Hussars. . . . At Hussars with mustaches. . . . That hussar with the moustache was riding down Tverskaia. I thought about him again across from Gur'ev's. . . . Old man Gur'ev" (chap. 13). These two monologues serve different purposes. That of the first is to break down the experience of a hero (Prince Andrei) into its components; that of the second is to investigate the process of internal discourse in a half-awake state, to look at a real-life phenomenon as it is registered in Nikolai Rostov.

The brilliant interior monologue of Anna Karenina before her suicide anticipates (as many others have written) the stream of consciousness of twentieth-century novelists. But the remarkable thing about Anna's monologue is that both kinds of internal discourse—both purposes—are in conflict in it. On the one hand there is the famous 'Tiut'kin Coiffeur' . . . *je me fais coiffer par* Tiut'kin"—an alternation of disjointed but linked thoughts emerging as a result of the intermittent intrusion of accidental impressions from the street and the pressure of the character's obsessive inner awareness of her misfortune. And then in the midst of all this, the persistent and familiar sound of Tolstoian "rationality" is suddenly audible: "'Well, I shall obtain a divorce and become Vronskii's wife. Will

Kitty then stop looking at me the way she did today? No. Will Serezha stop asking and wondering about my two husbands? And what new feeling can I invent between Vronskii and me? Is any kind of feeling, not happiness even, but merely freedom from torment, even possible? No, it is not,' she answered herself without the slightest hesitation" (pt. 7, chap. 30). This clearly articulated discourse is necessary because Anna has come to see everything "in that piercing light that now revealed to her the meaning of life and human relations" (Levin made the acquaintance of that piercing light during his own crisis). But the stream of tortuous, alogical associations is also necessary to give expression to the increasing spiritual confusion that threatens Anna and that draws her toward her death. Tolstoi, boldly combining the alogical interior monologue with the logical variety, understood the conventional nature of what he was doing. But what he was doing was concerned more with artistic cognition of the principles of internal discourse than with an attempt to reproduce it—something that in any case would have been impossible by means of external language intended for intercourse among people. Tolstoi had no wish to undertake naturalistic tasks that were incapable of solution.

If such tasks did later on become an issue in twentieth-century literature, they were still incapable of solution in practical terms. L. S. Vygotskii has observed that internal speech "is not speech minus sound" but rather a special structure (characterized by predication, abbreviation, and the "fusing" of words) that if transcribed would be "unrecognizable and unintelligible."[6] Hence the notorious and predictable conventionality of all subsequent attempts to represent stream of consciousness. This pertains as well to even the most daring of Joyce's innovations. Molly Bloom's interior monologue in *Ulysses*—a vast interweaving of unpredictable associations—is elaborated over the space of dozens of pages without a single punctuation mark. Nevertheless, the way in which the words and phrases of that monologue are combined is based on a model of external discourse intended as a medium of communication between one person and another.

Tolstoi's writings not only contain a multitude of different types of discourse rarely captured with such completeness by any other writer; they also represent an unprecedented artistic cognition of the *motives* underlying the individual utterance. And that is no less appropriate. The depiction of discourse as such followed from the Tolstoian principle of depicting the processes of life itself in terms of their individual manifestations. Tolstoi's keen interest in the motives governing direct discourse, however, was tied to his investigation of the conditionality of all that exists—to his desire to represent that discourse in the most precise and detailed fashion, even to the point of revealing the determined nature of every one of the character's verbal reactions.

For what reason and with what purpose—"why" and "what for"—does a person say precisely what he says? The special nature of this question is defined by the deceptive freedom of the speech act. Any act changes the surrounding world, however slightly, and it therefore always encounters the resistance of that world. The utterance of a word is by its very nature also an act. Sometimes this is obvious, but by no means is it always so. There are utterances that on the surface seem to be determined by nothing and connected to nothing, that appear to depend merely on the whim of the speaker. He has evidently said whatever came into his head. But why did just that "come into his head" and not something else?

There are forms of intercourse and speech situations that presuppose a defined conversational content (to a greater or lesser degree). Utterances having a business or practical function are predetermined and bound in this sense. Conversations stipulated by the etiquette of a given situation (such as exchanges among guests or in the lobby of a theater) may lack a precisely defined content, but they are usually, in their different social varieties, characterized by rather strict and stable stereotypes and by a circumscribed choice of themes—social, theatrical or literary, society, professional, family, and so on. But there are freer and more accidental forms of verbal interchange that attend a person's whole existence. Sometimes the most difficult thing of all is to elucidate the motives and purposes of precisely these forms of unregulated everyday dialogue.

All of the impulses enumerated above are characteristic of everyday dialogue as well: practical communication intending to convey information (or sometimes disinformation) to an interlocutor or to stimulate him to some action, the expression of affects and emotions, and the objectification of the inner contents of consciousness. But such dialogue also has its own special mechanisms without which the appearance of a rejoinder would in many situations remain incomprehensible.

We have very few linguistic works devoted to the study of dialogue. Those researchers who have touched on this issue have so far invariably appealed to L. P. Iakubinskii's article "On Dialogic Speech," in which he notes the importance and the undeveloped nature of the question of "the *purposes* of the speech utterance."[7] In his article, however, Iakubinskii examines not so much the conscious motives and purposes of the utterance as the psychophysiological and daily social mechanisms that make dialogic intercourse a necessity. He gives a great deal of weight to the automatism of such intercourse, to its stable routines, and to its reflexivity (not so much in regard to the "purpose" of the utterance as to its "cause"), that is, to the ability of "the *speech* act to elicit a *speech* reaction, that circumstance frequently having an almost reflexive character. Just as a question, thanks to the stable connection between thoughts and their articulation, almost involuntarily or 'naturally' engenders an answer . . . , so every speech irritant . . . , by stimulating thoughts and feelings in reaction to itself, necessarily impels the organism into a speech reaction."[8]

At the end of his article Iakubinskii complains about the lack of "dialogue transcribed from reality rather than from literary works." He is forced to use literary material, and in the overwhelming number of cases that material comes from Tolstoi (*Anna Karenina*), so great is the range of functions in the direct discourse of Tolstoi, and so confident is the reader's sense of its authenticity. The following is one of the examples cited by Iakubinskii. "The friends were silent the whole way. Levin was thinking about what the change in Kitty's expression meant. . . . Stepan Arkad'evich during the ride was composing the menu for their dinner. 'You like turbot, don't you,' he said to Levin, as they drove up to the restaurant. 'What?' Levin asked. 'Turbot? Oh yes, I'm *terribly* fond of turbot' " (pt. 1, chap. 9). This is an automatic response to another's question, and the content of the utterance would therefore seem to be merely accidental and without consequence. Speech acts of this kind were beyond the reach of pre-Tolstoian prose, where everything had to serve the purpose of depicting personality, milieu, and circumstance. This kind of direct discourse did, however, have a great future in late nineteenth and twentieth-century literature (Tolstoi and Chekhov directly influenced the structure of dialogue in Hemingway, for example). The "meaninglessness" of such dialogue should not, of course, be taken literally. The conversation about turbot is, to be sure, a characteristically Tolstoian investigation of the dialogic process, but it is also a portrayal of the spiritual state of Levin, who is preoccupied with his love for Kitty. A writer (a real one) cannot say anything accidental or meaningless, even if he wants to. The work of art gives meaning and symbolic significance to everything falling within its context.

Skaftymov has written very truly of the pointed semantic significance of "meaningless" dialogue in the Chekhovian drama of mood: "When Chebutykin, immersed in his newspaper, announces in act 2 of *Three Sisters*, 'Tsitsikar. Smallpox is raging here . . . ,' that phrase addressed to no one in particular has of course no communicable meaning whatever, but is present merely as an expression of the dull placidity, idleness, absentmindedness, and listlessness of the prevailing atmosphere. When Solenyi and Chebutykin get into an argument in the same place about what *chekhartma* or *cheremsha* is, whether it is a kind of meat or an onionlike plant, the meaning of that brief episode is to be found not in its subject matter, but in the triviality and concealed half-irritation to which it gives utterance."[9] The meaningless dialogue acquires meaning by virtue of the fact that it expresses the meaninglessness of the existence of Chekhov's characters. Direct discourse in literature thus has a dual function relating both to the system of the character's consciousness as it is depicted by the author and to the system of the work regarded as a whole.

Tolstoi relentlessly traces the verbal interplay that accompanies the internal and external life of the individual. A basic problem for Tolstoian psychologism is therefore the conditionality and intentionality of his characters' discourse, of that microcosm of personalities, characteristics, impulses, events, and situations.

The "reflexive" dialogic discourse that in the absence of transcriptions of actual conversations was studied by Iakubinskii on the basis of quotations from Tolstoi is the consequence not only of the need to respond to one utterance with another but of a number of other kinds of impulses as well. It may emerge spontaneously as a surface manifestation of the ceaseless operation of internal discourse (as the "thinking out loud" that is sometimes so astonishing to interlocutors who are unprepared for it). Such discourse may also be a consequence of human abhorrence of a vacuum, and of the fact that speech provides an outlet for energy by taking the place of action. And, lastly, such dialogic discourse may be a consequence of individual social habits. Remaining silent with other people is oppressive and awkward; it is socially unacceptable.

In all of these instances the content of the conversation is not determined by an explicit purpose; rather, it appears as something free and "accidental." It arises from the stream of inner conceptions and associations, from impulses derived from the speech of others, and from external impressions impinging on the field of consciousness (so that the attention of one's interlocutor is suddenly directed to a detail in the landscape or to the appearance of a passerby), and it adapts itself to verbal clichés whose purpose is merely to fill a void—whether they be the simplest of expressions (such as "How are you?"), or standard exchanges about the weather, or the complex formulas of society and literary conversation.

The Tolstoian artistic cognition of dialogue involves these forms too. Nikolen'ka Irten'ev enters his brother Volodia's room. The latter is lying on the couch, reading a book. "I went over to the desk and picked up a book too, but before I started to read it, it occurred to me that there was something ridiculous about the fact that we had not said anything to each other, even though we had been apart all day. 'So, will you be home tonight?' 'I don't know. Why?' 'No reason,' I said, and realizing that the conversation was not going anywhere, I took the book and started reading" (*Boyhood*, chap. 26).

It is not at all necessary for Nikolen'ka to know whether his brother will be home that evening. In *Anna Karenina* Levin asks unnecessary questions during his distressing meeting with his brother Nikolai. "'You were at Kiev University?' Konstantin Levin asked Kritskii in order to break the awkward silence that followed" (pt. 1, chap. 24). "'Is this your first time in Moscow?' Konstantin said to her [to Masha, Nikolai's companion], merely to have something to say" (pt. 1, chap. 25). Tolstoi required these pointless utterances too, since he needed to have the widest possible range of individual verbal manifestation, just as he needed the widest possible range of life's other manifestations. But he did not overuse them, and they are glimpsed only fleetingly in his texts in order to remind the reader of "how it is" in life.

The true subject of Tolstoi's artistic investigations, however, is not "reflexive speech" but rather those verbal forms whose conditionality and intentionality are so deeply concealed that only analysis is able to bring them out.

Tolstoi's interest in the problem of conversation as such is apparent in his very first literary effort, one not yet fully detached from the fabric of his early diaries.

In the unfinished and experimental "Story of Yesterday" (1851), the master of the house, while accompanying his guests to the door, says, "When will we see you again?" This phrase "is meaningless, but from vanity the guest involuntarily interprets it as follows: 'when' means 'as soon as you can, please'; 'we' means 'I and my wife, who would also enjoy seeing you very much'; 'again' means 'we have just spent the evening together, but one could not be bored with you'; and 'see' means 'give us the pleasure once more.' And the guest carries away a pleasant impression." This early fragment also contains a curious theoretical disquisition on the nature of conversation itself:

> People born in the last century complain that "there is no more conversation now." I do not know what people in the last century were like (it seems to me that people have always been the same as they are now), but conversation can never have taken place. Conversation, as an activity, is the silliest of inventions. It is not because of insufficient intelligence that conversation is impossible, but because of egoism. Everyone wants to speak about himself or about what he is doing; and if one person is talking, then the other must listen, so that the result is not conversation but instruction. . . .
>
> I am not even talking about those conversations that take place because it would be as unseemly not to talk as it would be to turn up without a tie. One side thinks: "You know perfectly well that I do not have time to talk about what I am talking about, but it is necessary"; the other side thinks: "Talk on, talk on, poor fellow—I realize it is necessary."
>
> This is no longer conversation, but the same thing as a black frock coat, visiting cards, and gloves—a matter of decorum. (1:280)

This fragment bears witness both to Tolstoi's interest in the very process of verbal intercourse in its various forms and varieties (conversation "about oneself or about what one is doing," conversation that takes place because "it would be unseemly not to talk," and so on) and to his investigation of conditionality, since each variety of conversation is characterized by its own kind of conditionality.

For Tolstoi with his relentless investigation of all the stratagems of human pride and egocentricity, the conversation "about oneself" or "about what one is doing" also provides one of the main opportunities for exposing the impulses concealed in any utterance—for showing how the individual's need to realize his own personality, to realize his own potentialities and capabilities, stands as the principal impetus behind all the other motives of his speech.

The speech of the characters in the pre-Tolstoian novel was sometimes very complex, but it was still a direct expression of personality, epoch, milieu, and situation. For Tolstoi, a person's speech is above all a sign of his unceasing ulterior struggle for self-affirmation understood in the broadest sense—as extending from the satisfaction of egoistic desires to identification with the loftiest and most universal of values.

"Language is a variety of human behavior," says Iakubinskii.[10] And conversation, like any other behavior, is determined, although the regularity of its patterns may remain concealed from those who are engaged in it. It may seem to them that they are taking part in an act that is almost entirely free of the resistance of the objective world that weighs on every other act. Love and vanity, hope and malice, all may find realization in conversation, sometimes in illusory ways. Conversation can be a kind of wish fulfillment. In discussion over a cup of tea or a glass of wine, interlocutors may overcome otherwise insurmountable barriers or achieve goals that would require years of unsuccessful effort in the world of action. Tolstoi grasped these psychological mechanisms of dialogue and was the first to depict them in a fully conscious way.

Tolstoi shows how the individual raised in an artificial milieu[11] asserts himself in conversation with his intimates both directly and obliquely, in both overt and roundabout ways—from guileless pronouncements about himself and his affairs to concealed admiration for his own opinions about science, art, and politics, or for his own wit and eloquence and his power over his listener's attention.

Such are the direct, positive forms for defending one's position in life, although indirect, negative forms are possible as well. Examples of self-affirmation of the latter, inverted type are every sort of deliberate foolishness, self-abasement, and hysterical display. The individual seeks a way out of his inadequacy by raising it to the level of an aesthetic or an ideology. This is the position, the particularly *verbal* position, of the hero of *Notes from Underground* and of many of Dostoevskii's other characters. Tolstoi remained largely a stranger to phenomena of this kind. He reveals the concealed motives (concealed sometimes from the speakers themselves) in the direct discourse of his characters, and he traces the personal themes behind these motives. The expression of those themes may be unmediated and direct (conversation about oneself and one's own interests), or it may be mediated and oblique, lying deep within the objectively significant part of the conversation and finding realization either in the conversation's cognitive or in its aesthetic potentials. Oral discourse in such cases then becomes a prototype for the individual's scientific and artistic activity, for his irrepressible need to communicate whatever he knows or has created.

The individual personality makes its values known in a variety of different ways, and that variety is given extensive representation in Tolstoi. Following the engagement at Schön Grabern, and just after he has been promoted from cadet to lieutenant in a hussar regiment, Nikolai Rostov visits the guardsmen Berg and Boris Drubetskoi. The characters' discourse in this scene directly serves their need for self-affirmation. "The two friends gave accounts of themselves to each other, the one of his hussar's revels and of his life as a combat soldier, the other of the pleasures and advantages of service under those of high rank. . . . As usual, Berg was silent whenever the subject did not touch on him personally" (vol. 1, pt. 3, chap. 7). Berg's own discourse is essentially a frank expression of egoism, smugness, and bragging about his successes. "'I am, Count, already quite settled in my new apartment now,' Berg said [to Pierre Bezukhov], confident that the information could not fail to be agreeable" (vol. 2, pt. 3, chap. 20).

In the scene describing the meeting of the three comrades, all talk openly "about themselves." Drubetskoi boasts like a careerist, Berg like a prosperous money-grubber, and Rostov like a passionate and noble youth. The discourse of each reveals his character. But Tolstoi proceeds beyond such characterological functions to an investigation of the verbal routines of youthful boasting itself. "He began his story intending to tell everything exactly as it happened but imperceptibly, involuntarily, and inevitably lapsed into falsehood. If he had told the truth to these listeners, who like himself had many times before heard stories about attacks and had formed definite ideas for themselves about what an attack was, and who were expecting just such a story from him, either they would not have believed him, or worse, they would have thought that Rostov was himself to blame for the fact that what usually happens to the narrators of cavalry attacks had not happened to him. . . . It is a very difficult thing to tell the truth, and young people are rarely capable of it" (vol. 1, pt. 3, chap. 7).

In the middle of the story about the battle of Schön Grabern, Drubetskoi's patron Prince Andrei comes into the room, bringing with him an altogether different verbal position. Direct discussion of his own merits or accomplishments is obviously out of the question for Bolkon-skii, with his acute sense of his failure to accomplish the great deeds he believes he is destined for. There is an element of Pechorin in him (Pechorin too is choked by "boundless strength") that is somewhat ahead of its time, since the "Byronic" type actually began to take shape in Russian society later on, at the end of the 1810s and the beginning of the 1820s, along with the activist Decembrist type with which it was sometimes combined in individual personalities.[12] Given Prince Andrei's cult of Napoleonic methods, however, and his hunger for a great deed or cause in which to achieve glory, his skepticism, contemptuous indifference, and aristocratic superciliousness are merely a mask, a well thought-out mask consisting of words, facial expressions, and gestures. Such he is at the moment of his first appearance in the novel (at the salon of Anna Pavlovna Scherer), and such he is in the episode of his encounter with Nikolai Rostov and Boris Drubetskoi. The youthful Rostov is also engaged in constructing an image for himself, one in keeping with his model of the ideal hussar, and in the scene of his meeting with Drubetskoi and Berg all of his words and actions are in fact directed toward that end. He takes pride in the military cross of St. George he wears and in his mud-spattered riding breeches; he throws away under the table a letter of introduction to Bagration sent to him from Moscow, since he has no need of the "lackey's job" of adjutant; he at once demands, "Send for some wine," and upon seeing the German landlady, he says "with a wink," "What is it, my pretty?" Taken all together, these gestures constitute a complex of signs expressing Nikolai Rostov's notion of the ideal "hussar." Just as Tolstoi's attention was drawn to the various other functions of dialogic discourse, so was it attracted to verbal self-modeling as one of the several means by which a personality may affirm itself.

I shall confine myself to one more example. There is in *Anna Karenina* a minor character, the Princess Miagkaia, "famous for her simplicity and for the rudeness of her manners, and nicknamed *l'enfant terrible*." Everything the Princess Miagkaia says in polite society is in performance of this role.

> "They [the banker Schuzburg and his wife] invited my husband and me to dinner, and I was told that the sauce for that dinner cost a thousand rubles," the Princess Miagkaia said loudly, sensing that everybody was listening, "and a very nasty sauce it was too, something green. We had to return the invitation, and I made a sauce for them for eighty-five kopecks, and everyone was satisfied. I cannot make thousand-ruble sauces."
>
> "She is unique!" said the hostess.
>
> "Marvelous!" said somebody else.
>
> The effect produced by the Princess Miagkaia's speeches was always the same, and its secret lay in the fact that although she often did not speak quite

to the point (as now), what she did say was simple and made sense. In the society in which she lived, words of that kind had the effect of the wittiest joke. The Princess Miagkaia could not understand why her words produced such an effect, but she was aware that they did and took advantage of it. (Pt. 2, chap. 6)

"Masks" and roles of this kind allow a person to avoid too direct conversation "about himself." Such conversation in its unconcealed forms is in fact proscribed in society, and one needs to be a thick-skinned Berg not to notice the mockery it provokes. "Conversation about oneself" is usually located at some remove from its initial personal motivation. Tolstoi derives that motivation analytically. He shows how an individual's "conversation about himself" may manifest itself as conversation "about what he is doing." He shows, in other words, how interlocutors may find cognitive satisfaction in socially significant themes or in aesthetic forms of discourse with which their own personal theme has in some way become identified. The art of society conversation in particular consists of presenting what is subjectively interesting as objectively significant.

The aesthetic principle, the experience of verbal form, is usually present to some degree in ordinary conversation (figurative speech, jokes, bons mots, and the like). Tolstoi, however, frequently portrays dialogic speech that has been transformed into a kind of specialized aesthetic activity. This above all involves his depiction of cultivated society conversation, which has its own masters. The diplomat Bilibin in *War and Peace*, for example, is portrayed exclusively in terms of this capacity. "In society he always waited for an opportunity to say something remarkable and took part in conversation only when that was possible. Bilibin's conversation was continually sprinkled with wittily original and polished phrases possessing general interest. Those phrases were prepared in the inner laboratory of his mind as if in an intentionally portable form, so that insignificant society people could carry them around from one drawing room to the next" (vol. 1, pt. 2, chap. 10). Tolstoi gives examples of Bilibin's phrases, and he gives examples too of the speech of such salon talkers as the vicomte de Mortemart at the salon of Anna Pavlovna Scherer. In the initial serial version of *War and Peace* the art of telling "interesting stories" is depicted in particular detail in the vicomte de Mortemart's account (abridged in the book's final edition) of the fateful chance encounter of the Bourbon scion the duc d'Enghien with the usurper Bonaparte at the house of the actress Mademoiselle George. The vicomte de Mortemart has two purposes—to recount in a skillful way a fascinating and politically relevant episode, and at the same time to make clear his own intimacy with this last representative of the house of Condé whom Napoleon has had executed. Yet even when the content of an interesting story or clever joke has no direct connection with the storyteller, that story may still serve as a means of self-affirmation for him. It gives him control over his listeners, creative satisfaction, a feeling of participation in events, and association as narrator with the values of whatever he happens to be narrating. Tolstoi shows that people are less willing to listen to interesting information they are unfamiliar with than they are to tell something that is already known not only to them but also to their listeners. It is as if Tolstoi, the tireless exposer of vanity, is saying that vanity is stronger even than curiosity.

Bilibin, the vicomte de Mortemart, and the other society talkers are depictions of the experience of one's own speech as a formal entity. Also extensively represented in Tolstoi is the individual's self-realization in conversations that have an intellectual and cognitive meaning for him. These representations are of great variety—from the sixteen-year-old Nikolen'ka Irten'ev in *Youth*, naively proud of the fact that he and Nekhliudov have "intelligent conversations," to the conversations in *War and Peace* of Prince Andrei and Pierre, which register the successive stages of their spiritual development, and thence to the disputes on philosophical, political, economic, and moral themes that permeate the text of *Anna Karenina*. Tolstoi is aware in all of this that the need to argue, generalize, and put one's cognitive potentialities into action is by no means the exclusive lot of thinkers—that that need is inherent in any person and may assume a number of different forms, depending on the nature of the person's occupation in life. The specifically feminine conversation that takes place on the terrace at the Levins' estate in *Anna Karenina* is an interesting one in this regard. Its participants—Kitty, Dolly, and the old Princess Shcherbatskaia—continually generalize and discuss, although the topics of their discussion are how to cook jam, what sort of gift to give to a servant, and how men propose to their future wives.

People realize themselves in conversations about their intellectual, business, and domestic interests. But Tolstoi penetrates beneath that layer, seeking out the still more personal, intimate themes concealed in the depths of those objective interests. Sergei Ivanovich Koznyshev in *Anna Karenina* expected a great deal from the publication of his book, but it was met by silence and even ridicule. Yet in that "for him most difficult time," he "gave himself up entirely" to the Slavic question. "'The nation's soul has become articulate,' as Sergei Ivanovich put it. And the more he delved into that issue, the more obvious it seemed to him that it was one that would necessarily attain enormous, epoch-making proportions. He devoted himself completely to the service of that great cause and forgot to think about his book" (pt. 8, chap. 1). Such is the unconscious personal theme concealed in the persistent theoretical wrangling about the war with Turkey and the Slavic question that Koznyshev engages in with Konstantin Levin. Koznyshev cannot permit the needs of the nation's soul to be understood otherwise than he himself understands them, because to do so would be to destroy the position in life that he has wrested from failure.

Levin's brother Nikolai comes to visit him in the country. Nikolai Levin is mortally ill, but he vainly attempts to convince both himself and others that he is much better. Levin "sensed that if neither of them pretended, but said . . . exactly what he was thinking and feeling and nothing else, then . . . Konstantin would only have said, 'You are dying, you are dying, you are dying!' and Nikolai would only have answered, 'I know I am dying, but I am afraid, I am afraid, I am afraid. . . .' One could not live like that, however." In order not to remain silent (silence would be terrifying), and in order not to say what is actually on their minds, the two brothers discuss abstract subjects. An argument about Konstantin Levin's economic ideas ends in a quarrel and in Nikolai's departure. Nikolai reproaches his brother for taking his thought from the communists but distorting it, thereby depriving it of its consistency and meaning. "'I am looking for a way of working that will be productive both for me and the worker. I want to organize. . . . ' 'You don't want to organize anything; you . . . want to show that you are not merely exploiting the peasants, but doing so according to an idea'" (pt. 3, chap. 32). The brothers are arguing about something that is objectively interesting and important, yet their dialogue here has become a struggle between two hidden and very personal themes. Konstantin loses his temper because "deep down in his soul" he is afraid that his brother is right in his criticism of his economic projects, projects that reflect in idealized form the way that he in fact manages his estate. He defends the position he has taken in life from whatever threatens to destroy it. Nikolai Levin is embittered because in the course of his slow death, "life has become intolerable to him"; he is irritated by plans for the future and by every kind of activity that is no longer possible for him. In condemning the affairs and ideas of others, he defends himself against life, which now causes him only pain. This human drama is played out behind words regarding the best way to employ the labor force.

Tolstoi combined extreme conversational determinism, or the conversation's actual, empirical connection to a given situation, and *disjunction*, or the indirect relationship that obtains between a situational utterance and its ulterior personal motive. There is a dual conditionality (both external and internal) in Tolstoian dialogue that is the source of the poetics of submerged dialogue that extends from Chekhov to our own day.

The situation elicits a verbal reaction (frequently automatic) to an external impression or to an interlocutor's remarks; it compels one to speak, to adhere to canonical themes or verbal clichés, even though one may wish to remain silent. Tolstoi enjoyed depicting the disjunction between the external veneer of speech and its inner content. Why does Pierre years later remember with repugnance and shame saying "Je vous aime" to Hélène? He torments himself because he, a person of complex spiritual life, had used a hackneyed society cliché at a decisive moment, and had done so precisely because it was impossible to translate into words what was actually taking place: one the one hand, sensual arousal, and on the other, crass calculation. Nikolai Rostov must inform his father of his huge loss to Dolokhov. "'What is there to be done! It has happened to everybody!' said the son in a bold and careless tone, while in his heart he thought himself a scoundrel and a villain. . . . Count Il'ia Andreich dropped his gaze upon hearing his son's words and began busily looking for something. 'Yes, yes,' he muttered, 'it will, I am afraid, be difficult to obtain. . . . Who has it not happened to! Who has it not happened to'" (vol. 2, pt. 1, chap. 16). Il'ia Andreevich is embarrassed for his son. With a different intonation he repeats his words, the first ones that occur to him, in order to avoid saying what he does not wish to say. And that meaningless repetition, concealing the inner direction of the conversation, causes Nikolai to break into tears and beg for his father's forgiveness.

The dying Prince Andrei maintains relations with those around him (relations that for him have already become superfluous) by means of verbal formulas that have no connection to his state of inner lucidity. "'Did you see Count Nikolai, Mary?' Prince Andrei said all of a sudden, apparently wishing to be kind to them. 'He wrote in his letter that he has taken a great liking to you,' he went on simply and calmly, evidently incapable of fully appreciating the complex significance his words had for living people. 'If you like him too, then it would be a good thing . . . for you to get married,' he added a little more quickly, as if happy to have at last found words that he had been seeking for a long time. Princess Mary heard his words, but they had no meaning at all for her, other than as proof of how remote he now was from everything living" (vol. 4, pt. 1, chap. 15).

Karenin loves Anna in his own way and has grown used to her and misses her. Yet he is unable to say so directly, since the private man in him is unable to detach himself from the model of the statesman that stands opposed to the expression of feeling. Aleksei Alekseevich finds an indirect path, however: "'Yes, as you see, the tender husband, as tender as he was in the first year of his marriage and consumed by the desire to see you,' he said in his thin, drawling voice in the tone that he almost invariably used whenever he addressed her, a tone that made fun of those who would actually speak that way" (pt. 1, chap. 30). The structure of disjunction is complex here. Karenin says what he thinks, and Anna must understand that it is in fact what he thinks, but he says it as if it were not.

We find verbal ploys of the converse variety in *The Death of Ivan Il'ich*. Ivan Il'ich's wife has asked a "famous doctor" to look in. "'Now please do not start objecting. I am doing it for myself,' she said ironically, giving him to understand that she was doing it all for him, so that he would have no right to refuse. . . . He felt that the mendacity surrounding him had become so tangled that it was very difficult to sort anything out. Everything she did for him, she in fact did only for herself and told him that she was doing it for herself, yet told him as if that were such an incredible thing that it could only mean the opposite" (chap. 8).

In the same passage in *The Death of Ivan Il'ich*, the wife and the daughter and the daughter's suitor drop in on the dying man before going out to the theater to see Sarah Bernhardt. A conversation begins about some opera glasses they are unable to find and about Sarah Bernhardt, "the kind of conversation that is always exactly the same." The conversation breaks off when they notice the suddenly motionless, indignant gaze of Ivan Il'ich. "It was necessary to set things right, but there was no way at all of doing so. Somehow that silence had to be broken. . . . All were seized with fear that the decorous lie would somehow be exposed, and that what was in fact the case would suddenly become clear to all. Liza was the first to take things in hand. . . . She wanted to conceal what they were all feeling, but she let it out. 'Anyway, *if we are going* [italics mine], it is time,' she said, glancing at her watch, a gift from her father." The phrase "if we are going" expresses the true content of the situation, which is that suffering and death keep others from living the way they ordinarily would and from enjoying life.

Tolstoi persistently deciphers the verbal codes of different spiritual states in terms of their multileveled conditionality, their dual significance both for the external situational context and for the internal psychological one. Tolstoian dialogue is analytical dialogue. It is a complex structure in which direct discourse is accompanied by authorial judgments of that discourse. To be sure, there are instances when Tolstoi permits the reader himself to make the necessary analytical maneuver, but such instances are a departure from the specifically Tolstoian form of dialogue. Much more characteristic of him, for example, is the famous intuitive conversation between Natasha and Pierre in the epilogue to *War and Peace*. What would be the result if, as an experiment, one were to "disconnect" the individual rejoinders of that conversation from their accompanying analysis, giving them something like the form they might have in a play? In the following quotation I have put the direct discourse in italics in order to set it off from the indirect discourse pertaining to it.

Natasha told Pierre *about what her brother had been doing, about how she had suffered rather than lived during his own absence, about how she had become even fonder of Mary, and about how Mary was better than she was in every way.* In saying this, Natasha was sincere in her acknowledgment of what she saw as Mary's superiority, but by saying it she was also demanding of Pierre that he still prefer her to Mary and to all other women, and that he now, after having seen so many women in Petersburg, tell her so once again.

Pierre, in responding to Natasha's words, told her *how intolerable it had been for him to go dinners and parties in Petersburg where ladies were present.*

"*I have quite forgotten how to talk to ladies,*" he said. "*It was simply boring. Especially since I was so busy.*"

Natasha looked at him intently, and then continued:

"*Mary is such a delight!*" she said. "*How well she is able to understand children! It is as if she can see right into their hearts. Yesterday, for instance, Miten'ka was misbehaving . . .*"

"*He is just like his father,*" Pierre interrupted.

Natasha understood why he mentioned Miten'ka's resemblance to Nikolai: the recollection of his argument with his brother-in-law was an unpleasant one, and he wanted to hear Natasha's opinion about it.

"*Nikolen'ka has the weakness that if something is not accepted by everyone, he won't agree with it on any account. But I understand that you yourself value whatever helps* ouvrir une carrière," she said, repeating words that Pierre had once used. (Pt. 1, chap. 16)

Tolstoian dialogue collapses without this system of analytical connections that establish why and to what end a person says what he says, and that consequently confirm the determined nature of what is being said (in the same way that they confirm the determined nature of every other phenomenon).

Dialogue for Tolstoi is still raw material; its meaning is formulated only through the accompanying authorial explanation, which frequently alters that meaning by removing the dialogue to another, hidden context. After the steeplechase and the moment when Anna gives herself away through her despair at Vronskii's fall, the Karenins take their seats in their carriage.

He saw that she had behaved indecently and considered it his duty to tell her so. But it was very difficult for him to say only that and nothing more. He opened his mouth to tell her she had behaved indecently, but involuntarily he said something quite different.

"How inclined we all are to these cruel spectacles, after all," he said. "I notice . . ."

"What? I fail to understand," Anna said contemptuously.

He was offended and at once began to say what he meant to say.

"I must tell you . . . ," he said.

"Here it comes now," she thought, and felt frightened. (Pt. 2, chap. 29)

The authorial analysis changes the meaning of the spoken words, referring them to the movement of the character's thoughts and feelings and of his internal discourse. Anna's apparently meaningless reply ("What? I fail to understand") releases the terrible, life-destroying confrontation that might not have taken place at that moment, had she not replied in precisely that way.

Tolstoian dialogue proceeds under psychological control of such intensity that the reader is provided with an account of every one of the character's words. Before her suicide, Anna drives by the Oblonskiis', where she finds Kitty. Here is their conversation in pure "theatrical" form: "'Yes, I am very glad to have seen you. I have heard so much about you from everybody, even from your husband. He called on me and I liked him very much. Where is he?' 'He has gone to the country.' 'Give him my regards, be sure to give him my regards!' 'I will be sure to!'"

And here is the same conversation with the authorial commentary restored:

> Kitty sensed that Anna was looking at her with hostility. She explained that hostility by the awkward position that Anna now felt herself to be in in regard to her as someone she had once patronized, and she began to feel sorry for her. . . .
>
> . . . Anna . . . turned to Kitty.
>
> "Yes, I am very glad to have seen you," she said with a smile. "I have heard so much about you from everyone, even from your husband. He called on me and I liked him very much," she added, with obvious ill intent. "Where is he?"
>
> "He has gone to the country," Kitty said, blushing.
>
> "Give him my regards, be sure to give him my regards."
>
> "I will be sure to!" Kitty naively repeated, looking compassionately into her eyes. (Pt. 7, chap. 28)

Tolstoian dialogue is antidramatic. The discourse of the characters in a play carries the full weight of psychological and expository meaning (the author's remarks having only accessory significance), and it therefore cannot entirely rid itself of explanation. Even Chekhovian drama was unable to. It is for this reason that the "meaningless" dialogue in Chekhov's plays is frequently more "meaningful" than the dialogue of Tolstoi's characters, after one removes the authorial explanation. Strakhov wrote of *War and Peace* in this regard, "There is no bare story; it is all in scenes."[13] And this is true in a way. The main thing, however, is not to confuse the novelistic scene with the dramatic kind,[14] just as one should not, for example, confuse a verbal image with one that is visual or imagined pictorially (since a metaphor that simultaneously combines ideas from two different levels, the direct and the figurative, is antipictorial).

Tolstoi certainly is all "in scenes," and the significance of dialogue in his novels is indeed extraordinarily great, but it would have been impossible for him to realize in purely dialogic form his authorial voice, the voice of the "observer and judge," as Eikhenbaum characterized it.[15]

Analysis ("ratiocination," "generalization") was essential to Tolstoi, as was an absolutely concrete object of analysis—above all an individual possessing an internal and external life complete with gestures and speech. The hero who is subjected to analysis in Tolstoi is always located within the physically dense world of objective reality. The nonbeliever Levin is required to fast before his marriage (the ceremony cannot take place otherwise). "There was no one in the church except an indigent soldier, two old women, and the clergymen. The young deacon, the two halves of his long back clearly visible beneath his thin undercassock, met him, and going at once to a small table next to the wall, began reading the precepts" (pt. 5, chap. 1). The scene with the young deacon is needed here as a reminder of the material three-dimensionality of life, as one of a number of different means of creating that illusion of truth to life that so captivates the reader of Tolstoi.

It is that illusion that is the essence of Tolstoian theatricalism, a theatricalism made up of external appearance, physical accessories, words, and gestures, but having nothing in common with theatricality.[16] Konstantin Leont'ev in his book on Tolstoi wrote in precisely this nontheatrical sense of the "theatricalism of the exposition" of the natural school of his day, condemning it as formless "superfluity of observation":

> Only *certain* images, *certain* words and sounds, *certain* of our own and other people's movements and utterances, remain in our memories, even from the day before. They—those images, colors, sounds, movements, and words—are *scattered* here and there against a general background of sadness or joy, suffering or happiness, or else they shine like occasional lights in the universally dark abyss of indifferent oblivion. No one can remember a conversation exactly from even the day before in its entirety or its development. All that is remembered are its *general spirit and certain individual* words and ideas. I therefore find that the old-fashioned mode of narration (a little more from the author and in a general way, and a little less in the form of conversations and of descriptions of all the characters' movements) to be more *real*, in the proper sense of the word—to be more truthful and natural, that is, according to the basic laws of our spirit.[17]

It was, however, precisely that level of elusive perception that Tolstoi wanted to proceed beyond. He wanted to extricate human psychological experience from the "abyss of indifferent oblivion," whatever the cost. And it was for this reason, and not for the sake of naturalistic description (he had in fact already expressed doubts in his early diaries about the possibility of describing individual people), that he needed the details of life in their exaggerated vividness and clarity.

Different epochs have differently interpreted the physical dimensions of human self-expression, have differently regarded the matter of individual appearance, facial expression, and gesture. For centuries a kind of deductive principle prevailed in literature, whereby individual gestures and speech were characterized by an *ideal* relation to the situations in which they occurred. Whatever the circumstances, the literary hero's physical behavior followed the precepts of the given style. This was true of the precisely calculated harmonious conventionality of the gestures of classical theater, just as it was of the demonstrativeness of romanticism that provided such abundant nourishment for parody. In essence, realism replaced deduction with observation—replaced, in other words, the typical with the individual. Yet the realists, though basing their descriptions on observation, also saw things in a variety of different ways, depending on their particular artistic orientations. In Gor'kii, for example, the vivid materiality of the Tolstoian depiction of individual physical features and manifestations became hyperbolic and symbolically ambiguous.

[Klim Samgin] was sitting a couple feet higher than Liutov and saw his irregular, disjointed face not convexly but concavely, like a plate—a dirty plate. The shadows of the boughs on the short pine trees trembled on Liutov's face, and his slanting eyes rolled across it like two nuts. His nose moved and his nostrils flared; his rubbery lips smacked, revealing the vicious row of his upper teeth and exposing the tip of his tongue; his sharp, unshaven Adam's apple leaped; and two small ivory balls twirled around his ears. Liutov gesticulated, the fingers of his right hand flashing like those of a deaf-mute, and his whole body jerked like a marionette on strings. It was repulsive to look at him. (19:343–344)

Gor'kii's tracing of the physical manifestations of internal states as the latter follow the movement of the dialogue is in the same spirit.

"Klim Ivanovich," Mitrofanov exclaimed at the top of his voice, his face swelling unnaturally and turning red, and even his ears seeming to move. "I understand you. Really, I do! . . ."

Samgin leaned over against the table too, painfully resting his chest on its edge. . . . Above the table in front of Samgin rose up a head as if severed and laid in the palm of a hand, a head with a familiar though altered face, scowling, its lips tightly pursed, its dark eyes as if full of the intense effort of somebody trying to read something printed in letters either too blurred or too tiny.

"The government cannot cope with either the working class or the student movement," Samgin whispered.

"Oh Lord," sighed Mitrofanov, relaxing his tensed face, so that it became ridiculously broad and mournful, its blue cheeks turning brown. (20:371–372)

In Chekhov, on the other hand, facial expressions, gestures, and other manifestations are outwardly muted and carefully limned. The Chekhovian and post-Chekhovian realistic theater and cinema of the mid–twentieth century (Italian neorealism, the films of Jean Gabin, and much else) have convinced their audiences of the meagerness of external signs of internal states. The artist once again saw something new—the human face that reacted to every shock with changes that were barely perceptible yet full of meaning.

Tolstoi's conscious interest in the very process of conversation is especially obvious whenever he creates complex, intersecting dialogic structures consisting of several or even many participants. It is then that his heightened feeling for conversational genres with their stable situations and verbal routines stands out in full measure. Presented in Tolstoi are everyday social conversations of the most diverse kind, from the family variety to those of polite society, and from the "professorial" to those of the "military officer."

Depicted in part 7 of *Anna Karenina* is a series of model conversations that succeed one another in the course of a single, meticulously traced day spent by Levin in Moscow. Each situation is accompanied by its own set of verbal routines. Levin's friend Professor Katavasov arranges for him to meet the celebrated scholar Metrov, who has taken an interest in Levin's agricultural theories. Levin and Metrov converse, each trying to expound his own ideas, but without attempting to understand what the other is saying. Nonetheless, Levin's vanity is "flattered by the fact that so learned a man should explain his opinions to him so willingly, so considerately, and with such confidence in Levin's knowledge of the subject. . . . Levin attributed this to his own value, not realizing that Metrov had exhausted the matter with all his intimates and spoke about it with particular eagerness to every new acquaintance" (chap. 3). Tolstoi creates a phraseological model of the "scholarly conversation" and at the same time reveals its motive springs of vanity, egoism, and personal interest. After parting with the professor, Levin goes to a morning concert to hear [Balakirev's] "King Lear of the Steppe" fantasia. And here the model of the scholarly conversation is replaced by a model of the sort of aesthetic conversation that takes place during an intermission. After the concert, there is a visit to the home of the Countess Bol' (which Levin makes at Kitty's request). This visit consists of an exchange of words whose only meaning is that in certain situations certain words must not fail to be spoken. Levin then has dinner at his club, and Tolstoi depicts the good-natured banter that takes place there with its purpose of obtaining aesthetic satisfaction from bons mots, jokes, and quick responses to whatever topics happen to come up.

After dinner at the club, Oblonskii induces Levin to visit Anna. The conversation at Anna's (which, besides Anna, Oblonskii, and Levin, includes the literary man Vorkuev, who intends to publish a children's book Anna has written) also has its standard decorum—that observed by guests. But Tolstoi examines the peripeties concealed in the conversation's everyday typology, taking into account the logic and conditionality of each of their different motivations. We shall trace that movement.

Levin is examining the portrait of Anna painted in Italy by the artist Mikhailov.

"It is exceptionally good, is it not?" Stepan Arkad'evich said, upon noticing that Levin was looking at the portrait.	The excerpt begins with a phrase elicited by an external impression—of the portrait and of Levin looking at it. There is also hidden exultation in Oblonskii's question. He wants Anna to conquer Levin (Levin's family principles secretly irritate the wicked Stepan Arkad'evich).
"I have never seen a better portrait."	Levin answers Oblonskii's question.
"It is an exceptional likeness, is it not?" said Vorkuev.	Vorkuev interferes in the conversation in order to say something pleasant to his hostess.
Levin glanced from the portrait to the original. A special brilliance lit up Anna's face when she felt his gaze upon her; Levin blushed, and in order to hide his confusion was about to ask her if it was a long time since she had seen Dar'ia Aleksandrovna, but Anna started talking just as he did:	Levin, confused by the impression Anna has made on him, looks for another topic in order to change the subject. Dolly surfaces logically, both because he is reminded of her by the presence of her husband, and because she is closely related to him and to Anna.
"Ivan Petrovich and I were just now talking about Vashchenkov's latest pictures. Have you seen them?"	Anna continues a conversational line associatively linked to her portrait.
"Yes, I have," replied Levin.	An answer to her remark.
"But excuse me, I interrupted you. You were going to say . . ."	A phrase prompted by the requirements of courtesy.

Levin asked her if she had seen Dolly lately.	Now that the discussion no longer concerns Anna's portrait but Vashchenkov's pictures, Levin no longer needs Dolly as a topic, but he is forced to return to her anyway.
"She visited me yesterday. She is very angry with the gymnasium because of Grisha. The Latin master has apparently been unfair to him."	Anna picks up the topic suggested by Levin.
"Yes, I have seen the pictures. I did not really care for them," Levin said, returning to the subject she had started.	

Levin prefers the topic of Vashchenkov with its ensuing discussion of the "new direction in art" to that of Dolly and her children, and he prefers it because he now wants to say "intelligent things" so that Anna will hear them. "This time Levin did not speak in anything like the mechanical way he had spoken that morning. Every word of his conversation with her took on a special meaning" (chap. 10).

One may find in *Anna Karenina* depictions of situations in which the conversation, even though it is the primary purpose of the encounter and of the time spent together by the participants, has rigorously predetermined topics and organized forms—as in the novel's assemblies and meetings (the portrayal of the nobility elections, for example), its business appointments (between Karenin and his lawyer, for example), and so on. Of greater importance for Tolstoi, however, are those situations that require the presence of conversation but do not prescribe its content—situations in which the conversation itself constitutes a kind of formal requirement. Since their topics are not predetermined (or are only partially predetermined), such conversations easily lend themselves to the investigation of what it is that conditions their emergence and their subsequent development. Belonging to verbal intercourse of this type are the discussions of friends and acquaintances who have just met, conversations among guests, and conversations at banquets and soirees.

Tolstoi explicitly portrays the society soiree as a mechanism (or machine). Fräulein Scherer's attention to her guests in *War and Peace* is compared to the care with which a spinning-mill foreman watches over the mill's operation. "So Anna Pavlovna . . . , with a word or a slight rearrangement, once again set the conversational machine in uniform, regular motion" (vol. 1, pt. 1, chap. 2). In addition to the "conversational machine" of high society, there is another variety—the soiree of average quality at the new apartment of the recently married Bergs:

> Vera, having decided on her own that Pierre was best occupied with conversation about the French embassy, at once initiated that conversation. Berg, having decided that masculine conversation was what was required, interrupted his wife's remarks, and touching on the question of war with Austria, leaped without realizing it from the general subject to personal considerations about suggestions made to him to take part in the Austrian campaign and about the reasons why he had decided not to do so. . . . Both husband and wife sensed with satisfaction that, although only one guest was present, their "soiree" had begun very well and was as like as two drops of water to every other soiree with its conversations, tea, and lighted candles. (Vol. 2, pt. 3, chap. 20)

If the topics are not completely predetermined in such situations, the choice among them is nonetheless limited by the strict typology of the society conversation. In his portrayal of the soiree at Betsy Tverskaia's in *Anna Karenina*, Tolstoi is explicit about this: "The conversation around the hostess and the samovar, after wavering for some time . . . among the three inevitable topics, the latest public news, the theater, and criticism of one's intimates, . . . finally settled down, having hit on the last of these, on slander, that is" (pt. 2, chap. 6). Of the standard topics available to society conversationalists, gossip is especially attractive, since it combines the pleasures of self-assertion (the condemnation and belittling of other people) with a variety of emotional effects.

The mechanisms of general conversation, since they are not so standardized or ritualized as salon *causerie*, are more complex and flexible. Take dinner conversations, for example. Described in great detail in *Anna Karenina* are two dinners involving several guests and household members (at the Oblonskiis' and at Vronskii's estate). The conversation at the Oblonskiis' (it is at this dinner that Levin and Kitty declare their love for each other) has a complex and universal structure that simultaneously serves a number of different functions. Above all there is the usual Tolstoian typological investigation of the "conversational machine," which Stepan Arkad'evich sets in motion by starting his guests off on the "inevitable topics" of the day. The movement of "intelligent conversation" is carefully traced here with its associative shifts from the Russification of Poland, to the advantages of a classical versus a practical education, and thence to the woman question.[18] At the same time, the dialogue contains within itself the psychological characteristics of its different participants, just as their individual spiritual states are reflected in the personal motives that drive it, motives that are sometimes concealed and that sometimes break through the surface.[19] Thus, the theoretical argument about the rights of women at once brings personal motives into play—those of Karenin, who is about to initiate divorce proceedings against Anna; of Oblonskii, who while defending emancipation thinks of his mistress Chibisova; of Dar'ia Aleksandrovna, who while condemning emancipation is thinking about the same thing as Oblonskii; and of Kitty, who sympathizes with women's rights and education because she herself has experienced the "terror of spinsterhood and humiliation."

Of particular interest, however, are those exchanges that appear to be more accidental in nature.

> "This cheese is not bad. May I give you some?" asked the host. "Have you really been doing gymnastics again?" he went on, turning to Levin and feeling his muscle with his left hand. Levin smiled and tensed his arm, and beneath Stepan Arkard'ich's fingers a lump like a round cheese and as hard as steel emerged from under the fine cloth of Levin's coat.
>
> "Now that is a bicep! What a Samson!"
>
> "I suppose you have to have great strength for bear hunting," said Aleksei Aleksandrovich, who had only the vaguest ideas about sport, as he broke off a piece of bread as delicate as a cobweb and spread some cheese on it.
>
> Levin smiled.
>
> "None at all. On the contrary, a child could kill a bear. . . ."

Kitty then approaches the appetizer table. "Did I hear that you have killed a bear? . . . Do you have bears on your estate, then?" From the sound of her voice and the movement "of her lips, eyes, and hands," Levin understands that he is loved, and he is overwhelmed with happiness. He recounts how, while returning from his hunting trip and still dressed in a sheepskin coat, he burst into Karenin's compartment (with whom he was still unacquainted), and the conductor, judging him by his dress, tried to escort him out, but Aleksei Aleksandrovich stood up for him. " 'Generally speaking, the rights of passengers with regard to their choice of seats are quite ill-defined,' Aleksei Aleksandrovich said, while wiping the tips of his fingers with his handkerchief."

Hearing his brother, Sergei Ivanovich Koznyshev thinks: "What has happened to him today? He is behaving like a conqueror" (pt. 4, chap. 9). This is of course the key to the preceding dialogue. Levin is in fact a conqueror. And Oblonskii, encouraging Levin's love for Kitty, takes pleasure in his vitality and admires his bicep. The center of attention is the bear that Levin has killed, and Kitty speaks of the bear. She is listening to Levin, and he therefore gives a "gay and entertaining" account of the adventure he had on his way home, although in society he is usually morose. There are no submerged themes in the conversation next to the appetizer table, nor is there any direct relationship on the part of the speakers to the subject occupying their attention, yet the motives for each remark are firmly tied to the content of the situation. It is not difficult to see what those motives are, once one has made a few associative connections.

Conversation around a family dinner table contains more surprises, is less predetermined, than the conversation at a society soiree. Yet there are forms of general conversation in *Anna Karenina* that are even less constrained. People linked to each other through a variety of different relationships are also brought together in situations where they cannot avoid conversation that is unrestrained, associative, and therefore especially imbued with covert personal themes. After a day spent hunting, Levin and his guests, Oblonskii and Veslovskii, spend the night in a hay barn belonging to a peasant. None of them is able to sleep. "After moving back and forth among recollections and stories about shooting, dogs, and other hunting trips, their conversation finally settled on a topic of interest to all three of them." That topic, introduced by Oblonskii, concerns "the pleasures of a hunting trip he had been on at Malthus's estate the summer before. Malthus was a well-known railroad magnate." Their conversation emerges from the impressions the day has made on each of them, and it is motivated by a chain of associations ultimately leading to Malthus. Their amiable chatter is eventually replaced, however, by an unpleasant argument between Levin and Oblonskii about dishonest profit and honest labor. Stepan Arkad'evich teases Levin about his inconsistency: although he is aware of the injustice of the advantages he himself enjoys, he is still unwilling to give his estate to his peasants. It "is just as dishonest as my earning more than my head clerk, or Malthus's getting more than one of his railroad mechanics." Tolstoi then reveals the submerged theme of the conversation, its underlying conditionality. "A sort of concealed hostility had lately grown up between the two brothers-in-law, as if the fact that they were now married to two sisters had produced a rivalry as to which of them had arranged his life in the best way, and that hostility now found expression in the personal tone the discussion was taking." A change in the conversation's direction is imparted by the singing of women's voices from outside the barn. Oblonskii prepares to follow Veslovskii in the direction of the singing, but Levin refuses to go. This provokes another argument, this time about the relationship between a husband and a wife. "'A man should be independent; he has his own masculine interests. A man should be manly . . . .' 'What is that supposed to mean, that he should go running after servant girls?' Levin asked. 'Well, why not, if he enjoys it?'" (pt. 6, chap. 11).

The real theme concealed in the argument about Malthus and social injustice—defense of one's attitude toward life—has now reached the surface.

Dialogue in which "accidental" impressions are recorded reminds the reader of the "tonus of the individual's average, everyday state" (in

Skaftymov's phrase). Kitty, Dolly, the old princess, and the Levins' housekeeper Agaf'ia Mikhailovna are talking on the porch about matters of general interest to them, including how to make jam in a new way introduced by the Shcherbatskiis (much to Agaf'ia Mikhailovna's dismay). "'Well, I think it is ready now,' Dolly said, dripping syrup from the spoon. 'When it begins to string, it is ready. Let it boil a little more, Agaf'ia Mikhailovna.' 'Oh, these flies!' Agaf'ia Mikhailovna said angrily. 'The result will be just the same,' she added. 'Oh, how sweet—don't scare him away!' Kitty said unexpectedly, gazing at a sparrow that had alighted on the railing and was pecking at a raspberry nub it had turned over" (pt. 6, chap. 2).

The references to the flies and the sparrow have different meanings here. The flies serve as a pretext for Anna Mikhailovna to vent her anger about the Shcherbatskiis' breach of a Levin tradition. The reference to the flies is conditioned both by an external impulse and by the interconnections of the conversation itself. The sparrow, on the other hand, is an accidental event, an impression that stimulates a verbal reaction. In the scene in the apiary at the end of the novel, a wasp appears in exactly the same way during an important argument involving Levin, Sergei Ivanovich Koznyshev, and Katavasov about the Slavic question and the war with Turkey. "'Kost'ia, look! There's a bee! It's liable to sting us!' Dolly said, waving away a wasp. 'That isn't a bee, it's a wasp,' Levin said. 'Well, sir, what is your theory then?' Katavasov asked with a smile" (pt. 8, chap. 15). The sparrow and the wasp are needed in order for the conversation to take place just as it would "in life," and they lead directly to Chekhovian dramaturgy.

The different purposes of Tolstoian dialogue are deployed at different depths. The range here is immense—from automatic reactions in response to accidental impressions or to the remarks of an interlocutor, to picking up a theme on the spur of the moment in order to fill a void, to utterances that reflect the crucial life decisions of an individual personality.

Another kind of analytical approach to the direct discourse of literary characters, although obviously one with a different point of view than Tolstoi's, was subsequently realized by Proust in his vast novel *A la recherche du temps perdu*. There can be no possibility here of addressing that work in its entirety or of entering into the controversies connected with it. My observations will therefore be restricted to a single topic— Proust as the culmination of the classical analytical novel (at the same time that he uncovered new principles for the depiction of the individual human being). Proust stripped the explanatory method bare, carrying it to a level of intensity that rendered further elaboration unnecessary, so that twentieth-century Western prose, although it did inherit individual themes and methodological features from Proust, largely failed to inherit what was most important in him—the tradition of a literature that explains and reflects out loud.

Great works of art are always subject to a variety of interpretations, since each student seeks in them whatever he needs. Proust is especially susceptible to this, by virtue both of his multidimensionality and his penchant for continual theorizing and systematizing in the absence of a genuinely systematic worldview. One can find support in Proust's theoretical formulations for judgments of the most diverse and contradictory kind.[20]

Proust's vast, many-volumed novelistic meditation has an extraordinary intonational and stylistic unity, although the heterogeneous strata that have been absorbed and reworked in it are still evident. There are echoes of the aesthetic, modernist enthusiasms of the early Proust, of the vigorous tradition of the seventeenth century (the investigation of the mainsprings of behavior),[21] of the culture of impressionism, of the doctrines of irrationalism and the unconscious that were contemporaneous to him and that became the explicit philosophy of his novel, and of his unique assimilation of the experience of the great nineteenth-century novelists, of whom he invariably spoke with admiration.

Proust does not, to be sure, resemble Tolstoi, but there is much in Proustian analysis that would probably not have been possible without him. Proust's thought frequently turned to Dostoevskii, and in *A la recherche du temps perdu* there is a whole digression devoted to him, but in structural terms Proust remained closer to Tolstoi, closer, that is, to the principle of explanatory, analytical prose.

There is in Proust (besides the references in the novel and in his articles) an essay on Tolstoi in which it is apparent that he read him very attentively, had boundless admiration for him, and saw in him just what he needed to see. It is this last point that explains his surprising inversion of the relationship between concreteness and generalization in Tolstoi. "The impression of power and vitality," Proust says of Tolstoi, "comes precisely from the fact that it is not observed, but that every gesture, every word, every action, has only the meaning of a law, so that one has the sense of moving within a multitude of laws."[22] This is quite wrong, of course, but it is interesting that Tolstoian "generalization" and "ratiocination" have somehow been captured. Probably the main thing here for Proust was concealed self-judgment (as frequently happens whenever one writer evaluates another)—an effort to project onto Tolstoi his own conception of the relationship between sensuous concreteness and "intellectual constructs."

Analysis in Proust is not authorial interference, as in Tolstoi, nor is it the focal point of a refraction of the objective world, as in the Herzen of *My Past and Thoughts*. Rather, it is an unceasing, all-consuming extended meditation that has itself become an object of depiction. The Proustian monologic element, however, is not the same thing as "stream of consciousness." The effort to imitate the disjointedness of internal discourse (one of Joyce's main tasks in *Ulysses*) was alien to Proust. If the story told by the Proustian narrator is nonetheless circuitous, if it is deflected by peripheral issues and abruptly surfacing details, then that is not so much the consequence of a particular conception of the category of time, as it is of the fact that Proust is depicting the very movement of thought with its associative twistings and turnings.

Given its immensity and the fact that its author's voice is continually and insistently audible, it is natural that *A la recherche du temps perdu* should have been regarded as a memoir. Its memoir orientation is so strong that critics have more often than not used the measure of authenticity in approaching the novel, virtually accusing Proust of suppressions and of "juggling" the facts. What we are actually dealing with here, however, is a pseudomemoir. Proust is in essence no more autobiographical or autopsychological than other novelists, and he is documentary to a lesser degree than many, for despite all the efforts to do so, no actual prototypes for his characters have ever been found. Nevertheless, the novel's pseudomemoir quality or mimicry of authenticity does have profound structural importance. In the soil of twentieth-century relativism and subjectivism, the analytical method grew to the point where the partitions surrounding the "second reality" of the classical novel had begun to break down. All that remained was the voice of the author and his direct conversation with the reader. The memoir orientation of *A la recherche du temps perdu* is thus the Proustian form of reality.

Proust understood the novel as the writer's conversation about life. A writer is given but one life, and there is therefore no point in writing several different novels. In the course of the time allotted to him, the novelist must create the one novel that is his, and it will therefore be a long one. The many-volumed character of his novel was therefore a matter of principle for Proust. One of the essential characteristics of that novel's infinitely prolonged lyrical and investigatory monologue (it really belongs to the narrator, but we apprehend it as the author's) is its persistent reversion to the great themes that define its philosophy: time, memory, habit, impermanence, the subjective isolation of the individual human being, and the essential unattainability of his desires. Lyrically meditative variations on formulations already familiar to the reader are interspersed with cognitive formulations that crop up at any pretext (both great and small), formulations in which Proust establishes the "general laws" that are of such importance to him. Those who have written about Proust, especially those Soviet scholars who have done so, have stressed that if the object of depiction in the novel is subjective consciousness, then included in that consciousness is a highly variegated world of people and things.[23]

Continuously replacing each other, these latter phenomena accompany and shore up the author's reflections, whereas in the classical analytical novel, it was the authorial reflections that accompanied the depiction of phenomena. Pure narrative and description are completely absent in Proust. "The copiable he does not see," as Beckett wrote of him in his essay.[24]

Proust speaks several times in the course of his novel about the agitation his hero, Marcel, felt as a youth at the sight of phenomena of the natural world, of objects whose beautiful integument remained impenetrable to him and tormented him with the mystery of its unknowable meaning. "I used to fix before my mind for its attention some image . . . , a cloud, a triangle, a church spire, a flower, a stone, because I had the feeling that perhaps beneath these signs there lay something of a quite different kind which I must try to discover, some thought which they translated after the fashion of those hieroglyphic characters which at first one might suppose to represent only material objects. . . . The task was to interpret the given sensations as signs of so many laws and ideas, by trying to think—that is to say, to draw forth from the shadow—what I had merely felt, by trying to convert it into its spiritual equivalent. . . . And this method, . . . what was it but the creation of a work of art?"[25] The work of art was the only means for Proust of arresting and giving meaning to the ephemeral traces of time. Artistic creation secures the objects of memory in an eternal present, thereby overcoming the elusiveness of the present and the unreality of the past. All the same, Proust is closer to the impressionists than he is to the symbolists; "hieroglyphs" and correspondences for him are not signs of another world but expressions of the essence of objective and psychological phenomena belonging entirely to this one.

The flowering hawthorn is undoubtedly beautiful in its pink and white magnificence, but for the young Marcel its beauty is agonizing and empty, since he has not yet discovered its symbolism, its intellectual equivalent. Everything that arises in the course of the narrative, everything that is drawn into it by way of association and analogy, sometimes close at hand and sometimes of the most unexpected and remote variety, is step by step subjected to this Proustian intellectual transformation.

The plot consists of an endless chain whose links are highly diverse in content, in the quality of the events they contain, but that are combined and made equivalent by the unified tone of reflection. Any phenomenon—spiritual states, the personalities and relationships of individuals, objects, landscapes, works of art—that has been caught up in the current of the novel and located at a given moment within its field of attention may be interpreted as an expression of its all-embracing patterns. It is precisely for this reason that Proust speaks of phenomena of the most diverse kind—of things great and small, of watershed events and of details lodged in the memory—as if they were all of material of the same order. He does not alter his tone.

To break through to the content that things conceal in themselves but reveal to the artist is to apprehend (by artistic methods) the "meaning" of a thing or phenomenon in one or another vital connection, and to correlate that meaning with the elements of a new context that derives its organization and meaning from "general laws." Until the artist finds that meaning, he languishes before the mute surface of things. The authorial meditations of Proust are a continuous translation of everything that he encounters into the language of the new meanings he has discovered. Proust regarded metaphor as the principal method for this transformation of things into *something else*, describing it in *Le temps retrouvé* as an analytical mechanism: "Truth will be attained by [the writer] only when he takes two different objects, states the connection between them—a connection analogous in the world of art to the unique connection which in the world of science is provided by the law of causality" (3:889; 3:924–925). Proust then calls these analytical operations "metaphor." Obviously, they are far from always being metaphor in the strict sense of the word, but they invariably do involve the discovery of new relationships between things. Proust uses this method, for example, to reveal the psychological significance of the telephone and the automobile, which were just then coming into use: they alter the perception of time and space and create new kinds of relationships among people. A detailed description of Odette Swann's attire ends with the sentence, "Kept alive beneath the concrete form [was] the unfinished likeness of other, older forms which one would not have been able to find effectively reproduced by the milliner or the dressmaker . . . ; she was surrounded by her garments as by the delicate and spiritualized machinery of a whole civilization" (1:619–620; 1:666–667). The constituent parts of a thing have here been "chemically compounded" (in Proust's formulation) with ideas of a culturohistorical order. Odette's attire takes on historical significance as an expression of the aesthetic and material culture of an age.

Proust created his own model for the metaphorical transformation of the sensuously concrete—the work of the invented artist Elstir, which incorporates the principles of impressionist and postimpressionist painting. Thus, one of Elstir's pictures depicting the harbor of a small town is described in all of its color and objective materiality. At the same time, however, the picture is also described as a "metaphor," as an *idea* of the complete interpenetration of sea and dry land in that town of fishermen and mariners. In one of Proust's own landscapes, a water lily buffeted by the current of a river is compared to certain victims of neurasthenia (and to Marcel's Aunt Léonie, in particular) and to the sinners in the *Inferno*. The "meaning" of the water lily is a metaphorical node in which a psychological excursus on neurasthenics is combined with the cultural allusiveness (Dante) that is so characteristic of Proust. But these correspondences are all preceded by the visual, observed representation of the plant: "Thrust towards the bank, its stalk would uncoil, lengthen, reach out, strain almost to [the] breaking point until the current again caught it, [and] its green moorings swung back over their anchorage and brought the unhappy plant to what might fitly be called its starting point" (1:168–169; 1:184). Proust's materiality is not of the unthinking variety. It is a sensuousness that invariably gives way to intellectual symbolism.

Sometimes the transfiguration of things in Proust is accomplished by means that are essentially nonmetaphorical. "The two crocketed, rustic spires of Saint-André-des-Champs, themselves as tapering, scaly, checkered, honeycombed, yellowing and friable as two ears of wheat," the rays of sunlight under an apple tree, which Marcel's father slashed at with his stick "without ever making them deviate," the minutely described raindrops, "each one keeping its place and drawing its successor in its wake" (1:146, 150; 1:159, 164)—in all these images the basic objects remain unchanged, remain *spire*, *apple tree*, and *raindrop*. They are not allegorical, but representational. Their symbolic meaning emerges from the context, inasmuch as they belong to the hallowed landscapes of the "lost paradise" of Combray ("the true paradises are the paradises we have lost," in Proust's pivotal formulation [3:870; 3:903]). And a single poppy growing on a slope "betokens" to Marcel "the vast expanse of waving corn beneath the fleecy clouds" (1:138; 1:151).

Proust's ideas and general laws are nourished by impressions. Proust maintained theoretically that he was concerned not with impressions but with memories, and that is often regarded as his singularly Proustian feature. But it is not in fact so very singular. Impressions in art are always conditioned by memory and imagination. Proust merely made creative memory one of the basic philosophical and aesthetic concerns of his novel; he turned it into an object of depiction.

Marcel, though still a boy, is deeply affected by his first encounter with Gilberte. From a distance he sees a little girl with fair, reddish hair, pink freckles, and black eyes. Yet whenever he thinks of her, "the memory of those bright eyes would at once present itself to me as a vivid [blue], since her complexion was fair; so much so that if her eyes had perhaps not been quite so black—which was what struck me most forcibly on first seeing her—I should not have been, as I was, so especially enamored of their [blueness]" (1:141; 1:153).[26] A love that would be the source of so much torment in the future is precipitated by a characteristically Proustian mechanism: a vivid sensuous impression that has been transformed by an idea. That idea required the eyes to be blue.

In portraying the illness and death of Marcel's grandmother, Proust investigates with great power the condition of pity—the pity that Marcel and his mother try not to show, or even to feel, since they dare not admit to themselves that they are witnessing the humiliating physical devastation of a beloved and revered being (the servant Françoise's sincere attachment to the grandmother, on the other hand, is expressed through her need to show her pity and horror). The pity that so frightens the hero is not limited to the mere fact of suffering. Like art, it works by details— by the memory of the grandmother's helpless, gray head in the arms of Françoise, who has decided that the dying woman needs to have her hair done, by the memory of the grandmother being photographed in a big hat with the brim pulled down so that her grandson will not remember her disease-ravaged face, while he, unaware of her purpose, gives her to understand that he regards the pose as "childish coquetry." The desires and sufferings of love and the torments of pity are alike nourished by impressions derived from the external world.

It has frequently been observed that the Proustian depiction of spiritual life is not homogeneous, that the narrator shown from the inside, and the other characters rendered (with the partial exception of Swann) from the outside, all belong to different categories, both social and otherwise.

The main hero (the narrator) is the scion of a very clearly defined bourgeois milieu, although he himself is free in a way of social conditionality. He is also free, in essence, of personality, since his personality consists merely of hypertrophied nervous reactions to any influence, of hypertrophied perceptiveness and intellectual refinement. He is therefore the best field for applying general laws and internal psychological analysis. That internal analysis assumes a form in Proust that is extraordinary for its extent and continuity and for the scrupulous way in which it traces the line from one psychological situation to another. Yet Proust never loses sight of the tradition of classic psychological analysis. The psychological entity is broken down into its constituent parts, distributed among a variety of causal sequences, and then shaped into a new structure with its own surprising logic. At work here are "apparent contradictions," the same ones that Rousseau spoke of.

> What she [the hero's mother] regretted was not so much seeing me abandon diplomacy as the prospect of my devoting myself to literature. "Don't worry," my father told her. . . . "He's no longer a child. . . . He's quite capable of deciding for himself what will make him happy in life."
>
> . . . Thanks to the freedom of choice which they allowed me . . . my father's words caused me great uneasiness. . . . Now, as an author becomes

alarmed when he sees the fruits of his own meditations, which do not appear to him to be of great value since he does not separate them from himself, oblige a publisher to choose a brand of paper, to employ a typeface finer, perhaps, than they deserve, I asked myself whether my desire to write was of sufficient importance to justify my father in dispensing so much generosity. But apart from that, . . . he aroused in me two very painful suspicions. The first was that (at a time when, every day, I regarded myself as standing upon the threshold of a life which was still intact and would not enter upon its course until the following morning) my existence had already begun, and that, furthermore, what was yet to follow would not differ to any extent from what had gone before. The second suspicion, which was really no more than a variant of the first, was that I was not situated somewhere outside Time. . . . In saying of me, "He's no longer a child," "His tastes won't change now," and so forth, my father had suddenly made me conscious of myself in Time, and caused me the same kind of depression as if I had been . . . one of those heroes of whom the author, in a tone of indifference which is particularly galling, says to us at the end of a book: "He very seldom comes up from the country now. He has finally decided to end his days there." (1:481–483; 1:519–520)

The psychological episode is very Proustian, with its metaphor of the selection of paper and typeface and its appeal to literature (the heroes of books one has read) and to the novel's great pervading theme, the theme of time. But behind all this we recognize the classic mechanism of the apparent contradiction. The hero is distressed when he should be pleased. An evidently straightforward relationship among the elements of a spiritual state is broken down, and the separated elements are traced back to their causes and recombined in a new set of relationships. The artistic structure here is *explanation* both of a general law and of a uniquely individual concrete instance.

In the section of the novel entitled *La fugitive*, Proust analyzes the mechanisms of forgetfulness. Marcel is charmed by a park where he once spent time with the dead Albertine.

The reason for this charm seemed to me to be that I still loved Albertine as much as ever, whereas the true reason was on the contrary that oblivion was continuing to make such headway in me that the memory of Albertine was no longer painful to me, that is to say had changed; but however clearly we may discern our impressions, as I then thought that I could discern the reason for my melancholy, we are unable to trace them back to their more distant meaning. Like those symptoms which the doctor hears his patient describe to him and with the help of which he works back to a deeper cause of which the patient is unaware, similarly our impressions, our ideas, have only a symptomatic value. (3:560–561; 3:572).

This passage also follows the characteristic pattern of Proustian analysis: the breaking down of an elementary relationship and the reassembly of its constituent parts into a new structure, and the transition from an individual to a general law supported by a metaphor (doctor and patient), all of it involving the novel's great, pervading themes: time, memory, and forgetfulness.

Internal analysis accompanies the main hero. The other characters are rendered from the outside within the limits of what the narrator is capable of knowing (although that principle is not in fact followed with complete consistency), and rendered moreover in terms of social categories. Sometimes those characters are the products of combinations of the social and the biological, especially in regard to the sexual peculiarities that determine their behavior.

Swann's appearance in the novel is immediately accompanied by detailed information about his place in society, an unusual one since this son of the wealthy Jewish bourgeoisie has as the rarest of exceptions become a friend of the Prince of Wales and "one of the men most sought after in the aristocratic world of the Faubourg Saint-Germain." Marcel's family knows nothing of Swann's double life and applies to him "a social coefficient peculiar to himself, as distinct from all the other sons of other stockbrokers in his father's position" (1:16; 1:16–17). It is with attendent personal "coefficients" of this kind that the novel's main characters are introduced into it. It has frequently been observed in the Proustian scholarly literature that his sociology, however narrow in scope it may be, is nonetheless an anachronism, since the fin-de-siècle aristocracy portrayed in the novel was for all practical purposes no longer a genuine social force. Yet for all the inadequacy of Proust's political and economic ideas, the social character of his artistic method is remarkable for its discriminating inventory of a highly complex, ramified hierarchy of principles and relationships. In a certain sense, that social character anticipates the interest of contemporary microsociology in the most minute social groups and "roles." The particularity of the social character of Proust's artistic method is of course what makes it so psychological: its detailed blueprint shapes the characteristics of individual personalities. A case in point is the peasant and servant Françoise, with her combination of hierarchical deference and animosity toward her employers, with her code of conduct that "provided for social complexities and refinements of etiquette," so that one was "obliged to assume that there was latent in her some past existence in the ancient history of France, noble and little understood" (1:29; 1:31). Located at the other pole is Odette, in whom the bourgeois principle is combined with the ideals of a Parisian coquette and the habits of a semieducated bohemian. Every word and movement of Odette's is socially colored when she receives Swann at her house amidst the "chic" orchids and the cushions of Japanese silk that she puts under her guest's feet in an affectation of prodigality. At the same time, "she had kept a sharp eye on the servant, to see that he set the [lamps] down in their appointed places. . . . And . . . she followed the man's clumsy movements with feverish impatience, . . . when he passed too close to a pair of jardinières" (1:221; 1:241).

In contrast to Balzac, such nuances are more important for Proust than are general socio-economic considerations. His microsociology is, however, combined in a distinctive way with psychological hyperbolism. Françoise, Charlus, and the Verdurins are rendered in extremely grandiose terms, and we sometimes encounter grandiose depictions of whole "races," such as the vast sociopsychological characterization of the Guermantes family.

Apparent in that characterization's nineteenth-century social definitions are the same qualities that La Bruyère ascribed to the powerful of this world. The whole race shares a "coefficient" that predicts its generic behavior, even though, for example, the personal organic characteristics of Charlus (his inversion, artistic bent, intellectualism, and even potential insanity) differ from those of his brother, the duc de Guermantes, who is narrow-minded to the point of obtuseness. Such is the way in which the Proustian character is constructed.

One of the most intensely debated issues in the critical literature devoted to Proust is whether his characters are two- or three-dimensional. Gaëtan Picon in particular has insisted on their two-dimensionality and unreality, although not as a defect but as one of the structural peculiarities of the Proustian novel.[27]

The characters' two-dimensionality is connected with their fluidity, with the fact that they disintegrate into a myriad of aspects that cannot be brought together in a unity. Yet that fluidity is not absolute. It is circumscribed by Proust's conception of love as a subjective striving that creates its own object. If one looks not at Proust's pronouncements but at the structure of his images, it will be seen that the people in his world are elusive only for those who love them: Albertine or Gilberte for Marcel, Odette for Swann, or Morel for Charlus. To all the other characters these people are fully "capturable" in their petit-bourgeois or bohemian greed, narrow-mindedness, and cruelty. The real Odette whom Swann agonizes after is the one who keeps a sharp eye on her clumsy servant.

If one measures Proust by a Tolstoian standard, then his characters might indeed seem unreal. But those characters have a different purpose than Tolstoi's do. The people and things in Proust's world of unceasing authorial meditation are illustrations, arguments, examples (however elaborated). The investigatory tone of the authorial discourse turns them into something like *specimens*, although without depriving them of their material concreteness. Their function as exempla of "general laws" required that they be concentrated and then sharply delineated and magnified as objects. Sometimes Proust's hyperbolism verges on the grotesque. Social analysis passes involuntarily into satire (although satire by its very nature is the polar opposite of analysis). All this is particularly applicable to his depiction of the direct discourse of his characters. That discourse plays a prominent role in the novel in both quantity and function. It provides material that lends itself especially well to direct observation by the narrator, and it therefore continually accompanies and illustrates his monologue. And this is true whether it involves the dozens of pages devoted to the depiction of intersecting conversations at receptions and dinners, or to the analysis of individual verbal behavior, or to the discussion of separate words and expressions.

Gaëtan Picon regards the speech of Proust's heroes as no less unreal than their personalities. He maintains that the protagonists speak in stereotypes that invariably give expression to their essence, which is moreover not even the essence of an individual but of a type.[28] This is true to a certain extent, but it by no means exhausts the significance of direct discourse in Proust.

Proustian dialogue is analytical dialogue, and one must suppose that he examined Tolstoi's practice closely. But direct discourse in Tolstoi belongs both to the character with his individual personality and to life in general—to that unprecedentedly three-dimensional "second reality" that he created. In Proust, on the other hand, the character's discourse is a specimen as well, and the attitude taken toward it is almost experimental. The investigator selects and amplifies whatever is able to support his conception. This is a principle diametrically opposed to Chekhovian dialogue, for example, where the significant is embedded in the apparently accidental. That illusion of the actual flow of life was not, however, what Proust was after; he wanted striking examples. The Proustian analysis of speech therefore verges at times on a kind of dialectology. Whole excurses are devoted to the magnificent language of the servant Françoise, with its ancient national substrata. It is on the one hand contrasted in detail with the aristocratic "colloquialisms" of the speech of the duchesse de Guermantes, and on the other with the slang of the urban petite bourgeoisie used by Françoise's daughter, who takes pride in what she regards as her enlightenment. "'Mountains aren't really interesting,' said the daughter, giving to the adjective a new and terrible meaning" (2:148; 2:149).

The "social coefficient" of a person's use of language is related to his individual character. Proust's dialectology is therefore also psychological. The elevator boy at the Balbec hotel, in a conversation with the narrator, informs him "that in the 'situation' he was supposed to 'rejoin,' he would have a smarter 'tunic' and a better 'salary,' the words 'livery' and 'wages'

sounding to him obsolete and unseemly" (1:799; 1:857). A person's lexicon is a reflection of his position in life, and not only in regard to the
utterances of the elevator boy but also to the speeches of Marcel's friend
Bloch, which combine poor breeding with bookish snobbism, including
in particular a supposedly "witty" imitation of the Homeric style.
"'Whelps,' said Bloch, 'I present to you the cavalier Saint-Loup, hurler of
javelins. . . . Come, draw closer your pepla with the fair clasps. What's all
this fandangle? Does your mother know you're out?'" (1:770; 1:826).
Phenomena of the same kind are Odette's manner, adopted from "distinguished people" after she becomes Madame Swann, of "suppressing the
definite article or demonstrative pronoun before an adjective qualifying a
person's name" (1:511; 1:550), or her daughter Gilberte's habit of employing a phrase very popular at the time: "I can see I'm not having much
of a success with my tea!" (1:507 ; 1:546), if one of her girlfriends happened to turn down a cup.

Probably the clearest example of Proust's treatment of such word-spec-
imens is the celebrated episode in which Albertine (after a lengthy absence) visits Marcel in Paris. Marcel is struck by "the advent of certain
words which had not formed part of her vocabulary," words that give
evidence of new experiences in her life. "It did not seem possible to me
that Albertine's natural environment could have supplied her with 'distinguished' in the sense in which my father would [speak] of a colleague. . . .
'Selection,' even when used of a golf club, struck me as being as incompatible with the Simonet family as it would be, if preceded by the adjective
'natural,' with a text published centuries before the researches of Darwin.
'Lapse of time' seemed to me to augur better still." And further on:

> This was so novel, so manifestly an alluvial deposit leading one to suspect
> such capricious wanderings over ground hitherto unknown to her, that on
> hearing the words "to my mind" I drew Albertine toward me, and at "I
> regard" sat her down on my bed.
>
> . . . There was a world of difference between the new expressions and the
> vocabulary of the Albertine I had known of old—a vocabulary in which the
> most daring flights were to say of an unusual person: "He's a type," or, if
> you suggested a game of cards to her: "I don't have money to burn," . . .
> expressions dictated in such cases by a sort of bourgeois tradition almost as
> old as the *Magnificat* itself. . . . All these expressions Madame Bontemps had
> imparted to her at the same time as a hatred of the Jews and a respect for
> black because it is always suitable and becoming. (2:354–356; 2:367–370)

If Proust is interested in phraseology as such, he strives even more to
grasp the idiom of an individual as an expression of the hidden mainsprings and general laws of his spiritual life.[29] At its highest level, this
involves the representation of immense intersecting dialogues and the

tracing of their associative logic with its social stereotypes and personal themes, and the analysis of the discourse of each of his characters in a search for its hidden motives and true "meaning." The artistic practice of Tolstoi undoubtedly stands behind all this.

The Proustian device of continuous simultaneous translation, so to speak, of the direct discourse of his characters into the language of revelatory authorial commentary requires space if it is to be properly displayed. I shall therefore limit myself to examples of the Proustian analysis of individual expressions, an analysis that is not so much lexical as psychological. Marcel conceals his desire to meet Albertine's aunt from Andrée, who is in love with him.

> Why then did she blurt out suddenly one day: "Oh, by the way, I happen to have seen Albertine's aunt"? It is true that she had not said in so many words: "I could see through your casual remarks all right that the one thing you were really thinking of was how you could get to know Albertine's aunt." But it was clearly to the presence in Andrée's mind of some such idea which she felt it more becoming to keep from me that the phrase "happen to" seemed to point. It was of a kind with certain glances, certain gestures which, although they have no logical rational form directly devised for the listener's intelligence, reach him nevertheless in their true meaning, just as human speech, converted into electricity in the telephone, is turned into speech again when it strikes the ear. (1:928; 1:990)

A similar role is played in another instance by the words "very well" [très bien]. After Swann's death the duchesse de Guermantes decides to invite his daughter Gilberte to visit her. "At the end of the meal, Gilberte said timidly: 'I believe you knew my father quite well.' 'Well, of course we did,' said Madame de Guermantes in a melancholy tone which proved that she understood the daughter's grief and with a spurious intensity as though to conceal the fact that she was not sure whether she did remember the father very clearly. 'We knew him very well, I remember him *very well*.' (As indeed she might, seeing that he had come to see her almost every day for twenty-five years.)" (3:580; 3:592). Swann had at one time charmed and diverted the duchess, nurturing in her the illusion of friendship. But the dead Swann for her was merely someone of a lower social status.

Proust probed in different social forms the same classic mainsprings of self-interest, egotism, and vanity, which work in essentially the same way at different levels in his book, although he added the new motive of "snobbism," which was of particular importance to him. This fact really does link him, as Albert Thibaudet believes, to the tradition of the great French moralists.[30] That is why attempts to represent Proust as a writer who stands aloof from good and evil remain unconvincing. Ramon Fernandez, for example, has asserted that there can be no hierarchy of values in Proust, that the main hero representing the author's point of view is governed only by sensation and intellect and is therefore utterly passive from an ethical point of view.[31] There is a certain logic in this, but in spite of that logic Proust does spontaneously distinguish between good and evil. His social analysis, like any other social analysis, involves judgment. The social reality depicted in Proust's novel is presented as a world of cruelty, mendacity, indifference, and betrayal, qualities that are, moreover, combined with narrow-mindedness, or at best with intellectual shallowness and sterility.

The reader can have no doubt, for example, about the author's attitude toward the duchesse de Guermantes's decision to become friends with Swann's widow and daughter in order to spite the deceased, someone to whom she had refused the fulfillment of that ardent wish with a kind of refined sadism while he was alive, or toward the evil done by her when at the first available pretext she orders a servant who is planning a tryst with his fiancée to remain at home. "Her heart sank" from envy of the servant whose happiness in no way depended on her.

Fernandez is right in the sense that Proust could not find within the limits of his worldview an objective basis for his depiction of good and evil. But he did do something else; he introduced into his novel the world of blissful childhood, of the lost paradise of Combray, and he introduced two figures—the narrator's mother and grandmother—who are the incarnation of goodness, purity, devotion, subtlety of mind, and intellectual elegance. Those two images are intended to take the place in the novel of the logical requirement of a moral criterion. Their presence serves as that standard of value that is inevitable in any artistic work.

Part Three

ETHICAL VALUATION

LITERATURE is concerned with characteristics, personalities, and actions—with every conceivable form of generalized human behavior. And whenever behavior is involved, all basic life values are at the same time ethical values. There is therefore an indissoluble bond between literature and ethics. The artistic creation of the image of an individual is inevitably a judgment of him, a judgment that shapes his image from within. No literature has ever succeeded in escaping its valuational functions—even when it has proclaimed the lofty impartiality of the author (the school of Flaubert, for example) or confounded the criteria of good and evil (decadence at the end of the nineteenth century and the beginning of the twentieth). Ethical criteria, albeit in confused and paradoxical form, were operative as well in later literary "immoralism," inasmuch as every school linked with that tendency advocated its own *model of behavior*. For decadence, the category of evil was one of the most fundamental and structurally significant. Decadence might glorify evil, but it could not remain ethically indifferent. Indeed, it could not even avoid reliance on the idea of sin, which is why it so easily accommodated itself to dogmatic religion, although the latter would seem to have been fundamentally opposed to it.

Literature is bound up with ethics, but the literature of the modern age has not simply reproduced the norms and dogmas of dominant ethical systems unequivocally.[1] Art is much too dynamic for that. Classicism is especially instructive in this regard, and precisely because it seems to have been so completely dominated by norms, whether ethical, political, aesthetic, or logical. Norms had a profound structural significance for classical art (just as the struggle against them had for romanticism), but that significance was by no means a mathematically precise one. Tragedy (the supreme creation of French classicism) depicted human beings in the grip of passions. According to the prevailing norms of seventeenth-century thought, passion was opposed to duty and virtue; it was a weakness that frequently led to vice and crime.[2] Yet it was precisely through the depiction of that passion that the dramatist was able to move and delight his audience. That delight was not something the spectator introduced on his own; it was contrived by the author and constituted an aesthetic fact. Racine says in his preface to *Phèdre* that it was only "the wrath of the gods" that ensnared his heroine in "an unlawful passion by which she is the very first to be horrified." The passions in his tragedy, he declares, "are . . . offered for view merely to exhibit all the disorder of which they are the cause; and vice is everywhere depicted in colors that make one know and hate its deformity."[3] This was partly intended to mollify the Tartuffes of church and society, and it also partly reflects Racine's own religious views as a disciple of the ascetic Jansenist movement. Nevertheless, Racine knew very well that he would touch the hearts of his contemporaries not with an edifying dissection of vice but with a spectacle portraying the current of passion in all of its twisting and turning. In the third canto of *L'Art poétique*, Boileau provides a theoretical foundation for this contradiction between the dominant ethical norm and the artistic practice of classicism, especially the Racinian variety:

> A sensitive portrayal of that passion is
> The surest way to reach into the human heart.
> Well then, agreed, depict your amorous heroes,
> But do not turn them into cloying shepherds.
>
> . . . .
>
> And see that love, often contended from regret,
> Appears as a weakness and not as a virtue.[4]

For rationalism, which broke the individual down into various capacities and existence into discrete realms, there was, in addition to the realm of religious values and of ethical values prescribed by reason, that of the social judgments worked out by the milieu to which the first audiences of Racine's tragedies belonged, a milieu dominated by the cult of passion and the rules of gallantry that the literature of *préciosité* had celebrated in its day. However far Racine's probing humanistic investigation of passion and feeling went beyond courtly gallantry, both the moral habits of that milieu and the pluralism of rationalist judgmental criteria were still an important part of his aesthetics, just as they were of the aesthetics of classicism in general. Indeed, an ordered pluralism was embodied in the very hierarchy of classical genres, since each genre was in essence a form for expressing one or another system of values, each of which belonged to a distinct realm of existence. One and the same poet could therefore render the Psalms in spiritual odes and yet glorify feasting and sensuality in Anacreontics.

We find echoes of this multileveled ethicoaesthetic system in Russian culture too, even among the people of Pushkin's generation. Educated in the values of seventeenth- and eighteenth-century French rationalism, Pushkin and his coevals retained certain features of its thought at every subsequent stage of their development. For the romantic mind, on the other hand, true value lay in the infinite, or in the finite spiritually transfigured by the infinite, and everything located outside that sphere was regarded as base. Rationalism, however, could conceive of the coexistence of diverse valuational levels and of different kinds of boon. And in this sense too it reflected, if only in abstract form, the reality of the social existence of a particular milieu. In addition to Christian boons, there were those of the state, which was remote from Christian charity and the renunciation of earthly cares. Associated with state values (which in the 1810s and the 1820s were effectively beyond dispute for all Russians, whatever their individual views) was the realm of nobility values with its distinctively feudal conception of honor, its cult of military valor, and ultimately its cultivation of society qualities based on passion ("the science of tender passion" [as Pushkin put it *Eugene Onegin*]). Located on another level was the Epicurean world of youthful daring, feasting, and intellectual and sensuous pleasure. Higher and lower boons were assigned their different places, and those places were not interchangeable. For Pushkin, national character, freedom, and creativity were the highest social and ethical values, yet he did not as a consequence unconditionally reject, say, the world of high society. Pushkin's attitude toward that world was ambivalent. He ruthlessly condemned its vanity and deceit, at the same time valuing the most highly cultivated forms of social intercourse practiced in its educated milieu.

Subsequently, in the climate of bourgeois positivism, rationalist ethical pluralism would turn into the eclectic chaos of the "dead morality" that Herzen wrote of with such aversion. But the ethical hierarchy of Pushkin's classically proportioned mind remained harmonious and continued to find reflection in the direct relationship between theme and form in his art and in its diverse stylistic levels long after he had abandoned the generic system of his youth.[5]

Literature is imbued with ethical problems and judgments, but the nature of their relationship to dominant norms of behavior cannot be encompassed in a simple formula. This is even more apparent in romantic material. Early German romanticism had a religious hue, although of a religiously subjectivist variety. From the point of view of religious dogma, sin and temptation were implicit in the ideas of romantic individualism, irony, the arbitrary rule of genius, and the idolization of sensuality and the flesh (Friedrich Schlegel's *Lucinde*, Schleiermacher's *Vertrauten Briefe*). Later romanticism in its Byronic phase was concerned to the highest degree with the problems of good and evil, but its own solutions were polemical and contradictory. Instead of virtue, there was the individualistic category of election, which was ethical to the extent that it placed the individual under definite obligations without which election could not be realized. The elect individual was the bearer of freedom, of a supreme value that found its expression in romantic irony and subsequently in romantic demonism. The romantic demon was, after all, a kind of positive hero. He did not deny the existence of higher moral purposes but rather lamented the impossibility of ever achieving them. He understood the beauty of the laws of virtue, even though he neither wished nor was able to follow them. His evil was the tragic reaction of a freedom-loving spirit to a world order that excluded true virtue. "*Who* covets evil for its own bitter sake?" asks Byron's Lucifer (in *Cain*). "Evil begets evil," says Pechorin. The demonic hero was always a victim of his own evil; that was his decisive feature. That Balzac made his demonic convict Vautrin a grandiose but base villain signified a departure from romantic ideology.

The solutions of romanticism and even of classicism were not dogmatic, but neither the one nor the other questioned the necessity of ethical precepts. The commandments of God and the absolute transcended the individual and were therefore beyond dispute. Even the metaphysically understood requirements of the elect personality transcended his individuality, inasmuch as they were requirements of his spirit, to which the empirical individual was obliged to submit. Even ethical naturalism and natural morality, which were based on innate individual qualities and on the principles of pleasure and utility, assumed a transcendental sanction for their premises. Natural morality was even combined on occasion with positivist religion, usually with Deism.[6] Nature, reason, and the essence of man were conceived as having been engendered by a supreme creative force, and their laws were therefore regarded as absolute in their own way. Subsequent Western utopian socialist ethics, despite its hedonism, also originated in religious notions that were not susceptible of further proof. Even early positivism in its Comtian phase sought a converted religious form for itself. It was as a consequence of all this that minds in the second half of the nineteenth century, whether atheist or wavering between belief and doubt, were faced with a difficult new task: to establish fresh criteria of value and fresh principles of individual human behavior—to discover, in other words, the reasons for their *necessity*. It was this that in fact became the greatest problem of nonreligious ethics.

Individualism no longer counterbalanced by absolutes or able to enjoy the transcendental consolations of romanticism acquired tragic features (if it did not merely degenerate into Philistine egoism). In the climate of emerging positivism, the fundamental contradictions of individualist thought brought the individualist mind to a critical impasse. How was it to resolve the contradiction between the unconditional value of the individual and his biological nature (suffering, old age, and death), or the contradiction between the individual and his social nature? In other words, how was it to deal with the impossibility of deriving the individual's ultimate value from the qualities of a single, isolated personality? The atheistic pessimism of Schopenhauer that took form in the second decade of the nineteenth century had by its second half become dominant. The idea that individual consciousness possessed self-sufficient value and

yet was finite was a contradiction that individualism was unable to resolve, and one that became a fundamental premise of pessimist ethics.
The fact of death (without the promise of personal immortality) served as
a basic argument for the meaninglessness of existence. The contradiction
did not end there, however. The formula "life is meaningless because man
is mortal" was by itself logically incomplete. Did it imply that a meaninglessness lasting an eternity would be better than one that was only temporary? The idea of immortality was adopted only in terms of the immortality of the soul—in terms, that is, of a different mode of existence beyond
human comprehension. The idea of an eternal empirical life for individuals was, as such, not only no consolation but in fact unthinkable and even
awful. Swift makes short work of that dream in the third part of *Gul-
liver's Travels* with his image of the appallingly decrepit Struldbruggs,
who have been given the gift of earthly immortality.

What the atheistic mind required was not an eternity of life, but its
meaning as a permanent link [*sviaz'*] present at any point in the life process. An immensely important document for the nineteenth-century atheistic mind's quest for meaning and for its psychological and moral experience is Tolstoi's *A Confession*.

On April 13, 1855, Tolstoi entered in his diary, "I have been writing a
great deal about the fourth bastion [one of the most dangerous sectors of
the Sevastopol' defense], a place I am beginning to like very much. . . .
The constant charm of danger and of observation of the soldiers I live
with and of the sailors and the war itself are so enjoyable that I not only
do not want to leave but would even like to remain here during the as-
sault, if it should ever come." The fear of death given such extensive treatment in *A Confession* was thus a philosophical terror that was in no way
incompatible with the personal fearlessness that was so characteristic of
Tolstoi.[7] "Is there any meaning in my life that the inevitable death awaiting me will not destroy?" (chap. 5). Such is Tolstoi's formulation in *A
Confession* of the substance of the crisis he had gone through. The only
answer that contemporary positivism in all its wisdom was able to give to
Tolstoi's question about the meaning of life was, "You are a transitory,
accidental agglomeration of particles . . . , a little clump of something.
That little clump rots. The little clump calls the rotting its life. The little
clump will disintegrate, and the rotting will stop and along with it all the
questions" (Chap. 6).

Tolstoi never had a thought that did not bear on the actual practice of
his life. In *A Confession* he says that the true philosophers of every age—
Solomon, Buddha, Socrates, Schopenhauer—have maintained that life is
meaningless. If life is meaningless, then suicide is the only consistent conclusion to be drawn from that claim.[8] Tolstoi was near suicide, but he first
wanted to examine what it was that prevented him and others from tak-

ing that logical step. "To live in the condition of Solomon and Schopenhauer—to realize that life is a stupid joke played on me, and yet to go on living all the same, washing myself, dressing, dining, talking, and even writing books—was repellent to me and a source of torment, but I nevertheless remained in that condition. . . . Life is a senseless evil, there is no doubt of it, I said to myself. But I have lived and am still living, just as the human race has lived and continues to do so. How can that be? Why does it go on living, when it is possible not to?" (Chap. 7). Tolstoi sought a logical error and found one in the fact that he had overlooked the laws of the life of the countless numbers of ordinary people. Many of those people (primarily the folk or the peasantry) were endowed with a spontaneous religious feeling, with faith, although, as it turned out, even those people who had lost their religion still retained faith in something. The word "faith" is therefore construed in very broad terms in *A Confession*: "And I understood that faith in its most vital sense . . . is not only the relationship of human beings to God . . . ; faith is a knowledge of the meaning of human life, in consequence of which a person does not destroy himself, but goes on living. . . . If a person lives, then he believes in something. . . . If he does not see and does not realize the illusory nature of the finite, then he believes in the finite; if he does realize the illusory nature of the finite, then he has to believe in the infinite" (chap. 9).

Tolstoi the moralist reaches a justification of life in *A Confession* by proceeding from his new religious views, but Tolstoi the psychologist says there that for the human being in society living means having interests and purposes, and that the experience of values for such a person is an indivisible part of his apprehension of the world. It is in fact his "faith in the finite," according to Tolstoi. The social human being is caught in a highly elaborate mechanism of goals, interests, problems requiring solution, and creative impulses. He lays his track of choice and judgment among all of these. A choice of behavior for him (if it is not a purely reflexive act) necessarily involves preferring the better to the worse and the higher to the lower. The diverse interests of the individual therefore inevitably acquire ethical meaning as well.

Tolstoi also addresses the fact that pessimists and skeptics have found it necessary to assert the very idea of the meaninglessness of life in written form.[9] If life has no meaning, then writing has no meaning either. Why then does a man write? In order to write that if life is meaningless, then writing is too. Such is the objection of logic. But the equally undeniable necessity of giving one's thought and one's creativity and labor to the outside world bears witness to the social human being's primary awareness of communal bonds and of himself in terms of those bonds. Whether he wants to or not, a person acquires that awareness along with the social and cultural contents of his mind and with his language as the carrier of shared meanings. To be sure, that sense of connection excludes neither the conditions of loneliness and isolation that are psychologically opposed to it, nor the most cruel and powerful of egoistic impulses. The sense of connection, that "faith in the finite," as Tolstoi put it, may be empirical or elemental, and it may be directed toward conscious goals—above all, social goals—taking the form of unconditional certainties that transcend the merely personal and that are therefore ethically obligatory.

The individualist personality regards itself as unconditionally valuable, even though it is at the same time unable to derive that value from itself, since whatever an individual may regard as significant in himself is always generally significant—it exists, that is, within the shared consciousness of a particular time and place. Yet how can that general significance be established without resorting to transcendental premises? The nineteenth century searched intensively for the answer to that question, and its solutions were various. There was Western bourgeois utilitarianism, there was the Russian revolutionary democratic version of utilitarian morality, and there was the new natural morality of Hugo. In addition to these, scientific socialism worked out its own ethical solutions, basing them on materialist dialectics. None of these solutions, however, was adopted by nineteenth-century realist literature, whether Western or Russian.

The ethical quest at issue here encountered the resistance of religious thought, which usually denied the very possibility of a nonreligious ethics. In Russia in the second half of the nineteenth century this last issue acquired particular poignancy, both political and philosophical. If there is no immortality of the soul, then human existence is meaningless, and if human existence is meaningless, then it follows that "everything is permitted." This was Dostoevskii's idea. The thinking of the Slavophiles came close to it as well. In his article "With Regard to Humboldt," Khomiakov cites Max Stirner's *Der Einzige und sein Eigentum* with considerable satisfaction, dismissing the absurdity of Stirner's literal conception of individuality as the inevitable consequence of the whole history of individualist thought.[10]

In an 1847 polemic with [the historian] Konstantin Kavelin, Iurii Samarin maintained that it was impossible to derive the law "necessary for all" by nonreligious means,[11] and in letters written to Herzen at the end of the 1850s and the beginning of the 1860s, he argued that those atheists whose behavior is moral are characterized by an unconscious religiousness, and that Herzen himself had not "made a clean break with religion."[12] The idea of "unconscious religiousness" persisted until the very end of the nineteenth century. It may be found (along with a rejection of all the conclusions of atheistic morality) in Vladimir Solov'ev's book *The Justification of the Good*.[13]

"Unconscious religiousness" was ultimately unprovable, however, even if the facts themselves left no doubt. The actual practice of Russian social life demonstrated that atheists and nihilists were capable of great deeds and sacrifices. Tolstoi, who was even more interested in human behavior as such than he was in the reasons for it, speaks directly in *A Confession* of the fact that the nonbelievers among his contemporaries were more moral than the believers were. "Then as now, the conspicuous profession and confession of Orthodoxy was most often met among people who were dull, cruel, and immoral, and who regarded themselves as very important. Intelligence, honesty, candor, good nature, and morality were most often met among people who professed to be nonbelievers" (chap. 1).

The revolutionary situation, with its zeal for struggle and service, spontaneously manifested itself in the behavior of democratic youth. Theoretical thought, however, sought the laws of that behavior as something present in the nature of the individual personality itself, regarded both biologically and socially. The utilitarianism that was so influential in the eighteenth and nineteenth centuries sought to strike a balance between the individual's egoistical and altruistic motives—from Bentham with his "greatest happiness of the greatest number" to the evolutionist morality of Spencer, who believed that altruistic qualities (those benefiting the interests of the species) were fixed in the individual by heredity. But an ethics of personal interest as such remained powerless to demonstrate the *necessity* of the transition from private utility to that of the "greatest number." The ethics of Russian revolutionary democracy, first formulated by Chernyshevskii as the theory of "rational egoism," certainly felt the influence of utilitarian philosophy, but its historical essence was entirely different, since it was a practical program of conduct for "new people." Despite its utilitarian veneer, "rational egoism" assumed the unconditional supremacy of shared social interests and goals; it was in fact in the service of such goals that the individual would discover the highest pleasures attainable to him. Addressing people who were inclined to follow his character Rakhmetov [in *What Is to Be Done?*] and those like him, Chernyshevskii warned, "I say, 'Do not follow them, righteous people, since the path to which they summon you is lacking in personal joys, but the righteous people do not listen to me and say, 'No, it is not lacking; it is very rich.'"[14] In theoretical terms, however, rational egoism was unable to make both ends meet: that which demanded sacrifice and suffering could not be measured by the standards of pleasure. The idea of someone who would find it more *pleasurable* to go to his execution or to penal servitude than to remain at home with every convenience was psychologically untenable. Marxism, on the other hand, maintained something quite different. It spoke of the process of "alienating" personal interests from class interests, which were viewed as "ideal" and "universal" and were experienced as such by the individual personality.[15]

The ethics of Herzen constitutes a unique phenomenon among the nonreligious ethical systems of the mid–nineteenth century. Discernable in it are a number of different strata: the hedonism that was generally characteristic of utopian socialism, an individualism that had been transformed by realism (as Herzen termed his philosophy) but that still was not obsolete, the traditions of the Russian nobleman's revolution, and criteria of behavior that were a direct outcome of the antifeudal, revolutionary movement in Russia and the actual practice of the revolutionary struggle in the West. The contradictory nature of these combinations kept Herzen from resolving the issues he raised, although he did raise them with extraordinary urgency and force.

The young Herzen was a romantic, and he accordingly accepted the idea of the romantic personality as something absolutely valuable, since it bore within itself the values of the whole world. In an 1836 sketch entitled "The Second Meeting," Herzen placed in the mouth of an exiled Polish revolutionary the sacred formula of a heroic conception of life: "One thought—that I have endured this—fills me with pride and joy. . . . Yes, that one thought is enough to raise me above the crowd that so fears all sensations, and that would rather consent to live the life of a beast than suffer the unhappiness that human life entails" (1:29). This formula contains both contempt for the "crowd" and certainty that the hero is distinguished from it precisely by the fact that he is ruled by the cause of its liberation. The solution to the problem of the hero and the "crowd" is a revolutionary one here, although it still remains romantically subjective: the burden of lofty moral obligations is not destined for everyone but only for an elect. It is in essence not so much a burden of obligations as of conditions for the hero's self-realization—the iron law of the ordeals "that human life entails."

Herzen broke with romanticism at the end of the 1830s, but there are echoes of his earlier romantic solutions in the conception of human behavior he worked out in his articles of the 1840s and the early 1850s. Herzen's most straightforward and developed pronouncements on ethical problems are concentrated in the works of this period—in the cycle of articles contained in Caprices and Meditations, in From the Other Shore, and in the Letters from France and Italy. In the last two uncensored books, ethics is linked directly to politics. Herzen develops the theory of "higher egoism," which he opposes to lower "vile egoism." Herzen's conception of egoism is polemical, simultaneously taking into account a number of different opponents: official church morality, the Philistine moral routine, the Slavophiles with their scholastic Orthodoxy and militant anti-individualism, and the Hegelians with their dominion of the absolute and the abstractly universal over the private and the individual. The polemical import of Herzen's ethics of "higher egoism" is obvious enough, but just what is its positive content? By means of what criteria does one distinguish "higher idealism" from "vile egoism," and where is its moral imperative to be found? There are judgments in Herzen's works that anticipate the theory of "rational egoism," but his "higher egoism" is an idea of an altogether different order. Despite the somewhat hedonistic coloration of his views, Herzen sought his basic criteria neither in utility, nor in pleasure, nor in Feuerbachian love, but in *action* (the demand for "creative action" was a principal one for him in the 1840s). That action was of course not conceived as mere activity without an object, but as an act that had historical and social significance. Herzen was unable, however, to substantiate the *necessity* for the humanistic goals of that action, although that necessity remained obvious to him, reflecting as it did the practical concerns of the liberation movement.

For Herzen, the individual's life attained its highest meaning when the realization of social values and goals became at the same time a personal creative act. Herzen sought a harmony between the interests of the individual and the needs of society that would at the same time preserve the equal rights and status of both principles: "There is in the very oscillation between the worlds of the individual and the universal an irresistible attraction; the person feels himself to be a vital, conscious linking of the two" (2:64).

By means of his theory of two worlds—equal in status and separate but seeking to be joined—Herzen left his system open to the fictive notion of a pure individual who enters into a relationship of reciprocal interaction with a society that in a sense remains independent of individuals. Herzen maintained that the individual was sovereign and ought not to be sacrificed to "universal concepts," whether advanced by the church, the Hegelian doctrine of the state, or even a revolution in the course of which the bourgeois deceives the people with the words "freedom," "equality," and "motherland." "The individual, the true and authentic monad of society, has always been sacrificed for some universal concept or abstract noun. . . . No one asked for whom they worked, for whom they were sacrificed, who exploited whom, or who was liberated by ceding individual freedom. Everyone sacrificed (in words, at least) both himself and others" (6:126). This is in *From The Other Shore*. Yet in the same book Herzen calls for revolution and even for the annihilation of the old world. And in a personal letter written at the same time to Moscow friends in which he describes episodes in the Paris street fighting of 1848, he tells of a woman with a banner in her hands whom the national guard shot on the barricades, "and a girl of about twenty went over to her, kissed her, picked up the banner, and proudly took her place in front of the rifles. A national guardsman put a bullet through her, and she bent over, like a flower, with her banner in her hands" (23:90). Herzen of course had no doubt that the woman on the barricades and the girl who took the banner from her knew "for whom they were sacrificed." He was in fact using a double standard. He rejected universal concepts that had been formulated by the church or the state (whether feudal or bourgeois), and he accepted universal concepts that reflected the revolutionary needs of the people.

The ethics of revolutionary action in essence required values that were independent of and superior to the individual. Herzen was reluctant to take that theoretical step out of respect for the sovereign rights of the individual. Nevertheless, he did in practice accept the "abstract nouns" "people," "freedom," "motherland," and "social justice" in their revolutionary and democratic meaning, and moreover without reservation, as something self-evident. His subsequent ethical constructs therefore all presupposed an individual in whom a definite system of social and moral values was already inherent, and for whom that system implied certain obligations and, if necessary, even sacrifices. But it was logically impossible to derive the universal necessity of those obligations from the sovereign individual himself. The Herzenian ethics of revolutionary activity that took shape in the 1840s thus could not serve as a model for mass conduct. It was aimed at those for whom the political cause with its dangers and sacrifices had become a free and conscious creative act.

The Herzenian ethics of action was one of the most remarkable episodes in the history of the mid-nineteenth-century atheistic mind. It was diametrically opposed to the other atheistic system that became dominant in the second half of the century—Schopenhauer's ethics of empathy. Schopenhauer's philosophy as a whole and his doctrine of the unity of the world as will and of the individual as the manifestation of that will served as the basis of his ethics. The individual grasps the unity of the world intuitively, although it remains concealed from the disintegrating work of his reason. "If the veil of Maya, the *principium individuationis*, is lifted from the eyes of a man to such an extent that he no longer makes the egotistical distinction between his person and that of others, but takes as much interest in the suffering of other individuals as in his own, and therefore is not only benevolent to the highest degree, but even ready to sacrifice his own individuality whenever such a sacrifice will save a number of others, then . . . no suffering is any longer strange to him."[16] The necessity of Schopenhauer's ethics of empathy was thus predicated on the metaphysical constitution of the individual, and the condition from which it proceeded was an understanding of life as evil and full of suffering.

Nonetheless, people continued to live and to pursue social and personal goals. The wide dissemination of pessimistic doctrines could not therefore eliminate the necessity for a theoretical justification of life. As far as Herzen was concerned, that justification was to be found in goal-directed action, in the act that had historical significance. At the end of the 1870s and the beginning of the 1880s, Guyau attempted to establish morality on a biological and naturalistic basis as something inherent in human nature. Guyau sought his ethical criteria in the very fact of life. The instinct for self-preservation is the source of the individual's egoistic strivings, and the irrepressible need to extend and increase life (Guyau called it "moral fecundity") is the source of altruism. The life force is realized only when the individual "emerges from himself" by means of love, creativity, or heroism. In love, something that is external to the individual absorbs him; in the act of creation, he himself becomes something external. Guyau transformed the individual's potentialities into a moral obligation: "That I can means that I must." In contrast to many positivist agnostics who permitted faith in the transcendental, Guyau was a confirmed atheist. He entitled his programmatic book *Esquisse d'une morale sans obligation, ni sanction*.[17] It has already been noted in the philosophical literature that Guyau anticipated Nietzsche, although the difference between them is fundamental. While repudiating the positions of traditional morality (especially of the Christian variety), Nietzsche in essence replaced it with other, quite rigorous demands based on the future *Übermensch*. Guyau, however, wanted to ground the classical morality of altruism and love for other people in a new way by divorcing it from transcendental premises. Guyau's doctrine exemplifies the impossibility of proving obligation in an ethics that relies on naturalistic criteria. For where does it follow that a man will necessarily transform the extension of his feeling for life into altruism and not into a Nietzschean "will to power" or simply into oppression of the weak?

Behavior based on biological premises or on individual abilities and potentialities is threatened by the relativity of all its values and goals. Instead of objective meaning, one finds a more or less regulated system of illusions, illusions so necessary for life that they sometimes continue to operate even in those who are already aware of their falseness.

Later on in twentieth-century Western sociology there emerged a tendency to regard man as a being controlled not by conscious moral choice but by various mechanisms that instilled group values and norms in him. This represented a rejection of the ethical alternatives formulated by Dostoevskii—either absolute values or "everything is permitted." Someone may deviate from social norms in his conduct, but he cannot wholly depart from the criteria accepted by his milieu, since they have already become an inalienable part of his mind and the form according to which he makes his judgments.

Attempts to turn subjective ethical goals into a kind of imperative have also been characteristic. Such, in particular, was the ethics of French atheistic existentialism with its conception of the individual as someone who himself determines the norms of his behavior and who acts accordingly on the strength of his own spiritual organization.

In Camus's novel L'Étranger life is doubly absurd—both life in general and the life of the hero in particular who wakes up, eats breakfast, goes to work, eats lunch, returns home, etc. But the hero likes the meaningless fragmentation of his life and the equivalence of its different moments (since there are no universal values, there can be no hierarchy). He wants to live, especially after he has been sentenced to death. The novel's line of reasoning ends at this point. In his essay Le Mythe de Sisyphe, however, Camus makes a logically unjustified leap from that point to heroic self-affirmation. Sisyphus hurling a challenge to the gods is happy. In his hopeless struggle Sisyphus the mortal is surrounded on all sides by truth, freedom, pride, and courage. Where do they all come from? And how does it follow that they are good? And what do "good" and "bad" mean anyway? Actually, we do know where they come from. Much has been written about the fact that the ethics of 1940s French existentialism reflected the practical concerns of the French Resistance.[18] This is a historical and psychological explanation. A logical basis for it is impossible, however, since all that Sisyphus asserts may have value only within the coherent hierarchy of some shared consciousness that, without asking the individual's permission, shapes his life experience. Without such a hierarchy, the spiritual wealth of Sisyphus is merely a condition required by self-affirmation, a system of necessary and therefore consciously accepted illusions.

But let us return to the nineteenth century. Even a cursory glance at certain aspects of the ethical quests of the second half of the century reveals how contradictory, disparate, and complicated were the moral issues with which realistic psychologism, both Russian and French, had to contend. That psychologism was the creation of minds that had rejected religion or that had irrevocably lost the integrity and certainty of their belief. The movement of atheistic ethics between social and naturalistic criteria, between the search for a moral imperative and the impartial study of the mechanisms of judgment, and between determinism and individual responsibility, provided the material that sustained the artistic analysis of motives and of different types of behavior.

The hyperintensity of individual self-consciousness did not diminish with the passing of the romantic period; on the contrary, it became more complex through the scrupulous exposure of details. The atheistic mind rejected ready-made solutions to the questions of life and death. Ethical problems were thereby exacerbated to a painful degree, values were reexamined, and psychological analysis became ever more refined, since in the process of moral searching it was necessary to reveal the conditionality of every spiritual operation.

Tolstoi created one of the greatest of his works, The Death of Ivan Il'ich, during the period of his religious orientation. Yet it is remarkable that in reading *The Death of Ivan Il'ich* we all circumvent or discount the tale's ending, where harmony is restored in that joyous suffusion of light to which Tolstoi brings Ivan Il'ich in his final moments. *The Death of Ivan Il'ich* remains for us the psychological discovery of a nineteenth-century nonreligious mind, and it could only have been written by someone who had experienced the crisis of belief that Tolstoi depicts in *Anna Karenina* and in *A Confession*.

Realism's characteristic ethical differentiation was just as inseparably a part of it as its differentiation of personalities, language, and the like. Instead of a summary model of behavior based on a religious or metaphysical conception of the soul, it proposed one derived from a multitude of variable criteria that had been historically formed and socially determined. The instability of valuational criteria and the difficulty of finding a logical basis for them were combined with their necessity, since without them no social activity would in fact be possible. The contradiction between the harsh value judgments of the great French novelists of the second half of the nineteenth century and the dogma of naturalistic objectivity and impartiality they promulgated has frequently been observed. But that contradiction is in essence only illusory. None of the nineteenth-century realists ever preached ethical nihilism. Their concern was not the *attitude* of the writer toward the facts of existence but the means used by him to represent those facts, and those means were intended to be objective and "impartial"—were intended, in other words, to leave it to the reader to draw his own conclusions from the valuational possibilities placed before him by the writer.[19] As the epigraph from Taine included in the [first] edition of Zola's *Thérèse Raquin* has it: "Vice and virtue . . . are products in the same way that sulfuric acid and sugar are."[20] Though the inspirer of positivism, Taine still retained in his provocative formula the categories of vice and virtue. He does not say that facts are ethically indifferent, but speaks instead of the manner of studying their genesis and their cause-and-effect relations. Later, in *Le Roman expérimental*, Zola would go on to describe the novelists of the naturalist school as the future "masters of good and evil."[21]

Even the greatest minds could not, on merely positivist grounds, escape the eclecticism of their ethical foundations. Humanistic criteria accepted unquestioningly and without addressing the fateful problem of the reasons for their necessity, Spencer's evolutionist morality instilled by heredity, and Schopenhauer's morality of empathy were all three combined with each other and with those other values, both ethical and cognitive, that determined behavior and that therefore acquired ethical meaning. In Flaubert, for example, everything was sacrificed to a combination of creativity and the scientific cognition of truth.

In the midst of these interconnected but variable criteria of social and moral valuation, the novel of the second half of the nineteenth century attempted to solve the problem of the analysis of spiritual life, and, in particular, to come to terms with the basic sociopsychological issue of how to reconcile determinism with the fact of guilt and individual responsibility. The question of free will with which philosophical, theological, and scientific thought had wrestled for centuries had its artistic aspect as well. The individual is physiologically and socially conditioned; his personality and behavior are the results of an infinite concatenation of cause and effect. The individual therefore is not guilty, since guilt and responsibility have been transferred to his environment. Yet that environment is also historically conditioned and therefore evidently "not guilty" either. And history in its turn is even less guilty. This logic could not, however, be the logic of artistic creation. The characters created by determinist writers are subject to judgment and evaluation in the same way that a living person is, and for the same reason—the impossibility of any kind of spiritual life at all or of any practical activity without the conviction that human beings have free choice in their actions, however much that choice may actually be limited by circumstances. A person cannot act—cannot live, that is—without regarding himself as free. And without that working hypothesis, a literature that investigates spiritual life cannot go about its business either. In contrast to mechanical, biological determinism, Marxist determinism regarded the individual's choice of behavior as the act of a socially conditioned consciousness.

For naturalistic literature, and in part for the school of Flaubert, the environment or milieu was seen as the most concentrated form of social evil. Yet any milieu necessarily consists of individuals and is cognized through an individual who is himself implicated in that evil. Is such an individual then a passive embodiment, or is he an actively evil force? This question was solved in a number of ways. The dominant tendency was the humanistic one of removing responsibility from the oppressed and the weak and placing it on the oppressors and the powerful of this world, although the behavior of those oppressors was also regarded as determined. Maupassant's peasants are not responsible for the cruel and grotesque features of their everyday social life, but the same certainly cannot be said of his bourgeoisie—from the "honest scoundrels" portrayed in the early story "Boule-de-suif," to the loathsome husband of the heroine in the novel Une Vie, to the triumphant villain Duroy in Bel-Ami. Duroy is guilty. The reader does not reach that conviction on his own; it is set before him by the very structure of the novel—by the disposition of its valuational accents. In the nineteenth-century social novel, a character's free will and consequent moral responsibility increased in direct proportion to his privileged status. Membership in the ruling class was apprehended as involving greater freedom of choice in one's actions.

Another aspect of the issue of guilt and truth and of individual moral responsibility was the historical one. The historical method was supposed to take note of the dependence of moral decisions on the historical situation and on the place of the individual in the actual disposition of social forces. This approach was especially characteristic of early realism, which emerged during a period of intensive development in historiographical thought soon after the advancement of the idea of class conflict by the French historians of the 1820s (Thierry, Guizot, Mignet, and Barante). It above all applied to the writings of Pushkin. The political ideas of the mature Pushkin took shape under very difficult circumstances in the years immediately following the collapse of Decembrism. Pushkin was aware that an objective ideal of social justice might not be consistent with what a person regarded as most appropriate for his own social group, that those group norms might not in their turn be identical with the best that was practically possible, and that even a conceivable practical possibility might not be fully consistent with the unreasoning reality that one might be compelled to deal with (for Pushkin the regime of Nikolai I was just such a reality). Each of these different levels had its own characteristic set of values and judgments.

The monolithic quality of Decembrist thought did not, however, simply dissolve in Pushkin's mind. Its place was taken by the interconnections of Pushkinian historicism, by its new correlation of contradictory elements. Pushkin always conceived of the historical method in its artistic transformation as a "Shakespearean view," as one that comprehended things in their full diversity and that moreover understood the appropriateness and necessity of that diversity and lack of consistency. Pushkin's historicism could therefore appreciate the different truths of opposing historical forces. Thus, in *The Bronze Horseman* there is the truth of Peter and the truth of Evgenii, and in *The Captain's Daughter* there is the truth of Pugachev and the truth of Captain Mironov.[22] Shvabrin, however, has no truth, for he does not represent a stratum in the history of Russia in the same way that Pugachev and Mironov do, but rather stands for interests that are self-seeking and personal. He serves first the tsars' and then Pugachev's Russia without believing in either. He is, in essence, outside history.

Later nineteenth-century realism concentrated its attention on social definitions of the individual and on the analysis of his spiritual life. In defiance of abstract logic, realistic determinism was in practice combined with the ethical attitude of the writer toward his subject, with the condemnation of evil and the acceptance of the ideas of guilt and responsibility. But that ethical attitude assumed a variety of different forms and was embodied in a variety of different methods for depicting the individual.

Of decisive importance for the differentiation of ethical judgments in realism were the methods of *external* and *internal* depiction. The polar extremes of these two methods in artistic expression are satire, which is always synthetic with its stereotypes imposed from outside on the ever-changing flux of life, and psychological analysis, which ruthlessly exposes hidden motives from within, at the same time explaining them in a way that to a certain extent "absolves guilt."

The artistic cognition of spiritual life covered enormous ground in moving from from the typological masks of rationalism to the fluctuating states and impulses of the nineteenth- and twentieth-century novel. And in the process the relationship between the thing depicted and its evaluation steadily changed. The rationalist trait was at the same time a judgment; that judgment was in fact inherent in it. The rationalist act was uninterested in knowing about the possibility of its origin in a variety of different motives or in the possibility of its having different meanings in different real-life contexts. A man lied; therefore, he was a liar. And if he was a liar, then he was a negative character.

Rationalist poetics took no note at all, in other words, of the difference between retrospective or summary judgmental traits (liar, miser, ambitious man, coquette, etc.) and the organic reactions of individuals or their acquired social habits. The main subject of the nineteenth-century psychological novel, however, was precisely those biological and social principles whose interaction produced the personalities and behavior of its literary characters.

The primary characteristics of an individual's nervous organization—his intelligence, will, and sensitivity—were in themselves not yet aesthetic facts. They were merely material capable of being molded into forms of social behavior that might be judged in diametrically opposed ways. The individual also had other characteristics of a different order, secondary characteristics that had been instilled in him by his milieu. One could be brave *by nature*, but one could not by nature be courteous, say, or conscientious.

The demise of classicism meant the departure from literature of a unified system of qualities, including the unity of motive, action, and ethical judgment. Nevertheless, the relationship of motive to action in prerealistic literature remained a direct one, regardless of its degree of complication. Judgments in their general features were assigned in advance on the basis of a sentimentalist or romantic ideal of natural feeling, the elect personality, and so on. Both sentimentalism and romanticism devoted an extraordinary amount of attention to the feelings and experiences of their characters, although not so much attention that moral issues assumed a new structural meaning in the work. For that to happen, the principle of internal depiction needed to be combined with a new conception of the conditionality of spiritual operations that was both multifaceted and detailed; it needed, in other words, to take the form of realistic psychologism.

Nineteenth-century psychology relied on introspection as its principal means of understanding the conditionality of spiritual events. The psychological novel of the era took the point of view of its hero, who was depicted from within. Its material was the self-aware and self-observant individual. The point here, of course, is a distinctive kind of conscious- ness and not that the hero of every nineteenth-century psychological novel necessarily had to engage in self-observation.

That which on the outside appears as a trait or action, on the inside takes the form of processes and motives, and therefore exists in terms of a different kind of valuational nexus. Psychological analysis demon- strated that the individual is not internally aware of himself as the posses- sor of precisely named qualities—that internally he does not say to him- self, "I am a selfless person" or "I am someone of crystalline purity," and that he does not do so not merely from humility but also because he can- not say such things about himself and still remain within the limits of his own inner experience with its host of conflicting tendencies.

In precisely the same way, the individual does not say to himself, "I am a scoundrel, a toady, a troublemaker, an envious person." He does not believe that the diverse reasons (which he sees from within) for his diverse actions leading to diverse consequences can be identified with a single term. If he does apply an unambiguous formula to himself, it is because he has looked at himself from the outside with a kind of sideways glance. This happens whenever a person constructs an image for himself, in the process sometimes modeling not only his nobler but also his more humil- iating features. Such is the roundabout path by which even base actions may acquire their own aesthetic and become interesting and "meaning- ful." In a number of works (beginning with *Notes from Underground*), Dostoevskii investigated the ways in which this kind of synthetic relation- ship to oneself may coexist with brutal self-analysis.

In addition to this, psychological literature has persistently shown how an individual's internal view of himself may be different from the external view of others. Take the envious person, for example. His enviousness is known to all of his acquaintances, and it is not open to doubt, since con- tact with anyone else's good fortune invariably elicits a reaction of protest from him. Internally, however, he sees the validity (as he imagines) of his protest in each instance, inasmuch as the other person's success reminds him of old offenses and therefore seems to him to be unfair. In making his protest he even feels righteous indignation. And others wish to exhaust that whole structure of alternating feelings with a single crude concept by calling it "envy"! Yet those around him are for their part certain that the reemergence of an unchanging, uniform reaction does indeed signify the presence of the quality they have noted. The scandalmonger or trouble- maker sees from within how he arrived at each scandal by some (for him) convincing path. In one situation he "could not tolerate" the injustice; in another, his nerves gave out; in a third, it was the boorishness that he resented; and so on. As if they were indeed all the same thing and could merely be called "quarreling."

That which when regarded from the inside is seen as a process and as an individual instance incapable of being captured in a single unambiguous term, is regarded from the outside as a form requiring a summary designation. Such general ethical concepts, such word definitions and word condemnations, are socially necessary. Without them, it would be impossible for people to understand one another. Without them, society would not be able to oppose those forces that are destructive to it. The nineteenth-century sociopolitical novel was very mindful of universal ethical requirements, but it wanted to comprehend the individual in all the newly revealed diversity of his conditionality, and it therefore set up the apparatus of psychological analysis on the inside, so to speak, in order to see spiritual phenomena exactly as they would appear to the person himself in the process of his own self-observation. Depiction from within (in conjunction with the new principle of conditionality) changed the ethical status of the novel, and not merely because analysis replaced evil, but because good and evil no longer appeared in pure form. Instead, they were seen as deriving from a variety of different sources and as set in motion by a variety of different motives.

Arguments about Kant's moral imperative had been proliferating for several decades, and yet the moralists of the nineteenth century were still unable to agree on whom to consider a good man—someone who was capable of suppressing his own appetites for the sake of principle, or someone of pure mind whose spontaneous inclinations deviated as little as possible from the norm. Whatever the answer to this question, the nonequivalence of motive and action opened up to analytical psychologism possibilities of the most varied kind.

The analytical method derived from the fact that within the mind not only of the bad man but also of the good one there are a great many improper impulses, including some that are egoistic, selfish, hostile, envious, vain, and so forth. These fleeting internal motives may be common to both the good man and the bad. Their behavior is different, however, because that of the good man is linked to a system of social prohibition, moral habits, conscience, and responsibility, whereas that of the bad one is free of them. The bad man is often dangerous not because of any particular criminality in his desires but because of the sheer unencumbered simplicity of his actions, which are in no way separable from his desires.

Tolstoi, as has frequently been observed, showed the bad thoughts of good people. The loving mother, Countess Rostova, has hostile feelings about her daughter's future marital happiness; Nikolai Rostov, remembering his first meeting with Princess Mary, whom he has taken a liking to, cannot keep his thoughts from her huge estate; and Princess Mary does not have the power to suppress her wish for the death of her father, who torments her. But desire is separated from behavior in these instances by an uncrossable line. The old countess does everything possible for her daughter's happiness, and Princess Mary devotedly cares for her dying father. Yet Anatole Kuragin, who is not lacking in a kind of animal good nature (unlike the cruel Dolokhov), is frightening precisely because of the absence in him of any distance between desire and action. During the period of Natasha's infatuation with him, his frightening simplicity and freedom are transmitted to her as well. At her very first meeting with Anatole (in a theater box), "it frightened her to realize that between him and her there was nothing of that barrier of modesty she had always felt between herself and other men. Without herself knowing how, in five minutes she felt terribly close to that person. When she turned away, she was afraid he would grab her from behind by her naked arm and kiss her on the neck" (vol. 2, pt. 5, chap. 10). Tolstoi shows us the mechanism that separates action from impulse or that brings them closer to the boundary between them. Extreme proximity of the two is not merely frightening; it is also unnatural: they should not be conjoined.

The analytical psychological method was also aware of disjunction of another kind—that between an action and its sociomoral judgment. An action that is judged positively by one milieu or another, an action that is even objectively heroic and selfless, may have motives that are negative from the perspective of the same milieu (vanity, spite, or gross calculation). On the other hand, good intentions and even lofty qualities of mind may lead to externally negative results. The objective social function of an individual's behavior becomes detached from him and takes on different, even opposed meanings in different real-life contexts.

In the nineteenth-century realistic psychological novel, the particular artistic identity of ethical solutions is based on the dissection of things that had previously formed an indivisible whole. The individual's social function, his place in the historical disposition of forces, is distinct from his actual behavior in every concrete situation, and that behavior in its turn does not always correspond to his personal characteristics. Motives are examined from within, and actions are regarded as if at the point where the internal and the external meet. Finally, the definition of the individual's social function may also be built up on the basis of external empirical evidence about his inner manifestations—the approach that is most characteristic of satire. Satire strives for hyperbole, for the deliberate destruction of proportion. But something like satire may sometimes inadvertently emerge even when the writer is seeking analytical exactness in his definitions. It emerges precisely at the moment when the depiction of the individual's social function is divorced from his inner states, from the contradictory unity of his subjective consciousness.

The notion that good deeds are unfailingly done by good people, and vice versa, is the kind of naively realistic ethical thinking that psychological literature wanted to reexamine. In Leonid Andreev's 1906 short story "The Governor," for example, there is a characteristic attempt to depict a man who is not bad in his own way but who has done a particularly black and terrible deed for which there can be no forgiveness. The governor has ordered soldiers to open fire on workers who were complaining about their intolerable lives. The governor is depicted internally with all his doubts and regrets regarding his ill-considered, impulsive command, his human terror, and his unique courage. Yet none of this alters the *external* judgment of him. The governor's action is an absolute evil that follows logically from the evil of the social role he performs. The governor will be killed. Everyone around him knows this and expects it, and the reader also expects it as a necessity. The governor himself knows it, and he knows too that it is justified and that it cannot be otherwise. Andreev formulates this schematically using the governor's own words: "The only pity is that no one will find out about these honorable and brave thoughts of mine. They know all the rest, yet this remains. They will kill me like a scoundrel." No one has any interest in the honorable and courageous private thoughts of the governor-murderer. He is a scoundrel in his social role, and as such he will be destroyed.

Leonid Andreev joins the nineteenth-century tradition here. Having condemned the governor as a fact of social existence, he simultaneously maintains that when regarded analytically the inner life of his character is not one of pure evil. Gor'kii went even further. One of the tasks he consciously set himself in the 1920s and 1930s was the internal depiction of absolute evil, an explanation that would be divorced from justification, even one that was partial and relative. The provocateur in his 1924 short story "Karamora" is examined in detail in relation to his inner movement toward betrayal and in terms of the full logic of that movement. But the reader's sympathy and compassion are excluded from the piece by design. Tolstoi had already shown the potentiality of such constructions. He demonstrated that internal analysis does not always remove the question of guilt, that it can sometimes even do without the psychological reservations that mitigate guilt. Such, for example, is the ethical-psychological structure of his image of Nikolai I in *Khadzhi Murat*. Nikolai I is a minor figure in the tale, although essential to it. Gor'kii, however, depicts his Klim Samgin from within in all the ramifications of his thoughts and spiritual states over the space of four volumes. In contrast to Karamora or Andreev's governor, Klim Samgin does not do anything particularly criminal. Yet potential treachery accompanies him like a shadow. It is a *possibility* without which the structure of his character would collapse, and without which it would be impossible to represent internally as absolute evil an individual who has passed his life on approximately the level of external behavior that is accepted by his milieu.

Gukovskii believed that post-Gogolian Russian realism, by releasing the individual from his milieu, transferred all responsibility to the latter (Gogol' himself, in Gukovskii's opinion, still judged both the milieu and the individual). "A profound and for its time progressive understanding of the issue at hand, although not without a certain mechanical quality," is the general tendency of nineteenth-century deterministic realism. Twentieth-century revolutionary thought, according to Gukovskii, brought a new solution to the problem. Gor'kii was the first to combine conditionality with responsibility in a fully conscious way, since for him "the human being was not merely the result of his milieu, but also its creator."[23]

Such is Gukovskii's conception. It is accurate enough when applied to Gor'kii, whose firmness of political purpose led to extremely pointed value judgments, but one cannot agree with Gukovskii's characterization of the ethical position of nineteenth-century realism as a whole. In spite of its determinism, nineteenth-century social and psychological literature did judge individuals, although there was perhaps a certain illogic in doing so. In any event, condemnation and approbation are not, when applied to the artistic work, something that the reader derives from the writer's explicit declarations or from his worldview to the extent that it may be known. Condemnation and approbation are given to the reader within the context of an artistic system.

The historical conditions in which nineteenth-century Russian literature developed prompted it to make extremely sharp value judgments—and not only negative ones. The concept of goodness, of positive life values, was especially important for Russian literature with its interest in truth. Yet a literally understood determinism carried to its logical conclusion would not only have eliminated evil but also good, turning it into a mere product of physiological and social factors.

Nineteenth-century Russian literature had to address in one way or another the issues raised by the liberation movement. The apportionment of responsibility between the powerful and the weak, between the oppressors and the oppressed (even though both groups might appear to be equally determined), therefore acquired a special, distinctively structural meaning in that literature. This pertains above all to the antiserfdom literature of the 1840s (Turgenev's *A Sportsman's Sketches* or Grigorovich's *Anton Goremyka*).[24]

As psychological analysis became more complex, so did ethical judgments, and their significance grew accordingly. The Russian psychological novel defined itself in ideological terms. It is impossible to imagine the actions of any of its ideological heroes—Pechorin, Bazarov, Pierre Bezukhov—without reference to the issues of responsibility and freedom of choice. The basic conflict of the nineteenth-century ideological or intellectual hero was no longer a conflict between hostile external circumstances, nor did it derive from a predetermined and uniform opposition between the individual and society (romanticism). It was instead a "free" conflict, in the sense that it emerged from the intellectual hero's own intellect and conscience.[25]

Dostoevskii (for whom guilt and free will were key themes) did not share the era's dominant deterministic viewpoint. Tolstoi did accept it, however. But if there is no writer in the nineteenth century whose works are as imbued with conditionality as Tolstoi's are, there is also no writer who posed the questions of moral responsibility with greater intensity than he did. The poignantly personal manner in which he addressed such questions was tied to his understanding of the relationship between a writer's art and his life—as has already been discussed. Tolstoi's diaries and his "rules" and programs for self-improvement all bear witness to the fact that there was nothing in his life that remained beyond the threshold of ethical judgment. In this sense Tolstoi is the culmination of the moral movement initiated by Belinskii with his defense of the importance of "kopecks" against the indifference of romantic ethics with its selectiveness and its division of things into those that are subject to moral judgment and those that are not. Belinskii's unlimited extension (in principle at least) of the range of Russian moral responsibility also had decisive significance for Tolstoi the writer. It corresponded to the breadth of realism's practical grasp of objective reality, to its treatment of any phenomenon as a potential bearer of artistic meaning.[26]

Tolstoi revealed both the highly detailed nature of individual conditionality and the all-encompassing range of individual responsibility. He understood that he had to account both as a thinker and as an artist for the contradiction between the two. In an attempt to resolve that contradiction, he drew a distinction in the epilogue to *War and Peace* between individual reason, which operates in terms of the categories of causality and necessity, and "consciousness," which is aware of its own freedom:

> The question comes down to the fact that in regarding the human being as an object of observation from whatever standpoint—theological, historical, ethical, or philosophical—we find a general law of necessity to which he is subject in the same way that everything else is. But regarding him from within ourselves as something we are conscious of, we feel ourselves to be free. . . .
>
> You say: I am not free. But I have lifted my arm and let it drop. Everyone understands that that illogical reply is an irrefutable demonstration of freedom.

That reply is an expression of consciousness, which is not subject to reason.

... Every person, be he a savage or a thinker, is aware that however incontrovertibly reason and experience may demonstrate to him the impossibility of imagining two different actions taking place under the very same circumstances, ... the fact remains that he can, however impossible it may be, for without that notion of freedom, he not only could not understand life; he could not live for a single moment. (Pt. 2, chap. 8)

Tolstoi's enthusiasm for Schopenhauer began when *War and Peace* was already largely completed. On May 10, 1869, he wrote to Fet, "The things I have written, especially in the epilogue, were not invented by me but torn painfully from my womb. There is additional support in the fact that Schopenhauer in his *Wille* says the same things I do, although he comes at them from a different direction." Tolstoi may have regarded Schopenhauer's doctrine of determinism and free will as one such concurrence. According to Schopenhauer, in the phenomenal world as it is apprehended by reason, causality is unquestionably dominant (the law of sufficient grounds). Yet the will (the thing in itself) may achieve an intuitive self-awareness that leads it to self-denial and to a liberation from motives—from causality, that is.

Schopenhauer opposed reason to will, whereas Tolstoi opposed it to "consciousness." I shall not go into the particulars of this philiosophical issue. The important point here lies elsewhere—in the fact that it was indispensable for Tolstoi to jettison unconditional mechanistic determinism if he was to conceive of the human being as simultaneously conditioned and morally responsible.

Evil in the Tolstoian character is condemned as something conditioned by his social milieu. Yet it is Tolstoi's conviction that there is also in the individual a certain shared human essence, a kind of free humanity that comes to light not only in Bolkonskii after he has seen the sky at Austerlitz, but also in Karenin at the bedside of the sick Anna. That is why that individual can be guilty. He could, after all, have chosen something loftier—renunciation of vanity, or love and forgiveness—but once he has chosen vanity or malice, he is guilty.

From the point of view of realism, the view of the positive hero as a virtuous hero was completely outmoded. That fact did not of course prevent realism (including the Tolstoian variety) from having its own positive heroes whose fundamental aspirations corresponded to the political, social, and moral ideals of the writer himself, although such heroes were never turned into mere formulas for those ideals.

Tolstoi assumed that even the best people of the spoiled "ruling" milieu were incapable of ridding themselves of conceit, vanity, sensuality,

and malice. Therefore, in order to have a positive role in the world created by Tolstoi, it is not necessary that a character be without faults,
although it is necessary that he choose to strive for truth and virtue. Pierre
Bezukhov has led a profligate life in his youth, but that does not keep him
from being a positive hero. Pierre is "likable." But Nekhliudov in *Resurrection* is not, is indeed even unpleasant, although that does not hinder
him, given the place he occupies in the novel, from being a positive hero
either. The dissolute Pierre, the egoistic Nekhliudov, and the stingy landowner Levin are all truth seekers and therefore people with a positive
function. Yet Stiva Oblonskii, who is kind, or rather intelligent and well-
intentioned, but devoid of any moral aspirations, is not a positive hero. In
contrast to the irresponsible Oblonskii, Vronskii is a man of strict responsibility and limited but precise generosity. Vronskii, however, is utterly
circumscribed. Unlike Levin or even Karenin, he is incapable of breakthroughs to spiritual freedom. Within the limited viewpoint of a definite
social milieu, his behavior is irreproachable. Even his passion, which
transcends those limits, is still comprehensible to that milieu with its society ethics (it mocks Karenin whose wife has abandoned him, and it regards Levin as an amusing though harmful eccentric). Only after Anna's
suicide does Vronskii cease to be an exact replica of the model of the
Russian gentleman. The mechanism of that model has been exploded by
guilt and responsibility.

The relationship between conditionality and freedom in Tolstoi varies
from character to character. Usually the freer a Tolstoian character is, the
more problematic and ideological he becomes. At one pole, say, there is
Pierre Bezukhov, and at the other, Berg or Napoleon. Neither Berg nor
Napoleon has any moral concerns. But to deprive Pierre Bezukhov and
Levin of their freedom of choice would be to deprive them of all meaning
and to destroy their link to the plot, which is after all the story of the
decisions taken by them.[27]

As has already been said, Tolstoi made a theoretical distinction between the world comprehended by reason, where causal relationships
have full sway, and the internal world of "consciousness," which is dominated by the individual's conviction in spite of all logic that he is free to
choose his own actions. This philosophical duality has its own form of
artistic expression in Tolstoi. The free spiritual decisions taken by his
intellectual heroes are at the same time tightly woven into the general
fabric of actual cause-and-effect relations. Bolkonskii twice experiences
periods of spiritual illumination, periods in which he reevaluates all his
relationships, *because* he has been wounded (the second time mortally).
Pierre Bezukhov's moral about-face takes place *because* he has been captured, *because* he has been subjected to the effect of incredible, previously

unexperienced events, has met Karataev, and so on. These are strictly causal lines, but ones that have been set in motion only as a result of their encounter with another line, one consisting of motives arising from the inner laws of the individual himself.[28] Levin spending a sleepless night before proposing to Kitty, Levin hunting and mowing with his peasants, and Levin in numerous other circumstances is examined by Tolstoi as a psychic mechanism that is extremely sensitive to the most varied external impressions and that reacts to them instantly and with great adaptibility. How then is the moral crisis that is depicted in the last part of *Anna Karenina* and that completes the image of Levin as ideologist conditioned? Two kinds of impulse are given, one that initiates the process of anguished seeking, and another that brings about a resolution of that process. The first impulse is the illness and death of Levin's brother Nikolai, which forces Levin to face the issues of life and death. The second impulse is a chance conversation with the thresher Fedor about a peasant who "has remembered God" and who "lives for his soul." In both instances, the turning points are indeed impulses, pretexts, or stimuli that do not so much engender a spiritual event as precipitate it. Tolstoi himself speaks of this: "The words spoken by the peasant let loose an electric spark in his mind that suddenly transfigured and welded into a single whole a swarm of disparate, feeble, uncoordinated thoughts that had never ceased to trouble him" (pt. 8, chap. 12).

The autobiographical basis of the eighth part of *Anna Karenina* (which concerns Levin's spiritual conversion) and its textual similarity to *A Confession* and "Notes of a Madman" (also autobiographical) are well known, although Tolstoi did permit himself in *Anna Karenina* to make his characteristic departures from autobiographical chronology. In 1862 he married and entered a period of protracted absorption in creative, family, and estate life. The feelings evoked by the death of his brother Nikolai Nikolaevich in 1860, and in particular by the "Arzamasian horror" that he experienced in 1869 (and later on in 1897) and that is described in detail in "Notes of a Madman," were a portent of the coming crisis. Nevertheless, Tolstoi's professional and domestic life followed its normal course until approximately 1876, when his work on *Anna Karenina* was already nearing completion. The crisis whose torment he describes in *A Confession* occurred at this time: "And it was then that I, a happy man, removed a rope from my room where I spent every evening getting undressed alone, lest I hang myself from the crossbeam of the partition, and stopped going hunting with a gun, lest I be tempted by so easy a way of delivering myself from life" (chap. 4). *A Confession* was written at the beginning of the 1880s. Several years earlier, however, Tolstoi had already given that suicide that never took place to Levin: "And though a happy family man and a healthy person, Levin was several times so close to suicide that he hid a rope, lest he hang himself with it, and was afraid to carry a gun, lest he shoot himself" (pt. 8, chap. 9).[29]

What in fact has happened here? At the time of his own crisis Tolstoi already had behind him fourteen years of family life, many years of estate management, vast experience as a writer, and a fame that was already beginning to cloy, whereas Levin contemplates suicide after taking only the very first steps on the road of his new and to him fascinating family life. There is in fact a certain discrepancy between Levin the "logical suicide" and the Levin who takes part in Kitty's confinement, who is present at Mitia's bath, and who hurries with a blanket to the woods where his family has been caught in a downpour. The contours of the two images do not coincide. But that did not matter to Tolstoi, who was not afraid of inconsistency. The psychological anachronism allowed Tolstoi to detach Levin's moral choice to a certain extent from the conditions of his everyday life. "If there is a reason for goodness, then it is no longer goodness," Levin muses. In order to assert the full extent of his ideological hero's freedom and responsibility, Tolstoi weakens the system of his motivations at precisely those points where the issue concerns his loftiest moral experience.

The psychological stereotype in literature evolved from static qualities to the stable yet dynamic features of the realistic personality; the basis for the subsequent detailed elaboration and dynamization of that personality was the individual "impulse" regarded in terms of its purposefulness and conditionality. The artistic investigation of individual impulses had existed long before Tolstoi, of course, but as always with him a general premise of classical realism was carried to the point of a qualitative change. In Tolstoi's system, the impulse became an unprecedentedly significant unit of psychological analysis, or more accurately an ethicopsychological unit, inasmuch as ethical judgments are applied in Tolstoi not only to his characters' (relatively) stable aspirations but also, and just as intensively, to those impulses that continually flare up and die out within them.

Impulses in Tolstoi are only partly determined by the character's personality. The rest of the time they are neither predetermined nor predictable, since the infinite variety of life situations and of possible reactions to them is not predetermined. The pre-Tolstoian sociopsychological novel was still dominated by a predetermined relationship between personality or social type and the impulses and motives for its actions. That "logical" connection is very clear and strong, for example, in the historical types created by Turgenev and in the heroes of Goncharov. Actions and motives in the nineteenth-century novel are probably least predetermined in Dostoevskii. That, however, is a phenomenon of a different order. Dostoevskii employs a fundamentally different logic of motivation that is subordinate to the movement of the ideas embodied in his heroes.

Tolstoi, then, does not limit himself to a set model of character behavior, but instead offers a fresh ethicopsychological resolution for each situation, even the most transitory. His world, however, in no way disintegrates into a series of separately solved problems. On the contrary, it is imbued with connections and organized on the basis of a comprehensive view of spiritual life. Tolstoi depicts individual behavior as a process of continuously alternating impulses and at the same time as a system that is defined by the individual personality's basic aspirations, which are themselves distributed among a variety of different ethical levels. This mechanism is intended to struggle at once for the individual's material existence and those interests connected with it, for the realization of his capabilities and potentialities, and for access to those universal values and ideals without which he cannot regard himself as fully human. Tolstoi was always concerned with the issues of good and evil, and both for him were subject to a single method of investigation. He transferred the analytical method, which had been used primarily for the examination of weaknesses, conflicts, and vices, to goodness as well in the process of locating its different levels and testing its reality.

Foundations and conditions are needed in order for an ethical act, understood as the rejection of the lower for the sake of the higher, to triumph over the spontaneous power of egoistic strivings. Using analytical means, Tolstoi sought the moral foundations of actions, even of those actions he had pronounced free. If he did not find them, he boldly lowered himself over the hierarchical cliff, confident that in the absence of higher interests, lower ones would be at work.

There is a pronounced ethicopsychological parallelism in Tolstoi. His investigation of the levels of goodness is at the same time an investigation of the motives underlying individual behavior. For Tolstoi, love of other people and a sense of direct connection to something outside of and higher than the individual (whether God, motherland, national unity, or the peasant community) is regarded as unconditionally good. In examining actions that are directed toward the good understood in this sense, Tolstoi seeks to discover whether goodness or a camouflage of entirely different impulses is actually operative in each instance. Yet the answer to this, for him, cardinal question is not unambiguous—either goodness or its counterfeit. He is aware of the elusive movement between egoism and selflessness. He is also aware of the possibility of their coexistence and their psychological combination.

Several times in this book—in relation to Rousseau, Tolstoi, and Gor'kii—the discussion has concerned those psychological discoveries that follow from the conception of spiritual life as the dynamic and simul-

taneous coexistence of different levels, of different planes of conditionality. This conception of spiritual life has its ethical aspect as well. The
ethical problem is connected here with the fact that a person may perform
some action and yet condemn it at the same time. From a rationalist point
of view, this fact is explainable as either a contradiction or as hypocrisy;
from a dynamic point of view, it is seen as a consequence of the multileveled conditionality of behavior. In his "Western Arabesques" [interpo-
lated in *My Past and Thoughts*], Herzen wrote of the Middle Ages that
"knights and believers often failed to fulfill their obligations, but the
awareness that they were thereby violating a social bond that they themselves acknowledged kept them both from being unconstrained in their
aberrations and from raising their own conduct to a norm. They had their
festive garb and their official performances, which were not so much
falsehood as their ideal" (10:129).

Even when he is behaving egoistically, the individual judges actions
(especially those of others) in accordance with generally accepted norms.
He feels superior to those who in performing the same actions remain
unaware of those norms and who lack a higher perspective as to what is
appropriate and what is not. Some actions take place under the influence
of passions, momentary insanity, terror, and every other kind of external
pressure. Once those conditions have passed, however, ethical values return to their place, and then, as if nothing had happened, the individual
condemns in other people or "in general" what he himself has done. He
now views his previous bad action as a temporary and accidental fact that
did not follow from his particular human essence and that therefore has
no bearing on the moral ideas and values that he has worked out in his
life. Now and then in the midst of moral deviations provoked by circumstances, people may sincerely hold on to their old habits of value or to a
customary phraseology of goodness that still seems to them to be consistent with their "permanent" spiritual character. As a consequence there
emerges a defensive illusion of the irreversibility of a moral position once
it has been adopted. The individual as it were freezes a previous model
from which his behavior has long detached itself.

The issue here is the alternation of coexistent psychological states. But
those states may be coexistent in an even more narrow sense. Someone
may yield to his desires and passions at the same time that he subjects
them to judgment and condemnation. Involved here are two different orders of experience, each with its own source and its own conditionality,
and each entailing its own kind of satisfaction.

In *A Confession*, Tolstoi provides an ethicopsychological formula for
combinations of this kind: "My life—one of pandering to desire—was
meaningless and evil, and the answer, 'Life is evil and meaningless,' therefore applied to my own life alone and not to human life in general. . . .

That truth had always been the truth, in the same way that $2 \times 2 = 4$, but I did not acknowledge it, because if I admitted that $2 \times 2 = 4$, then I would also have been obliged to admit that I myself was bad. And to feel that I was good was of greater importance and necessity to me than that $2 \times 2 = 4$" (chap. 11). The individual not only wants things to be good for him; he undoubtedly also wants to be good himself—and not only Lev Tolstoi, but in principle every normal human being.

The experience of value is both centrifugal and centripetal. It combines the universality of the object and as personal an apprehension of that object as possible. The act of realization therefore has numerous ethical gradations. Someone may accomplish a feat from conceit, ambition, or calculation, or from a desire to experience his own human significance. He may accomplish it out of a feeling of love or a sense of shared bonds. Yet even in such a condition of supreme moral effort, the individual is in his way not completely disinterested. It is already necessary for him that he make the sacrifice rather than someone else, even if that other sacrifice would be no less useful to the cause. Tolstoi knew that love, selflessness, and compassion are just as inalienably facts of spiritual life as egoism, self-interest, and conceit, but he rigorously tested them each time, checking their reality. Examining various spheres of life, he sought *foundations for the good* capable of withstanding an analysis that would strip impulses of their verbal masks.

For Tolstoi, there is a hierarchy of spheres in which the motives for an individual's behavior take shape. At the very bottom is the sphere of primary biological urges governed by the law of pleasure and pain, a sphere that would appear to be located outside the domain of ethics. There are characters in Tolstoi who barely rise above the motives of that sphere, and who by introducing its motives into social life and into their relationships with other people spread evil and destruction. Such a character is Anatole Kuragin, for whom desire and action are equivalent. Anatole may be deflected from an action only by fear or by a different desire. Pierre therefore first grabs him by the collar and then promises him money.

Located above the world of unconcealed appetites is the social world. For Tolstoi, that world is a system of conventional values worked out by a clearly defined milieu. The system is complex and heterogeneous, and it includes everything—from conscious cynicism to a feeling for the conventional as something that transcends individuals and that is therefore obligatory.

Tolstoi was endowed with an extraordinarily acute sense of the conventional. He tracked down conventionality everywhere, dragging it to the surface wherever it was concealed and destroying its customary forms in order to do so. Such are Tolstoi's celebrated depictions of the theater, of the church liturgy, of the law court, and the like, and a great deal has been written about them. But Tolstoi did something else as well. He depicted the whole course of "artificial" life, of the life of people belonging to privileged circles, as a linking of relative and conventional values properly regarded as "rules of a game," although while the game is in progress, there is nothing more obligatory for its players than those rules. Relative values acquire their reality in proportion to the pressure of the milieu that carries them in its consciousness. In the milieu that was the subject of Tolstoi's artistic investigations, mockery was paid for with a duel, and losing at cards, with a self-inflicted bullet in the forehead. The strength of that milieu's pressure was determined by what it could give to those who lived by its laws, and by what it could withhold. That was its reality, although that reality might be concealed behind a veneer of automatically employed phraseology. If he wants to remain an active member of any given milieu, the individual must draw a very precise distinction between verbal functions and the situation he is actually faced with. Tolstoi depicted this mechanism repeatedly, but he explained it with particular clarity in regard to Vronskii:

> Vronskii's life was a particularly happy one, thanks to the fact that he had a set of rules that determined beyond any doubt everything that should and should not be done. That set of rules encompassed a very small circle of conditions, but on the other hand the rules themselves were not open to doubt, and Vronskii, who always remained within that circle, never hesitated for a moment about doing whatever had to be done. The rules determined beyond any doubt that a cardsharp ought to be paid, whereas a tailor need not be; that one should not lie to a man, although one could lie to women; that one should not deceive anyone, although one could deceive a husband; that one must not forgive insults, although one could insult others; and so on. These rules might all be unreasonable and bad, but they were not open to doubt, and in complying with them Vronskii felt at ease with himself and was able to carry his head high. (Pt. 3, chap. 20)

Described here is the code of conduct of a milieu whose members knew very well that the stricture "thou shalt not commit adultery" was merely church phraseology (although very respectable), whereas failing to pay a gambling debt really was something that you should not do: it would be civil death. Such norms are compulsory for the individual when from his point of view they have objective existence, when they are, in other words, part of the shared consciousness of the circle to which he belongs.

Herzen, proceeding from his ethics of action, spoke in the 1850 article "Omnia mea mecum porto" (in *From the Other Shore*) about the different kinds of relationship that may obtain between an individual and his social milieu. There are epochs of upsurge, of historical activity, when "the action to which every energetic nature aspires coincides . . . with the aspirations of the society in which that nature resides. . . . At such times, those actions that seem to onlookers to be sacrifices consist of simple fulfillments of the will, of natural forms of behavior." There are other epochs in which social forms that have outlived their usefulness begin to break down, and "violence, mendacity, ferocity, cunning servility, narrow-mindedness, and the loss of any feeling of human dignity become the general rule for the majority." And finally, there are still "other times, the most common of all, times that are peaceful, even somnolent, in which the relations of the individual to his milieu *continue* on in forms that were instituted in the last upheaval. . . . Everything . . . is lost without a trace in the established order, and the recognized relationships remain firm, resting on custom, on human unconcern, on indolence, and on an insufficiency of the demonic principles of criticism and irony." This "somnolent" time, in Herzen's term, is thus one that is ruled by "ethical routine," by that eclectic, senselessly contradictory, and feeble morality that he would speak of several years later in *My Past and Thoughts*: "Analyze the moral precepts that have existed for half a century—what do they not include? Roman ideas about the state along with a Gothic division of its powers, Protestantism and political economy, *salus populi* and *chacun pour soi*, Brutus and Thomas à Kempis, the Gospel and Bentham, and profit-and-loss bookkeeping and J.-J. Rousseau. With such a muddle in the head and the magnet in the heart that is eternally drawn to gold, it was not difficult to reach those absurdities that have been reached by the advanced countries of Europe" (10:126).[30]

Herzen's younger contemporary Tolstoi scrutinized that eclectic moral routine just as intently, although from a different point of view and on the basis of different social and psychological material. The routine was necessary not only to the Western bourgoisie but also to the Russian bureaucratic state, since it served them both as an auxiliary means of control. Yet it also suited the individual member of the "ruling" milieu. He could not find a basis for the meaning and necessity of moral prohibitions, although at the same time he was afraid of finding himself in the dangerous and difficult position of someone for whom "everything is permitted." Thanks to the routine, everything became more convenient and required less thought. What, besides unconditional obligation, could constrain an individual's desires? Such things as a sense of reality, fear, calculation, habits, persistent ideas of good and bad instilled in childhood and accepted unquestioningly, irrational holdovers, relics of past moral systems that had lost their content but preserved their form (Herzen had these in mind too), the powerful pressure of milieu, and a natural striving to remain on the level of prevalent norms of behavior. Moreover, these constraints promised strength, dignity, and a sense of superiority—promised, in short, the possibility of "carrying one's head high," as Tolstoi says of Vronskii. It was out of this confused medley that the moral routine emerged. The man of moral routine was a creature of situations, from the greatest historical to the most ordinary and transitory. Tolstoi depicts a great many people of this stamp in *War and Peace*, in *Anna Karenina*, and with particular harshness in *Resurrection*. He sets forth their different species: the liars who consciously engage in dissembling, people given to automatic bureaucratic thinking who execute the norm and are completely satisfied with that, and people who are in their own fashion intelligent and honest—Sviiazhskii in *Anna Karenina*, for example, who timidly conceals sham values from his own and others' analysis.

For Tolstoi, these characters are all different species of the human type that remains on the surface of social life. And all of them are condemned by him in their social functions. But there is another type, the one exemplified by Nikolai Rostov. Nikolai Rostov thinks in terms of established precepts, whether those of the church, the landowner milieu, or his regiment. He is immersed in daily life, in professional military and domestic concerns and interests. Yet he is unconsciously connected through feeling with other spheres of life and with other systems of value that in Tolstoi's view are more organic. In this sense, Rostov stands higher than Vronskii, although Vronskii is superior to him in intellect and in the elegance and force of his personality. Vronskii, however, requires a model of behavior. He is the ideal Petersburg guardsman, and then, after he is forced to repudiate that model, he attempts to become the ideal reform-minded large landowner of liberal tendencies. But his catastrophic and doomed relations with Anna inevitably destroy that form as well.

In Tolstoi's ethical hierarchy, the sphere of the individual's spontaneous and unquestionable inner experience ranks higher than that of artificial social conventions. Reaching beyond oneself or breaking out of oneself is the core of the ethical act. A person who does not believe in absolutes or in the absolute objectivity of social requirements seeks within himself that which is superior to himself. He finds there the spontaneously conferred reality of love and compassion and the reality of the need for action and creativity, which, being immanent, still do not satisfy his need to find ultimate grounds for the universal moral law. The individual's irrepressible striving to realize his own creative potential is an unquestionable psychological reality. Romanticism created the image of the artist who endures poverty, persecution, and obscurity for the sake of his art. Creative impulses, being immanent, may control a person in ways that the strictest laws of the external world are not always capable of doing.

Tolstoi addressed this theme in 1857–1858 in an unsuccessful story called "Al'bert," which later caused him considerable embarrassment with its almost romantic treatment of the figure of a dissolute but inspired musician. In *Anna Karenina*, the man of creative achievement (the artist Mikhailov) is depicted in an entirely different, authentically Tolstoian manner. This was not, however, one of Tolstoi's principal themes. The cult of the artist and the idea of art as a special kind of activity detached from everything else was alien to Tolstoi, and not only when he wrote his treatise *What Is Art?* and repudiated his own creations but throughout his career. His own artistic work was something that Tolstoi viewed within the highly complex unity of his spiritual and practical life—which explains the circumstance that in portraying himself, Tolstoi never even once made himself a writer. Levin is Tolstoi minus his writer's profession and his genius. Yet Tolstoi did not doubt that there was indeed a *resemblance*, and that what remained in Levin was in fact the main part—so much greater was Tolstoi's interest in the natural than in the exceptional. It was not heroic moral solutions that he valued, but those that lay within the reach of everyone, and the more within reach they were, the greater their validity. It is here that Tolstoi's ethical conception closes ranks with his principle of psychological cognition of the individual. For Tolstoi, the highest ethical condition, higher than intuitive compassion or intuitive closeness to the earth (Nikolai Rostov) or than immanent creative energy, was a condition of faith that was accessible to all, but especially to simple, uneducated people, a condition of faith in the absolute validity of the experience of shared bonds that is given to Tolstoi's unbelieving intellectual heroes only as a *possibility*.

The complex hierarchical system of motives of behavior originating in different spheres of life assumes a dynamic and mobile form in Tolstoi's work, and it could not have been otherwise, given his conception of the fluidity of human nature. Motives of different quality intersect with each other, and his characters oscillate between different spheres. Levin moves from the vague and intuitive to a conscious grasp of absolute values, and in the process he acquires new motives of behavior. Tolstoi endows Prince Andrei with talent and a will for practical activity, and the latter responds to the temptations of conventional values engendered by the world of fame and power with ambitious dreams of his own "Toulon" and with participation in [the reformer] Mikhail Speranskii's liberal bureaucratic committees. Yet Prince Andrei is always on the point of grasping lofty, absolute values that are sometimes near at hand and sometimes remote, but that finally take full possession of him in the last days before his death.

In "Master and Man" (1895) an individual moral conversion is presented with the particular tendentious clarity that was typical of the late Tolstoi. That presentation, however, is accompanied by a depiction of the interpenetration of motives of diverse conditionality that is remarkable for its psychological power. Brekhunov at first abandons the freezing Nikita and tries to find the right road on horseback in order to save himself. He is unsuccessful and is forced to return to his starting point. Nikita, who has in the meantime regained consciousness, says that he is dying and bids Brekhunov farewell:

> Vasilii Andreich stood silent and motionless for half a minute, and then suddenly slapping his hands together the same way he used to do after a profitable purchase, he took a step backwards, pushed up the sleeves of his fur coat, and with both hands started brushing the snow off Nikita and the sleigh.

Vasilii Andreich begins warming Nikita's body with his own, and Nikita begins to stir.

> "Aha, and you tell me you are dying. Lie still and warm up, and then this is what we will do . . . ," Vasilii Andreich started to say.
> But to his great astonishment he was unable to go on, because the tears had started to well up in his eyes and his lower jaw had begun to tremble. . . .
> "This is what we will do . . . ," he said to himself, experiencing an oddly jubilant tenderness. . . .
> "He won't wriggle out of this, anyway," he said to himself of the fact that he was warming the peasant, using the same boastful tone he used whenever he talked to himself of his purchases and sales. (chap. 9)

Brekhunov passes from impulses that are openly and cruelly egoistical (his attempt to save himself after abandoning his freezing companion), to self-affirming consciousness of his own strength (he can do anything, including save another human being), and thence to tender feelings about himself—to an ethical state that is completely new to him, but that still retains traces of egoism. He does not yet have words for his new spiritual experience, and he therefore speaks of his great sacrifice in the language of the merchant: "This is what we will do" and "He won't wriggle out of this, anyway." Starting from self-affirmation in an action that is deserving of general astonishment and approbation and that strengthens his sense of his own significance, Vasilii Andreich is drawn ever deeper into the sphere of love. Toward the end of this process he no longer brags about his goodness but blissfully experiences the truth of bonds that transcend the individual: "It seemed to him that he was Nikita and Nikita was him, and that his life was not in himself but in Nikita." "Master and Man" is a structure of centrifugal and centripetal impulses. Those impulses are mutually permeable, and there is a continuous exchange between them.

The early Tolstoi was attracted to incisive psychological unmasking. In the trilogy *Childhood, Boyhood,* and *Youth* (but especially in *Boyhood* and *Youth*) and in the Caucasian and Sevastopol' stories, egoism, vanity, and conceit—especially conceit—are relentlessly tracked down. In the period of *War and Peace* and *Anna Karenina,* that analysis is softened and complicated by the intersection of different ethical motives. The "national idea" and the "family idea" promote a process whereby the analytical dissection of the positive hero loses some of its implacability. Positive motives are particularly important in *War and Peace,* with its dominant atmosphere of partriarchal life and national warfare. Tolstoi's last period with its explicit value judgments and its counterposing of different social principles is marked once more by cruel psychological unmasking of the impulses of the "dominant" consciousness.

Whatever its negative function, however, the power of Tolstoian analysis and unmasking does work at the same time to make goodness convincing. The reader knows that the slightest stirring of pride, egoism, or self-interest will not escape Tolstoi's notice, so that if he does show unalloyed bravery and authentic selflessness and love, then that is indeed *what they are*—that there is in fact an internal and an external foundation for them.

Speaking of this from his own point of view, which despite his admiration for Tolstoi required that he reproach him at every opportunity for the habits of the natural school, Konstantin Leont'ev wrote:

> Given our . . . inclination always to be suspicious of whatever is in ourselves and to see everything about ourselves as poor and weak instead of good and strong, Count Tolstoi's most outward devices, subtle and caviling to the point of strain one moment and of crudeness the next (I would not call them real, but "realistic" or "naturalistic"), are very useful. Had it all been written in a slightly more ideal, simple, and general way, we probably *would not have believed* it. But when the Russian reader sees that Count Tolstoi is a great deal more attentive and caviling than he himself is, when he, that disciple of the "Gogolian" and "quasi-Gogolian" period, sees that in Lev Tolstoi one hero (a *real* hero) "started sniffling," and another "started sobbing," and yet another "started howling," or that one hero was intimidated, while another was engaged in intrigues, and a third was simply a scoundrel, even though he died for his country (young Kuragin, for example) . . . , then he, the reader, is already disposed as well to believe everything that is good, lofty, and ideal.[31]

What Leont'ev says here in regard to *War and Peace* is also fully applicable to the unmasking analysis of the *Sevastopol' Stories.* The analytical dissection of the psychology of the staff officers who belong entirely to the world of artificial interests is carried out unreservedly. The analysis exposing First Lieutenant Mikhailov ("Sevastopol' in May"), however, is an analysis of base impulses exposing the weakness of a good man (in terms of his social function) and a good officer. Mikhailov is fearful, he is vain in his dealings with those ranking above and below him, and he is caught up in the trivial concerns of military service and daily life. But that whole set of impulses intersects with others that Mikhailov himself draws together in simple-hearted fashion under the term "duty." Though wounded in the head, Mikhailov does not take himself to the medical station, because there are "many severely wounded" people there. Instead of sending soldiers to do it for him, he himself goes to the most dangerous place to look for Praskukhin's body. "'And in fact it may be that he is dead already, so there is *no reason* to endanger people needlessly, and it was my fault anyway for not having taken the trouble. I shall go myself and see whether he is still alive. It is my *duty*,' Mikhailov said to himself." Mikhailov, "almost at a crawl and trembling with fear," returns under hostile fire. And the reader has no doubt that that is precisely how First Lieutenant Mikhailov (and consequently any other human being) would have thought and behaved, and that if all the concerns about advantages and rewards that so preoccupy him had suddenly been removed, he would still have fought in precisely the same way.

Here is the death of Ensign Kozel'tsov (in "Sevastopol' in August"):

> The priest . . . recited the prayer and gave the cross to the wounded man.
>
> Death did not frighten Kozel'tsov. He took the cross in his weak hands, pressed it to his lips, and started to weep.
>
> "Have the French broken through everywhere, then?" he asked the priest.
>
> "Everywhere victory is ours," the priest answered . . . , concealing from the wounded man, in order not to distress him, the fact that the French flag was already waving over the Malakhov redoubt.
>
> "God be praised, God be praised," muttered the wounded man, not feeling the tears that were running down his cheeks, and experiencing ineffable joy at the knowledge that he had done something heroic.
>
> The thought of his brother flashed for an instant in his head. "May God grant him the same happiness," he thought. (chap. 25)

Hardly any other nineteenth-century realist would have dared to depict the death of one of his characters with such unmitigated heroic pathos. Tolstoi permitted himself to do so, however, precisely because his older Ensign Kozel'tsov is a cruel man who has grown coarse, who is extremely proud, who dreams about his career, who envies the success of the light-fingered supply officers, and who tries to ingratiate himself with his superiors.

How does the miracle of Tolstoian truth happen? How is it that Tolstoi's egoists under certain circumstances not only behave unselfishly (which is possible for any number of reasons) but even have unselfish impulses? The fact is that Tolstoi distinguishes not only levels of good but also levels of egoism. He recognizes both inorganic and organic egoism. Inorganic egoism is the egoism of society people, of staff officers, of bureaucrats, and in general of the most artificial people in an artificial society—those people of whom Prince Andrei says on the eve of the Battle of Borodino: "'They only care about their own petty interests.' 'At a moment like this?' Pierre asked reproachfully. '*At a moment like this*,' Prince Andrei repeated. 'For them it is merely something that gives them the opportunity to undermine a rival and obtain an extra cross or ribbon'" (vol. 3, pt. 2, chap. 25). Yet Tolstoi knows another kind of egoism too, one that has an organic, often unconscious foundation, be it in family ties, the land, or the common cause of a national war. That foundation imperceptibly subordinates the individual's private impulses to its own ends. The situation, especially if it is a protracted one, adapts the individual to itself while revealing higher ethical levels to him. Such is the national war in *War and Peace*, whose moment of greatest tension is the Battle of Borodino. The battle situation draws into its circle not merely the people (the soldiers), and not merely the positive heroes, but also those who live according to the laws of the lower artificial sphere, in the process engendering impulses in them that even they find surprising. Boris Drubetskoi considers it an advantageous thing for his career to stick close to the different headquarters and to the main billets, but after unexpectedly finding himself in battle (near Austerlitz), he smiles in conversation with Rostov "that happy smile that may be seen on the faces of young men who have come under fire for the first time." Whereupon Berg makes his appearance: "'Count! Count!' shouted Berg, no less animated than Boris. . . . 'Count! My right arm was wounded . . . and I stayed at the front. I held my sword in my left hand, Count—all the von Bergs have been knights!'" (vol. 1, pt. 3, chap.17). In order to obtain a promotion, Berg later on shows his bandaged arm to every possible superior while repeating that he remained at the front. Tolstoi, however, views Berg's state at this moment as a simultaneous conjunction of different impulses. He wants decorations, and he wants to feel like a Knight von Berg, and he is sincerely enthusiastic and glad because he has in fact behaved in a commendable way. Berg wants things to be good for him, and he wants to be good himself.

The theme of organic egoism is tied to the Tolstoian problem of "swarm life" and to the intuitive grasp of the truth that is such a fundamental part of the conception of *War and Peace*. This theme is directly formulated in the novel's fourth volume: "Most of the people of that time paid no attention whatever to the general course of events but were guided merely by their own private interests in the present. And it was just those people who were the most useful at the time." The prototype of these "useful people" is Nikolai Rostov.

> In Petersburg and in the provinces far from Moscow, ladies and gentlemen in reserve uniforms wept for Russia and its capital and spoke of self-sacrifice and so on, but in the army, which had retreated beyond Moscow, almost no one spoke or thought about the city, and no one gazing at its great fire swore revenge on the French, but thought instead about the next pay period, or the next bivouac, or Matreshka whose husband ran the canteen, or things of that kind. . . .
> . . . Had [Rostov] been asked what he thought about the current situation of Russia, he would have said that it was not his business to think about it, that Kutuzov and the others were there for that purpose, but that he had heard that the regiments were being brought up to full strength, that the fighting would undoubtedly go on for a long time yet, and such being the case, it would not be surprising if he got his own regiment in a couple of years. (Vol. 4, pt. 1, chap. 4)

The story of the desertion of Moscow by its residents has a similar meaning: "Rostopchin suggested in his *affiches* that it was shameful to leave Moscow. They were ashamed to be called cowards and ashamed to go, but still they went, knowing that it was necessary to do so. . . . They left, each for his own reason, and yet it was only as a result of their leaving that that magnificent event took place that will always remain the greatest glory of the Russian people." Tolstoi then identifies the organic principle that regulated private interests and put them to work on its own behalf: they "acted that way as a result of the concealed (*latent*) patriotism that expresses itself . . . unobtrusively, simply, and organically, and therefore in a way that always produces the most powerful results" (vol. 4, pt. 3, chap. 5).

Organic egoism unconsciously does what is necessary for "life in general." But life in general triumphs when that egoism is replaced by organic altruism and its impulses are elevated to a higher ethical plane. This happens to the Rostovs. Motivated by "latent patriotism," they desert Moscow along with everyone else, intending at first to take their most valuable possessions with them. At the last moment, however, they abandon almost everything (which for them is tantamount to complete ruin) and seat the wounded on their carts. The sight of the wounded left to the mercy of the enemy prompts Natasha to demand this sacrifice from her parents—Natasha, whose concern has always been with "individual interests," but who like her brother Nikolai is intuitively linked to the organic foundations of life.

At work here is a mobile mechanism of coincident and mutually transferable impulses from different levels, one that Tolstoi traces unrelentingly regardless of the ethical level his characters happen to be on at the moment. Psychologism and ethics are tightly interwoven in Tolstoi's analytical investigation of impulses.

Ethicopsychological mechanisms are stripped bare in Tolstoi's later, frankly tendentious work. *Resurrection* is especially remarkable in this regard. [In a foreword to the work] Bakhtin noted the peculiarities of the structure of *Resurrection* in comparison with Tolstoi's earlier novels. Bakhtin attributed those peculiarities to the novel's generic specificity, which he defined as "socioideological" (a category to which he also assigned Herzen's *Who Is to Blame?*, Chernyshevskii's *What Is to Be Done?*, and the novels of George Sand).[32]

In tearing the mask from phenomena that are social and therefore psychological as well, Tolstoi does not in *Resurrection* merely return to the ruthlessness of his earlier brand of analysis; he abandons himself to it with even greater severity. The reasons are clear. The world of conventional, artificial relationships has now been irrevocably condemned in all of its manifestations. Moreover, a way out has been indicated, one leading along definite paths toward resurrection. Those who remain within the world of evil are therefore *guilty*; they have been spoiled by that world, and proceeding step by step Tolstoi exposes bad impulses even in the best of them, even in those who are themselves the victims of social evil.

The sentence has not yet been pronounced, but Nekhliudov already realizes that because of the obtuse decision of the jury, the completely innocent Katiusha Maslova is threatened with penal servitude. And Nekhliudov is incapable of suppressing a fleeting sense of relief in himself: "But Siberia and penal servitude had immediately destroyed any possibility of a relationship with her. The wounded bird would stop fluttering in the game bag and reminding him of its existence" (pt. 1, chap. 23). For Katiusha, however, Nekhliudov begging her forgiveness the first time is "merely one of those people who, whenever they needed to, exploited creatures like herself, and whom creatures like herself had exploited no less profitably in their turn. And for that reason she smiled alluringly at him. She remained silent for a moment, considering how she might take advantage of him" (pt. 1, chap. 43). Such are the first natural impulses of people brought up in an unnatural world, impulses that are as yet uncurbed by any higher moral principles. But in Tolstoi those other, higher principles are always urgently intruding on the order of things. And by virtue of that intrusion, the characters of *Resurrection* are deployed in a particularly clear-cut way among a variety of different ethical levels.

There is the very lowest level, the level of Nekhliudov's bailiff, who after hearing of his employer's project to turn his land over to the peasants, "did not in essence understand anything, and obviously not because Nekhliudov had expressed himself badly, but because the plan meant that he was renouncing his own advantage for the sake of others, and the axiom that everybody is concerned only with his own advantage at the expense of others was so rooted in the bailiff's consciousness that he assumed he had failed to grasp something" (pt. 2, chap. 6). The bailiff is a kind of model for the world of inorganic bureaucratic egoism and camouflage by means of mendacious phraseology.

For Tolstoi, however, the bailiff's is not the most typical form of human behavior. More typical still is the striving for self-justification, the wish to combine comforts, advantages, and the gratification of one's desires with the sense of social worth and importance and the approval of one's milieu that sustain a personality's self-affirmation.

There is in *Resurrection* a remarkably clear-cut formulation of these correlations:

> What astonished [Nekhliudov] was that Maslova was not only not ashamed of her position (not her position as a prisoner, since she was ashamed of that, but as a prostitute) but even seemed to be satisfied with it and almost proud of it. It could not have been otherwise, however. Everyone, in order to function, has to regard his own activity as important and worthwhile. And therefore, whatever his position may be, he invariably devises for himself a view of human life in general that will make his own activity seem important and worthwhile. . . .
>
> For ten years, wherever she was, beginning with Nekhliudov and the old police superintendent and ending with the jailers in prison, she saw that all men needed her, and she did not see or did not notice those men who did not need her. And therefore the whole world seemed to her to be a collection of lust-obsessed people who were keeping a close watch on her from all sides. . . .
>
> That was how Maslova understood life, and according to such a view she was not only not the lowest, but in fact a very important person. And Maslova prized that view of life more than anything else on earth. . . . Sensing that Nekhliudov wanted to take her away to a different world, she resisted him, realizing that in the world he was drawing her to, she would necessarily lose that place in life from which she derived her confidence and self-respect. (Pt. 1, chap. 44)

Here the model of self-affirmation is the mind of a prostitute (just as the model for the behavior of those in power is the bailiff who "does not understand" disinterested impulses). The predictable patterns traced in that mind extend to the whole world of artificial interests, in Tolstoi's understanding of them, and to higher intellectual activity as well. Katiusha Maslova has devised a "conception of life" for herself in which she is a "very important person." Earlier in *A Confession* Tolstoi said of writers (including himself): "We could not do anything except write books and newspaper articles. . . . But in order to do such useless work and to assure ourselves that we were *very important people*, we required a theory that would justify our activity. And we invented the following: 'Everything that exists makes sense'" (chap. 2).[33] And everything that makes sense evolves and develops through the enlightenment of others.

When we speak of Tolstoi's depiction of the "mechanisms" of spiritual life, we are not merely ascribing our own ideas to him. In addition to breaking down the workings of the soul into their most particularized and individual components, Tolstoi was also fond of investigating the soul's mechanisms in terms of their predictable patterns and the constancy of their operation (his great interest in eighteenth-century rationalism and didacticism was not without purpose).

Depicted in *Resurrection* are the efforts of "artificial" people of a variety of different social strata to preserve their "confidence and their self-respect." Tolstoi was well acquainted with the mechanism of "displacement" that would later acquire such decisive importance for psychoanalysis. Maslova had never given Nekhliudov any thought, and his appearance now threatens to destroy defensive postures that are essential to her. "Nekhliudov sensed that there was something in her that was directly hostile to him and that protected her as she now was" (pt. 1, chap. 43). Nekhliudov had never given Katiusha any thought either, because he knew "deep down in his soul" that he had acted in a "base and cruel manner" and that he could not reconcile the "knowledge of that act" with his sense of "himself as a fine, noble, generous . . . person. . . . Yet he needed to regard himself as such a person in order to go on living his life cheerfully and happily. And there was only one way to do that—not think about it" (pt. 1, chap. 18).

Operating alongside displacement is another mechanism: the defensive replacement of a base reality with ideal concepts. The old general, the commandant of the fortress where political prisoners are kept so that half of them will perish, says of himself, "The tsar has need of honest men . . . ," and of the convicts in the fortress, "'These people are all of the most immoral sort. . . .' And he . . . did not doubt it, and not because it was true, but because it if had not been true, he would have had to admit that he was not a respected hero commendably living out the last days of a good life, but a scoundrel who had sold his conscience and who was continuing to do so in his old age" (pt. 2, chap. 19).

In an argument with his sister's husband, a bureaucrat in the justice department, Nekhliudov sharply attacks capital punishment as "an absurd and cruel business." "'But, you see, I happen to be involved in it,' Ignatii Nikiforovich said, turning pale" (pt. 2, chap. 33). And Nekhliudov is astonished to see tears in the eyes of this callous, unpleasant man. Through Nekhliudov, Tolstoi has examined Ignatii Nikiforovich from the outside and seen a complacent magistrate, but now he looks at him from the inside and sees a frightened man defending the meaning of his life and clinging to the one thing that he is able to do and that gives him significance.

Nekhliudov's university friend Selenin, once a fine youth, has transformed himself from an atheist into a *sincere* churchgoer, since unbelief would interfere with his career as an official and continually force him to hide the fact and dissemble, which would be repellent to him. He has obtained books by Hegel and Khomiakov and "naturally found in them just what he needed—something like peace of mind and a vindication of the religious doctrine . . . that his reason had long ago ceased to tolerate, but without which his whole life had been filled up with difficulties, although they had been eliminated as soon as he accepted it" (pt. 2, chap. 23). Tolstoi was as a general matter interested in tracing the subterfuges of reason in the employ of desires. Nekhliudov has returned to the estate where he was born, and under the pressure of his memories he is suddenly filled with regret for the house, the orchard, and the land, and along with them the half of his income that he stands to lose. "And all at once arguments appeared at his service to show that it was an unreasonable thing to give the land to the peasants and break up his estate" (pt. 2, chap. 1).

In *A Confession* Tolstoi traces the "subterfuges" of theorizing reason in himself, intentionally simplifying his own spiritual life for the sake of the experiment. He thus maintains that his fascination with schools for peasant children was unconsciously intended "to satisfy my desire to teach, although deep down in my soul I knew very well that I could not teach anything that would be needed, since I myself had no idea what it was" (chap. 3). Tolstoi also says in *A Confession* that he was satisfied with the doctrine of the growth and development of everything that exists so long as his own organism "was growing more complex and evolving," but when that growth stopped there came with age a diminution of strength, and he saw that "there never had been, nor could there ever be such a law" (chap. 5). Tolstoi observes how rationalizations and ideas turn up "at the service" of desires and interests, and how, depending on the absence or presence of an interest, values may change in an instant and new impulses arise.

Evil in *Resurrection* is always both moral and social evil. Yet another mechanism is therefore very important, that of adapting evil to a certain norm of behavior sanctioned by the ruling milieu. Tolstoi speaks of this through Nekhliudov: "If one were to undertake the psychological problem of learning how to make the people of our time, whether Christians, humanists, or merely good people, commit the most terrible crimes without feeling any remorse, then . . . what would be needed is that things be exactly as they are now—that those people be governors, inspectors, and policemen," so that "the responsibility for the consequences of their actions with regard to others should not fall on any one of them alone" (pt. 2, chap. 40). This, according to Tolstoi, is how ethical alienation takes place: the abstractness of social functions obscures the reality of the relationship between one individual and another. Shown in *Resurrection* is the continual interconnection and clashing of impulses belonging to different levels. One of the basic artistic tasks of the novel is to embody that ethical hierarchy in concrete psychological terms. Selenin with his religious and philosophical fabrications designed to trick his conscience already stands higher than those who simply have no conscience. Nekhliudov with his conscience that has atrophied but who is ready to undertake an action that will destroy his whole way of life stands still higher. Vasilii Brekhunov in "Master and Man" manages in the few hours before his death to move from the crudest form of self-love to self-admiration and ultimately to identification with something beyond himself—to move, that is, to what Tolstoi regarded as the highest reality of love and compassion. That process is compressed in "Master and Man"; in *Resurrection* it is elaborated over the full extent of the novel. The psychological content of Nekhliudov's image is located in his transitions from one level to the next and in the intermittent nature of his impulses, including impulses of a lower order that he is unable to rid himself of completely, despite his gradual improvement.

The situation of Katiusha Maslova's trial, the starting point for the action of the whole novel, also contains the seeds of the motives for Nekhliudov's future behavior. At first, the strongest of those motives is "fear of the disgrace he would be covered with if everyone here in the courtroom were to learn of his action" (pt. 1, chap. 21). But already simultaneously at work in him is increased loathing for the spectacle of social evil and for "his own idle, depraved, cruel, and willful life" (pt. 1, chap. 22). The motives for Nekhliudov's future behavior are pity, duty, disgust at his own baseness and a consequent desire to be good, and vain self-admiration. Nekhliudov's tears are both good and bad, and "bad . . . because they were tears of tender feeling for himself and for his own virtue" (pt. 1, chap. 28). But Nekhliudov can no longer remain on that level, and the situation draws him ever further along, producing motives that are at once less gratifying and more compelling. "If he had not attempted to smooth over and atone for his action, he would never have sensed its full criminality. . . . Earlier Nekhliudov had played with his admiration for himself and his feeling of repentance; now it was simply repellent to him" (pt. 1, chap. 49). Nekhliudov's impulses emerge continuously from his initial desire for self-purifying sacrifice and his subsequent wish to avoid that sacrifice. Hence his envy of the calm, uncomplicated life of the landowner and the sense of revulsion that alternates with that envy. But more complex spiritual states are also shown in *Resurrection*, as when Nekhliudov realizes the value of the new thoughts and feelings revealed to him and *simultaneously* succumbs to the usual temptations of society. Mariette, the wife of a prominent Petersburg official, without herself knowing why, flirts with Nekhliudov. "Many times thereafter Nekhliudov remembered with shame his whole conversation with her—remembered her words, which were not so much false as counterfeits of his own. . . . They had talked of the injustice of power, of the sufferings of the downtrodden, and of the poverty of the people, although covertly during the conversation their eyes had in essence been continually asking each other, 'Can you love me?' and answering, 'Yes, I can,' and the sexual feeling, taking the most unexpected and pleasurable forms, drew them toward each other" (pt. 2, chap. 24). In the course of this erotic interlude Nekhliudov speaks with utter sincerity and seriousness of the "horrors of prison" and the poverty of the peasants. Such highly disparate impulses may be combined in a unity because they are simultaneously conditioned by elements belonging to the different levels of Nekhliudov's psychic life—his moral enlightenment, his sensuality, and his habits as a man of society.

An even more complex conjunction of simultaneous but differently conditioned reactions takes place in Nekhliudov's mind at the very end of the book, when Simonson confides in him his desire to marry Katiusha.

> What Simonson told him had freed him of the self-imposed obligation that in moments of weakness had seemed so difficult and terrible to him, but at the same time there was something about it that was not only unpleasant, but even painful to him. Contained in that feeling was the fact that Simonson's proposal had deprived his own action of its exceptional character, had lessened the value of his sacrifice in his own and others' eyes. . . . There was also, perhaps, a feeling of ordinary jealousy: he had gotten so used to her love for him that he could not admit that she might come to love another. And then too there was the fact that the plan he had once formed of living close by her while she served out her term was now ruined. If she married Simonson, his own presence would become superfluous, and he would have to make new plans for his life. (Pt. 3, chap. 17)

Along with alarm at the prospect of the ruin of his plan for a new life, there is ordinary jealousy and vain regret that his sacrifice has now lost its significance. This complex of feelings is as logical as it is contradictory: the individual lives simultaneously in a number of different spheres, on a number of different levels, and in accordance with a number of different sources of his being that condition his different impulses. Nekhliudov is a truth seeker, but he is also an egoist, and not merely an egoist, but an intellectual egoist used to skimming cream even from his own spiritual sufferings.

The Tolstoian investigation of ethical levels and their corresponding impulses is presented in *Resurrection* in its most clear-cut form. This is especially true of his portrayal of the revolutionaries.

> Among them were people who had become revolutionaries because they sincerely considered it their duty to fight existing evil, but there were also those among them who had chosen that activity from motives that were egocentric and vain; the majority, however, were attracted to the revolution by a thirst for danger, risk, and the pleasure of playing with their lives, feelings that were familiar to Nekhliudov from his time in the military, and that are characteristic of energetic young people of the most ordinary kind. What distinguished these people from ordinary ones, however, and what was certainly in their favor, was the fact that the moral standards accepted among them were higher than those accepted among ordinary people. Not only were self-control, a strict mode of life, truthfulness, and unselfishness regarded as duties among them, but so was a readiness to sacrifice everything, even life itself, for the common cause. And therefore those among them who were above the average level were far above it, and models of an uncommon moral loftiness, while those among them who were below the average, were far below it, and people given to dishonesty and pretense, yet at the same time arrogant and proud. (Pt. 3, chap. 5)

What Tolstoi is in fact interested in here is a typology of impulses, and he first of all identifies in his members of the People's Will those traits that are political and those that are personal and common to all human beings. The revolutionary leader Novodvorov consists primarily of "political" traits, and Tolstoi condemns this intelligent man for his love of power, his arrogance, and his narrow views. The "political" in the "deacon's daughter," the pathetic and homely Vera Bogodukhovskaia with her naive talk about "propagandizing, disorganization, and groups, sections, and subsections" (pt. 1, chap. 55), is handled with mockery. But in human terms Vera Bogodukhovskaia is meek, kind, honest, and selfless. And lastly, there are among the members of the People's Will in *Resurrection* some frankly positive heroes, heroes of a type so completely positive, in fact, as to be rarely found in Tolstoi. There is Maria Pavlovna, for whom the revolution is subjectively a form of loving service to other people, and there is Kryl'tsov, who is completely consumed by compassion for the unfortunate and hatred of their oppressors. Tolstoi condemns the political goals and methods of the People's Will and he condemns certain individual members of it, or rather he condemns one or another type of revolutionary activist, while approving the moral function they share. That judgment is presented in the name of and from the point of view of Katiusha: "Such 'marvelous' people, as she put it, as those she was now with, she not only had never known but could not even have imagined. . . . She understood very easily and without effort the motives that guided them, and as someone who herself belonged to the people, she was in complete sympathy with them. She understood that they were for the people and against the masters, and the fact that they had sacrificed their privileges, their freedom, and their lives for the people even though they themselves belonged to the masters made her especially cherish and admire them" (pt. 3, chap. 3).

These words belong to the author, of course. Do they contradict his earlier assertion that many of the revolutionaries brought to the struggle personal and even frankly egocentric passions—love of power, vanity, and a hunger for strong sensations? In the final analysis, they do not contradict it. Involved here again is a very Tolstoian posing of the question, one not unlike the posing of the moral question in *War and Peace*: a certain general life situation has drawn the self-centered strivings of individual people into its service. The difference here is a fundamental one, however. The national war for Tolstoi was an objectively great fact of communal life, of life in general, whereas he denies the objective meaning of the People's Will, although he is prepared to acknowledge the moral value of its orientation of popular service. Individual human beings bring to its cause the impulses of self-esteem and love of power that are an inalienable part of them, and some of them even strive for a kind of revolutionary "career." Of course, to make a "career" by setting off to prison for the sake of the people is quite different from making one by means of baseness, treachery, and servility (and there are many careerists of this kind in *Resurrection*).

Resurrection gives a strict classification of the different impulses that have drawn people into the circle of the People's Will: Novodvorov—love of power, Kryl'tsov—hatred originating in wounded compassion, Simonson—a utopian cast of mind, Maria Pavlovna—love for other people, Rantseva—love for her husband, and Grabets—a desire to be pleasing to men.[34] The energy of these and many other impulses are transformed by the historical situation into the energy of sacrifice. In conferring on the revolutionary point of view, which was so alien to him, that capacity and that strength, Tolstoi paid it the tribute of lofty recognition.

In the last section of *War and Peace* Tolstoi propounded a metaphysical doctrine of the dual nature of the human being—determined in the material realm comprehended by reason, yet free and therefore responsible in the realm of "consciousness." In the artistic structures of Tolstoi, conditionality and responsibility are interrelated. Operative in the spiritual mechanisms of his characters are spontaneous and natural defensive reactions and egoistic desires. That which stands opposed to those reactions and desires is rooted just as naturally in the individual's innate sense of shared bonds. Serving as the concrete psychological expression of this sense of bond is the condition of love, tenderness, and pity "for all people" that is experienced by Tolstoian heroes of the most varied kind, whether Prince Andrei, Pierre, Levin, Nekhliudov, or Vasilii Brekhunov. For Tolstoi, this condition constitutes the highest ethical state (he called it religious). It is, moreover, a condition of happiness that eliminates the questions "What for?" and "What next?" that so tormented him during his period of crisis. Yet love and compassion, Tolstoi suggests, do not merely give themselves of their own accord to whoever desires them. They must be obtained by the individual himself. In a milieu that is incapable of fostering and cultivating them, they atrophy, disappearing with fearful ease, thereby opening the way for evil and cruelty. Tolstoi applied his terrible analytical test to the highest ethical acts as well, with their conditions, gradations, and masks. Free moral choice for him is therefore not one that is made independently of the causes and conditions that dispose and stimulate individuals to do good (or evil). Tolstoi requires not only the individual's organic predisposition to love and compassion, but also situations—from the broadest historical events to the most private and ephemeral of impressions—that, as they impinge on that individual and become ever more evident to him, painfully heighten his sense of pity.

Ethics showed what ought to be within the perspective of a free moral decision; nineteenth-century realism analyzed the real in terms of its social and biological conditionality. Ethics regarded behavior as involving *choice*; psychologism viewed that behavior as a simultaneity of logically contradictory impulses. Yet both ethics and psychologism sought to comprehend behavior, and it is therefore no coincidence that the greatest genius of psychological analysis was his whole life a tireless moralist who judged every movement of the characters he created.

Literature has always engaged in the depiction of human behavior, and ethics has therefore always been one of its internal, structural principles. The correlation between the two has taken an infinite variety of forms. The writings of Tolstoi are material of incomparable importance for the formulation of this theoretical question, since there is no other writer who concentrated so organically and so consciously on the connections between moral judgment and the psychological process.

While bringing about changes in the cognition of the individual human being, time has also introduced those changes into the artistic structures that have embodied that cognition, whether as the features of historical personality or as the maximally particularized motives of individual behavior.

Using literary material, both canonically artistic and documentary, I have traced in this book a sequence of transitions: from characteristics to personality, and thence to the psychological process; from paired oppositions to multifaceted historical and social conditionality; from direct relationships between feeling and word, between quality (motive) and action, and between action and its ethical value, to relationships that are complex and multivalent; and from the logically formal contradictions of rationalism and of romantic contrasts and polarities to the dynamic contradictions of the sociopsychological novel of the second half of the nineteenth century.

NOTES

Translator's Preface

1. L. Ia. Ginzburg, *O psikhologicheskoi proze* (Leningrad, 1971; rev. ed. Leningrad, 1977). The translation follows the revised edition.

2. For discussions of these and other matters see the collection of essays edited by Sarah Pratt in *Canadian-American Slavic Studies* 19, no. 2 (Summer 1985): 121–199; the introduction by Boris Gasparov to *The Semiotics of Russian Cultural History*, ed. A. D. Nakhimovsky and A. S. Nakhimovsky (Ithaca, 1985), 13–29; the contributions by various hands in *Literaturnoe obozrenie* 10 (October 1989): 78–86; and the corpus of Ginzburg's autobiographical and memoiristic writings contained in her *Literatura v poiskakh real'nosti* (Leningrad, 1987) and *Chelovek za pis'mennym stolom* (Leningrad, 1989).

Introduction

1. The works of D. S. Likhachev, especially his *Chelovek v literature drevnei Rusi* (Moscow, 1970), play an important methodological role in this regard.

2. G.W.F. Hegel, *Sämtliche Werke*, ed. Ludwig Boumann et al., 2d ed., 20 vols. (Stuttgart, 1927–1940), 14:244; English translation by T. M. Knox, G.W.F. Hegel, *Aesthetics*, 2 vols. (Oxford, 1975), 2:968–969. (Tr.)

3. V. G. Belinskii, *Polnoe sobranie sochinenii*, 13 vols. (Moscow, 1953–1959), 10:318, 316. Subsequent references to this edition are given in the text.

4. Characteristic too is the interdependence of the memoirist's own level and his rendering of the opinions of a remarkable contemporary. The naive and limited memoirist, even when he thinks he has transcribed everything scrupulously, is still unable to convey those opinions adequately. Tolstoi's conversations in the last years of his life are reflected in a number of memoirs and were immediately written down by the memoirists in the most painstaking way. Yet compare what Tolstoi says in the recollections of some of the Tolstoians, for example, with everything that he says—so exceptional in the power and freshness of its thought—in the memoirs of Gor'kii (*Lev Tolstoi: Zametki*). This discrepancy may of course be partly explained by the fact that people speak differently with different interlocutors, but only partly.

5. In practical terms, there is of course no definite boundary between documentary and artistic literature; only the extreme tendencies of each are intended here. Obviously there are a great many documentary works that make no claim whatever to having aesthetic significance.

6. A. I. Gertsen, *Sobranie sochinenii*, 30 vols. (Moscow, 1954–1964), 18:87. Subsequent references to this edition are given in the text.

7. Devoted to the specific nature of "literary personality" is S. Bocharov, "Kharaktery i obstoiatel'stva," in *Teoriia literatury: Osnovnye problemy v istoricheskom osveshchenii: Obraz, metod, kharakter* (Moscow, 1962).

8. S. L. Rubinshtein, *Printsipy i puti razvitiia psikhologii* (Moscow, 1959), 134. In regard to personality as a "functional and dynamic structure," see in particular K. Platonov, "Lichnostnyi podkhod kak printsip psikhologii," in *Metologicheskie i teoreticheskie problemy psikhologii* (Moscow, 1969), 197–198.

9. Rubinshtein, *Printsipy i puti*, 170.

10. Hegel, *Sämtliche Werke*, 12:112; *Aesthetics*, 1:73. I have slightly adjusted Knox's rendering here. (Tr.)

11. *Goethes Werke*, ed. Erich Trunz et al., 14 vols. (Hamburg, 1948–1960), 9:588; English translation by John Oxenford, *The Autobiography of Johann Wolfgang von Goethe*, 2 vols. (Chicago and London, 1974), 2:218. (Tr.)

12. William James, *The Principles of Psychology*, 2 vols. (1890; repr. New York, 1950), 1:294. (Tr.)

13. C. G. Jung, *Psychologischen Typen* (Leipzig and Stuttgart, 1925), 663–664; English translation by R.F.C. Hull, *Psychological Types* (Princeton, 1950), 464. (Tr.)

14. *Filosofskaia entsiklopediia*, 5 vols. (Moscow, 1960–1970), 3:481–483. (Tr.)

15. V. Shtoff, *Modelirovanie i filosofiia* (Moscow and Leningrad, 1966), 33.

16. *Goethes Gesprache mit Eckermann*, ed. Edith Zenker (Berlin, 1955), 212; English translation by John Oxenford, *Conversations of Goethe with Eckermann* (London, 1874), 154. (Tr.)

17. For a more detailed discussion of this issue, see my "O strukture literaturnogo personazha," in *Iskusstvo slova* (Moscow, 1973), 376–388.

18. I have in mind here the typological and psychological identification of the literary character. The phrase "identification of the hero" is commonly used in another sense to mean the discovery of his name, birth, social position, and family connections.

19. For a discussion of this issue, see my *O lirike* (Leningrad, 1974), especially chap. 3, "Problema lichnosti."

20. In his *Biografiia i kul'tura* (Moscow, 1927), G. Vinokur defines biography as "personal life in history," at the same time emphasizing that the personality studied by the biographer is a structure with its own expressive forms and style of behavior.

21. K. Marks and F. Engel's, *Sochineniia*, 2d ed., 50 vols. (Moscow, 19551981), 8:120. The text in question is Marx's *Der achtzehnte Brumaire des Louis Bonaparte* (1852). (Tr.)

22. S.-A. Sainte-Beuve, *Causeries du lundi*, 15 vols. (Paris, 1851–1870), 3:389 (Tr.). Although Saint-Beuve uses the word "model" [*modèle*], his understanding of the term obviously differs from that of contemporary usage.

23. H. Taine, *Essais de critique et d'histoire* (Paris, 1887), 209.

24. In *M. Iu. Lermontov v vospominaniiakh sovremennikov* (Moscow, 1964), 37.

25. Beketova even devoted an article to this topic: "Veselost' i iumor Bloka"; see the collection *O Bloke* (Moscow, 1929).

26. *M. Iu. Lermontov v vospominaniiakh sovremennikov*, 287.

27. Ricarda Huch, *Die Romantik: Blütezeit, Ausbreitung und Verfall* (Tübingen, 1951); see especially the chapter "Der romantische Charakter."

28. V. M. Zhirmunskii's *Religioznoe otrechenie v istorii romantizma* (Moscow, 1919) is to a considerable extent devoted to the "life-art" of the late German (Heidelberg) romantics. Louis Maigron in his *Le Romantisme et les moeurs: Essais d'étude historique et sociale d'après documents inédits* (Paris, 1910), a book that made quite a stir in its day, examines romanticism in everyday social life from a sharply antiromantic position. A Russian translation was published in 1914. The book's subjects are men and women who have reproduced a series of romantic clichés in their lives (a game with frequently fatal results); Maigron calls these people "reflected beings" (*créatures de reflet*). I touch on the problems of "life-art" in connection with Russian romanticism in the 1830s (especially with respect to the young Herzen) in my *Byloe i dumy Gertsena* (Leningrad, 1957), 110–119.

29. N. Evreinov sought to draw theoretical conclusions about its consequences in his *Teatr dlia sebia* (Petrograd, 1915–1916), as well as in his *Teatr kak takovoi (Obosnovanie teatral' nosti v smysle polozhitel'nogo nachala stsenicheskogo iskusstva v zhizni)* (Moscow, 1923). In *Teatr dlia sebia* Evreinov even suggests a number of brief scenarios that might be acted out in life by a single character.

30. Letter to L. I. Volkonskaia, May 3, 1885, in L. N. Tolstoi, *Polnoe sobranie sochinenii*, 90 vols. (Moscow, 1928–1958), 61:80. Subsequent references to this edition are given in the text.

PART ONE

BAKUNIN, STANKEVICH, AND THE CRISIS OF ROMANTICISM

1. For a discussion of the Herzen-Ogarev circle and of the problem of personality as it was understood by the young Herzen, see my *Byloe i dumy Gertsena*, especially the chapter "Evoliutsiia geroia."

2. The "wisdom lovers" of the 1820s would become the Slavophiles of the 1840s. Anti-individualism was a fundamental part of the Slavophile worldview, and the working out of the problems of the contemporary introspective personality was therefore impossible in that circle.

3. The most sentimental of the sentimentalists, Prince Shalikov, was in command of the military unit that was most brutal in suppressing the peasant uprising in the Tula province in 1797.

4. A. N. Veselovskii, *V. A. Zhukovskii: Poeziia chuvstva i "serdechnogo voobrazheniia"* (Petrograd, 1918). (Tr.)

5. John Mason, *Self Knowledge: A Treatise Showing the Nature and Benefit of That Important Science and the Way to Attain It* (Boston, 1800; first published in London in 1745), pt. 1, chap. 1; published in Russian as *Ioanna Masona poznanie samogo sebia* (Moscow, 1783). All citations in the text refer to the 1800 English version. (Tr.)

6. *Dnevniki V. A. Zhukovskogo* (St. Petersburg, 1903), 12.

7. Ibid., 27–28.

8. V. A. Zhukovskii, *Sobranie sochinenii*, 4 vols. (Moscow and Leningrad, 1959–1960), 4:453.

9. Ibid., 4:476–477.

10. Ibid., 4:454.

11. Michel Montaigne, *Oeuvres complètes*, ed. Albert Thibaudet and Maurice Rat (Paris, 1962), 959; English translation by Donald Frame, *The Complete Essays of Montaigne* (Stanford, 1958), 750. (Tr.)

12. M. A. Bakunin, *Sobranie sochinenii i pisem*, 4 vols. (Moscow, 1934–1935), 1:42. Subsequent references to this edition are given in the text.

13. Cited in A. A. Kornilov, *Molodye gody Mikhaila Bakunina* (Moscow, 1915), 9, 30–32.

14. V. M. Zhirmunskii, *Nemetskii romantizm i sovremennaia mistika* (St. Petersburg, 1914), 109–110.

15. N. P. Ogarev, *Izbrannye sotsial'no-politicheskie i filosofskie proizvedeniia*, 2 vols. (Moscow, 1952–1956), 2:262.

16. *Russkaia mysl'* 10 (1889): 7–8. M. Gershenzon has adduced data demonstrating that while he was a student in St. Petersburg at the beginning of the 1830s, Pecherin was experiencing similar moods: M. Gershenzon, *Zhizn' V. S. Pecherina* (Moscow, 1910), 11.

17. Ogarev, *Izbrannye . . . proizvedeniia*, 2:273.

18. Ibid., 2:306.

19. All of these episodes have been elucidated in detail in the Bakunin literature, especially by Kornilov in *Molodye gody*.

20. Ibid., 155–156.

21. Tat'iana Bakunina's letters to Turgenev have been published by N. L. Brodskii in "'Premukhinskii roman' v zhizni i tvorchestve Turgeneva," in *I. S. Turgenev* 2 (Moscow and Petrograd, 1923); see also L. V. Krestova, "Tat'iana Bakunina i Turgenev," in *Turgenev i ego vremia* (Moscow and Petrograd, 1923).

22. I. S. Turgenev, *Polnoe sobranie sochinenii i pisem*, 28 vols. (Moscow and Leningrad, 1960–1968); *Pis'ma*, 1:220–221. Subsequent references to this edition are to Turgenev, *Pis'ma* or *Sochineniia*.

23. Kornilov, *Molodye gody*, 666–667.

24. An extremely small number of Bakunin's letters to his friends and acquaintances in the 1830s has in fact survived. Obviously, the addressees or their families destroyed his letters after he was declared a state criminal. Lost too are his immense letters to Belinskii, documents of great importance for the history of the spiritual development of both figures. One is therefore compelled to base one's evaluation of the young Bakunin's correspondence on the few extant letters to A. Afremev, Stankevich, Ketscher, Neverov, and S. N. Murav'ev (see Bakunin, *Sobranie sochinenii i pisem*, vols. 1–2).

25. Written in 1840. One should mention that Bakunin's letters not infrequently had an ulterior motive. In this instance he needed to elicit Stankevich's sympathy, since he hoped to obtain his help in connection with his proposed trip abroad.

26. Kornilov, *Molodye gody*, 162, 165.

27. *T. N. Granovskii i ego perepiska*, 2 vols. (Moscow, 1897), 1:375, 383, 403.

28. *Literaturnoe nasledstvo* 56 (Moscow, 1950), 117.

29. N. G. Chernyshevskii, *Polnoe sobranie sochinenii*, 16 vols. (Moscow, 1939–1953), 7:449.

30. Turgenev, *Pis'ma*, 5:47; see N. Ostrovskaia, *Vospominaniia* (Petrograd, 1915), 95, for similar statements by Turgenev.

31. See L. P. Grossman and V. P. Polonskii, *Spor o Bakunine i Dostoevskom* (Leningrad, 1926), and A. Borovoi and N. Otverzhennyi, *Mif o Bakunine* (Moscow, 1925).

32. M. M. Bakhtin, *Problemy poetiki Dostoevskogo* (Moscow, 1972), 151–154.

33. P. V. Annenkov, *Vospominaniia i kriticheskie ocherki*, 3 vols. (St. Petersburg, 1877–1881), 3:382.

34. Turgenev, *Sochineniia*, 6:393.

35. *T. N. Granovskii i ego perepiska*, 2:101.

36. K. Aksakov, *Vospominaniia studentstva* (St. Petersburg, 1911), 19.

37. Turgenev, *Sochineniia*, 6:394.

38. Letter to A. A. Tolstaia (60:274). In a letter written at the same time to Chicherin, Tolstoi also said of Stankevich, "Here is someone I could have loved as I do myself" (60:272).

39. Stankevich's letters attest to a steady movement toward "simplicity and normality." An elevated romantic phraseology still shows through in the earliest of his letters (especially those to Neverov written in the first half of the 1830s), but thereafter it rapidly decreases, and when it does reemerge, it does so only in relation to specific situations and addressees—for example, the 1840 letter to V. A. D'iakova in which Stankevich's last love is reflected. Generally speaking, the language of Stankevich's letters is the language of unconstrained friendly conversation in which "humorous banter" alternates with philosophical meditation.

40. Stankevich's attempts at verse (which he quickly abandoned) are typical, if rather unsuccessful, specimens of the romantic poetry of the 1830s.

41. See the commentary to "Andrei Kolosov" in Turgenev, *Sochineniia*, 6:546, for a discussion of this matter.

42. An earlier phenomenon was the "George Sandism" of the 1830s and 1840s to which both Belinskii and Herzen and the people of Herzen's circle paid tribute.

43. A. V. Druzhinin, *Sobranie sochinenii*, 8 vols. (St. Petersburg, 1865–1867), 6:307.

44. *Perepiska N. V. Stankevicha (1830–1840)* (Moscow, 1914), 626–627. Subsequent references to this edition are given in the text.

45. Devoted to Belinskii's letters in particular are "Perepiska Belinskogo (kritiko-bibliograficheskii obzor)," in *Literaturnoe nasledstvo 56* (Moscow, 1950); and Mark Poliakov, "Vsia zhizn' moia v pis'makh," in *Poeziia kriticheskoi mysli* (Moscow, 1968).

PART TWO
BELINSKII AND THE EMERGENCE OF REALISM

1. A. N. Pypin, *Belinskii, ego zhizn' i perepiska*, 2 vols. (St. Petersburg, 1876). (Tr.)

2. For a discussion of Belinskii's letters to Bakunin in reference to the history of the relations between the two men, see V. G. Berezina, "Belinskii i Bakunin v 1830-e gody," Uchenye zapiski Leningradskogo universiteta 58, no. 17 (1952).

3. In an 1840 letter to Botkin (2:573), for example, Belinskii spoke of his "fantastic and ridiculous nature."

4. Annenkov, *Vospominaniia*, 3:327, 329, 340.

5. Ibid., 3:334.

6. K. Rosenkranz, *Psychologie, oder die Wissenschaft vom subjektiven Geist* (Königsberg, 1837). In his preface Rosenkranz writes that his book is a concise elaboration of the principles of Hegelian "Psychologie" (as the third part of the first section of Hegel's *Philosophie des Geistes* is called).

7. G.W.F. Hegel, *Enzyklopädie der philosophischen Wissenschaften im Grundisse*; the English translation is from *Hegel's Philosophy of Subjective Spirit*, ed. and trans. with an introduction and notes by M. J. Petry, 3 vols., rev. ed. (Dordrecht and Boston, 1979), 1:6–8. (Tr.) Bakunin could not have known these lines in 1837, since they are part of the addenda included in the 1845 edition of the *Philosophie des Geistes*.

8. Subsequently, in his 1843 review of the works of Nikolai Polevoi, Belinskii wrote of vain attempts to introduce the term *prekrasnodushie* into current usage, even though it was "a clumsy one in Russian translation" (6:671–672).

9. Kornilov, *Molodye gody*, 467–468. I have italicized the circle terminology.

10. Ibid., 491.

11. Ibid., 515–516. We also find Hegelian terminology in Botkin's love letters to A. A. Bakunina: "It seems to me that I shall never be able to give that infinite content that fills me a definite, real form. What is necessary is that the reality that must surround you become a reflection of the gossamer poetry of your inner world" (ibid., 527).

12. For a characterization of Botkin's personality and his socio-political and aesthetic views, see B. F. Egorov, "V. P. Botkin—literator i kritik" 1–3, *Uchenye zapiski Tartuskogo universiteta: Trudy po russkoi i slavianskoi filologii* 6 (1963), 8 (1965), 9 (1966).

13. Ibid., vol. 9 (1966): 42–43. (Tr.)

14. Ibid., vol. 6 (1963): 27. (Tr.)

15. Kornilov, *Molodye gody*, 555.

16. I am quoting from the first edition of *The Inspector General*; the 1841 version was revised.

17. *T. N. Granovskii i ego perepiska*, 2:383.

18. These questions had already been posed at the beginning of the 1830s in Herzen and Ogarev's circle under the influence of the idea of the "rehabilitation of the flesh" that was a fundamental part of Saint-Simon's philosophy and of early utopian socialism in general.

19. Belinskii's most important declarations on this matter belong to his articles from the beginning of the 1840s on the issue of the ideal and the real to which Russian aesthetic thought of the 1820s and 1830s had given such close scrutiny. See my "Gertsen i voprosy estetiki ego vremeni," in *Problemy izucheniia Gertsena* (Moscow, 1963), 122–146.

20. Herzen usually understood materialism as mechanical materialism, whereas he gave the term "realism" to the worldview he adopted in the 1840s.

21. B. O. Korman examines the problem of shyness in the psychic life of the plebeian intellectual and the social conditionality of that phenomenon in connection with Nekrasov's poem "Shyness." Though primarily concerned with later

phenomena, Korman touches on Belinskii as well. See his *Lirika N. A. Nekrasova* (Voronezh, 1964), 127–142.

22. It is curious that some two years later Belinskii discovered "ugliness" in Bakunin. This occurs in a letter to Botkin describing a confrontation between Bakunin and Katkov that ended in blows: "His face was pale, although two unpleasantly crimson spots decorated his cheeks, and his already disgusting lips were simply turned into a parallelogram. I had long held his ugliness in contempt, but I became utterly convinced then that he is extremely ugly. It is hard to imagine any woman loving him, and to tell the truth I do not understand how his sisters can kiss him" (11:543).

23. This is treated in more detail in my article, "Belinskii v bor'be s romanticheskim idealizmom," in *Literaturnoe nasledstvo 55* (Moscow, 1948), 185–202.

24. Apollon Grigor'ev, *Polnoe sobranie sochinenii i pisem*, 12 vols. (Petrograd, 1918), 1:127.

25. Even the concrete content of the moral-psychological problems faced by Belinskii was very "Tolstoian." "We shall now investigate," he wrote to Bakunin in 1837, "more fundamentally and profoundly the reasons for my insignificance despite an abundance of the life principle. . . . There are two main deficiencies in me: vanity and sensuality" (2:168). This is very similar to the entries in Tolstoi's early diaries.

26. In his article "Iz studencheskikh let L. N. Tolstogo," B. M. Eikhenbaum notes that D. I. Meier, the University of Kazan' professor who had such influence on Tolstoi as a student, was ideologically linked to Belinskii's circle and the journal *National Annals*. Tolstoi's highly interested and sympathetic reading of Belinskii's articles is discussed in Eikhenbaum's "Nasledie Belinskogo i Lev Tolstoi." Both articles are included in his *O proze* (Leningrad, 1969).

27. In 1864 Turgenev wrote in the lyrical essay "Enough" that to man "alone is it given to 'create' . . . , but it is a strange and terrible thing to say, 'we are creators . . . for an hour,' just as it is a strange and terrible thing to be caliph for an hour, as the phrase has it. . . . Everyone more or less vaguely understands his significance, and senses his kinship to something lofty and eternal, but knows that he lives, and must live, in the moment and only for a moment."

28. Speshnev was to a certain extent the prototype of Stavrogin, and Petrashevskii, of Petr Verkhovenskii.

29. F. M. Dostoevskii, *Dnevnik pisatelia za 1873 i 1876 gody* (Moscow and Leningrad, 1929), 8.

30. Letter of 1839 concerning Anna Shchepkina and Katkov.

31. See A. S. Dolinin, *Poslednie romany Dostoevskogo* (Moscow and Leningrad, 1963), 233ff.

32. A. N. Pypin, "V. G. Belinskii: Opyt biografii," *Vestnik Evropy* 2 (1875): 617.

PART ONE
SAINT-SIMON'S *MÉMOIRES* AND THE RATIONALIST SCHEMA

1. The text used in the following discussion is Saint-Simon, *Mémoires*, ed. Gonzague Truc, 7 vols. (Paris, 1953–1961). Subsequent references to this edition are given in the text.

2. Sainte-Beuve, *Causeries du lundi*, 3:274.

3. In this sense their fate was not unlike that of *My Past and Thoughts*. Herzen's great work remained proscribed for decades in Russia and was known to only a relatively small circle of readers.

4. That archive consists of 277 bound volumes, folders, and portfolios with documents, including the eleven autograph volumes containing the finished text of the *Mémoires*.

5. *Journal du M. de Dangeau . . . avec les additions inédites du duc de Saint-Simon*, 19 vols. (Paris, 1854–1860).

6. There are a number of investigations devoted to the creative history of the *Mémoires*. See A. Chéruel, *Saint-Simon considéré comme historien de Louis XIV* (Paris, 1865), chap. 9; and Yves Coirault, *Les "Additions" de Saint-Simon au "Journal" de Dangeau: Perspectives sur la genèse des Mémoires* (Paris, 1965) and *L'Optique de Saint-Simon: Essai sur les formes de son imagination et de sa sensibilité d'après les Mémoires* (Paris, 1965), 479–482.

7. Chateaubriand, *La Vie de Rancé*, as quoted by Gonzague Truc in the Introduction to his edition of the *Mémoires* (1:xxi). (Tr.)

8. Chéruel, *Saint-Simon considéré comme un historien de Louis XIV*. (Tr.)

9. Sainte-Beuve, *Causeries du lundi*, 15:424.

10. Taine, *Essais de critique et d'histoire*, 241.

11. See André Le Breton, *La Comédie humaine de Saint-Simon* (Paris, 1914), and J. de La Varende, *Monsieur le duc de Saint-Simon et sa comédie humaine* (Paris, 1955).

12. Charles Sarolea, *La Cour de Louis XIV* (Paris,1911), 20.

13. Herbert De Ley, *Marcel Proust et le duc de Saint-Simon* (Urbana and London, 1966), 122.

14. Taine, *Essais de critique et d'histoire*, 249–250.

15. Though the memoirs of La Rochefoucauld are memoirs of the chronicle variety, but they are nonetheless distinguished by the art of psychological characterization. This is even more true of the brilliant portraits in the memoirs of Cardinal Retz.

16. Even earlier René Doumic had asserted that Saint-Simon in essence applied to reality images that had been informed by his imagination: *Saint-Simon: La France de Louis XIV* (Paris, 1920).

17. The preface warns against exaggeration and underestimation, against all the traps of "feeling, taste and imagination. . . . All . . . must give way to the smallest and least significant truth" (1:5). In other words, Saint-Simon condemns everything that constitutes his own strength as a writer.

18. The English translation of this passage is by Lucy Norton: *Historical Memoirs of the Duc de Saint-Simon*, 2 vols. (New York, 1968), 2:135–141. I have adjusted her version slightly. (Tr.)

19. "The king discusses the rank of his bastards gravely and at length, as if it were an affair of state," Taine writes. As a consequence, a number of intricate differences between them and the peers and the princes of the blood are devised. For example, the president of *Parlement*, "in asking the [Duc du Maine's] advice, will call him by his name, just as he does the peers, but with his hat in his hand and held a little less low than it would be for the princes of the blood, who are merely

looked at without being named. . . . He will be met and escorted in a coach by a single usher, in contrast to the princes of the blood, who are met and escorted by two ushers, and to the peers, who are neither met nor escorted" (*Essais de critique et d'histoire*, 217–218).

20. See Le Breton, *La Comédie humaine de Saint-Simon*, 163.

21. *Correspondance complète de Madame, la duchesse d'Orléans*, trans. M. G. Brunet, 2 vols. (Paris, 1863), 1:15. Subsequent references to this edition are given in the text.

22. De Ley, *Marcel Proust et le duc de Saint-Simon*, 34.

23. Bussy-Rabutin, *L'Histoire amoureuse des Gaules*, 2 vols. (Paris, 1868), 1:105. (Tr.)

24. Let me cite one more scene in the spirit of a kind of burlesqued Saint-Simonian naturalism: "At the dauphine's funeral," Madame writes, "when I was I going up to make my offering, I was carrying a candle and, nota bene, gold pieces for the bishop who was singing the high mass and who was sitting in an armchair close by the altar. He wanted to give the candle to the priests from the king's chapel who were serving the mass, but the monks from Saint-Denis ran up at full speed, claiming that the candle and the gold pieces belonged to them. They threw themselves on the bishop, causing his armchair to rock back and forth and knocking his miter off his head. If I had lingered an instant longer, the bishop and all his monks would have fallen on me, and so I quickly jumped down the four steps of the altar . . . and watched the battle; it was impossible to keep from laughing, and everybody else did too" (*Correspondance*, 2:141–142).

25. *Mémoires de Madame de la Fayette precédés de la Princesse de Clèves* (Paris, n. d.), 262–263.

26. Gustave Lanson, *L'Art de prose* (Paris, 1909), 127–128.

27. La Bruyère, *Oeuvres complètes*, ed. Julien Benda (Paris, 1951), 271. Subsequent references to this edition are given in the text. (Tr.)

28. We also find textual coincidences in the characterization of the great adventuress and intriguer, the princesse des Ursins, a feminine version of the predatory type. Of Barbezieux: "The best and the most useful friend . . . ; and as an enemy the most dangerous, the most terrible, . . . the most implacable, and naturally savage" (1:818); of des Ursins: "She was an ardent and excellent friend, whose friendship was weakened neither by time nor separation, and who in consequence was a cruel and implacable enemy, ready even to follow her hatred into hell." Immediately following this are formulas that coincide with the characterizations of both Barbezieux and Harcourt: "She was uniquely endowed with charm, art, and niceness of judgment, and with an eloquence that was simple and natural" (1:955).

29. François, duc de la Rochefoucauld, *Oeuvres complètes*, ed. L. Martin-Chauffier and Jean Marchaud (Paris, 1964). The quotations are from La Rochefoucauld's "Reflexions ou sentences et maximes morales" (1678), nos. 2, 472, 301, and 18 respectively. (Tr.)

30. Beginning with Sainte-Beuve, it has been noted in the literature devoted to Saint-Simon that individual characters in the *Mémoires* frequently consist of two moieties: first the character's good qualities are enumerated, then his defects. That duality, however, frequently turns out to be illusory in those instances where the

character's good qualities are calculated merely to conceal his defects. It is then that both moieties serve, in essence, a single-dimensional negative depiction in which the character's other sins are dominated by hypocrisy. Hypocrisy, along with self-interest and vanity, was a principal sin in the seventeenth-century moral code.

31. It is interesting to compare Saint-Simon's attitude toward Louis XIV with his high regard for the personality and accomplishments of Peter I, whom he calls a great monarch.

32. For a discussion of the significance of form and etiquette in Saint-Simon's depiction of the "Versailles machinery," see De Ley, *Marcel Proust et le duc de Saint-Simon*, 31–35, 95. De Ley says in particular, "Examples of [the king's] insensitivity are at the same time examples of [his] concern that the succession of ceremonies and amusements continue without interruption—of concern, that is, for the form of aristocratic life" (31).

33. "To obtain an audience with her was no easier than to obtain one with the king," Saint-Simon notes (4:1037).

PART TWO
ROUSSEAU'S *CONFESSIONS* AND THE
MODIFICATIONS OF PERSONALITY

1. J. Guéhenno, *Jean-Jacques: Histoire d'une conscience*, 2d ed., 2 vols. (Paris, 1962). Guéhenno's book was first published in 1948.

2. Jean-Jacques Rousseau, *Oeuvres complètes*, ed. Bernard Gagnebin and Marcel Raymond, 3 vols. (Paris, 1959): vol. 1, *Les Confessions: Autres textes autobiographiques*, 277–278; English translation by J. M. Cohen, *The Confessions of Jean-Jacques Rousseau* (Baltimore, 1954), 261–262. Subsequent references to these editions are given in the text, the French cited first. (Tr.)

3. Montaigne, *Oeuvres complètes*, 358; *The Complete Essays*, 273. Subsequent references to these editions are given in the text, the French cited first (Tr.). Rousseau engages in a polemic with Montaigne precisely because it was Montaigne (with his Renaissance interest in personality) who was his rival, and not the moralists of the seventeenth century. For La Rochefoucauld, it was the mainsprings of the individual's behavior—of the generalized individual, that is—that were the chief thing; for Pascal, it was the generalized individual taken at the very foundations of his moral and spiritual being. Pascal did not approve of Montaigne's empiricism, especially his endeavor to investigate individual personality. Pascal spoke of Montaigne's "silly project of describing himself," and declared that Montaigne "talked too much about himself" (Pascal, *Oeuvres complètes*, ed. Jacques Chevalier [Paris, 1954], 1103–1104 [Tr.]).

4. This unrealized plan was conceived in 1756. For the significance of the idea of *morale sensitive* in Rousseau's oeuvre, see Marcel Raymond, *Jean-Jacques Rousseau: La Quête de soi et la rêverie* (Paris, 1962), 42. Raymond observes that a "sensationalist morality" coexisted in Rousseau with moral rigorism. See also G. May, *Rousseau par lui-même* (Paris, 1961), 70.

5. Claude Adrien Helvétius, *Oeuvres complètes*, intro. Yvon Belaval, 14 vols. (Hildesheim, 1967–1969), 8:41. (Tr.)

6. Rousseau, *Oeuvres complètes*, 1:1051. Subsequent references to this edition of the *Rêveries* are given in the text. (Tr.)

7. Jean-Jacques Rousseau, *Les Confessions*, ed. Jacques Voisine (Paris, 1980), 790–792. (Tr.)

8. This of course does not include those pages in the second part of the *Confessions* that are distinguished by Rousseau's morbid suspiciousness and his hatred of his enemies.

9. Rousseau, *Oeuvres complètes*, 1:820. Subsequent references to this edition of the *Dialogues* are given in the text. (Tr.).

10. Rousseau offers a justification of sensuality in passing: the sensual person is natural rather than rational.

11. Rousseau, *Oeuvres complètes*, 1:1134. (Tr.)

12. I. V. Pavlov, *Izbrannye trudy* (Moscow, 1954), 276.

13. Her main reason for fleeing to Savoy was of course the scandalous failure of one of her enterprises (a silk-stocking factory).

14. Rousseau speaks of Anet, a talented self-taught botanist, with respect and sympathy.

15. The duchesse de Longueville was famous for her energetic activity during the period of the Fronde.

16. Rousseau's biographers have even been of the opinion that these sentiments of Madame de Warens exercised an influence on Rousseau's religious thought and were in part the basis for his celebrated *Profession de foi du vicaire savoyard*.

17. Havelock Ellis, *From Rousseau to Proust* (Boston and New York, 1935), 51.

18. I have in mind primarily the late romantics here. For the early, Jena romantics the duality of the flesh and ideal love was not yet characteristic, as is demonstrated for example by Friedrich Schlegel's novel *Lucinde*.

19. Arthur Chuquet, *Jean-Jacques Rousseau* (Paris, 1893), 198–199.

20. The reference is to the fact that in the *Republic* the rearing of children was left entirely to the state.

21. She meant women of the upper classes whom Rousseau had inspired with the need to renounce the use of wet nurses.

PART THREE

HERZEN'S *MY PAST AND THOUGHTS* AND HISTORICAL IDENTITY

1. *My Past and Thoughts* is examined here mainly in terms of the problems that are the subject of the present book. Some of the questions touched on in this section are treated in more detail in my *Byloe i dumy Gertsena*.

2. See B. M. Eikhenbaum, *Lev Tolstoi*, 2 vols. (Moscow and Leningrad, 1928–1931), 1:80–96.

3. See *Dnevniki S. A Tolstoi, 1860–1891* (Moscow, 1928), 8–29; and P. Biriukov, *Lev Nikolaevich Tolstoi: Biografiia*, 3d ed., 2 vols. (Moscow and Petrograd, 1923), 1:232–235.

4. B. G. Reizov, *Frantsuzskaia romanticheskaia istoriografiia (1815–1830)* (Leningrad, 1965), 367.

5. Annenkov, *Vospominaniia*, 91.

6. Eikhenbaum regarded as convincing Bartenev's argument that the proto-type of old Prince Bolkonskii was in large measure Count M. F. Kamenskii (*Lev Tolstoi*, 2:263).

7. *Literaturnoe nasledstvo* 61 (Moscow, 1953), 674. *My Confession* remained unfinished. The surviving text covers only Ogarev's childhood and adolescence.

8. M. O. Gershenzon, ed., *Russkie propilei*, 6 vols. (Moscow, 1915–1919), 4:263–266. (Tr.)

PART ONE
CAUSAL CONDITIONALITY

1. *Les Lettres françaises* 764 (March 12–18, 1959): 4. (Tr.)

2. G. A. Gukovskii, *Pushkin i russkie romantiki* (Moscow, 1965), 45. (Tr.)

3. Through an analysis of the novels of Jean-Paul Richter, M. L. Tronskaia shows how unsuccessful at this level early attempts to create a contradictory unity of ironical personality were; that personality inevitably disintegrated into sepa-rate elements (*Nemetskii sentimental'no-iumoristicheskii roman epokhi Prosve-shcheniia* [Leningrad, 1965], 132ff).

4. I have addressed the issue of the significance for the development of realism of romantic irony with its changeable values and shifts between the sublime and the quotidian and the tragic and the ridiculous in my works of the 1930s: "K postanovke voprosa realizma v pushkinskoi literature," in *Pushkin: Vremennik Pushkinskoi komissii* 2 (Moscow and Leningrad, 1936), 387–401, and *Tvorch-eskii put' Lermontova* (Leningrad, 1940). Of particular concern in these works is the significance of irony in the artistic system of *Eugene Onegin*.

5. In Shoderlo de Laklo, *Opasnie sviazi* (Moscow and Leningrad, 1965), 343.

6. V. P. Grib has noted that in La Fayette's novel there are (in the spirit of La Rochefoucauld) "permanent links between the lofty and base impulses of human nature: between egoism, self-love, and self-preservation, on the one hand, and the most sublime feelings, on the other" (in his *Izbrannye raboty* [Moscow, 1956], 344).

7. Madame de la Fayette, *Romans et nouvelles*, ed. Émile Magne (Paris, 1961), 388. (Tr.)

8. Benjamin Constant, *Oeuvres*, ed. Alfred Roulin (Paris, 1957), 22. Subse-quent references to this edition are given in the text. (Tr.)

9. Anna Akhmatova in her article "*Adol'f* Benzhamena Konstana v tvorch-estve Pushkina" noted that "in *Adolphe* Constant showed for the first time the duality of the human psyche, the relationship of the conscious to the unconscious, and the role of suppressed feelings, and he revealed the true impulses behind human actions. It is for this reason that *Adolphe* has been called 'the father of the psychological novel.'" In *Pushkin: Vremennik Pushkinskoi komissii* 1 (Moscow and Leningrad, 1936), 98–99.

10. In his own copy of *Adolphe* Pushkin underlined the last word of this sen-tence ("plaisir") and in the margin wrote "bonheur."

11. Werther of course also has a personality. He is someone given to "storms and stresses," and it is no accident that he became a prototype and idol for *Sturm*

und Drang. In the context of the novel, however, Werther's *Sturm und Drang* qualities are a mechanism that is set in motion by his passion for Lotte. It is this feeling that is the novel's true object of depiction.

12. Stendhal, *Romans et nouvelles*, ed. Henri Martineau (Paris, 1952), 541; English translation by C. K. Scott-Moncrieff, *The Red and the Black*, 2 vols. (New York, 1926), 2:146. Subsequent references to these editions are given in the text, the French cited first. (Tr.)

13. Honoré de Balzac, *La Comédie humaine*, ed. Marcel Bouteron, 10 vols. (Paris, 1948–1952), 2:918. (Tr.)

14. Ibid., 4:588–589. (Tr.)

15. B. G. Reizov, *Tvorchestvo Flobera* (Moscow, 1955), 137.

16. Ibid., 414–415ff.

17. Gustave Flaubert, *Oeuvres*, ed. A. Thibaudet and R. Dumesnil, 2 vols. (Paris, 1951–1952), 2:34; English translation by Perdita Burlingame, *The Sentimental Education* (New York, 1972), 8. Subsequent references to these editions are given in the text, the French cited first. (Tr.)

18. The classical prototype in this regard is Rousseau's *La Nouvelle Héloïse*. Saint-Preux's passion at first meets the obstacle of Julie's virtue; that obstacle is then replaced by social obstacles that are the consequence of the aristocratic prejudices of her father. After her marriage to Wolmar, the obstacle is once again Julie's virtue, this time that of a wife and mother. It is at this point that internal obstacles appear for the first time in Saint-Preux: duty, honor, and respect for the domestic hearth. Aspirations and obstacles are arranged in Rousseau's novel along a straight line that follows the sequence of events.

19. Turgenev, *Sochineniia*, 12:303.

20. Hjalmar Hjorth Boyesen, "A Visit to Tourguéneff," *The Galaxy* 17 (April 1874): 462. (Tr.)

21. L. V. Pumpianskii, "Romany Turgeneva i roman 'Nakanune,'" in I. S. Turgenev, *Sobranie sochinenii* (Moscow and Leningrad, 1930), 6:11.

22. Turgenev's striving for images that were characterologically stable and socially and historically definitive understandably precluded psychologism of the Tolstoian or even of the Flaubertian variety. Turgenev's numerous antianalytical statements are well known, as is his irritated criticism of Lev Tolstoi's "quasi-subtle reflections and cogitations." These statements may be found in A. G. Tseitlin's *Masterstvo Turgeneva-romanista* (Moscow, 1958) in the chapter entitled "Romany Turgeneva: Rabota nad obrazom."

23. *Les Lettres françaises* 839 (September 1–7, 1960): 2. (Tr.)

24. Tolstoi's diaries had a variety of purposes. In the early entries, along with self-cultivation and moral exercises, one finds the professional exercises of the writer—Tolstoi's first experimentation with his future methods. Included at this point are notations that register in summary fashion his day-to-day activity. As the writing becomes more professional, this experimentation assumes preparatory forms of another kind: preliminary drafts, plans, and rough drafts. The concern of the diaries is now to fix the passage of life, sometimes in its "accidental" phenomena, but phenomena that are in any case important for the individual's moral development.

25. Apparently the only time he ever said anything directly about himself was

in an 1870 letter to Maikov in connection with his projected *Life of a Great Sinner*: "The main question addressed in all these parts is the same one I have been consciously and unconsciously tormented by all my life—the question of the existence of God"; F. M. Dostoevskii, *Pis'ma* (Moscow and Leningrad, 1930), 2:263. And in another letter written the same year to Katkov, there is a phrase about Stavrogin: "I took him from my own heart" (*ibid.*, 2:289).

26. P. L. Biriukov, *Lev Nikolaevich Tolstoi: Biografiia*, 2:96.

27. The problem of "life in general" in Tolstoi is addressed in my article "O romane Tolstogo *Voina i mir*," *Zvezda* 1 (1944): 125–138.

28. Konstantin Leont'ev, *Sobranie sochinenii*, 12 vols. (Moscow, 1912–1914), 8:283, 291.

29. Prince Andrei's aristocratic background in combination with his self-possession and reserve yield different derived qualities. There are also supplementary social nuances: Bolkonskii is a scion of the old aristocracy, whereas Bezukhov belongs to the new nobility created by Ekaterina II.

30. Nikolai Strakhov, *Kriticheskie stat'i ob I. S. Turgeneve i L. N. Tolstom* (St. Petersburg, 1895), 362.

31. Eikhenbaum, *Lev Tolstoi*, 2:375–378ff. For a discussion of Tolstoi's philosophical digressions as an organic "superstructure" of the artistic text of *War and Peace*, see S. G. Bocharov, *Roman L. N. Tolstogo "Voina i mir"* (Moscow, 1963), 33–35.

32. A. A. Saburov, *"Voina i mir" L. N. Tolstogo: Problematika i poetika* (Moscow, 1959), 448–464ff.

33. A. V. Chicherin, *Idei i stil'* (Moscow, 1965), 239.

34. A. Skaftymov, *Nravstvennye iskaniia russkikh pisatelei* (Saratov, 1972), 149, 136.

35. For a discussion of Dostoevskii's novels as a special type of the novel of ideas, see B. M. Engel'gardt, "Ideologicheskii roman Dostoevskogo," in F. M. Dostoevskii, *Stat'i i materialy* 2 (Leningrad and Moscow, 1924); and M. M. Bakhtin, *Problema tvorchestva Dostoevskogo* (Leningrad, 1929) and *Problema poetiki Dostoevskogo* (Moscow, 1972).

36. N. M. Chirkov, *O stile Dostoevskogo* (Moscow, 1964), 56. See also the chapter "Pisatel'-psikholog," 50–67.

37. F. M. Dostoevskii, *Diary of a Writer* for January 1876; *Polnoe sobranie suchinenii*, 30 vols. (Moscow, 1972–1986), 22:8. (Tr.)

38. In I. T. Bzhalava, *Psikhologiia ustanovki i kibernetiki* (Moscow, 1966), 32ff.

39. D. N. Unadze, *Psikhologicheskie issledovaniia* (Moscow, 1966), 253.

40. M. Gor'kii, *Sobranie sochinenii*, 30 vols. (Moscow, 1949–1955), 29:430. Subsequent references to this edition are given in the text. (Tr.) There are similar formulations in a March 15, 1925, letter to Stefan Zweig (29:428).

PART TWO
DIRECT DISCOURSE

1. Great, although fundamentally different, discoveries in this regard obviously belong to Dostoevskii. They are examined in detail by Bakhtin in connec-

tion with his idea of Dostoevskii's polyphonic novel. See his *Problema poetiki Dostoevskogo*, chap. 5.

2. V. O. Vinogradov, "O iazyke Tolstogo (50–60-e gody)" in *Literaturnoe nasledstvo* 35–36 (Moscow, 1939), 196–201ff.

3. Ibid., 179–189.

4. There are individual exceptions, but they do not constitute a system.

5. Michel Aucouturier, "Langage intérieur et analyse psychologique chez Tolstoi," *Revue des études slaves* 34 (Paris, 1957): 8.

6. L. S. Vygotskii, "Myshlenie i rech'," in his *Izbrannye psikhologicheskie issledovaniia* (Moscow, 1956). V. N. Voloshinov regards "total impressions" ("integral" units that are not resolvable into grammatical elements) as the components of internal discourse; see his *Marksizm i filosofiia iazyka* (Leningrad, 1930), 42.

7. L. P. Iakubinskii, "O dialogicheskoi rechi," in *Russkaia rech'* 1 (Petrograd, 1923), 100. Among the more recent works in this connection are A. Kholodovich, "O tipologii rechi," in *Istoriko-filosofskie issledovaniia* (Moscow, 1967); and A. Balaian, "Problemy modelirovaniia dialoga," in *Materialy 3-go vsesoiuznogo simpoziuma po psikholingvistike* (Moscow, 1970). The work of the Americans J. Jaffee and S. Feldstein in *Rhythms of Dialogue* (New York, 1970) is based on an experimental investigation of the rhythmic factors of dialogue abstracted from their meaning.

8. Iakubinskii, *Russkaia rech'* 1, 134.

9. Skaftymov, *Nravstvennye iskaniia*, 417.

10. Iakubinskii, *Russkaia rech'* 1, 96.

11. Tolstoi's approach to popular speech was determined by his understanding of the man of the people as someone whose natural impulses had not bifurcated into overt and concealed motives.

12. For a discussion of this issue, see my article "O probleme narodnosti i lichnosti v poezii dekabristov," in *O russkom realizme XIX veka i voprosakh narodnosti literatury* (Moscow and Leningrad, 1960), 52–93.

13. Strakhov, *Kriticheskie stat'i*, 279.

14. Not only is the Tolstoian scene not theatrical; neither is the Dostoevskiian variety with its vast, uninterrupted dialogues.

15. B. M. Eikhenbaum, *Molodoi Tolstoi* (Petrograd and Berlin, 1922), 59, 121ff. Bakhtin comes close to a similar opinion in examining the reasons why dramatic form was "not relevant to Tolstoi's basic artistic intentions"; see his preface to Tolstoi's plays, in L. N. Tolstoi, *Polnoe sobranie khudozhestvennykh proizvedenii* (Moscow and Leningrad, 1929), 11:iii–iv.

16. Vinogradov in the above-cited article on Tolstoi's language ("O iazyke Tolstogo") examines Tolstoi's "pantomime" language in combination with the actual verbal utterances of his heroes. He emphasizes the existence in Tolstoi's writing of persistent gestures, of physical reactions that are common to all of his characters (as Tolstoi's contemporaries had already noted), and at the same time the presence of individual objects that become the "'signals' and symptoms of a particular image."

17. Leont'ev, *Sobranie sochinenii*, 8:321–322.

18. In *L'Éducation sentimentale* (which was written in 1864–1869, almost

simultaneously with *War and Peace*) there is a detailed description of a dinner at the Dambreuses' with elaborate intersecting dialogue and interwoven social and personal themes. Nevertheless, the structure is different than in Tolstoi. What Flaubert needs in this scene is the socially and psychologically characteristic; he is not interested in the mechanism of conversation *as such* as his object of depiction.

19. For a discussion of the significance of disputes and discussions on abstract themes in *Anna Karenina*, see E.-D. Goy, "The Role of Topic and Opinion in *Anna Karenina*," *Annali istituto universitario orientale: Sezione slava* 6 (Naples, 1963).

20. For example, Samuel Beckett in his *Proust* (New York, 1970) regards Proust as the epitome of anti-intellectualism, whereas [René] Étiemble has written an article proclaiming Proust's intellectualism and taking issue with the theory of his Bergsonism: "Proust et le crise de l'intelligence," in his *C'est le bouquet!* (Paris, 1967), 150–212. In an anthology of essays published in the United States and edited by René Girard, Proust appears within the covers of a single volume as the exponent of religious intuition, as an extreme relativist, as a skeptic, as a romantic, and as a rationalist heir of the national classical tradition (the viewpoint of Albert Thibaudet and of Proust's friend Jacques Rivière); see *Proust: A Collection of Critical Essays*, ed. René Girard (New York, 1962). This list of contradictory opinions could easily be extended.

21. In his introductory article to the Russian edition of Proust, A. V. Lunacharskii links him with the rationalistic "sensationalist subjectivism of the seventeenth century"; Marsel' Prust, *Sobranie sochinenii*, 4 vols. (Leningrad, 1934–1936). In an article included in the third volume of the same edition, N. Ia. Rykova speaks of Proust's rationalistic impressionism.

22. Marcel Proust, *Contre Sainte-Beuve, précédé de pastiches et mélanges et suivi de essais et articles*, ed. Pierre Clarac and Yves Sandre (Paris, 1971), 658 (Tr.). The question of Tolstoi and Proust (in regard to this article) has been addressed by T. L. Motyleva in her "Tolstoi i sovremennye zarubezhnye pisateli," in *Literaturnoe nasledstvo* 69, no. 1 (Moscow, 1961).

23. For a discussion of the problem of the relationship in Proust of subjective consciousness and objective reality, see V. Dneprov, *Cherty romana XX veka* (Moscow and Leningrad,1965), 207–216; L. Andreev, *Marsel' Prust* (Moscow, 1968), 53–55; and S. G. Bocharov, "Prust i 'potok soznaniia,' " in *Kriticheskii realizm XX veka i modernizm* (Moscow, 1967).

Erich Auerbach in his famous book *Mimesis* (first published in Bern in 1946) maintains that Proust overcame subjectivism in his own way by depicting things that had been resurrected in the memory, that had been liberated, that is, from the subjectivity of their spontaneous apprehension in a particular present. See *Mimesis: The Representation of Reality in Western Literature*, trans. Willard Trask (Princeton, 1953), 541–542. (Tr.)

24. Beckett, *Proust*, 63. (Tr.)

25. *A la recherche du temps perdu*, ed. Pierre Clarac and André Ferré, 3 vols. (Paris, 1954), 3:878–879; English translation by C. K. Scott Moncrieff and Terence Kilmartin, *Remembrance of Things Past*, 3 vols. (New York, 1981), 3:912. Subsequent references to these editions are given in the text, the French cited first. (Tr.)

26. A. Frankovskii translates this last phrase into Russian as "her imagined

blue eyes" (Leningrad, 1934–1936); N. Liubimova has the very similar "those eyes which appeared blue to me" (Moscow, 1973). It seems to me, however, that one ought to retain the paradoxical character of Proust's French text. He speaks directly of blue eyes: "amoureux, en elle, de ses yeux blues."

27. Gaëtan Picon, *Lecture de Proust* (Paris, 1963), 68–76.

28. See ibid., 61–63. Ramon Fernandez, on the other hand, emphasizes the importance of experience and reality in the formation of Proustian "general laws": *Proust* (Paris, 1943), 91–92, 98.

29. See Rykova's discussion of Proust's "pathology of behavior": Prust, *Sobranie sochinenii*, 3:14–15.

30. Albert Thibaudet, "Faces of Proust," in *Proust: A Collection of Critical Essays*, 47–52. (Tr.)

31. Ramon Fernandez, "In Search of the Self," ibid., 136–149.

PART THREE
ETHICAL VALUATION

1. In contrast, that is, to the basic principles of medieval ecclesiastical literature with its direct link to dogma.

2. Descartes in his *Traité des passions de l'ame* (1649) called for moderating and circumscribing those passions and affects that may act in a destructive way.

3. Jean Racine, *Oeuvres complètes*, ed. Raymond Picard (Paris, 1950), 763, 765. (Tr.)

4. Nicolas Boileau, *Oeuvres complètes*, ed. Françoise Escal (Paris, 1966), 171. (Tr.)

5. The mature Pushkin's harmonious hierarchy of socioethical ideas is very clearly set forth in his letters in French and in Russian. The letters in French to women or to Chaadaev or Raevskii, his society and familiar correspondence [in French and in Russian], and his letters to his betrothed [in French] and thereafter his wife [in Russian] all concern different aspects of life, and each of them has its own appropriate style. Pushkin retained in his letters a special language for things that were important.

6. "The will of a God who is just and good is that the sons of the earth be happy and that they enjoy all the pleasures that are compatible with the public good," as Helvétius formulated it (*Oeuvres complètes*, 7:96 [Tr.]).

7. Tolstoi's position is reminiscent of one of Pascal's *pensées*: "To be afraid of death not when in danger but when the danger has passed, since one must be a man" (*Oeuvres complètes*, 1147 [Tr.]).

8. Tolstoi failed to notice that Schopenhauer took measures against the practical interpretation of his statements. He denied the advisability of suicide on the basis that the individual still cannot extirpate the principal evil—the world as will.

9. "No one prevents Schopenhauer and me from denying life. Go ahead and kill yourself, then . . . , and stop fooling around in this life, talking and writing about how you don't understand it" (chap. 7).

10. A. S. Khomiakov, *Polnoe sobranie sochinenii*, 4th ed., 5 vols. (Moscow, 1911–1914), 1:150–151. (Tr.)

11. Iu. F. Samarin, *Sochineniia*, 12 vols. (Moscow, 1900–1911), 1:41.

12. *Rus'*, No. 1 (1883), 38.

13. V. S. Solov'ev, *Opravdanie dobra* (St. Petersburg, 1897). (Tr.)

14. N. G. Chernyshevskii, *Polnoe sobranie sochinenii*, 11:210.

15. See Marks and Engel's, *Sobranie sochinenii, op. cit.*, 3:234. The text in question is from *Die deutsche Ideologie: "Neues Testament: 'Ich,' " 2. Phänomenologie des mit sich einigen Egoisten. . . .* (Tr.)

16. Arthur Schopenhauer, *Die Welt als Wille und Vorstellung*, 2 vols. (Wiesbaden, 1961), 2:447; English translation by R. B. Haldane and J. Kemp, *The World as Will and Idea*, 3 vols. (London, 1896), 1:489. (Tr.)

17. Jean-Marie Guyau, *Equisse d'une morale sans obligation, ni sanction* (Paris, 1885). (Tr.)

18. See, for example, E. Iu. Solov'ev, *"Eksistentsializm (stat'ia vtoraia)," Voprosy filosofii* 1 (1967): 126–39.

19. Flaubert's correspondence is indicative of his passionate interest in the events of social and personal life. In her book devoted to this issue, Marianne Bonwit shows how variable and complex a phenomenon Flaubert's "impartiality" was, even in literary terms; see *Gustave Flaubert et le principe d'impassibilité* (Berkeley and Los Angeles, 1950).

20. Émile Zola, *Thérèse Raquin* (Paris, 1867); *Oeuvres complètes*, ed. Henri Mitterand, 15 vols. (Paris, 1966–1970), 1:514–515. (Tr.)

21. Émile Zola, *Le Roman expérimental* (Paris, 1880); *Oeuvres complètes*, 10:1188. (Tr.)

22. For a discussion of *The Bronze Horseman* in this connection, see I. M. Toibin, "Filosofsko-istoricheskaia poema A. S. Pushkin 'Mednyi vsadnik,' " *Uchenye zapiski Kurskogo pedogogicheskogo instituta* 55 (1968). The question of the truth of Pushkin's Pugachev is addressed in a unique way in Marina Tsvetaeva's article "Pushkin i Pugachev," in Marina Tsvetaeva, *Moi Pushkin* (Moscow, 1967).

23. G. A. Gukovskii, *Realizm Gogolia* (Moscow and Leningrad, 1959), 451–465.

24. See, for example, Turgenev's story "A Meeting" (in *A Sportsman's Sketches*), where the hero Viktor is an oppressed house serf, but is himself responsible for oppressing and taking advantage of a serf girl. Turgenev depicts Viktor with strong condemnation, even disgust, and he does so without making any allowance for his situation.

25. Twentieth-century Western literature partially returned to the linked conflict in its most extreme form. This is especially true of Kafka, with his individual stifled by an objective terror of external powers that try, judge, and convict him without his knowing why (*Der Prozess*), or his individual transformed into an insect by an unknown force for unknown reasons (*Die Verwandlung*).

26. Actually for Tolstoi, as for all nineteenth-century realists, there were practical limits to what might be depicted. A comparison of Tolstoi's diaries with his use of autobiographical material in his fiction shows that even he played down the psychological conflicts. Thus in the diary for 1863, the first year of Tolstoi's married life is sometimes depicted in very harsh and unattractive terms. That actual experience was later used in the portrayal of the initial period of Kitty's and Levin's married life, a difficult period of mutual adjustment. It is all much more

general in the novel than in the diaries, however, and the unattractive features have been omitted.

27. The internal "consciousness" of the Tolstoian man of the people is combined with his natural conditionality and stands opposed only to the artificial forms that constrain him (the conscript Karataev, for example).

28. Sometimes motives from both series enter into irresolvable conflict, as in *The Cossacks*—the story of a free choice for a new life that is defeated by the resistance of the social conditionality of the hero Olenin, on the one hand, and that of the Cossacks who expel him from their milieu, on the other.

29. Tolstoi's crisis reached its most extreme form in 1876. And it was in fact in 1876 that Dostoevskii in the *Diary of a Writer* (for October and December) in the articles "A Verdict" and "Unfounded Opinions" created his "logical suicide"—a person of such inordinately intense self-consciousness that he cannot endure the contradiction between his sense of his own value and his finiteness. Without faith in the immortality of the soul, only suicide is left: "For him it is all too obvious that he cannot go on living, and he also knows all too well that he is right and that he cannot be refuted" (*Polnoe sobranie sochinenii*, 24:48 [Tr.]). Ippolit's confession in the third part of *The Idiot* (1868) is already moving toward ideas of this kind. Dostoevskii in 1876 was writing about the same thing that Tolstoi was experiencing at that time.

30. Compare the version of this text in the drafts of 1854–1855 (11:474).

31. Leont'ev, *Sobranie sochinenii*, 8:236–37.

32. M. M. Bakhtin, "Predislovie," in L. N. Tolstoi, *Polnoe sobranie khudozhestvennykh proizvedenii*, 15 vols. (Moscow and Leningrad, 1928–1930), 13:viiiff. For additional discussion of the artistic forms in which the frank tendentiousness of the late Tolstoi was embodied, see Ia. S. Bilinkis, "Povestvovanie v 'Voskresenii,'" in *O tvorchestve L. N. Tolstogo* (Leningrad, 1959).

33. In his treatise "What Then Must We Do?" (1882–1886), Tolstoi explained the success of the ideas of Hegel by the fact that they "justified people in living bad lives."

34. In one of the first editions of chapter 13 of the third part of *Resurrection*, Tolstoi analyzed the motives for the behavior of the women revolutionaries with a harshness that he later rejected: "Their girlish enthusiasms and dreams whose basis was a desire for love took the form for others and themselves of a desire to serve humanity."

INDEX